Level 2
Language Arts

Teacher's Manual
for
Grand Tour I and Grand Tour II

Author

Sue Dickson

with
Jeanette Cason
and
Marjorie Knapp

ISBN 1-56704-748-3
Printed in the United States of America
13 18

1-800-321-3106
www.pearsonlearning.com

Editors
Sharon Rice, Managing Editor
Donna Francis, Editor
Susan Nitz, Senior Editor

Consultants
Deborrah Howes
Pauline Hord

Illustration and Graphic Design
Leigh Anderson, Art Director
Gregory Dyer
Jean Hamilton
Nathan Heim
Paul Rosado

Assessments and
Quick Placement Test
Martha Markham

Production Support
Jane Allen
Tangerine Serocki

SSR&W Level 1 Phonics Songs
Music and Lyrics by
Sue Dickson
Arranged and Produced by
Stephen Peppos

SSR&W Level 1 Singers
Bobby Dickson
Christina Dickson
Kaleigh Dickson
Kara Dickson
Brittany Fix
Bryan Fix
Dante Graham
Brittany Mayes

Level 2 Grand Tour Singers
*First Week Introduction Program
and Grand Tour Song
Written by*
Sue Dickson

*Grand Tour Music
Arranged and Produced by*
Danny Hamilton

*Southern Border Song
Eastern Border Song
Music, Lyrics and Arrangements by*
Kathy Troxel

Table of Contents

Grand Tour I

Spelling: Review Short Vowel Words,
Sing All Phonics Songs
Language Arts Skills: Letter Switch,
Rhyming Words, Word Fun, Word Clues,
Manuscript Writing Review
Additional Related Activities: Around the World
with Rhyming Words; Letter Switch

Spelling: Review Short Vowel Words,
Sing All Phonics Songs
Language Arts Skills: Compound Words, Syllables,
Sentence Scramble, Riddles, Using "is" and "are,"
Cloze, Rhyming Words, Word Scramble, Using
"don't" and "doesn't," Crossword Puzzle,
Handwriting Practice, Writing Connection
Additional Related Activities: Syllable Clapping;
Compound Words; Rhyming Words; Riddles
Process Writing: Lesson #1 — Writing a Story

Spelling: Review Short Vowel Words,
Sing All Phonics Songs
Language Arts Skills: Word Scramble,
Using "went" and "gone," Word Meanings,
Word Association, Compound Words,
Cloze, Syllables, Rhyming Words,
Using "came" and "come,"
Crossword Puzzle, Using "did" and "done,"
Handwriting Practice, Writing Connection
Additional Related Activities: Around the World
with Rhyming Words; Syllable Clapping;
Around the World with Compound Words
Process Writing: Lesson #1 — Writing a Story

Spelling: Two Vowel (ōȼ, ēȼ, ēȼ, āȳ) Words
Language Arts Skills: Cloze, ABC Order,
Complete and Incomplete Sentences,
Rhyming Words, Suffixes es and ing,
Compound Words, Crossword Puzzle,
Handwriting Practice, Short Stories,
Writing Connection
Additional Related Activities: Tell Me What
I'm Doing (pantomiming); Rhyming;
Illustrating Compound Words
Process Writing: Lesson #2 — Narrowing the Topic

Spelling: Silent e Words, c = s Words
Language Arts Skills: Rhyming Words, Cloze,
Suffixes ful and less, Subjects and Predicates,
Crossword Puzzle, Compound Words, Handwriting
Practice, Short Stories, Writing Connection
Additional Related Activities: Rhyming Word Families;
Hot Potato with Suffixes ing, ful, and less;
Hang an Apple with Suffixes; Alphabet Rummy
Process Writing: Lesson #2 — Narrowing the Topic

Spelling: "āȳ" Words, y = ī Words,
ge, gi, gy = Soft g Words, y = ē Words
Language Arts Skills: Cloze, Rhyming Words,
Word Meanings, Subjects and Predicates,
Word Scramble, ABC Order, Word Association,
Syllables, Word Search, Handwriting Practice,
Writing Connection
Additional Related Activities: Around the World
with ABC Order (alphabetizing); Riddle Time
Process Writing: Lesson #3 — Sequencing

(Continued on next page)

Grand Tour II

(Continued on next page)

Sing Spell
Read & Write

(Continued on next page)

Index to Additional Related Activities

Sing Spell Read & Write.

Overview • Teacher Tips
Phonics Skills
Quick Intervention • Handwriting

Overview

Sing, Spell, Read & Write (SSR&W) **Level 2** provides a complete and balanced multisensory Language Arts curriculum for students in grade 2. It is designed to build upon the SSR&W Level 1 program. While Level 1 is designed to teach **learning-to-read**, Level 2 reviews the learning-to-read skills, expands upon them, and then moves on to transition children into **reading-to-learn**.

Placement

A typical second grade classroom has students with a wide range of reading abilities from non-readers to advanced readers. *Sing, Spell, Read & Write* provides teachers with the "tools" necessary for teaching this typical second-grade classroom.

At the beginning of Level 2, all students will be checked for mastery of the skills taught in SSR&W Level 1 through the use of the Individual Skills Assessment Chart found on page 4 of the *Grand Tour I* Student Book.

During the first three weeks of school, all students are provided a review of the phonics lessons taught in Level 1. Students review the **learning-to-read** skills through songs, games, and activities. It is important that students master the **learning-to-read** skills before they enter the Level 2 **reading-to-learn** phase.

Administer the one-on-one *Sing, Spell, Read & Write* Quick Placement Test to *any* child:

- with incomplete school records,
- who has not completed the 36 Steps of *SSR&W* Level 1, or
- who may, in your judgment, be reading below grade level.

Follow the placement guidelines on the *Quick Placement Test* and refer to TM pp. 34-39 for intervention strategies that may be used to bring the child to independent reading ability before starting the *Grand Tour Storybooks*.

Overview

Sing, Spell, Read & Write Level 2 Teacher's Manuals

There are two Teacher's Manuals for *Sing, Spell, Read & Write* Level 2: a Teacher's Manual for Reading and a Teacher's Manual for Language Arts.

Level 2 Teacher's Manual for Reading

The SSR&W Level 2 Teacher's Manual for Reading provides Comprehension Instruction, Guided Reading discussion questions, Cultural Appreciation Activities, Additional Related Activities, Correlated Reproducibles, and a Recommended Reading Bibliography that includes suggested read-aloud and self-selected student reading. A complete overview of the *Grand Tour Storybooks* and related components is in the Level 2 Teacher's Manual for Reading.

Level 2 Teacher's Manual for Language Arts

The SSR&W Teacher's Manual for Language Arts provides directions for teaching the Spelling, Vocabulary, Grammar, Writing, Proofreading, Reference Skills, and Handwriting Lessons found in *Grand Tour I* and *II* Student Books. Also included are suggestions and/or directions for:

- Classroom preparation
- Daily and weekly schedules
- Phonics songs and games
- Intervention Strategies
- Grammar Chalkboard Lessons
- Manuscript and Cursive Writing instructions
- Speaking and Listening Activities, including crafts and games
- Process Writing Lessons, 18 lessons—one for every 2 weeks
- Evaluation techniques and tips for Process Writing
- Homework assignments to give students the opportunity to develop good study habits, and also to keep parents informed of the skills being taught
- Reproducibles

Answer Keys

Answer Keys for *Grand Tour I* and *Grand Tour II* Student Books are in separate booklets for teacher convenience.

Grand Tour I and *II* Student Books

The correlated Spelling, Vocabulary, Grammar, Reading, Writing, Proofreading and Reference Skills lessons presented in *Grand Tour I* (first semester) and *Grand Tour II* (second semester) are designed to lead students to mastery of Level 2 Language Arts skills. The lessons present skills in a continuum of increasing difficulty from simple to more complex. The curriculum meets or exceeds the most recent state guidelines.

Level 2 *continued*

Spelling and Vocabulary

The 144 phonics-based Spelling Lessons are presented in four 10-word lessons per week for 36 weeks (40 words per week). The spelling words serve as the core of *Grand Tour I* and *II* and are integrated within the Grammar and Vocabulary activities. A total of 1,440 spelling words are presented in an orderly and graduated sequence. Included are correlated lessons for compound words, multisyllable words, homophones, synonyms, antonyms, and contractions.

Each group of spelling words presents a phonetic-based grouping, which is taught and reinforced through games and songs with accompanying wall charts. Brain research has determined that long-term retention is increased by the use of music. Marilyn Adams, in her 1990 study stated, "Because the phonological processor (mentally perceiving sounds) is highly attuned to patterns of rhyme, rhythm and pitch, songs are much easier to learn than unintoned lists." The combination of phonetic groupings, songs, and games provides motivational practices to reinforce the correlated lessons in Spelling and Phonics and ensures success for all students.

A variety of activities including Crossword Puzzles, Word Searches, Spelling Codes, and Fill-in-the-Blanks are designed to ensure that learning is attainable, effective and enjoyable.

Reading in *Grand Tour I* and *II*

Once a group of spelling words is introduced and practiced, those same words are often incorporated into short stories. The stories provide opportunities for connected reading activities and the development of higher level thinking skills. In addition, the short stories provide motivation for The Writing Connection lessons. By integrating the teaching of Spelling, Vocabulary, Grammar, Reading, and Writing, students are given the opportunity to see the English language as a whole, rather than as unrelated, disjointed subjects.

Grammar

Grammar lessons include:

- Sentences, Complete and Incomplete
- Subjects and Predicates
- Nouns
- Verbs
- Adjectives
- Adverbs
- Pronouns
- Synonyms
- Antonyms
- Homophones
- Capitalization

- Punctuation
- ABC Order
- Suffixes
- Prefixes
- Root Words
- Verb Usage
- Rhyming Words
- Compound Words
- Contractions
- Possessives
- Singulars and Plurals

Level 2 continued

Writing

- The Writing Connection curriculum in *Grand Tour I* and *II* Student Books provides instruction in Creative Writing activities.

- The 18 Process Writing Lessons in the Language Arts Teacher's Manual assist teachers as they provide instruction in a wide variety of composition skills. Students learn to write effectively by learning and practicing these five steps:

  1. **Pre-Writing**—students generate ideas.
  2. **Composing**—students compose and write for a sustained period of time.
  3. **Revising**—students develop skills to improve their work. This step provides time for teacher-student conferences.
  4. **Editing**—students use their grammar, spelling, and proofreading skills to make corrections.
  5. **Publishing**—students publish their work in many different ways and share their finished work with others.

Pre-Writing

Composing

Revising

Editing

Publishing

Proofreading Skills

***Sing, Spell, Read & Write* Level 2** provides many specific proofreading lessons and frequent opportunities to practice and apply these skills. The *Grand Tour I* and *Grand Tour II* Student Books include instruction and practice in capitalization, punctuation, and recognition of incomplete sentences. Students learn simple proofreading marks and use them to correct text. Each of the 18 Process Writing Lessons has proofreading instruction. Students are taught to self-edit their compositions.

Reference Skills

***Sing, Spell, Read & Write* Level 2** provides many opportunities for students to practice using reference skills. Suggestions for teaching reference skills are found in the *Teacher's Manual for Language Arts*. Each lesson has suggestions for Additional Related Activities. These include ideas for research opportunities using library books, print or electronic encyclopedias, or Internet web sites.

***Sing, Spell, Read & Write* Level 2** provides instruction in dictionary skills in a variety of ways. The *Grand Tour I* and *Grand Tour II* Student Books provide lessons in using guide words, alphabetizing entry words, and choosing the correct meaning of multiple-meaning words. Dividing words into syllables and using diacritical marks as an aide to pronunciation of unfamiliar words is taught. The Process Writing Lessons introduce specific practice in using the dictionary to correct spelling errors. A vocabulary page with pronunciation and word meanings is in each *Grand Tour Storybook*. These assist students in using dictionary skills.

Handwriting

Manuscript Writing skills are reviewed in *Grand Tour I*. Students are introduced to cursive writing in *Grand Tour II*. Note that while **Sing, Spell, Read & Write** manuscript letter forms have been carefully designed to GUARANTEE students a smooth transition into cursive writing, the teaching of cursive writing is optional. You are the best judge to determine if your students are ready for cursive writing.

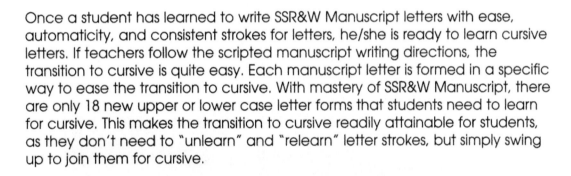

Once a student has learned to write SSR&W Manuscript letters with ease, automaticity, and consistent strokes for letters, he/she is ready to learn cursive letters. If teachers follow the scripted manuscript writing directions, the transition to cursive is quite easy. Each manuscript letter is formed in a specific way to ease the transition to cursive. With mastery of SSR&W Manuscript, there are only 18 new upper or lower case letter forms that students need to learn for cursive. This makes the transition to cursive readily attainable for students, as they don't need to "unlearn" and "relearn" letter strokes, but simply swing up to join them for cursive.

p. 5

Grand Tour II (Back Cover)

Sing, Spell, Read & Write Level 2

Classroom Kit Contents

- Grand Tour Curriculum Wall Chart with 6 movable bus icons
- Sets of 17 Readers in a Literacy Center Display
- Level 2 Grand Tour CD (with Introductory First Week Program, and Sing-Along and Point Level 2 Grand Tour Songs)
- Quick Placement Test
- Four Assessment Booklets (class packs with 25 of each)
- *Grand Tour I* Student Books and Answer Key
- *Grand Tour II* Student Books and Answer Key
- Teacher's Manual for Language Arts
- Teacher's Manual for Reading
- Desk Stick-Ons
- Phonics Games (5)
- Phonics Songs CD
- Phonics Wall Charts
- Treasure Chest and Prizes
- Dry-Erase Markers and Erasers

Level 2 *continued*

A to Z Phonics Song Cards

Short Vowel Cards

Long Vowel Cards

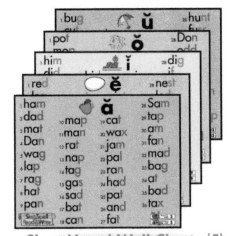

Short Vowel Wall Charts (5)

Wall Charts

Letter Cluster Wall Charts (4)

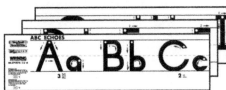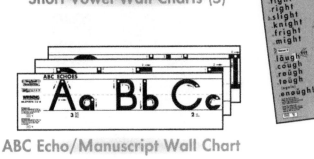

ABC Echo/Manuscript Wall Chart

Sound-O and Word-O Games

Cursive Wall Chart

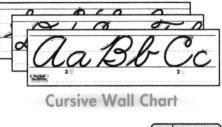

Treasure Chest with Toys

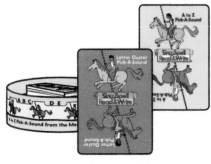

Pick-A-Sound Games (2)

Sing, Spell, Read & Write Level 2
Classroom Kit Contents

Teacher's Manual for Language Arts

The Level 2 Language Arts Manual contains program Overview, Teacher Tips, and Instructions for a full year of Phonics, Spelling, Vocabulary, Grammar, and Handwriting lessons found in *Grand Tour I* and *II* Student Books. Also included are Correlated Reproducibles, Additional Related Activities, and 18 Process Writing Lessons.

Teacher's Manual for Reading

The Teacher's Manual for Reading includes Guided Reading questions for *Grand Tour Storybooks*, Cultural Appreciation Activities, Additional Related Activities, and Correlated Reproducibles. Also provided is a Recommended Reading Bibliography that has suggested read-aloud and self-selected student reading.

Grand Tour I Student Book (consumable)

Grand Tour I includes lessons in Phonics, Spelling, Vocabulary, Grammar, Reading and Comprehension, Authentic Writing, Proofreading and Reference Skills, and Manuscript Writing for the first semester of second grade.

Grand Tour II Student Book (consumable)

Grand Tour II includes extended lessons introduced in *Grand Tour I* and introduces Cursive Writing (optional).

Answer Keys

Use *Grand Tour I* and *Grand Tour II* Answer Key Booklets to correct student papers. Student Book pages pictured in TM are for reference only.

Dry-erase markers and erasers

Dry-erase markers and erasers are included for each student for writing practice. The back cover of each student book is an erasable slate to use for handwriting practice.

Assessments

Four assessments are provided to be administered periodically throughout the school year to assess Language Arts and Reading Comprehension Skills.

SSR&W Quick Placement Test

The SSR&W Quick Placement Test allows for quick assessment of a child's decoding skills to assist the teacher in determining the level at which to begin instruction.

Manuscript/Cursive Desk Strips (one for each student) (consumable)

A removable vinyl desk stick-on features: the alphabet in both manuscript and cursive; Phonics Song pictures (for visual reference); and space for student's name. Easy reference builds child's confidence.

Grand Tour Wall Chart and 6 Movable Bus Icons

The oversized Grand Tour chart shows North America and the color-coded "highways" your students will travel this year on the Level 2 Grand Tour bus. Children sing along and point on the map as reading groups move their buses from one state and storybook to the next, visiting children along the southern and eastern borders of the United States. The static cling bus icons help track reading group progress through the program.

Level 2 Grand Tour CD

This CD features songs that will help children remember each of the states they "visit" on the Grand Tour. The Level 2 Grand Tour covers the southern and eastern borders of the United States. The CD includes: The Introductory First Week Program; the *Grand Tour Song*, the *Southern Border Song*, the *Eastern Border Song*; classic favorites such as *California Here I Come*, *Deep in the Heart of Texas*, *Oh, Susanna!*, *Georgia on My Mind*; and finally, an assortment of patriotic songs including *The Star Spangled Banner*, *America the Beautiful*, *This Land is Your Land*, and others.

Literacy Center Bookshelf with Grand Tour Storybooks (Reading-to-Learn)

Bookshelf display unit comes complete with sets of 17 Storybooks, and provides nearly 600 pages of fully illustrated stories and character tales.

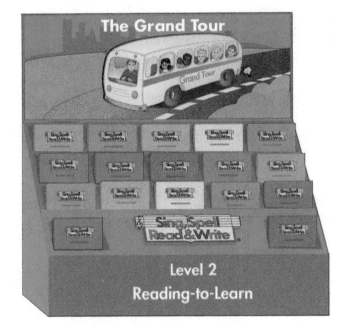

Level 2 *continued*

Interactive Phonics Wall Charts and Phonics Songs on CD

For large-group sing-along-and-point and echo routines. Provides phonics review and intervention. Correlates with phonics songs on Level 1 CD.

- *A to Z Phonics Song Cards* - Upper and lower case letters with key word pictures teach letter sounds.

- *ABC Echo Cards* - Provide manuscript writing model for upper and lower case letter formation and letter sounds.

- *Short Vowel Cards* (5) (ă,ĕ,ĭ,ŏ,ŭ) - Students manipulate cards while singing to gain familiarity with short vowel sounds.

- *Short Vowel Word Charts* (5) (ă,ĕ,ĭ,ŏ,ŭ) - Practice in reading and spelling short vowel words.

- *Ferris Wheel Chart & "Tickets"* - Practice in blending initial consonant sounds with short vowels to make short vowel words.

- *Long Vowel Cards* (ā,ē,ī,ō,ū) - Upper and lower case letters with key word picture.

- *Letter Cluster Phonics Song Charts* (4) - Builds knowledge of letter clusters (th-, ch-, sh-, etc.),

- *Pop the Balloons Chart* - Checks mastery of letter cluster sounds in large group activity.

- *Two Vowel Chart with Word Cards* - Practice reading, spelling, and singing two vowel words.

- *Silent ∉ Chart with Word Cards* - Practice in reading, spelling, and singing silent e words.

- *Gh Clown Chart* - Practice reading, pronouncing, spelling, and singing words with "gh."

- *Cursive Wall Charts* - Teach cursive letter formation.

Level 1 Phonics Songs on CD

Phonics Songs are used with the interactive wall charts in sing-along-and-point, and echo routines. The songs include:

A to Z Phonics Song
ABC Echoes
Short Vowel Song
Ferris Wheel Song
Letter Cluster Song

Long Vowel Marching Song
ABC Echoes (All Sounds)
Two Vowels Get Together Song
Silent ¢ Song
Gh Clown Song

Games (5) with Storage Containers

Large and small group games provide practice for review, and mastery of letter sounds, clusters, and sight words.

- *A to Z Pick-A-Sound* and *Letter Cluster Pick-A-Sound Games* are two small-group card games played like "Go Fish." Students practice knowledge of letter sounds A to Z and letter clusters.

- *A to Z Sound-O, Letter Cluster Sound-O,* and *Word-O Games* are three Bingo-like games. Students use Bingo-style cards and see-through chips to cover the letter, letter cluster, or sight word that corresponds to the letter sound and key word that is called by the teacher from caller cards.

Treasure Chest with Prizes

Treasure Chest Box containing prizes to be used for rewards.

A Letter from the Author

Sing, Spell
Read & Write ®

Dear Colleague:

*You are about to embark on another great year full of adventure with **Sing, Spell, Read & Write's (SSR&W)** **Level 2 Program, The Grand Tour**. Last year, your students hopefully completed Level 1 to achieve independent reading ability. Now that they have completed **learning to read**, they are ready to start **reading to learn**.*

*During my 27 years in the classroom, I experienced many trends in Reading and Language Arts. I found the only way for students to achieve mastery of required Language Arts skills was to correlate the instruction in one unified approach and theme. In **SSR&W** Pre-K, the Jolly Trolley theme and chart take 4-year-olds through readiness skills; in Kindergarten, the Kindergarten Express theme and chart help students begin reading; in Level 1, the Raceway theme and chart lead students to independent reading ability; in Level 2, the exciting Grand Tour theme and chart lead students towards reading to learn.*

In Grand Tour Language Arts, the lessons for Phonics, Spelling, Vocabulary, Grammar, Reference, Proofreading, Process Writing, and Handwriting are fully correlated. The Grand Tour I and II Student Books include Crossword Puzzles, Word Searches, Decoding Games, Spelling Codes, Riddles, Short Stories, Writing, and more. Your students will be having so much fun learning that they won't even think of it as school work! Teachers who piloted the Language Arts phase of the program last year have called it, "The best program for 2nd grade I've ever had."

*When it came to developing the Reading/Literature component for Level 2, I thought back to my days in the classroom. I remembered how electrified my students became when I gave chalk talks and told them dramatic stories of the Pilgrims' perilous journey across storm-tossed seas to the New World. I remembered how a simple story could take away their confusion about why Abraham Lincoln's birthday came before George Washington's in February when they knew that George Washington lived first. I remembered our discussing last night's news and weather report and seeing how mesmerized they were when I pulled down the map and showed them the places they had just seen on T.V., places that were so far away from their homes. And then I had the answer for the **Sing, Spell, Read & Write** Level 2 reading program. It would be a **reading-to-learn** program, a reading program that would tell stories — true stories — that would expand their horizons and help them learn about things they are probably hearing others talk about in the real world on a daily basis.*

I also remember when I taught second grade we teachers desperately needed to have the tools for intervention for those students who had not yet mastered the "learning-to-read" phase. Not only was an intervention program needed, but also a more stimulating reading program for everyone. The ideal would be a program that correlates all the Language Arts, Science, Social Studies, Geography, and even Music, into one thematic approach. Happily, you now have all this in the Level 2 Grand Tour Program.

Level 2 Grand Tour Curriculum includes a Quick Placement Test, an Intervention Program with songs, games, vocabulary lists, storybook readers, assessments and a complete Spelling, Writing, and Grammar Component to ensure a successful second grade experience for you and your students.

In Level 2, your students will take an imaginary trip aboard a Grand Tour bus. Together, you will travel along the southern and eastern borders of the United States of America.[1] Along the way, your students will read stories to learn what the children are like in all the places they visit. Many of the stories have been written and illustrated by students just like yours. Your students will find out what other children's families do for fun and for work, what their weather is like, what their favorite places are, and what it is that makes them most proud of where they live. These delightful, high-interest stories engage inquisitive young minds. Furthermore, the storybooks provide that gentle transition from narrative stories that are so prominent in primary grade classrooms to informational stories. This is done through fictional characters such as Bubba the Frog, Marty the Mockingbird, and Monty the Moose. Children are enthralled while at the same time gaining valuable knowledge that is essential for survival in the Information Age.

An article by respected reading researchers Hallie Kay Yopp and Ruth Helen Yopp published in <u>The Reading Teacher</u> supports such an approach.[2] In their article, the Yopps recommend the introduction of nonfiction texts to children early and regularly in the primary grades. The consistent exposure to nonfiction texts allows youngsters to develop a familiarity and comfort level with the informational texts that they will start to encounter by the fourth grade.

*And since music is always a major part of every program from **Sing, Spell, Read & Write**, your children will learn folk, popular, patriotic, and informational songs to help them remember in the most enjoyable way the places they've visited. We promise you a Grand Tour of reading — and learning — and singing — all rolled into one unforgettable school year!*

I look forward to hearing of your success.

Sue Dickson

Sue Dickson
Author/Teacher

---

[1] Children will continue the Grand Tour in the third grade, with Sing, Spell, Read & Write's Level 3 Program. Level 3 will be available for use in classrooms in Fall 2001.

[2] Ruth Helen Yopp and Hallie Kay Yopp, "Sharing Information Texts with Young Children," *The Reading Teacher*, Vol. 53, No. 5, February 2000

Teacher Tips

Layout for Model Classroom

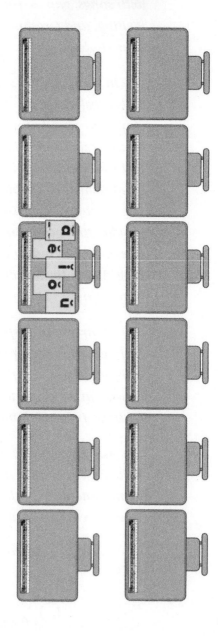

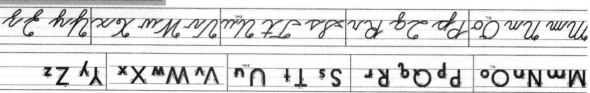

Sing, Spell
Read & Write

Teacher Tips

Layout for Model Classroom

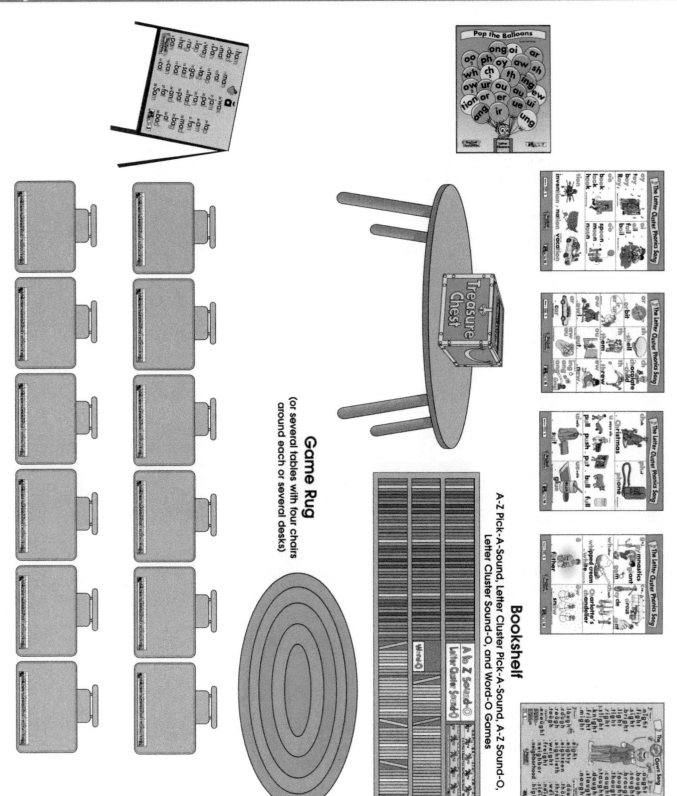

Game Rug
(or several tables with four chairs
around each or several desks)

Bookshelf
A-Z Pick-A-Sound, Letter Cluster Pick-A-Sound, A-Z Sound-O,
Letter Cluster Sound-O, and Word-O Games

Teacher Tips

How to Prepare Your Classroom

The classroom arrangement on pages 22 and 23 is an example of the way the room should look at the beginning of the school year. The phonics charts and materials will be used during the first three weeks of school for review.

Desk Arrangement

Choose a chalkboard for writing instruction this year and face desks toward that chalkboard for optimal directionality during instruction. Every student will have the door (or whatever) to the left, and the flag (or whatever) to the right. Therefore, the teacher can say "Put your pencil on the top line...go toward the flag or toward the door," when reviewing or teaching letter formation. This will provide for the oral as well as the visual pathway to the brain. Students will hear, see, and feel the writing instruction.

Teacher Tip ✓ Some students have trouble with directionality in forming letters and because of this should not have their desks moved around the room. Place their desks near the center and leave them there. Extreme left or right desks in the front row are the worst seats in the classroom because of the angle.

Desk Stick-Ons

Adhere a desk stick-on to each desk. Carefully write the student's first and last name in upper and lower case manuscript, using a fine felt-tip pen. The desk stick-on provides the student with:

1. The manuscript and cursive alphabet

2. A model for correct letter formation when practicing handwriting

3. Key pictures for the *A to Z Phonics Song*

Teacher Tip ✓ On the first day of school tell students you're having a contest to see who will have the smoothest, cleanest desk stick-on the last day of school, and those students will receive prizes. Praise nice clean desk stick-ons occasionally throughout the year.

Teacher Tips

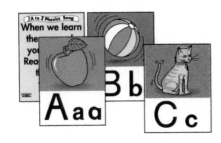

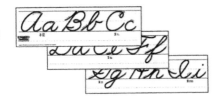

How to Prepare Your Classroom *continued*

Wall Charts and Cards

A to Z Phonics Song Cards

The *A to Z Phonics Song Cards* are to be used the first day of school. Place them directly above the chalkboard. Students will point to these cards so display them no more than one inch above the board. Follow the numbers so all your cards will be in order. The first card reads, "When we learn these sounds you'll see, ready to read then we will be."

Manuscript Wall Chart

The *Manuscript Wall Chart* (without pictures) must be displayed on a side wall, as shown in the classroom diagram, or on the back wall away from the *A to Z Phonics Song Cards*.

Cursive Wall Chart

The teaching of Cursive Writing in this program is optional. Cursive Writing is introduced in the second semester of second grade. If you choose to teach cursive writing, display the *Cursive Wall Chart* at the very beginning of the year when you set up your classroom. Place the *Cursive Wall Chart* directly below the *Manuscript Wall Chart* as shown in the diagram on TM pp. 22-23. This early exposure will help students establish a familiarity with and curiosity about this "new kind" of writing. Together, the *Manuscript and Cursive Wall Charts* correlate with the students' desk stick-ons.

Chalkboards

Prepare your selected chalkboard for writing lessons. You will need a waterproof marker, a yardstick, a steady hand and perhaps a helper (fellow teacher). Measure very carefully and rule in pencil the entire section of your board to look exactly like a sheet of beginning writing paper...one line ruled, one line broken. A spacing of two inches between lines is adequate for good visibility from the back of the room. Go over those penciled lines with a waterproof marker. It helps to have someone hold the other end of your yardstick as you guide your marker along, tracing over the penciled lines. You will find that you will have to go over the lines with the marker several times during the year as they fade away.

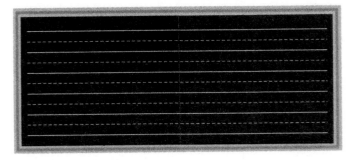

Teacher Tip ✓ Use thick chalk sticks (approximately one inch in diameter) for all your chalkboard writing. They are messy but give the best visibility.

Teacher Tips

CD Player

The CD player is most convenient when placed near the left side of the chalkboard, since that is where you begin pointing along with the music for the *A to Z Phonics Song* during the three-week phonics review. Once you start the Grand Tour, you may want to move the player nearer to the *Grand Tour Chart*. Each day, students will be singing a song while pointing along on the chart. They will learn a new song to help them remember each place they visit as they travel across the United States.

Grand Tour Wall Chart
and 6 Movable Bus Icons

Display the *Grand Tour Chart* in your classroom as shown in the diagram on TM p. 22. The year kicks off with the *Grand Tour Song*. This oversized chart is a map that shows the color-coded "routes" your students will travel this year in *Grand Tour I* and *II*. Children sing along and point on the map as your reading groups move their buses from one place and storybook to the next. As students start each new story, they will learn a new song that is linked to the place they are reading about. For additional details on how the *Grand Tour Chart* works with Level 2, refer to the *Teacher's Manual for Reading*.

Homework Chart

Make a *Homework Chart* on large lined paper and keep it on the easel. Each morning, immediately following opening exercises, call each student's name on the chart and make a large crayoned star if the student has the homework paper. Make a straight line if the student has no homework. Tell the student to bring the missing homework paper tomorrow, and the straight line will be changed into a star.

When the *Homework Chart* is filled with stars, cut it along the lines into strips, staple each strip into a circle to fit the student's head, and everyone has a crown to wear! Students who have all stars — no lines — on their crowns are on the All Stars Team. Call them to the front of the room, give them some applause (peer recognition) and let them choose a prize from the *Treasure Chest*. This helps EVERYONE remember homework! Accentuate the positive! It will motivate an almost 100% return on homework all year.

First Day Letter to Parents

A sample letter to send home the first day of school is shown below. It is found in the Reproducible Section, TM p. 469. It will help you feel well-organized and prepared. It will let parents know about **Sing, Spell, Read & Write**, and it will assure them that you welcome their participation in their child's learning experience this year.

The First Day of School

Dear _____,

Last year, I was **learning to read**. This year, I will be **reading to learn** with a program called **Sing, Spell, Read & Write**.

For the first three weeks of school, we will be reviewing our phonics and reading skills. You'll be hearing me sing some of the phonics songs that helped me learn to read last year.

This year, in Language Arts we will be learning more than 1,400 new Spelling and Vocabulary words, Grammar skills, how to use a dictionary, and how to write good stories.

In Reading, we will be taking an imaginary trip aboard a Grand Tour bus. We're going to travel along the southern and eastern borders of the United States of America. Along the way, we're going to learn what the children are like in all the places we visit. We'll find out what families do for fun and for work, what their weather is like, what their favorite places are, and what makes them most proud of where they live. We'll even learn some of the songs they like to sing. It will be a Grand Tour of reading — and learning — and singing — all rolled into one great school year! Next year in third grade, we'll finish the Grand Tour of the United States.

But before we get on board the Grand Tour bus to read about the United States, we're going to learn how our country began and where all these people came from! For one week, I'll be bringing home coloring pages each day. These pages tell the story of America. I'd like you to display the pages on the refrigerator or on my bedroom door. Each day, I'll share with you what I learned in the story about America.

During the year, every Monday through Thursday, I will bring home a Spelling homework paper. It should take me no more than 10-15 minutes to complete. This will help me learn to be responsible and will show you something I learned in school each day. Please initial my paper. My teacher will collect these papers each morning and give me a star on the *Homework Chart*. Please help me make this a good daily habit.

My Physical Education Day is _____.

My Media Center Day is _____.
(Please help me remember my library book, so I can get a new one.)

My Art Day is _____.

My Music Day is _____.

Lunch is at _____ and it costs $_____.

At Back-to-School Night my teacher, Mrs./Ms./Mr. _____, will explain our **Sing, Spell, Read & Write** Reading and Language Arts program. He/she is looking forward to meeting you.

Love,

_____

Sample Classroom Schedule

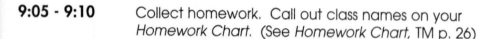

The following are three sample schedules you might want to write on a chalkboard or chart paper. They have approximate times.

WEEK 1

9:00 - 9:05 Flag salute, sing a patriotic song selection from the *Grand Tour* CD

9:05 - 9:10 Collect homework. Call out class names on your *Homework Chart*. (See *Homework Chart*, TM p. 26)

9:10 - 9:40 *Individual Skills Assessment Chart* (See *Grand Tour I* Student Book, p. 4)

9:40 - 10:00 Spelling - Step 1, *Grand Tour I* (See TM p. 99)

10:00 - 10:15 Go over and teach the remainder of the two-page daily lesson in the *Grand Tour I* Student Book. Teach these two pages as a total group, and have students write in answers the first week. Beginning the second week, the teacher will teach the lesson; however, students will **not** write answers at this time, as this will be part of their seatwork during reading groups.

10:15 - 11:25 Reading (Week 1 only)
- Audio/visual introduction to *Grand Tour Storybooks* with narration on CD and accompanying reproducibles. A complete description and transcript of the narration is found in the Teacher's Manual for Reading.
- Begin individual *Quick Placement Test* while students are coloring accompanying reproducibles mentioned above.
- Students will have self-selected reading from class library.

11:25 - 12:00 Select a storybook and read aloud to class, play phonics games, Additional Related Activities

Sample Classroom Schedule *continued*

WEEKS 2 - 3

9:00 - 9:05   Flag salute, sing a patriotic song selection from the *Grand Tour* CD

9:05 - 9:10   Sing state songs from *Grand Tour* CD for states where *Grand Tour* buses are parked (for each reading group)

9:10 - 9:15   Collect homework. Call out names on your *Homework Chart*. (See *Homework Chart*, TM p. 26.)

9:15 - 9:45   *Individual Skills Assessment Chart* (See *Grand Tour I* Student Book, p. 4)

9:45 - 10:00   Spelling Test

10:00 - 10:15   Introduce spelling words in *Grand Tour I* Student Book and teach the phonics skills and songs connected with the spelling lesson. Students will copy the 10 spelling words to take home, study, and write in sentences for homework.

10:15 - 10:30   Go over and teach the remainder of the two-page daily lesson in the *Grand Tour I* Student Book. Teach these two pages as a total group, but **do not** have students write answers in *Grand Tour I* at this time. Students will write in answers for seatwork while the teacher is meeting with reading groups.

10:30 - 11:30   Reading Groups
Suggestions for student seatwork while the teacher is conducting reading groups:
* *Grand Tour I*, 2 pages
* Grammar Chalkboard Lesson
* Additional Handwriting Practice
* Self-selected reading from class library
* Rereading stories from the *Grand Tour Storybooks*
* Journal Writing
* Additional Related Activity found in Teacher's Manual (last page of each step)
* *Pick-A-Sound* game
* If time permits, students may start Spelling Homework.

11:30 - 11:50   Process Writing

11:50 - 12:00   Select a storybook and read aloud to class, play phonics games, Additional Related Activities

Sample Classroom Schedule *continued*

WEEKS 4 - 36

9:00 - 9:05   Flag salute, sing a patriotic song selection from *Grand Tour* CD

9:05 - 9:10   Sing state songs from *Grand Tour* CD for states where *Grand Tour* buses are parked (for each reading group)

9:10 - 9:15   Collect homework. Call out class names on your Homework Chart. (See *Homework Chart*, TM p. 26)

9:15 - 9:30   Spelling Test

9:30 - 9:45   Introduce spelling words in the appropriate *Grand Tour* Student Book (weeks 4-18, *Grand Tour I*; Weeks 19-36, *Grand Tour II*), and teach the phonics skills and songs connected with the spelling lesson. Students will copy the 10 spelling words to take home, study, and write in sentences for homework.

9:45 - 9:55   Go over and teach the remainder of the two-page daily lesson in the appropriate *Grand Tour* Student Book. Teach these two pages as a total group, but **do not** have students write answers in *Grand Tour* Student Book at this time. Students will write in answers for seatwork while the teacher is meeting with reading groups.

9:55 - 11:25   Reading Groups
Suggestions for student seatwork while the teacher is conducting reading groups:
• *Grand Tour* Student Book, 2 pages
• Grammar Chalkboard Lesson
• Additional Handwriting Practice
• Self-selected reading
• Rereading stories from the *Grand Tour Storybooks*. Students should read each story three times: once in the reading group; once silently; and once with a peer.
• Additional Related Activity when appropriate
• Journal Writing
• *Pick-A-Sound* game
• If time permits, students may start Spelling Homework.

11:25 - 11:45   Process Writing

11:45 - 12:00   Select a storybook and read aloud to class, play phonics games, Additional Related Activities

Sing Spell Read&Write

Frequently Asked Questions

When do students start reading the Grand Tour Storybooks? And how do I place those students entering in the middle of the year?

Sing, Spell, Read & Write develops each program with the philosophy that learning should be fun and challenging for children, not frustrating. We want every child to experience success. The Level 2 *Grand Tour* Storybooks have been written specifically for children who have *successfully* completed all 36 Steps of **Sing, Spell, Read & Write** Level 1. The Level 2 curriculum includes three weeks of phonics review, during which time individual student assessments are done. All children in the class should participate in the three-week phonics review. In addition, we have provided a **Sing, Spell, Read & Write** Quick Placement Test.

Administer this one-on-one test to any child:

- with incomplete school records,
- who has not completed the 36 Steps of **SSR&W** Level 1, or
- who may, in your judgment, be reading below grade level.

Then, follow the placement guidelines on the *Quick Placement Test* and refer to TM pp. 34-39 for intervention strategies that may be used to bring the child to independent reading ability before starting the *Grand Tour Storybooks*.

A one-week Introduction to *Grand Tour* provides two or three coloring pages per day. These are correlated with a CD that prepares the children for the *Grand Tour* by giving them the true story of what happened long ago.

Should I use other curriculum materials with Sing, Spell, Read & Write Level 2?

Sing, Spell, Read & Write Level 2 is a complete Reading and Language Arts curriculum. You need no supplementary curriculum materials for Phonics, Spelling, Vocabulary, Grammar, Process Writing, or Handwriting. The 17 *Grand Tour* Level 2 Storybooks will provide a full year's worth of instructional-level reading. Throughout the *Teacher's Manual for Reading*, we have included themed bibliographies of Recommended Read-Alouds and self-selected reading that correlate with each story. We suggest that you work closely with your media specialist and take full advantage of the resources in your school's media center. Provide your media specialist with a copy of the Recommended Reading Bibliography found in the *Teacher's Manual for Reading*. Request that he/she set up a display or special shelf in the media center. If he/she knows the topics that you will be covering in the storybooks, he/she can request age-appropriate movies, film-strips, or other audiovisual materials from the district's media resource center.

Teacher Tips

When do I start having written Spelling Dictation Tests?

Written Spelling Dictation begins with Step 2, during the second week of school.

What is a "step" in the Level 2 program?

A "step" is a full week of instruction. Each step includes one full week of lessons and practice in: Phonics, Spelling, Vocabulary, Grammar, Proofreading, Reference Skills, Reading and Comprehension, Authentic Writing, and Handwriting. There are 36 steps in Level 2 *Grand Tour Language Arts*. These 36 steps provide one full school year of Language Arts instruction. There are also 18 *Process Writing Lessons*. Each of these lessons is designed to be used over a two-week period, and will provide one full school year of writing instruction and practice.

What do I do with students who are not yet independent readers?

Your first and most important goal should be to identify those children and get them "up to speed" and reading independently as quickly as possible. The Level 2 program includes the tools to help you achieve this goal. First, we provide the **Sing, Spell, Read & Write** *Quick Placement Test*.

Administer this one-on-one test to any child:

- with incomplete school records,
- who has not completed the 36 Steps of **SSR&W** Level 1, or
- who may, in your judgment, be reading below grade level.

Then, follow the placement guidelines on the *Quick Placement Test* and refer to TM pp. 34-39 for intervention strategies that may be used to bring the child to independent reading ability before starting the *Grand Tour Storybooks*.

Level 2 has a complete set of Phonics Charts, Games, and Songs for intervention and/or review in filling in the "gaps" in phonics/decoding/word identification skills. Available as a separate purchase are the Level 1 *Phonetic Storybook Readers*. We strongly recommend that you purchase one or more sets of the Level 1 *Storybooks* for your classroom, or arrange to "borrow" a set from a first-grade colleague.

Use Intervention Plan A if Level 1 *Storybooks* are available to you. If Level 1 *Storybooks* are not available, use Intervention Plan B. Teach the Intervention Vocabulary Lists in TM pp. 38-39 to give students word identification skills necessary for Level 2. Children MUST be able to score at least an 80% on the **Sing, Spell, Read & Write** *Quick Placement Test* to experience reading success in the Level 2 *Storybooks*. While these students are busy being brought up to independent reading level, they should continue their Language Arts instruction with the rest of the class in the *Grand Tour I* Student Book. Please be gentle with these students until they catch up in reading ability. Help them succeed with close assistance. The intervention program should make a big difference for them in three or four weeks. Also, the intervention students should participate in the group singing of all songs that are introduced along the *Grand Tour*.

When do students begin writing smaller?

Students may begin writing smaller after you have completed all the *Manuscript Writing Practices* (through Step 11), or when you are satisfied that the students have mastered correct manuscript letter formation. At that time, you can move students to one-spaced capital letters and half-spaced lower case letters. You do not need to order different paper. Just go through the alphabet from Aa to Zz in a direct writing lesson on the board. Show capital letters that start at the dotted line and small letters that go from an "imaginary dotted line" to the solid line "sidewalk." This is done for several reasons:

* Students are ready to write sentences now, and with the large writing each word almost takes up an entire line, making sentence writing difficult if not impossible. The smaller writing will help.

* Students who have struggled with the letters that go above or below the line (h, b, g, y, etc.), have much less trouble when you move to one-spaced capitals and half-spaced lower case letters.

* Students are capable of writing much more at this point, providing:
    a. The writing consists only of words they can sound-out and read, or
    b. The writing consists of a poem or song which they know well (so they can find and keep their place more readily when copying from the board).

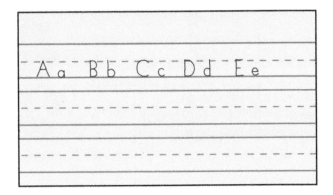

Note that although the writing lines provided in *Grand Tour I* and *II* have the dotted lines that primary grade writing paper has, their overall height is approximately that of regular lined notebook paper.

When students begin Cursive Writing (optional), you will want to use both spaces of the writing lines. This will be important, even critical, while students are learning correct cursive letter formation. Encourage students to practice this using the Writing Slate on the back of their *Grand Tour II* Student Books and the dry-erase markers and erasers provided with your classroom kit.

Phonics Skills

Quick Intervention

Your first and most important goal this year should be to identify those children who are not yet reading on grade level and get them "up to speed" as quickly as possible. The **Sing, Spell, Read & Write** Level 2 program includes the tools you need to help you achieve this goal.

You are encouraged to use the **Sing, Spell, Read & Write Quick Placement Test** (included in your Level 2 Program) to identify gaps in the decoding skills of any student.

Administer the one-on-one *Quick Placement Test* to any child:

- with incomplete school records,
- who has not completed the 36 Steps of *SSR&W* Level 1, or
- who may, in your judgment, be reading below grade level.

Score the *Quick Placement Test* as you administer it to each individual student. (See detailed Teacher Directions on the reverse side of the *Quick Placement Test*.)

Students who score 80% or better on each of the five lists can proceed directly into reading the Level 2 *Grand Tour Storybooks*. Students who have scored below 80% on any list should be given intervention before reading the Level 2 *Grand Tour Storybooks*.

Once you have identified students in need of intervention, select which of the following Intervention Plans you will be using:

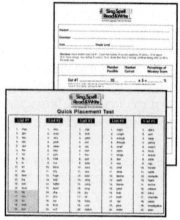

Quick Placement Test

Intervention Plan A

Intervention Plan A is based on the use of the Level 1 *Phonetic Storybook Readers*. These Storybooks are available as a separate purchase. We strongly recommend that you purchase one or more sets for your classroom, or arrange to borrow a set from a first-grade colleague. This plan is recommended if you have access to the Level 1 Phonetic Storybook Readers. Intervention Plan A is explained in detail on TM page 36.

*Level 1
Phonetic Storybook Readers*

Intervention Plan B

Intervention Plan B is based on the use of the **Quick Intervention Plan B Vocabulary Lists** found on TM pages 38 and 39. If the Level 1 *Phonetic Storybooks* are not available, the Intervention Vocabulary Lists will quickly give students the word identification skills they need in order to be successful in reading the Level 2 *Grand Tour Storybooks*. Intervention Plan B is explained in detail on TM page 37.

Note to teacher: The Level 2 Curriculum includes a one-week introduction to the *Grand Tour* Reading Program. **All** of your students should participate in the introductory activities and work in the *Grand Tour I* Student Books. The *Quick Placement Test* will help you identify students who are ready to "board the bus" and begin reading the *Grand Tour Storybooks* in their reading groups. Some of your students may need to complete the Intervention Program during reading group time **before** being placed in the *Grand Tour Storybooks*.

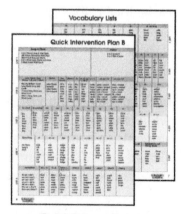

*Quick Intervention
Vocabulary Lists*

Quick Intervention Placement Chart

Quick Placement Test Five or more errors on:	Intervention Plan A Begin with:	Intervention Plan B Begin with:	Phonetic Skills Student needs instruction in:	Correlated Songs & Charts Have students sing and do these activities:	Correlated Games Have students play these games:
List #1	Phonetic Storybook Reader #1	Vocabulary List #1	Short Vowel Words	A-Z Phonics Song & Wall Cards ABC Echoes & Manuscript Wall Chart Short Vowel Song & Cards Ferris Wheel Song, Chart & Tickets Short Vowel Word Charts (5)	A-Z Sound-O A-Z Pick-A-Sound
List #2	Phonetic Storybook Reader #6	Vocabulary List #2	Letter Clusters Long Vowels Two Vowel Words Silent ǿ Words	Letter Cluster Songs & Charts (4) Pop the Balloons Chart Long Vowel Song & Cards Two Vowels Get Together Song, Chart & Word Cards Silent ǿ Song, Chart & Word Cards	Letter Cluster Sound-O Letter Cluster Pick-A-Sound Word-O
List #3	Phonetic Storybook Reader #9	Vocabulary List #3	Letter Clusters (continued)	(same as previous box)	
List #4	Phonetic Storybook Reader #13	Vocabulary List #4	Oddities of the English Language	Gh Clown Song	
List #5	Phonetic Storybook Reader #16	Vocabulary List #5	Contractions Silent Letters Multisyllable Words Rulebreakers & Wacky Words		

Quick Intervention *continued*

Intervention Plan A
Use if you have access to *SSR&W Level 1 Phonetic Storybook Readers.*

Available as a separate purchase are the *SSR&W* Level 1 *Phonetic Storybook Readers.* We strongly recommend that you purchase one or more sets for your classroom, or arrange to borrow a set from a first-grade colleague. With the phonics songs and accompanying wall charts, five games, and 17 storybooks, you have everything you need to bring students to independent reading ability.

How to Implement Intervention Plan A

1. Administer the one-on-one *Quick Placement Test* to any child:
   * with incomplete school records,
   * who has not completed the 36 Steps of *SSR&W* Level 1, or
   * who may, in your judgment, be reading below grade level.

   The *Quick Placement Test* will help you identify students who need intervention before being placed in the Level 2 *Grand Tour Storybooks.*

*Level 1
Phonetic Storybook Readers*

2. Use the Quick Intervention Placement Chart on TM page 35 to select the appropriate Level 1 *Phonetic Storybook Reader.* Also, make note of the correlated songs, charts, and games you should use to help students quickly learn the targeted phonetic skills.

3. Have students read and discuss the vocabulary words at the beginning of each story in the selected Storybook Reader. Ask students to use some of the words in sentences orally to help them develop their vocabulary.

4. Read and discuss the story.

5. Continue with the subsequent stories, moving through the remaining Level 1 *Phonetic Storybook Readers* as quickly as possible until the student has completed *Phonetic Storybook Reader 17.*

6. Give *Quick Placement Test* again to check for 80% or better mastery.

7. Once 80% or better mastery is achieved, that student is ready to begin reading *Grand Tour Storybook 1.*

Pack your bags, get on the bus . . .

80%

Grand Tour
Storybook 1

Sing Spell
Read & Write

Quick Intervention *continued*

Intervention Plan B

Use if you do not have access to *SSR&W* Level 1 *Phonetic Storybook Readers*.

If the *SSR&W* Level 1 *Phonetic Storybook Readers* are not available, use the *Quick Intervention Plan B Vocabulary Lists* on TM pages 38 and 39 to quickly give students the word identification skills they need in order to be successful in reading the Level 2 *Grand Tour Storybooks*.

How to Implement Intervention Plan B

1. Administer the one-on-one *Quick Placement Test* to any child:
   * with incomplete school records,
   * who has not completed the 36 Steps of *SSR&W* Level 1, or
   * who may, in your judgment, be reading below grade level.

   The *Quick Placement Test* will help you identify students who need intervention before being placed in the Level 2 *Grand Tour Storybooks*.

2. Use the Quick Intervention Placement Chart (TM page 35) to select the appropriate *Intervention Vocabulary List*. Also, make note of the correlated songs and games you should use to help students quickly learn the targeted phonetic skills.

3. Introduce students to the list of words to be learned. For example, if the student needs to start on List #1, write the first group of words from List #1 on the board.

4. Have students:
   * Sing the appropriate songs using the accompanying charts.
   * Play the appropriate games.
   * Read each word on the board and use in a sentence orally.
   * Write each word, marking the phonetic grouping as indicated in the first word of each list.
   * Spell the words orally (optional).

5. Continue through each subsequent group of words in each list as quickly as possible, using the songs, games, and charts to teach and/or reinforce each skill. Knowing these words will help the student gain decoding ability and prepare him/her for reading unknown words independently.

6. When student completes List #5, give the *Quick Placement Test* again to check for 80% or better mastery.

7. Once 80% or better mastery is achieved, that student is ready to begin reading *Grand Tour Storybook 1*.

Quick Intervention Vocabulary Lists

List #1

ă
căt
bat
hat
cap
map
can
bag
ran

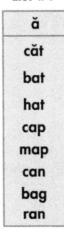

80%

Pack your bags, get on the bus . . .

Grand Tour Storybook 1

Quick Intervention Plan B

LIST 1

Songs & Charts	Games
A to Z Phonics Song & Wall Cards	A to Z Sound-O
ABC Echoes & Manuscript Wall Chart	A to Z Pick-A-Sound
Short Vowel Song and Cards	
Ferris Wheel Song, Chart and Tickets	
5 Short Vowel Word Charts	

LIST 2

Songs & Charts	Games	Two Vowels	Silent e	āy	ge, gi, gy = soft g	y = ē	ed says /t/	ed says /d/
Letter Cluster Song (Verses 1-4) and 4 Charts	Letter Cluster Sound-O	rain	bite	day	germ	pretty	pack = packed	hunt = hunted
Pop the Balloons Chart	Letter Cluster Pick-A-Sound	green	robe	lay	giant	funny	camp = camped	want = wanted
Long Vowel Song & Cards		each	made	pay	age	happy	pick = picked	dust = dusted
Two Vowel Song, Chart, & Word Cards		meat	fine	say	gym	penny	lock = locked	test = tested
Silent e Song, Chart, & Word Cards		teach	cute	stay	hinge	windy	jump = jumped	lift = lifted
		pie	take	may	huge	candy	mix = mixed	paint = painted
		dear	hope	play	gem	lady	kick = kicked	melt = melted
		soap	make		page	baby	fix = fixed	rest = rested

LIST 3

th voiced	th unvoiced	tch	ow	ou	ōw	ew	qu	wh	ar
the	thank	match	how	ground	own	new	quit	which	hard
this	thick	patch	brown	sound	snow	flew	quick	what	barn
that	thin	stitch	cow	round	slow	stew	queen	where	card
these	think	itch	owl	found	blow	threw	quack	why	yard
those	thing	switch	down	out	low	few	quiz	when	farm
them	three	ditch	town	scout	grow	grew	quiet	whip	star
then	both	catch	clown	loud	mow	chew	quite	white	park
they		pitch		mouth	show	drew	question	while	smart

LIST 4

Song/Chart	all	ar = or	dge	ue	x = cks	īe = ē	ēa = ā	ĕa
Gh Clown Song & Chart	ball	war	fudge	true	box	chief	bear	bread
	call	warn	judge	blue	mix	piece	pear	read
Sing until student can read all the words	all	warm	budge	Sue	ax	yield	wear	thread
	tall	swarm	edge	clue	wax	niece	tear	ready
	small	wart	hedge	glue	tax	believe	steak	head
	wall	reward	pledge	flue	ox	field	break	heavy
	fall	toward	ledge	due	fix		great	breath
	hall		dodge	Tuesday	fox			feather
					six			

LIST 5

contractions	āre = air	ä = ŏ	before e, i or y: c = s	silent w	silent k	silent l	silent b	silent g
do not = don't	bare	father	circus	write	knot	walk	crumb	sign
are not = aren't	rare	want	choice	wrote	knob	talk	limb	gnat
can not = can't	care	wash	circle	wrist	knee	chalk	thumb	gnaw
we are = we're	spare	wasp	cent	wring	knapsack	half	comb	gnash
did not = didn't	hare	watch	police	wrap	know	calf	lamb	resign
they are = they're	share	swamp	prince	wreath	known	could	climb	
have not = haven't	dare	swap	voice	wrench	knew	would	debt	
	stare	watt	city	wrong	knock	should		

Sing Spell Read & Write

Vocabulary Lists

ă	ĕ	ĭ	ŏ	ŭ	ă ĕ ĭ ŏ ŭ	
căt	wĕt	pĭn	tŏp	gŭm	hănd	milk
bat	pet	him	got	mug	snack	frog
hat	get	dig	hop	nut	mend	pond
cap	jet	big	box	cup	desk	rust
map	yes	win	pot	fun	hill	bump
can	egg	lid	doll	pup		
bag	mess	did	sock	jump		
ran	sent	swim	rock	dust		

ed says /ed/	if word ends in e, add d for ending ed	ed, er, ing		or	sh	ch	er	ir	ur
hunt = hunted	save = saved	hop = hopped, hopper, hopping		born	she	chain	her	sir	fur
want = wanted	time = timed	bat = batted, batter, batting		storm	ship	chilly	over	shirt	hurt
dust = dusted	hope = hoped	hum = hummed, hummer, humming		for	short	chin	term	girl	burn
test = tested	place = placed	drum = drummed, drummer, drumming		north	shut	inch	teacher	stir	turn
lift = lifted	rake = raked	stop = stopped, stopper, stopping		torn	rash	pinch	herd	dirt	purple
paint = painted	pile = piled	mop = mopped, mopper, mopping		fort	crash	each	were	first	curb
melt = melted	race = raced	scrub = scrubbed, scrubber, scrubbing		horn	shop	reach	sister	third	curl
rest = rested	trace = traced	pat = patted, patter, patting		sport	fish	cherry	thunder	bird	purse

aw	au	ing	ang	ong	oy	oi	ōō	ŏŏ	tion
draw	Paul	king	sang	song	boy	oil	boot	took	nation
law	haul	ring	hang	strong	joy	soil	tool	look	station
lawn	August	sting	gang	belong	enjoy	boil	roof	book	vacation
jaw	author	bring	rang	along	toy	join	food	hook	information
paw	fault	thing		long	royal	joint	soon	cook	addition
straw	sauce	wing			annoy	coin	cool	foot	action
dawn	because					point	tooth	good	election
saw	auto					moist	room	wood	investigation

ear = er	f to ves	long ī	long ō	u = ŏŏ	air	ui = ōō	or = er
pearl	leaf = leaves	kind	gold	put	chair	suit	worm
earn	wife = wives	bind	bold	pull	air	fruit	worry
learn	knife = knives	blind	cold	push	hair	nuisance	world
heard	thief = thieves	mind	fold	pudding	stair	suitcase	motor
earth	loaf = loaves	behind	hold	bush	fair	juice	word
search		grind	mold	bull	pair	cruise	work
		wind		full			doctor
							color

silent h	silent t	qu = k	ph = f	ch = k	ss = sh	ch = sh	Rulebreakers and Wacky Words	
hour	often	mosquito	phone	Chris	mission	Charlotte	ocean	friend
honor	fasten	croquet	phonics	Christmas	permission	Chicago	sugar	soup
honest	moisten	bouquet	photo	chord	admission		shoe	eyes
John	listen		elephant	school	discussion		busy	door
	castle		trophy	stomach			does	built
	whistle		Ralph	anchor			sure	
			alphabet	chorus				
			dolphin	ache				

Introduction

Many of your students will have been in a Sing, Spell, Read and Write classroom before coming to second grade. For these students, using the charts, singing the songs, and playing the games will be a review and reinforcement of the phonics skills taught in first grade. For students new to the program, it will be a new learning experience, and one that is vital to their success. The songs and games provide the phonetic keys for decoding.

Spend at least 30 minutes a day the first three weeks of school reviewing all the songs and games with the total group. After the three week review, use the songs and games suggested in the *Language Arts Teacher's Manual* and *Grand Tour I and II* Student Books, as you see the need.

Ă...ă...apple

A to Z Phonics Chart and Song

CD Track 2

Directions

Place the *A to Z Phonics Song Cards* (apple, ball, cat, etc.) across the front of the room above the chalkboard. There are numbers on the cards to help you place them in their proper position. Begin listening to the song together:

> **"When we learn these sounds you'll see, ready to read then we will be."**

Now point to the wall card with the apple, first pointing to capital **A**, then to little **a**, then to the picture of the **apple**, as the children sing:

> **"Ă, ă, ă**pple"

Then point to capital **B**, then to little **b**, then to the picture of the **ball**, as the children sing:

> **"Bh, bh, b**all"

Continue in this way through the song, pointing first to the capital letter, then to the small letter, then to the picture, for each card from **A** to **Z**. Your pointer will really be moving along to keep up with the music! Don't point to each word on the cards that have words only. After you learn the song well, you'll probably turn to look at the class when you come to these cards.

B...b...ball

After singing the song several times, ask if anyone in the room thinks he/she can be the leader and point the way you did:

First to the capital letter,   Then to the small letter, and   Then to the picture

Ask the children to be very careful to say the sounds the way they are on the CD and not to add an /ŭ/ for the umbrella sound with each sound they sing! This takes practice to do properly and is **very** important.

C...c...cat

After choosing someone to be the leader, tell the class that each child must keep his/her eyes at the tip of the pointer while singing this song. Tell them that the best readers are those who always keep their eyes at the tip of the pointer. You might add, "Let's see how many good readers we're going to have this year!" If you will compliment a few for watching carefully, you'll see how the rest start watching carefully, too. This is extremely important. **To sing without looking is a total waste of time**. Insist! This is Auditory-Visual training, both hearing the sound and seeing the shapes of the letters that make the sound. So Sing, Listen, and Look!

D...d...doll

A to Z Sound-O Game

TO BE PLAYED UNTIL MASTERED

Objective

A to Z Sound-O is a Bingo-like game which gives students practice in recall of letter sounds as taught in the *A to Z Phonics Song*.

Preparation

1. Cut apart the *Teacher Caller Card* found in the package of 25 *A to Z Sound-O Cards*.
2. Place the Teacher Caller Cards in the round plastic container labeled *A to Z Sound-O*.

Directions

1. Distribute the *A to Z Sound-O Cards* and see-through game markers.
2. Students will use the blue printed side of the card first.
3. Tell students to put a marker on the X on Gus-the-Bug in the center of the card. This is a free space.
4. The teacher will draw a Caller Card from the container and call that letter. Always say the word learned in the *A to Z Phonics Song* with each sound as you call:

   "Cover the letter **A** that says **ă** as in **ă**pple."
   "Cover the letter **E** that says **ĕ**, as in **ĕ**gg."
   "Cover the letter **O** that says **ŏ** as in **ŏ**ctopus," etc.

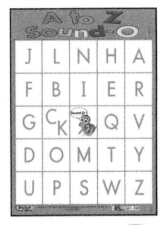

- Assure players that **every** card has **every** sound being called; keep looking -- it's there somewhere!

- **Important:** Be sure to go up to the front of the room and point to the letter on the *A to Z Phonics Song Cards* (in front of the class) as you call each sound. Watch their eyes. **When they no longer look up to check the letter, you know they know them all**. Turn the card over to the red side to practice the lower case letters.

- If someone says, "I can't find the **t** (or whatever letter) on my card," or "My card doesn't have it," give help. Let their neighbors help. **This is a game, not a test**. If you create the right atmosphere with this activity — laughing, helping, and even giving a prize to the winner, you will find your students choosing this educational game for rainy days or quiet play time.

5. Tell students to call out **"Sound-O!"** when they get a straight line vertically, horizontally, or diagonally. Have fun!

6. The winner gets to choose a prize from the Treasure Chest.

7. Follow these same directions for Side 2, red.

A to Z Pick-A-Sound Game

TO BE PLAYED UNTIL MASTERED

Objective

To play a game which will give students practice in identifying sounds as taught in the *A to Z Phonics Song*.

A to Z Pick-A-Sound is played with the **yellow** deck of cards. Two to five students may take part. The object is to make pairs from cards in each player's hand. The game ends when any player is completely out of cards. The player with the most pairs is the winner.

Directions

1. Place the **Merry-Go-Round** in the center of the table. Shuffle the deck of cards and deal one card at a time until each player has five cards. Place the rest of the cards face down in a pile inside the Merry-Go-Round container.

2. All players should then sort their cards, placing any pairs they have face-up on the table in front of them.

3. The player to the left of the dealer should begin the game by calling any player by name and asking for a card. *"Mary, do you have the letter m that says m-m-monkey?"* The player making the request **must** hold that card in his/her possession.

4. If Mary has the **Mm** card, she must give it to that player who will put the pair down. That player will get another turn, calling on another person for a sound. However, if Mary does not have the **Mm** card, she must call, **"Pick-A-Sound from the Merry-Go-Round."**

5. The player must then pick the top card from the pile of cards inside the Merry-Go-Round, and add that card to those in his/her hand. If the player picks the card with the sound called for, he/she makes a pair and takes another turn. When the player can no longer make a pair, the person on the left then becomes the next player. **When a player pairs all the cards from his/her hand, the game is over. The player with the most paired cards is the winner.**

6. The winner gets to choose a prize from the Treasure Chest.

Sing-Spell Read & Write.

ABC Echoes

CD Track 3

Directions

Teach the entire class at one time using the classroom *Manuscript Wall Chart* (marked *ABC ECHOES*). This alphabet strip should be displayed from A to Z in full view of the class on a side or back wall. This activity will serve as further sound-symbol reinforcement. It will also assess the student's ability to recall the sounds of the letters learned in the *A to Z Phonics Song* without the aid of pictures. Tell students to keep their eyes at the tip of the pointer and echo after the teacher as he/she goes along the wall cards from A to Z, pointing to the letters and saying each sound. Listen to the demonstration lesson on CD Track 3 to hear the *ABC Echoes*.

Teacher:	(Pointing to **Aa**) "ă!"
Class:	"ă!"
Teacher:	(Pointing to **Bb**) "bh!"
Class:	"bh!"
Teacher:	(Pointing to **Cc**) "ck!"
Class:	"ck!"

Manuscript Wall Chart

Continue along the alphabet strip saying each sound quickly so you will leave off the easily added /ŭh/ sound. After the teacher leads the class through the sounds from A to Z, ask whether anyone thinks he/she can use the pointer and lead the class. Tell students in row 1 (or table 1) to line up, one behind the other at letter **A**. Allow each student to have a turn being leader. The students in row 2 (or table 2) may be the next group to go up to take turns leading the class. Continue practicing this activity daily with five students, following the singing of the *A to Z Phonics Song*.

Aa Bb Cc Dd Ee Ff Gg Hh Ii

Jj Kk Ll Mm Nn Oo Pp Qq Rr

Ss Tt Uu Vv Ww Xx Yy Zz

Short Vowel Song

CD Track 4

<u>Directions</u>

- Tell students there are five letters of the alphabet more important than any others; **Aa**, **Ee**, **Ii**, **Oo**, **Uu**.

- Tell them the letters **Aa**, **Ee**, **Ii**, **Oo**, **Uu** are also known as **vowels**. (All the rest of the letters are known as **consonants**.)

- Tell students they learned these vowel sounds when they sang the *A to Z Phonics Song*. (There are long vowel sounds for **Aa**, **Ee**, **Ii**, **Oo**, **Uu** which they will learn later.)

- A scoop mark over a vowel (˘) means to say the short vowel sound. There is a song to help students remember the short vowel sounds. It is called the *Short Vowel Song*.

- Introduce the *Short Vowel Song* to everyone at once. Hold up, one by one, the large yellow cards with a short vowel (**ă, ĕ, ĭ, ŏ, ŭ**) printed on each. Tell children these letters are very important letters and we call them **vowels**. Hold up the one with a printed **ă** on it and ask the class what sound they have learned for this letter.

Continue in the same manner with each of the other vowel cards, having the class identify its sound. Tell children you're going to say a sound **four** times and you want them to tell you the picture they have learned for that sound, as:

Teacher:	"ă, ă, ă, ă!"
Class:	"apple!"
Teacher:	"ĕ, ĕ, ĕ, ĕ!"
Class:	"egg!"
Teacher:	"ĭ, ĭ, ĭ, ĭ!"
Class:	"inchworm!"
Teacher:	**"The short vowels we do sing"** — (See? I'm teaching you a song.) **"ŏ, ŏ, ŏ, ŏ!"**
Class:	"octopus!"
Teacher:	"Now, we're going to say this next sound only once — listen: **ŭ, umbrella, too.**"
Class:	"ŭ, umbrella, too."
Teacher:	**"Now I know my short vowel sounds, I'll sing them all to you."**
Class:	**"Now I know my short vowel sounds, I'll sing them all to you."**
Teacher:	"Wonderful! Now I want you to notice the little scoop mark printed over each vowel (˘). It is called the short vowel mark, and the sounds we have learned are the short vowel sounds. I need five students to line up, one behind the other, in front of this table (in center front of group and on which the short vowel cards are spread out, face up). I'll go first to show you how to do it."

Short Vowel Song *continued*

Play the *Short Vowel Song* on CD Track 4 and listen to children on the CD sing:

Short Vowel Song
(holding up vowel cards one by one)

ă, ă, ă, ă, 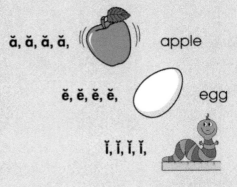 apple   (Teacher should hold up the ă card for class to see.)

ĕ, ĕ, ĕ, ĕ,   egg   (Teacher should hold up the ĕ card for class to see.)

ĭ, ĭ, ĭ, ĭ,   inchworm   (Teacher should hold up the ĭ card for class to see.)

The short vowels we do sing!

ŏ, ŏ, ŏ, ŏ,   octopus   (Teacher should hold up the ŏ card for class to see.)

ŭ,   umbrella too!   (Teacher should hold up the ŭ card for class to see.)

Now I know my short vowel sounds,
     I'll sing them all to you!

Copyright © Sue Dickson

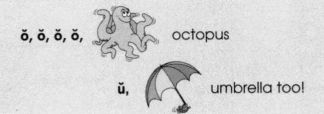

ă, ă, ă, ă, apple...

The first student in line should step up to take a turn holding up the correct vowel cards as the entire group sings the song through. Continue in this way until everyone has a turn holding up the cards. **The song repeats five times**.

The teacher may want to rearrange the cards quickly on the desk after each student's turn to see if she can "trick" someone into holding up the wrong card!

Ferris Wheel Song

CD Track 5

Directions

Review with students how to **slide together** (blend) two letter sounds, (one consonant and one short vowel) to make beginnings of words. Practice blending two sounds through the song in preparation for reading and spelling hundreds of short vowel words. (It is estimated that 62% of English is made up of short vowel words and syllables.)

Important: Place the *Ferris Wheel Chart* in the *left front of the classroom* so students who are seated will not have their view blocked by students who come up to "ride" the Ferris Wheel.

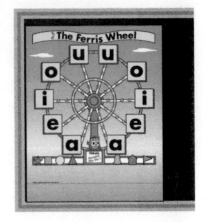

Place Ferris Wheel Chart in the left front of classroom

1. Point to the vowels around the *Ferris Wheel Chart* and have students say the short vowel sounds.

2. Sing the *Short Vowel Song* (to interlock with the previous step), pointing from lower left **ă** to **ŭ** at the top.

3. Pick up the ticket with a **star #1** and an **arrow**. With it, point to each vowel going clockwise from lower left **ă**, and sing the sounds of the vowels up the scale five notes and back down the scale five notes. (Listen to the *Ferris Wheel Song* on the CD Track 5.)

4. Pick up **star ticket #2** (with letter b) and ask for the sound of **b**. Tell students they are going to review putting two sounds together by "riding the Ferris Wheel," and **they will be making beginnings of words** as they "ride and sing" this game.

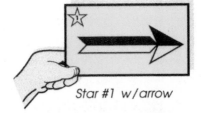

Star #1 w/arrow

Teacher:	(holding **b** ticket) "What is the sound of **b**?"
Class:	**"Bh!"**
Teacher:	"What is the sound of letter **a**?" (pointing to letter **ă** on the *Ferris Wheel Chart*)
Class:	**"ă!"**
Teacher:	(Holding **b** ticket to the left of the **ă** on the *Ferris Wheel Chart*) "Let's say the sound of **b** first, then slide to the **ă** sound. Ready? Watch! **Bh...ă!** Now put them together!"
Class:	**"Bă!"**
Teacher:	"Great! Can anyone think of a word that begins **bă**?"
Class:	**"Băt!"**
Teacher:	"Yes, and what do you hear after **bă** in bat?"

Star #2 w/letter b

Ferris Wheel Song *continued*

Class:	"T!"
Teacher:	"Can anyone write **băt** on the chalkboard for us?"
Teacher:	"Great! See, we're reading and spelling! Does anyone know another word that begins **bă**?"
Class:	"**Băg!**" (or **băd**, etc.)
Teacher:	"Yes, and what do you hear at the end of **bag**?"
Class:	"**G**," etc.
Teacher:	"Yes, the **g** as in goat."

You may continue with different tickets to let children see and understand the "sound-symbol-word-reading-writing" relationship.

1. Be sure you have secured your *Ferris Wheel Chart* on an easel or on the chalkboard **at a level the students can reach easily**.

2. Distribute the tickets with ★ ■ ○ ▲ symbols to students. The tickets with symbols 🔔 🏠 ▷ have *letter blends*, such as **st**, **bl**, and **gl**, and are used with the *Ferris Wheel Blends Song* later.

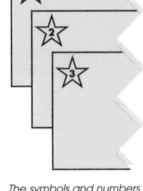

The symbols and numbers on Ferris Wheel Tickets

3. Tell students to find the symbol and number on their tickets.

4. Now point to the row of corresponding symbols which are printed across the *Ferris Wheel Chart*. Tell students to notice the **star** is first, the **square** next, etc., (from left to right), and this is the order in which groups will come to the *Ferris Wheel Chart*. Students with **star** tickets will come up first, then when they are through, those with **square** tickets, etc.

The symbols on the Ferris Wheel Chart

5. Before playing the *Ferris Wheel Song*, write numbers 1-5 on the floor in chalk as shown. Have children look at the number on their ticket. Tell them when the music begins, students with a **star** should come and stand on the corresponding number on the floor. This keeps the tickets in order with the recording.

6. Each of the "riders" should:

   a. **Hold ticket in left hand** as shown, with arm outstretched so all can see the ticket as they sing.

   b. Start at lower left vowel box with **a**.

   c. Move ticket clockwise, always holding to the left of vowel boxes.

Children in line at corresponding numbers

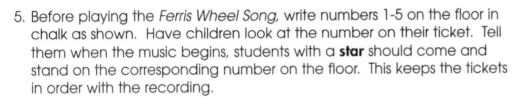

Ferris Wheel Song *continued*

7. Letters **c** and **k** have the same sound, and therefore are located on opposite sides of the same ticket. Students must flip the ticket over so that **c** appears only with **ă**, **ŏ**, and **ŭ**; and **k** with **ĕ** and **ĭ**. (This is because the **c** gives the **s** sound before **e** and **i**, as in cent and circus, but don't go into this with the children now!)
Just remember *k* goes with *e* and *i*.

8. Everyone should sing the *Ferris Wheel Song*. This will help students review blending initial consonant and short vowel sounds for reading words.

Ferris Wheel Song

"Round and round and up and down, the Ferris Wheel we go.
Round and round and up and down, come on now don't be slow.
Have your ticket in your hand, the ride will soon begin.
Do your best, your very best, go round and round again."

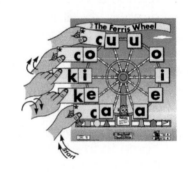

9. Using **Star Ticket #1**, sing vowel sounds only: ă, ĕ, ĭ, ŏ, ŭ, ŭ, ŏ, ĭ, ĕ, ă.

10. Then using **Star Ticket #2**, sing: bă, bĕ, bĭ, bŏ, bŭ, bŭ, bŏ, bĭ, bĕ, bă. Next: **c** and **k** (Flip ticket so **k** is with **e** and **i**.)

Continue in this way with all tickets. When students are proficient, go on to the *Ferris Wheel Blends Song* using tickets with 🔔 🏠 ▷. Ask someone to identify the **br** sound as you hold up that ticket. Do not accept **ber**. We do not say **berrush** (brush) or **berroom** (broom). Elicit **brh** as the sound for **br**. Do the same for **tr**. It's not **terruck**, it's **trh** truck. This will help them with spelling later. (Only **er**, **ir**, **ur**, can say **er**.)

Making Words with the Ferris Wheel

After singing the *Ferris Wheel Song,* have students sit in a group close to the *Ferris Wheel Chart* for "making words."

Teacher:	(Holding ticket **b** before **ă** on the chart) "What did we sing for these letters?"
Class:	**"Bă"**
Teacher:	"Can you add **t**?" (say letter name)
Class:	**"Băt"**
Teacher:	"Can you add **d**?" (say letter name)
Class:	**"Bad"**
Teacher:	"Can you add **g**?" (say letter name)
Class:	**"Bag"**
Teacher:	(Moving **b** ticket before **ĕ** on Ferris Wheel) "What did we sing for these two letters?"
Class:	**"Bĕ"**
Teacher:	"Can you add **d**?" (say letter name)
Class:	**"Bed"**
Teacher:	"Can you add **g**?" (say letter name)
Class:	**"Beg"**

Continue in this way using the tickets and chart to help students make hundreds of words!

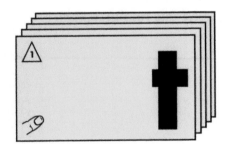

Phonics Skills

Short Vowel Word Charts

Directions

Use the *Short Vowel Word Charts* with students who need extra help in blending and reading. Point to the key letter and picture at the top center of the *Short a Word Chart*, then proceed:

Teacher: "Can anyone tell me why this chart is called the *Short a Word Chart*?"

Student: "Because there is an **a** in each word!"

Teacher: "Yes! Now we're going to read some of these **short a** words. I'm going to cover the last letter in the top word so we can just see the first two letters - **hă**. Now, what did we say on the *Ferris Wheel* when we saw these letters?" (Thus interlocking with the previous step.)

Class: "**Hă!**"

Teacher: "Right! Now let's say **hă** and then add the sound of this last letter to see what the word is. **hă**...mm. Together, **ham**! Yes, I had a **ham** sandwich. Now let's try the next one. What did we say on the Ferris Wheel for **d** and **a**?"

Class: "**Dă!**"

Teacher: "Right! Now let's add the last sound. What is it? Put it all together now, **da**...d! He is my **dad**."

NOTE: Say each word in a complete sentence after the children decode it together, so they will understand the full meaning. If a word has more than one meaning, the teacher should point this out and use it in a sentence. For example: Word #3, "mat," on the *Short a Word Chart* can be a <u>place mat</u> on the table or a <u>doormat</u> for wiping your feet.

Continue in this manner with the other short vowel charts for students who need this reinforcement.

Short e Word Chart

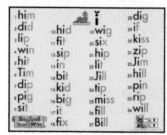
Short i Word Chart

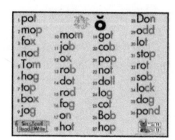
Short o Word Chart

Short a Word Chart

Letter Cluster Phonics Song

CD Tracks 8 and 9

<u>Directions</u>

Display the *Letter Cluster Phonics Song Charts*, verses 1-4, in front of the classroom.

Verse 1:

Teacher: I taught you that **o** says **ŏ** and **r** says **rh**, but whenever you see letters **o** and **r together**, don't say **ŏ-rh** to sound out the word...it won't work! Whenever you see **o-r** say **or** as in **or**bit. (Echo the **or** sound.) Who can think of a word that starts with **or**?"

Elicit:

orchestra-	The orchestra played beautiful music.
orchard-	Apple trees grow in the orchard.
organ-	She can play the organ.
orphan-	The child was an orphan.
order-	The waitress took our order.
orchid-	An orchid is a beautiful flower.
orbit-	An orbit is a circular pathway around the earth. The rocket was in orbit.

Talk about meanings and use these words in oral sentences, as shown above. Continue in this manner for the remaining letter clusters on the chart.

Tell students they are going to sing the *Letter Cluster Phonics Song*. Play the song and point to the letter cluster and the picture only. (The very small words are there for the benefit of the teacher.)

Play CD Track 8 and point along to the first chart. Have students join in singing.

For **th**, tell students that letters **t-h** have two sounds, and that **th** means "put your tongue to your teeth!" Have them do this and blow! Then say, "Three, think, threw," stretching out th at the start of every word. Now have students put their fingers on the front of their necks and with their tongues on their teeth again, practice saying voiced **th** stretching the "th" sound again: th—is, th—at, th—ese, th—ose, th—em, etc. Let them feel the vibration with their fingers.

Continue in this manner with CD Tracks 8 and 9 for the four *Letter Cluster Phonics Song Charts*.

Phonics Skills

Letter Cluster Sound-O Game

TO BE PLAYED UNTIL MASTERED

Objective

A Bingo-like game to give students practice in recall of letter cluster sounds as taught in the *Letter Cluster Phonics Song*.

Preparation

1. Cut apart the Teacher Caller Card found in the package of 25 *Letter Cluster Sound-O Cards*.

2. Place Teacher Caller Cards in the round plastic container labeled *Letter Cluster Sound-O*. The **blue** printed side is to be used with Side 1 of the *Letter Cluster Sound-O Card* to practice letter clusters taught in verses 1-2 of the *Letter Cluster Phonics Song*. The **red** printed side is used with Side 2 to practice letter clusters learned in verses 1-4.

Directions

1. Distribute the *Letter Cluster Sound-O Cards* and see-through game markers. Tell students to put a marker on Gus-the-Bug in the center of the card. This is a free space.

2. Students will place the **blue** printed side of the card face-up.

3. Teacher will draw a caller card from the container and use the **blue** printed side to read the **exact script**. The teacher will also go to the wall chart and point to the letter cluster(s) called. Watch the students' eyes. When they no longer look up to check the *Letter Cluster Charts*, you know they know them.

4. Students may call **"Sound-O"** when they have a straight line vertically, horizontally, or diagonally covered with chips.

5. Follow these same directions for Side 2, **red**.

NOTE: There are several letter cluster spellings of like sounds per box on Side 2, **red**. Assure players that every card has every sound called: "Keep looking. It's there somewhere."

Sing, Spell Read & Write

Caller Card Script

Side 1, blue:

1. Cover the three groups of letters that say /er/ ir/ ur/ the rooster's wild.

2. Cover the two groups of letters that say /ew/ for new and /o͞o/ for balloon.

3. Cover the letters that say /or/ for orbit.

4. Cover the two groups of letters that say /oy/ as in toy and /oi/ for oil.

5. Cover the two groups of letters that say /th/ as in them and /th/ as in threw.

6. Cover the letters that say /ar/ as in car.

7. Cover the letters that say /ing/ as in ring.

8. Cover the letters that say /ang/ as in rang.

9. Cover the two groups of letters that say /ow/ as in owl and /ou/ as in out.

10. Cover the letters that say /ung/ as in rung.

11. Cover the letters that say /sh/ as in shell.

12. Cover the letters that say /o͝o/ as in book, look, and hook.

13. Cover the letters that say /ch/ for chocolate.

14. Cover the two groups of letters that say /aw/ as in "we see a baby we say aw."

15. Cover the letters that say /ong/ as in song.

16. Cover the letters that say /shun/ for invention.

17. Cover the letters that say /o͞o/ as in balloon.

18. Cover the letters that say /qu/ as in quilt.

Caller Card Script *continued*

Side 2, red:

1. Cover the letters that say /**wh**/ for **whipped cream**.

2. Cover the letters that say /**ong**/ for **song**.

3. Cover the letters that say /**ung**/ for **rung**.

4. Cover the letters that say /**ew**/ for **new**.

5. Cover the letters that say /ŏŏ/ for **book** and **look** and **hook**, and the single letter /**u**/ as in **pull, push, put, bull,** and **full**.

6. Cover the letters that say /**ang**/ as in **rang**.

7. Cover the letters that say /**ss**/ as in **ci**rcus, **cy**cle and **ce**nt.

8. Cover the letters that say /ō/ as in **snow**.

9. Cover the letters that say /**ar**/ as in **car**.

10. Cover the letters that say /**ch**/ as in **chocolate**, /**ch=sh**/ as in **Charlotte's chandelier** and /**ch=k**/ for **Christmas**.

11. Cover the letters that say /**qu**/ as in **queen**.

12. Cover the letters that say /ōō/ as in **balloon**, /**ui**/ as in **suit**, and /**ue**/ as in **glue**.

13. Cover the letter that says /ä/ as in **father**.

14. Cover the letters that say /**oi**/ as in **oil** and /**oy**/ as in **toy**.

15. Cover the letters that say /**ow**/ for **owl** and /**ou**/ as in **out**.

16. Cover the letters that say /**or**/ as in **orbit**.

17. Cover the letters that say /**j**/ as in **gymnastics, giant** and **gem**.

18. Cover the letters that say /**shun**/ as in **invention**.

19. Cover the letters that say /**ing**/ as in **ring**.

20. Cover the letters that say /**aw, au**/ as in "we see a baby we say **aw**."

21. Cover the letters that say /**sh**/ as in **shell**.

22. Cover the letters that say /**ph**/ as in **phone**.

23. Cover the letters that say /**er, ir, ur**/ **the rooster's wild**.

23. Cover the letters that say /**th**/ for **them** and /**th**/ for **threw**.

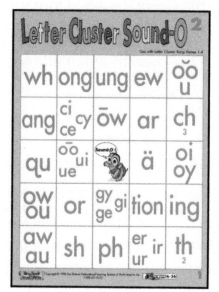

Letter Cluster Pick-A-Sound Game

TO BE PLAYED UNTIL MASTERED

Objective

To play a game which will give students practice in letter cluster sounds as taught in the *Letter Cluster Phonics Song.*

This game is played with the **blue** deck of cards. Two to five players may take part. The object is to make pairs from cards in each player's hand. The game ends when any player is completely out of cards. The player with the most pairs is the winner.

Directions

1. Place the Merry-Go-Round in the center of the table. Shuffle the deck of cards and deal one card at a time until each player has five cards. Place the rest of the cards face down in a pile inside the Merry-Go-Round container.

2. All players should then sort their cards, placing any pairs they have face-up on the table in front of them.

3. The player to the left of the dealer should begin the game by calling any player by name and asking for a card.

   "Mary, do you have the card that says **or for orbit**?" The player making the request must hold that card in his/her hand.

4. If Mary has the **or** card, she must give it to that player who will put the pair down. That player will get another turn, calling on another player for a sound. However, if Mary does not have the **or** card, she must call: **"Pick-A-Sound from the Merry-Go-Round."**

5. The player must then pick the top card from the pile of cards inside the Merry-Go-Round, and add that card to those in his/her hand. If the player picks the card with the sound called for, he/she makes a pair and takes another turn. When the player can no longer make a pair, the person on the left then becomes the next player. **When a player pairs all the cards from his/her hand, the game is over. The player with the most paired cards is the winner.**

6. Give prizes from the Treasure Chest to winners.

Phonics Skills

Pop the Balloons Chart

Pop the Balloons is an activity that tests a student's knowledge of the sounds of the letter clusters as taught in the *Letter Cluster Phonics Song,* verses 1-4.

<u>Directions</u>

Teach the entire class at one time using the *Pop the Balloons Chart* in the following manner:

- Ask if anyone thinks he/she can pop all the balloons by saying the correct sound for the letter cluster on each balloon.

- Balloons with the **numbers 2 or 3 have two or three sounds** which must be called in order to "pop" them.

- Choose a student to come up and take the pointer.

- Tell the class to echo the sound if it was called correctly and then clap their hands to indicate the popping of the balloon.

Long Vowel Song

CD Track 10

<u>Directions</u>

1. Tell the class there is a song about long vowels.
2. Select five students to form a line to the left of the *Long Vowel Cards*. The leader will lead the singing, point to the *Long Vowel Cards*, and march back to give the pointer to the new leader.
3. Play CD Track 10 for the *Long Vowel Song* with students singing.
4. Allow everyone to have a turn as leader. Leaders should point to each long vowel card, leading the class:

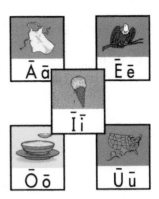

LEADER:	**CLASS ECHOES:**
ā for apron! (pointing to apron)	ā for apron!
ē for eagle! (pointing to eagle)	ē for eagle!
ī for ice cream! (pointing to ice cream)	ī for ice cream!
ō for oatmeal! (pointing to oatmeal)	ō for oatmeal!
ū for United States! (pointing to United States)	ū for United States!
So we do echo! (marking time facing class)	So we do echo!
(Singing together, as leader marches back to give pointer to next leader)	As we march along And we sing a song Learning our long vowels!

ā for apron   ē for eagle   ī for ice cream   ō for oatmeal   ū for United States ...

Word-O Game

TO BE PLAYED UNTIL MASTERED

Objective
A Bingo-like game to give students practice in reading the most frequently used sight words.

Preparation
1. Cut apart the Teacher Caller Card found in the package of 25 *Word-O Cards*.
2. Place Callers in the round plastic container labeled *Word-O*.

Directions
1. Distribute the *Word-O Cards* and see-through game markers.

2. Students will place the **blue** printed side of the card face up.

3. Students will put a marker on Gus-the-Bug in the center of the card. This is a free space.

4 Draw a caller card from the container and call that word. Use the word in a sentence. Example: "**has**" - "She **has** a book."

5. A student may call **"Word-O"** when he/she has a straight line vertically, horizontally, or diagonally.

6. Follow these same directions for Side 2, **red**.

7. Give prizes from the Treasure Chest to the winners.

All ABC Echoes

CD Track 12

Directions

Next, go to the *Manuscript Wall Chart* with your pointer and lead students through **every sound learned for each of the letters**. There are small numbers under the letters which have several sounds as demonstrated on CD Track 12. Tell students you will lead all the *ABC Echoes*.

LEADER:		CLASS ECHOES:
Pointing to **Aa**:	"ă"	"ă"
	"ā"	"ā"
	"ä"	"ä"
Pointing to **Bb**:	"bh"	"bh"
	"c (k)"	"c (k)"
	"c (s)"	"c (s)"
	"dh"	"dh"

(Continue in same manner for rest of alphabet.)

Two Vowels Get Together Song

CD Track 13

<u>Directions</u>

Tell students when two vowels are together in a word, as in **bo̅ǿt** (write it on the board), the second vowel is completely quiet (strike through it as shown), and it makes the first vowel say its name (the name of the letter). Put a long vowel mark over the first vowel as shown. Sound the word out: **bo̅ǿt**. Write several two-vowel words on the board marking the vowels and allow the students to decode them. Examples: **se̅ǿt, he̅ǿt, le̅ǿf**

Tell students you have a song/activity to help them learn many two-vowel words:

* Place the *Two Vowels Get Together Chart* just above the chalk ledge in the front of the room.

* Have students form two lines from the front toward the back of the room. Station the first two students at a line six feet from the chart.

* Stand by the chart and hold the first 10 cards in numerical order. Hold them in the space provided on the chart at the appropriate time with the song.

* Play CD Track 13.

* When the music begins, the two students at the front of the line skip to the chart. The student on the left is the **first vowel student** and the student on the right is the **silent vowel student.** The class will sing together with the music:

Two Vowels Get Together Song

> "Two vowels get together and they play a game
> The first vowel speaks; it says the letter name
> The vowel says e̅
> (to be called out by the student on left as he/she points to the first vowel in the word).
> And the word is se̅at."
> (to be called by child on right as he/she points to second vowel with his/her finger).
> Class echoes: "The vowel says e̅ and the word is se̅at."

* The two students separate and go to the back of their lines, and the teacher removes the card, exposing the next card with "beach." While this is taking place, the next couple skips up.

* Next, play CD Track 14 and use word cards #11 to #21. Then use word cards #22 to #32.

Silent e̸ Song and Dance

CD Track 15

<u>Directions</u>

* Place the *Silent e̸ Song and Dance Chart* at approximately teacher's eye level in the front of the room.

* Follow the same procedure used for the *Two Vowels Get Together Song*.

The class will sing together with the music:

Silent e̸ Song
"With a silent e̸, it's like a game
The first vowel speaks; it says the letter name
The vowel says ī   (to be called out by the student on left as he/she points to the first vowel in the word).
And the word is tīme̸."   (to be called by child on right as he/she points to silent e̸).
Class echoes: **"The vowel says ī and the word is tīme̸."**

Gh Clown Song

CD Track 17

<u>Directions</u>

* Go to the board and write the following words:

  n i(gh)t   l i(gh)t   s i(gh)t

* Draw a circle around the letters **gh**, as shown.

* Show students that **gh** is silent (or quiet) and doesn't say ANYTHING. Tell them **gh** always causes the vowel(s) to say a different sound. Look! There is just one vowel, and one vowel USUALLY says its short vowel sound, but not when **gh** is around! Look, the vowel is saying the long vowel sound!

* Put a slash mark through **gh**. n i(gh̸)t .

* Put the long vowel mark over each **i**. n ī(gh̸) t. Now sound out the words.

* Next, place the *Gh Clown Chart* in the front of the room.

* Read down through the **ight** words. When you get to "knight," cover the k at the beginning and say:

Teacher:	"This word matches the one at the top. What did it say?"
Student:	"Night."
Teacher:	"Who can think of another kind of **night** -- not the one when we get in bed and go to sleep." Elicit -- the one who wears armor, rides the horse, helps the **king**. Then take your hand away to expose the **k** and say: "That's why we put a **k** at the start. This is the **knight** that helps the king. **K** is for **k**ing. And it's silent!"

* Look next at the list that begins with **ought**. Say:

Teacher:	"Letters **ou** usually say **ou** as in **out**. But not when **gh** is around! It is saying **aw**. Read down through that list. Notice that **au** words are there too."

* Next, show the row of words that begins with **laugh**. Point out that letters **gh** are on the end and are saying **fff**! Notice, <u>EVERYTIME</u> **gh** is going to make the vowels say a different sound. After reading the list that starts with **laugh**, point to the words and have the class do what the word says:

laugh	(students laugh)
cough	(students cough)
rough	(students make believe they have steering wheels in their hands and bounce up and down as though on a rough road)

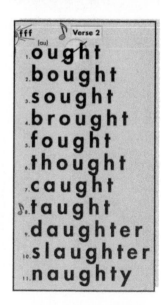

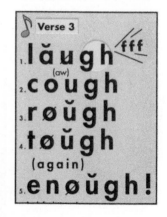

Gh Clown Song *continued*

tough   (students make fists with arms up at the elbows looking tough!)

enough   (students get stern looks on faces and point fingers as though someone is saying ENOUGH!)

* Go on to the next list that begins with **eight** (no song for this list) and say:

Teacher: "Look at this! **Gh** is making the letters **ei** say **ā**. Can you believe that? Read down through these words, covering letters **gh** with your fingers because they are silent."

1. e i g h t (ā)
2. e i g h t y
3. e i g h t e e n
4. e i g h t i e t h
5. w e i g h t
6. f r e i g h t
7. n e i g h b o r
8. n e i g h b o r h o o d

* Next, show the list that starts with **dough**, and say:

Teacher: "Look, here are letters **gh** on the end, but they are silent. What a trick!" Read the words and discuss.

* First, play CD Track 17 all the way through for students to hear, pointing to the letters and words on the chart (down to the note symbol on each list).

* Then sing the *Gh Clown Song*.

1. d ō u g h
2. t h ō u g h
3. t h r o u g h (o͞o)
4. w e i g h (ā)
5. n e i g h (ā)
6. s l e i g h (ā)
7. h ī g h

Gh Clown Song: Lyrics

Chorus

Look for letters gh
Help this happy clown,
Letters gh make the vowels
Say a different sound.
Look for letters gh
They will help you, friend,
They're silent in the middle
And go fff! at the end.

Verse #1

n-i-g-h-t says *night*
f-i-g-h-t says *fight*
s-i-g-h-t says *sight*
b-r-i-g-h-t *bright*
l-i-g-h-t says *light*
t-i-g-h-t says *tight*
r-i-g-h-t says *right*
s-l-i-g-h-t *slight*
(Back to chorus)

Verse #2

o-u-g-h-t says *ought*
b-o-u-g-h-t *bought*
s-o-u-g-h-t *sought*
b-r-o-u-g-h-t *brought*
f-o-u-g-h-t *fought*
t-h-o-u-g-h-t *thought*
c-a-u-g-h-t *caught*
t-a-u-g-h-t *taught*
(Back to chorus)

Verse #3

l-a-u-g-h says *laugh*
c-o-u-g-h says *cough*
r-o-u-g-h says *rough*
t-o-u-g-h says *tough*
Teacher: AGAIN!
(repeat verse #3)
(Back to chorus)
Chanting:
E-N-O-U-G-H **ENOUGH!**

Gh Clown Song: Motions

Directions

1. Display the *Gh Clown Chart* in front of the classroom.
2. Have students form a circle around the classroom.
3. Have one student at left of *Gh Clown Chart* pointing to words as class sings down through the list(s).
4. Play CD Track 17 and sing the *Gh Clown Song*.

Have students perform the motions below as they circle around the room:

Singing: "Look for letters gh"

Motions: Put hand on forehead like a "visor" over the eyes and move head from left to right searching for letters gh.

Singing: "Help this happy clown,"

Motions: Put hands out in front and pretend to be juggling.

Singing: "Letters gh make the vowels Say a different sound."

Motions: Arms out to the sides pretending to be balancing on a tightrope.

Singing: "Look for letters gh"

Motions: Put hand on forehead like a "visor" over the eyes and move head from left to right searching for letters gh.

Singing: "They will help you, friend,"

Motions: Put hands around mouth like a megaphone.

Singing: "They're silent in the middle"

Motions: Put index finger over lips to show silence.

Singing: "And go fff! at the end."

Motions: Put hands up to chest and make a fist, then quickly open hands at the "fff!" sound.

A student at left of **Gh Clown Chart** points to words as class sings down through the list(s).

Handwriting

Review for Manuscript Writing

Manuscript Writing Pages

There is a **Manuscript Writing** review for each letter of the alphabet.

The review pages appear in the *Grand Tour I* Student Book on pages 5, 15-16, 27-28, 39-40, 49-50, 59-60, 69-70, and 79.

On pages 68 –73 of this Teacher's Manual are directions for the formation of the letters. It is important to use the "script" provided. The teaching of manuscript writing using this method is designed to do away with difficulties such as:

- **Flipping of letters (Reversals).**

- **Inability to tell the difference between similar letters, especially little letters d and b, p and q.**

- **Inability to change to cursive writing.**

When students are taught to form all letters from "balls and sticks" it can be confusing to many students. The muscle movement is indeed simple, because every letter is formed from straight lines or complete circles, or both. However, the brain is confused when a child is taught, "Letter b is formed by making a straight line here and a ball down here, and letter d is formed by making a straight line down here with a ball over here." It is easy to see why a child may find it difficult to remember which one is which.

Another method teaches writing the lower case letters in one continuous stroke, not lifting the pencil from the paper except when writing a letter that has a cross stroke or a dot. This reduction in the number of strokes is ostensibly to help students transition from manuscript to cursive more easily in second or third grades. This method has slanted letter forms with letter "tails" and "curve ups." These letter forms are never seen in standardized tests, library books, or readers, so this teaches students one style of letters to write and another style to read, which is confusing.

Students are also confused when they are taught to write this **a** and then expected to read in their book this **a**; when students are taught to write this **g** and are expected to read this **g**. They stumble when the book prints letter **j** to look like letter **i**, without its identifying hook at the bottom of **j**. And they stumble when their books are filled with capital letter **I**'s that are identical to little letter **l**.

The **Sing, Spell, Read & Write** manuscript writing style offers the best of two worlds! You will find the method for teaching manuscript writing presented in this program is designed to:

- Always provide for assisting the student in remembering which letter is which: **b** or **d**, **q** or **p**, **i** or **j**.

- Have fewer touchdowns which transitions easily to cursive writing.

- Have students recognize just one alphabet form for both reading and writing.

p. 15

p. 27

p. 39

p. 49

Handwriting

What we say guides the way in teaching manuscript writing. Oral, visual, and kinesthetic avenues to the brain will be utilized in learning to write with the ***Sing, Spell, Read & Write*** method. So repeat, repeat, repeat the phrases provided as you form each manuscript letter, reviewing four letters each week in Steps 1-6 and concluding with letters **Yy** and **Zz** in Step 7.

(Left Handed)

To the Teacher: As you form each letter on the chalkboard keep repeating: (For **D**) Put your pencil on the start dot. Go straight down to touch the floor. Put your pencil on the start dot again. Go around and down to the floor. That's big letter **D**! (Say the name of the letter.) D, d, doll! (Say the letter sound as in *A to Z Phonics Song*.)

(For **d**) First make a little c from its start dot. Now put your pencil on the dot on the line above and come straight down to the floor, touching the edges of little c. "First little c, then little d". (Repeat and repeat this.) Little letter **d**! D, d, doll!

Teacher Tip ✓ The following illustrations provide an example of how students' writing paper should be slanted depending on whether they are right or left handed. The arm should rest on the paper, coming up from the bottom, not around from the side.

(Right Handed)

Procedure

- Using lined chalkboard, instruct students how to correctly form letters. Refer students to *Grand Tour I*, page 5.
- Use script on TM pp. 68–73 to review correct formation of manuscript letters.
- After teaching students the correct formation of letters, show an incorrect formation and ask students to tell you what is wrong.
- Have students complete Manuscript Writing pages in *Grand Tour I*, according to instructions in Steps 1-7 of TM.

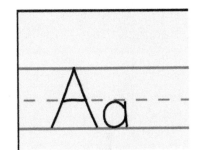

(correct)

(incorrect)

Writing Slate

- The back cover of *Grand Tour I* has an erasable writing slate for additional manuscript writing practice. Students use dry-erase markers and miniature felt erasers provided in your kit when practicing penmanship on the slate.

Writing Slate

Manuscript Handwriting

Teacher says:

Boys and girls, I know you learned how to write all your letters last year. Now, this year, we're going to concentrate on learning to make our handwriting look neat and beautiful on the page when we write our letters. But first, we're going to take a few days just to review each letter of the alphabet and the correct way to form each of those letters.

If you'll turn to page 5 in your *Grand Tour I* Student Book, you'll see the whole alphabet. Follow along with me right now and listen to these easy tips to help you remember how to form each letter.

Then, we'll practice four letters each week so that we can get our handwriting as perfect as possible. Remember that practice makes perfect. Let's start.

Teacher says:

Now, it's time for us to review manuscript forms of capital **A** and little **a**.

As you form each letter on the chalkboard keep repeating:
(For **A**) Put your pencil on the start dot. Go down the slide as shown by arrow #1 to the "floor line." Now put your pencil on the start dot again and go down the slide as shown by arrow #2 to the "floor line." Now put your pencil on the middle broken line and give Mr. A a nice belt ... and be sure to go the way the arrow points, from the first slide line we made to the second one. That's big letter **A**! (Say the name of the letter.) Ă, ă, apple! (Say the letter sound as in *A to Z Phonics Song*.)

(For **a**) Now we are going to make little letter a. Listen carefully and watch! Put your pencil on the start dot. First go up to touch the middle broken line, then curve around to touch the floor, then curve up, go all the way up to the start dot, and then come straight down to the floor with a stick. There we have it: Little letter **a**! Ă, ă, apple!

Teacher says:

Now, it's time for us to review manuscript forms of capital **B** and little **b**.

As you form each letter on the chalkboard keep repeating:
(For **B**) Put your pencil on the start dot. Go straight down to the floor. Now put your pencil on the start dot again, go around to the middle, then around to the floor! A big fat chest and a big fat tummy! That's big letter **B**! (Say the name of the letter.) Bh, bh, ball! (Say the letter sound as in *A to Z Phonics Song*.) Not buh, but bh.

(For **b**) Put your pencil on the start dot. Go straight down to the floor, bounce straight up to the middle dotted line, then around and down. Bh! Bh! Bounce up and around. Bh! Bh! Bounce up and around. (Repeat over and over.) Little letter **b**! Bh, bh, ball!

Teacher says:

Now, it's time for us to review manuscript forms of capital **C** and little **c**.

As you form each letter on the chalkboard keep repeating:
(For **C**) Put your pencil on the start dot. Go up to the ceiling, around to the floor, and swing up. That's big letter **C**! (Say the name of the letter.) C, c, cat! (Say the letter sound as in *A to Z Phonics Song*.)

(For **c**) Put your pencil on the start dot. Curve up to the middle broken line, then curve around and down to the floor line, then curve up just a bit. Little letter **c**! C, c, cat!

Teacher says:

Now, it's time for us to review manuscript forms of capital **D** and little **d**.

As you form each letter on the chalkboard keep repeating:
(For **D**) Put your pencil on the start dot. Go straight down to touch the floor. Put your pencil on the start dot again. Go around and down to the floor. That's big letter **D**! (Say the name of the letter.) D, d, doll! (Say the letter sound as in *A to Z Phonics Song*.)

(For **d**) First make a little c from its start dot. Now put your pencil on the dot on the line above and come straight down to the floor, touching the edges of little c. First little c, then little d. (Repeat and repeat this.) Little letter **d**! D, d, doll!

Teacher says:

Now, it's time for us to review manuscript forms of capital **E** and little **e**.

As you form each letter on the chalkboard keep repeating:
(For **E**) Put your pencil on the start dot. Go straight down to touch the floor, then across with his hat, across with his belt and across with his shoes. That's Mr. **E**! (Say the name of the letter.) Ĕ, ĕ, egg! (Say the letter sound as in *A to Z Phonics Song*.)

(For **e**) Put your pencil on the start dot which is in the middle of the space between the middle broken line and the floor and make a line straight over, the way we did for Mr. E's belt. Do not pick up your pencil, but curve up to the middle broken line and then make a "c." What do we have? Little letter **e**! Ĕ, ĕ, egg!

Teacher says:

Now, it's time for us to review manuscript forms of capital **F** and little **f**.

As you form each letter on the chalkboard:
(For **F**) Put your pencil on the start dot. Go straight down to touch the floor, then across with his hat, across with his belt. That's big letter **F**! (Say the name of the letter.) F, f, fan! (Say the letter sound as in *A to Z Phonics Song*.)

(For **f**) Put your pencil on the start dot. Go up, the way we begin c, then straight to the floor, then a belt all the way across. Little letter **f**! F, f, fan!

Teacher says:

Now, it's time for us to review manuscript forms of capital **G** and little **g**.

As you form each letter on the chalkboard:
(For **G**) Put your pencil on the start dot. First make big C, then curve up to the middle broken line. Now give him a tray to hold! That's big letter **G**! (Say the name of the letter.) G, g, goat! (Say the letter sound as in *A to Z Phonics Song*.)

(For **g**) Put your pencil on the start dot. First make little a, then go straight down through the floor and curve around to make a basket. Say: Gee, that's a good idea; a basket to catch the ball if it falls! Gee! Little letter **g**! G, g, goat!

Teacher says:

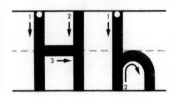

Now, it's time for us to review manuscript forms of capital **H** and little **h**.

As you form each letter on the chalkboard:
(For **H**) Put your pencil on the start dot and go straight down to the floor. Now pick up your pencil and make another line just like that one, just over a bit from the first one. Now make a bridge between the two. That's big letter **H**! (Say the name of the letter.) H, h, hand! (Say the letter sound as in *A to Z Phonics Song*.)

(For **h**) Put your pencil on the start dot. Go down to the floor, up to the middle broken line, then around and down. Little letter **h**! H, h, hand!

Teacher says:

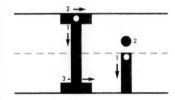

Now, it's time for us to review manuscript forms of capital **I** and little **i**.

As you form each letter on the chalkboard:
(For **I**) Put your pencil on the start dot and go straight down to the floor. Now give him a straight line for a hat and a straight line for his shoes. That's big letter **I**! (Say the name of the letter.) Ĭ, ĭ, inchworm! (Say the letter sound as in *A to Z Phonics Song*.)

(For **i**) Put your pencil on the start dot and go down to the floor. Now give him a dot just above the middle line. Little letter **i**! Ĭ, ĭ, inchworm!

Teacher says:

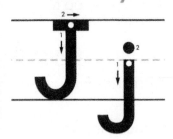

Now, it's time for us to review manuscript forms of capital **J** and little **j**.

As you form each letter on the chalkboard:
(For **J**) Put your pencil on the start dot and go straight down to the floor, then turn to make a basket just as you did for little g. Give it a straight line for a hat. That's big letter **J**! (Say the name of the letter.) J, j, jam! (Say the letter sound as in *A to Z Phonics Song*.)

(For **j**) Put your pencil on the start dot and go down through the floor to the basement and make a basket, just as you did for big letter J. Now give it a dot. Little letter **j**! J, j, jam!

Teacher says:

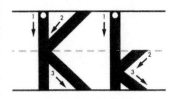

Now, it's time for us to review manuscript forms of capital **K** and little **k**.

As you form each letter on the chalkboard:
(For **K**) Put your pencil on the start dot and go straight down to the floor. Now put your pencil on the top line again a little bit away from the start dot. Come down to the middle, then down to the floor. That's big letter **K**! (Say the name of the letter.) K, k, kite! (Say the letter sound as in *A to Z Phonics Song*.)

(For **k**) Put your pencil on the start dot at the top line and go down to the floor. Put your pencil on the middle broken line and slant into the middle, as shown by arrow #2. Then slant out and down to the base line, as arrow #3 indicates. That's little letter **k**! K, k, kite!

Teacher says:

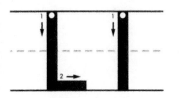

Now, it's time for us to review manuscript forms of capital **L** and little **l**.

As you form each letter on the chalkboard:
(For **L**) Put your pencil on the start dot and go straight down, then turn the corner. That's big letter **L**! (Say the name of the letter.) L, l, lamb! (Say the letter sound as in *A to Z Phonics Song*.)

(For **l**) Put your pencil on the start dot. Go straight down to the floor. Little letter **l**! L, l, lamb!

Teacher says:

Now, it's time for us to review manuscript forms of capital **M** and little **m**.

As you form each letter on the chalkboard:
(For **M**) Put your pencil on the start dot and go straight down to the floor. Put your pencil back on the start dot and go down the slide to the floor, up the slide to the top line, then straight down to the floor. Big letter **M**! (Say the name of the letter.) M, m, monkey! (Say the letter sound as in *A to Z Phonics Song*.)

(For **m**) Put your pencil on the start dot. Go down to the floor, then go up on the same line almost to the top, then arch over and down, then up on the same line, then over and down again. Be sure to have each arch touch the middle broken line. Little letter **m**! M, m, monkey!

Teacher says:

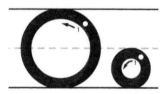

Now, it's time for us to review manuscript forms of capital **N** and little **n**.

As you form each letter on the chalkboard:
(For **N**) Put your pencil on the start dot and go straight down to the floor. Put your pencil back on the start dot and go down the slide to the floor. Put your pencil on the top line again and go straight down to the floor to touch the bottom of the slide. Big letter **N**! (Say the name of the letter.) N, n, noodles! (Say the letter sound as in *A to Z Phonics Song*.)

(For **n**) Put your pencil on the start dot. Go down to the floor, then go up on the same line almost to the top, then arch over and down to the floor again. Be sure you have the arch touch the middle broken line. Little letter **n**! N, n, noodles!

Teacher says:

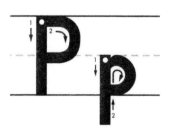

Now, it's time for us to review manuscript forms of capital **O** and little **o**.

As you form each letter on the chalkboard:
(For **O**) Put your pencil on the start dot. Curve up to touch the ceiling, then down to touch the floor, and up to where you started. Big letter **O**! (Say the name of the letter.) Ŏ, ŏ, octopus! (Say the letter sound as in *A to Z Phonics Song*.)

(For **o**) Put your pencil on the start dot. Curve up to touch the broken line, then down to touch the floor, and up to where you started. Little letter **o**! Ŏ, ŏ, octopus!

Teacher says:

Now, it's time for us to review manuscript forms of capital **P** and little **p**.

As you form each letter on the chalkboard:
(For **P**) Put your pencil on the start dot and go straight down to the floor. Put your pencil on the start dot again and curve around to the center line. That's big letter **P**! (Say the name of the letter.) P, p, poodles! (Say the letter sound as in *A to Z Phonics Song*.)

(For **p**) Put your pencil on the start dot and go down through the floor to the basement. Come right back up on that same line to the top and curve around to touch the floor line. That's little letter **p**! P, p, poodles!

Manuscript Handwriting

Teacher says:

Now, it's time for us to review manuscript forms of capital **Q** and little **q**.

As you form each letter on the chalkboard:
(For **Q**) Put your pencil on the start dot. Make a capital O and then give the queen a walking stick. That's big letter **Q**! (Say the name of the letter.) Q, q, quilt! (Say the letter sound as in *A to Z Phonics Song*.)

(For **q**) Put your pencil on the start dot. Make little letter a and go straight down through the floor to the basement and then curve to make a basket away from the ball. If the ball falls it won't go into the basket! That's little letter **q**! Q, q, quilt!

Teacher says:

Now, it's time for us to review manuscript forms of capital **R** and little **r**.

As you form each letter on the chalkboard:
(For **R**) Put your pencil on the start dot. Form capital P and then give it a leg down to the floor. That's big letter **R**! (Say the name of the letter.) R, r, rail! (Say the letter sound as in *A to Z Phonics Song*.)

(For **r**) Put your pencil on the start dot. Go down, then come up on the same line and hook over. Little letter **r**! R, r, rail!

Teacher says:

Now, it's time for us to review manuscript forms of capital **S** and little **s**.

As you form each letter on the chalkboard:
(For **S**) Put your pencil on the start dot. Form letter c up in the top space, then curve around and back. That's big letter **S**! (Say the name of the letter.) S, s, sun! (Say the letter sound as in *A to Z Phonics Song*.)

(For **s**) Put your pencil on the start dot. Form a very little c in the top of the space, then curve around and back. Little letter **s**! S, s, sun!

Teacher says:

Now, it's time for us to review manuscript forms of capital **T** and little **t**.

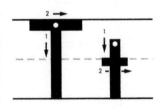

As you form each letter on the chalkboard:
(For **T**) Put your pencil on the start dot. Go straight down to the floor and then put his hat on. That's big letter **T**! (Say the name of the letter.) T, t, tail! (Say the letter sound as in *A to Z Phonics Song*.)

(For **t**) Put your pencil on the start dot. Little t is a teenager. He's not as tall as the capital letters nor as short as the small letters. Go down to the floor and then go across on the broken line. Little letter **t**! T, t, tail!

Teacher says:

Now, it's time for us to review manuscript forms of capital **U** and little **u**.

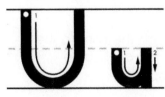

As you form each letter on the chalkboard:
(For **U**) Put your pencil on the start dot. Go straight down to the floor and curve over and up to the top. That's big letter **U**! (Say the name of the letter.) Ŭ, ŭ, umbrella! (Say the letter sound as in *A to Z Phonics Song*.)

(For **u**) Put your pencil on the start dot. Go down to the floor and curve over and up to the broken line then straight down to the floor again. Little letter **u**! Ŭ, ŭ, umbrella!

Teacher says:

Now, it's time for us to review manuscript forms of capital **V** and little **v**.

As you form each letter on the chalkboard:
(For **V**) Put your pencil on the start dot. Go down the slide to the floor and up the slide to the ceiling. That's big letter **V**! (Say the name of the letter.) V, v, vase! (Say the letter sound as in *A to Z Phonics Song*.)

(For **v**) Put your pencil on the start dot. Go down the slide to the floor and up the slide to the middle broken line. Little letter **v**! V, v, vase!

Teacher says:

Now, it's time for us to review manuscript forms of capital **W** and little **w**.

As you form each letter on the chalkboard:
(For **W**) Put your pencil on the start dot. Go down the slide to the floor then up the slide to the ceiling. Then go down the slide and up again to the ceiling. That's big letter **W**! (Say the name of the letter.) W, w, wagon! (Say the letter sound as in *A to Z Phonics Song*.)

(For **w**) Put your pencil on the start dot. Go down the slide to the floor, then up the slide to the middle broken line. Then go down the slide and up again to the middle broken line. Little letter **w**! W, w, wagon!

Teacher says:

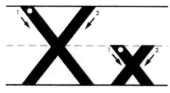

Now, it's time for us to review manuscript forms of capital **X** and little **x**.

As you form each letter on the chalkboard:
(For **X**) Put your pencil on the start dot. Go down the slide to the floor. Now put your pencil up on the ceiling line again and go back down and cross the slide at the broken line and continue to the floor. That's big letter **X**! (Say the name of the letter.) X, x, (ks!), box! (Say the letter sound as in *A to Z Phonics Song*.)

(For **x**) Put your pencil on the start dot. Go down the slide to the floor. Now put your pencil up on the middle broken line again and go back down and cross the slide in the middle and continue to the floor. Little letter **x**! X, x, (ks!), box!

Teacher says:

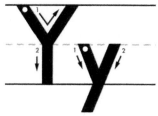

Now, it's time for us to review manuscript forms of capital **Y** and little **y**.

As you form each letter on the chalkboard:
(For **Y**) Put your pencil on the start dot. Go down the slide to the center, up the slide to the top and then put on the stem. That's big letter **Y**! (Say the name of the letter.) Y, y, yard! (Say the letter sound as in *A to Z Phonics Song*.)

(For **y**) Put your pencil on the start dot. Go down the slide to the floor line. Put your pencil on the middle broken line again and over a bit, then go down to touch the slide and keep going through to the basement. Little letter **y**! Y, y, yarn!

Teacher says:

Now, it's time for us to review manuscript forms of capital **Z** and little **z**.

As you form each letter on the chalkboard:
(For **Z**) Put your pencil on the start dot. Go across the ceiling, down the slide to the floor (like the number 7), and back across the floor. That's big letter **Z**! (Say the name of the letter.) Z, z, zoo! (Say the letter sound as in *A to Z Phonics Song*.)

(For **z**) Put your pencil on the start dot. Go across the middle broken line, down the slide to the floor, and back across the floor. Little letter **z**! Z, z, zoo!

Handwriting

Introduction to Cursive Writing—Optional

While the formation of manuscript letters in SSR&W is specifically designed to lead to cursive writing without a hitch, the teaching of cursive writing in the second semester of second grade with *Grand Tour II* is strictly optional. You are the best judge of your students' readiness to learn this skill.

However, if you choose to instruct students in cursive writing, you are urged to follow the teaching directions provided in TM pp. 75-83. **Once students have mastered the correct letter formation for manuscript letters with the SSR&W method, it is truly an easy transition to cursive writing.** With SSR&W, there are only 18 combined upper and lower case new cursive letter forms that children need to learn! Only A, b, F, f, G, I, J, L, Q, r, s, T, V, v, x, Y, Z, and z have distinctively different formations when going from manuscript to cursive writing. That means children start out with familiarity of 34 of the 52 upper and lower case cursive letter forms. What a way to instill confidence and success in your students!

Explain to children that once they have learned to write in cursive, they will be able to write faster. That means they will also be able to put their ideas down on paper faster! Introduce children to the concept of cursive writing and cursive letter formation using the scripted directions below. Remember, as with manuscript writing, **What we say guides the way.**

Teacher says:

Boys and girls, you have all done a good job learning how to form your manuscript letters in *Grand Tour I*. Now that we're starting *Grand Tour II*, we're going to be learning a new kind of writing. It's called cursive writing. If you look up here at this chart (point to Cursive Wall Chart), you'll see all the letters of the alphabet. They have been formed in cursive writing. We should be able to recognize most of these letters, boys and girls, because they look very much like they do when we write them in manuscript writing. There are capital letters and little letters, just like in manuscript writing. If you look closely, you'll see that there are arrows that show us which direction to move our pencil to form each letter. You have these same letters on your desk stick-ons, too, but without the directional arrows.

Now, I'm going to point to each of the letters on the chart and say them, and I want you to echo after me. Are you ready? (Teacher, point along, say the letter, and have children echo after you.)

Was I right? Did you recognize many of these cursive letters? Now, we're not going to learn to write all these letters at once. We'll be learning one or two new letters a week and practicing them. They'll be part of our Language Arts lesson each week for the rest of the school year.

You're going to like cursive writing because you'll soon discover that once you have learned how to form all the letters of the alphabet in cursive, you can write much faster and put your thoughts down on the paper much faster, too. In cursive writing, all the letters in a word are connected. You will only need to lift your pencil from the paper for each *word* instead of for each *letter*. Are you ready to learn cursive writing?

Cursive Writing Script

As each new letter is introduced, the teacher demonstrates all writing on chalkboard.

Teacher says: We are now ready to write the cursive forms of capital **A** and little **a**.

Put your pencil just below the top line. Now, go up to touch the top line and curve around to touch the base line, swing up to where you started and back down on that same line to the base line and swing up.

Now, little letter **a**. Put your pencil on the center dotted line. Curve around and down to touch the base line, curve back up to where you started, go down again on the same line, touch the base line and swing up.

Teacher says: Now, you are ready to write the cursive forms of capital **B** and little **b**.

Put your pencil on the center dotted line. Swing up to touch the top line, pull down to the base line, go up on that same line, to the top again, curve around and in to the center. Loop at the center and curve down to the base line and touch the first downward stroke, and swing over to form a little "boat."

Now, little letter **b**. Put your pencil on the base line, swing up to the top line, loop around and back down to the base line, then up to the center dotted line and swing out.

Teacher says: Now, you are ready to write the cursive forms of capital **C** and little **c**.

Put your pencil on the top line. Loop down, up and around and touch the top line again, curve out and around to the base line and swing up.

Now, little letter **c**. Put your pencil just below the center dotted line. Curve up and around to touch the dotted line, then down to the base line and swing up.

Cursive Writing Script *continued*

Teacher says:

Now it's time for us to write the cursive forms of capital **D** and little **d**.

Put your pencil on the top line. Slant down to the base line, bounce up and loop across the slanted line, touch the base line, curve out and up to the top where you started, loop around and swing up.

Now, little letter **d**. Put your pencil on the center dotted line, curve around, down to touch the base line, then go up on a slant all the way to the top line, and back down on the same line to the base, then swing up again.

Teacher says:

Now, it's time for us to write the cursive forms of capital **E** and little **e**.

Put your pencil on the top line. Loop down, up and around to touch the top line, curve in to the center line, loop around again to the base line and swing up.

Now, little letter **e**. Put your pencil on the base line. Swing up to the center dotted line, loop around to the base line and swing up.

Teacher says:

Now, it's time for us to write the cursive forms of capital **F** and little **f**.

Put your pencil just above the top line. Loop down, up and around to the top line, and along the top line. Lift your pencil. Put it down centered under the top line you have made. Go down on a slant to the base line, swing up and across to make a "boat" and down.

Now, little letter **f**. Put your pencil on the base line. Now, slant up to the top line, touch, loop around, pull down three spaces to the line below the base line, loop up to the base line and swing out.

Sing Spell Read & Write.

Cursive Writing Script *continued*

Teacher says: Now, it's time for us to write the cursive forms of capital **G** and little **g**.

Put your pencil on the base line. Slant up to the top line, loop around and down to touch the center dotted line, swing up to a sharp point, down to the base line, over to cross your first line, and make a "boat."

Now, little letter **g**. Put your pencil on the center dotted line. Curve around to form letter "a," go down to the line below the base line, loop around and swing up through the base line touching the bottom of the "a."

Teacher says: Now, it's time for us to write the cursive forms of capital **H** and little **h**.

Put your pencil just above the top line. Loop down, up and around to touch the top line, then curve down to the base line. Lift your pencil. Put your pencil on the top line again spaced over from your first stroke. Slant down to the base line, swing up and over touching the center line, loop down and around and swing across the center line.

Now, little letter **h**. Put your pencil on the base line. Swing up to the top line, loop around and down with a slant to the base line, bounce up on that same line to the center, arch over and down again to the base line and swing up.

Teacher says: Now, it's time for us to write the cursive form of capital **I** and little **i**.

This letter is easy to make if you first think of making letter "C," starting at the bottom and going up to touch the top line, loop over and back down to the base line, then up to the center line and make a little "boat."

Now, little letter **i**. Put your pencil on the base line. Swing up to the center line on a slant, go back down on the same line to the base line and swing up. Put a dot above it.

Handwriting

Cursive Writing Script *continued*

Teacher says:

Now, it's time for us to write the cursive forms of capital **J** and little **j**.

Put your pencil just below the base line. Now swing up all the way to the top line as though you were making capital letter "C," starting from the bottom, then curve over and go down with a slant to one space below the base line, loop around and up, crossing at the base line.

Now, little letter **j**. Put your pencil on the base line. Swing up to the center dotted line, go down to one line below the base line, loop around and cross at the base line.

Teacher says:

Now, it's time for us to write the cursive forms of capital **K** and little **k**.

Put your pencil just above the top line. Loop down, up and around, and slant down to the base line. Lift your pencil. Put your pencil on the top line again, spaced over from where you started, slant down to touch the middle of the first stroke, loop up and around and curve down to the base line and swing up.

Now, little letter **k**. Put your pencil on the base line. Swing up to the top line, loop around and down to the base line on a slant, go up on the same line to the center line, looping over and in, then slant down to the base line and swing up.

Teacher says:

Now, it's time for us to write the cursive forms of capital **L** and little **l**.

Put your pencil on the center dotted line. Swing up to the top line, loop around and down on a slant to the base line, bounce up and loop over, crossing the slanted line, touching the base line and swing up.

Now, little letter **l**. Put your pencil on the base line. Swing up to the top line, loop around and down to the base line and swing up.

Sing Spell Read & Write

Cursive Writing Script *continued*

Teacher says:

Now, it's time for us to write the cursive forms of capital **M** and little **m**.

Put your pencil just above the top line. Loop down, up and around to touch the top line, then slant down to the base line. Go up on the same line and arch over and down to the base line, back up and arch over and down to the base line again and swing up.

Now, little letter **m**. Put your pencil on the base line. Curve up to the center dotted line, then over and down to the base, up on the same line, arch over and down to the base line, up on the same line again, arch over and down to the base line and swing up.

Teacher says:

Now, it's time for us to write the cursive forms of capital **N** and little **n**.

Put your pencil just above the top line. Loop down, up and around, then slant down to the base line, back up on the same line, arch over to touch the top line, curve down to the base line and swing up.

Now, little letter **n**. Put your pencil on the base line. Curve up to the center dotted line, go over and down to the base line, back up to the center, arch over and down to the base line again and swing up.

Teacher says:

Now it's time for us to write the cursive forms of capital **O** and little **o**.

Put your pencil on the top line. Curve around and down to the base line, curve up to the starting place, loop around and up.

Now, little letter **o**. Put your pencil on the center line. Curve down to the base line, and up to the starting place, loop around and up.

Cursive Writing Script *continued*

Teacher says:

Now, it's time for us to write the cursive forms of capital **P** and little **p**.

Put your pencil at the center dotted line. Swing up to the top line, slant down all the way to the base line, go up on the same line almost to the top line, curve to touch the top line and circle around and down, touching at the center line.

Now, little letter **p**. Put your pencil on the base line. Swing up to the center dotted line, go down to one space below the base line, loop up again all the way to the center line crossing the downward stroke, curve around to touch in at the base line and swing up.

Teacher says:

Now, it's time for us to write the cursive forms of capital **Q** and little **q**.

Put your pencil just above the top line. Loop down, up and around and curve down to touch the base line, loop up and over across your downward stroke, touch the base line and swing up. It looks like a large numeral "2."

Now, little letter **q**. Put your pencil on the start dot. Make a little letter "a," continuing down to one line below the base line, touch it, and then curve up as in the printed letter **q**. Touch in at the base line and swing up.

Teacher says:

Now, it's time for us to write the cursive forms of capital **R** and little **r**.

Put your pencil just above the center line. Swing up to touch the top line, go down on a slant to the base line, back up on the same line, touch the top line, curve around to touch the center line, loop up and around and down to the base line, and swing up.

Now, little letter **r**. Put your pencil on the base line. Swing up to the center line. Dip down slightly from the center line, swing over and up and pull down to the base line and swing up.

Cursive Writing Script *continued*

Teacher says:

Now, it's time for us to write the cursive forms of capital **S** and little **s**.

Put your pencil on the base line. Slant up two spaces to the top line, then curve around to form a letter "S" (like the manuscript letter) down to the base line, then swing over to make a "boat."

Now, little letter **s**. Touch the base line. Slant up to touch the center dotted line, curve down to the base line, touch in and swing back out.

Teacher says:

Now, it's time for us to write the cursive forms of capital **T** and little **t**.

Put your pencil just above the top line. Loop down, up and across. Lift your pencil. Touch the center of the top stroke, pull down on a slant to the base line, swing out and back to make a "boat."

Now, little letter **t**. Put your pencil on the base line. Slant up to touch the top line, pull down on the same line almost to the base line, curve down to touch the base line and then swing up. Make a cross bar just above the center dotted line.

Teacher says:

Now, it's time for us to write the cursive forms of capital **U** and little **u**.

Put your pencil just above the top line. Loop down, up and around and down to the base line, swing over and up to the top line, back down on the same line to the base line, and swing up.

Now, little letter **u**. Put your pencil on the base line. Slant up to the center dotted line, back down to the base line, then curve up to the center line and down to touch the base line, and swing up.

Cursive Writing Script *continued*

Teacher says:

Now, it's time for us to write the cursive forms of capital **V** and little **v**.

Put your pencil just above the top line. Loop down, up and around, then down to the base line, curve over and up to the top line, and swing over.

Now, little letter **v**. Put your pencil on the base line. Slant up to the center dotted line, go down to the base line, curve back up to the middle dotted line and over.

Teacher says:

Now, it's time for us to write the cursive forms of capital **W** and little **w**.

Put your pencil just above the top line. Loop down, up and around, curve down to the base, go up sharply on a slant to the top line, back down sharply to the base line and swing up and over.

Now, little letter **w**. Put your pencil on the base line. Swing up to the center dotted line, go down to touch the base, and curve up to the center line again, down to the base again, swing up to the center line and over.

Teacher says:

Now, it's time for us to write the cursive forms of capital **X** and little **x**.

(The first stroke resembles a curved "9." The second stroke resembles a curved "6.") Put your pencil just above the top line. Loop down, up and around and curve down to the base line. Lift your pencil. Move over a space on the top line, curve down and touch the "9" at the center dotted line, curve down to the base line and loop the bottom of the "6."

Now, little letter **x**. Put your pencil on the first start dot on the base line and slant up to the center dotted line, curve over and slant back down to the base line, and swing up. Lift your pencil. Touch down on the center line and cross over on a slant to the base line.

Cursive Writing Script *continued*

Teacher says:

Now, it's time for us to write the cursive forms of capital **Y** and little **y**.

Put your pencil just above the top line. Loop down, up and around, curve down to the base line and on up to the top line, go down three spaces, loop around and up through the base line.

Now, little letter **y**. Put your pencil on the base line. Curve up to the center dotted line, over and down to the base line, curve up to center, slant down two spaces, loop up and through the base line.

Teacher says:

Now, it's time for us to write the cursive forms of capital **Z** and little **z**.

Put your pencil just above the top line. Loop down, up and around, curve down to the base line, loop at the base line and curve down to one line below the base line, loop around and swing up through the base line.

Now, little letter **z**. Put you pencil on the base line. Slant up to the center dotted line and curve down to the base line, then curve around and down to one space below the base line, loop up through the base line.

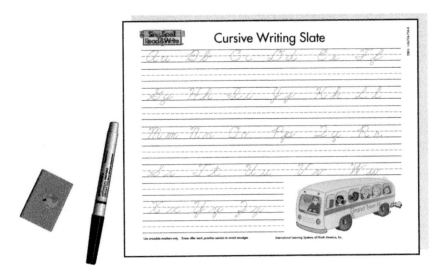

NOTES

Grand Tour I

Overview for Step 1

Objectives

Phonics: To sing *SSR&W Phonics Songs* and play *SSR&W Phonics Games*, providing review and/or new instruction for the phonics/decoding skills taught in SSR&W Level 1 Program

Spelling: To review the spelling of short vowel words

Grammar: To hear and understand rhyming words

Handwriting: To review the correct formation of manuscript letters

Suggested Pacing
1 Week

Materials
Grand Tour I, pp. 4-16
Desk Stick-Ons
Manuscript Wall Chart
Short Vowel Word Charts (ă, ĕ, ĭ, ŏ, ŭ)

Homework
Daily homework is described in TM p. 99.

Phonics Games
A to Z Sound-O (See TM p. 41.)
A to Z Pick-A-Sound (See TM p. 42.)
Letter Cluster Sound-O (See TM p. 52.)
Letter Cluster Pick-A-Sound (See TM p. 55.)
Word-O (See TM p. 58.)

Phonics Songs and Charts
A to Z Phonics Song, CD track 2 (See TM p. 40.)
ABC Echoes, CD track 3 (See TM p. 43.)
Short Vowel Song, CD track 4 (See TM p. 44.)
Ferris Wheel Song, CD track 5 (See TM p. 46.)
Ferris Wheel Blends Song, CD track 7 (See TM p. 48.)
Letter Cluster Phonics Song, verses 1-4,
    CD tracks 8 and 9 (See TM p. 51.)

Additional Related Activities
Additional activities are found in TM p. 96.

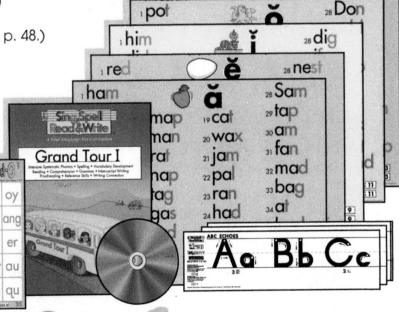

Individual Skills Assessment Chart

Phonics Review for Weeks 1-3 (30 minutes per day)

Directions:
(a) Have students sing song #1 with entire class.
(b) Have students pick a buddy and sing song #1 with their buddy.
(c) Have buddy initial and date box #1(Teachers check students new to SSR&W).
(d) Play Sound-O, Pick-A-Sound, and Word-O Games during the three review weeks.
(Continue in this manner for Goals 2-10.)

Goal 1
(a) Can sing A to Z Phonics Song
(b) Can play A to Z Sound-O Game
(c) Can play A to Z Pick-A-Sound Game

A...ă...apple

Initial / Date

Goal 2
Can lead ABC Echoes

Initial / Date

Goal 3
Can sing Short Vowel Song

B...b...ball

Initial / Date

Goal 4
(a) Can sing Ferris Wheel Song
★ ■ ○ ▲ Tickets
(b) Can sing Ferris Wheel Song
🔔 ⌂ ▷ Tickets

Initial / Date

Goal 5
(a) Can sing Letter Cluster Song
(b) Can play Letter Cluster Sound-O Game
(c) Can play Letter Cluster Pick-A-Sound Game

Initial / Date

Goal 6
Can Pop the Balloons

Initial / Date

Goal 7
(a) Can sing Long Vowel Song
(b) Can play Word-O Game

Initial / Date

Goal 8
Can sing Two Vowel Song

ā for apron

Initial / Date

Goal 9
Can sing Silent e Song

Initial / Date

Goal 10
Can sing Mr. Gh Clown Song

Initial / Date

Goal 11
Can write Manuscript Lesson #1 in Grand Tour I

Initial / Date

Sing, Spell Read & Write

Procedure for Step 1

Directions for Phonics Review Lessons and Individual Skills Assessment Chart

Steps 1-3 of **Grand Tour I** are designed for the first three weeks of school. They provide a review of the reading and spelling of short vowel words and syllables (which are estimated to comprise 62% of the English language). Students will also review the SSR&W Phonics Songs with accompanying wall charts as well as the SSR&W Phonics Games. These lessons were presented in SSR&W Level 1, but because it is unlikely that all of your students were in the program last year (or that all of them completed it, if they were), the key "learning-to-read" lessons of Level 1 are included. Success in Level 2 is dependent upon Level 1 skill success. This is the perfect opportunity for you to assess all of your students and intervene immediately on behalf of those in need of help in becoming independent readers. (In other words, fill in all the missing "learning-to-read" chunks.) Level 2 reviews Level 1 skills and then extends them to a higher level. For example, to review the spelling of short vowel words, the review list may include **sun**, **set**, **up**, **vent**, and **in**. These words will then be expanded to form **sunset**, **sunup**, **invent**, **upset**, etc.

> * The 11 goals listed on the **Individual Skills Assessment Chart**, *Grand Tour I*, page 4, should be the focus of instruction for **30 minutes every day** during the first three weeks of school.
>
> * Students must demonstrate competence and be signed off in the initial/date boxes on all 11 goals in order to successfully participate in the Level 2 Program.
>
> Initial
>
> Date

Individual Skills Assessment Chart

Directions for Goal 1

* As a class, have students sing the *A to Z Phonics Song* and take turns pointing to the *A to Z Phonics Wall Cards*. (See TM p. 40.)

* Pair up students and have the buddies take turns singing and pointing to the letters and pictures on their *Desk Stick-Ons*.

* If buddy #1 is successful in singing and pointing, have buddy #2 initial and date the box for **Goal 1**. Then have the buddies reverse roles.

* The **teacher** should listen to **students new to SSR&W** and, as needed, provide practices for them to master this goal as quickly as possible. Once the goal is mastered, the **teacher** initials and dates the box for **Goal 1**.

* Have students play *A to Z Sound-O* and *A to Z Pick-A-Sound* reinforcement games in order to provide ample practice for those students needing additional help with Goal 1. (See TM pp. 41-42.)

(Continued on next page)

Procedure for Step 1 *continued*

Directions for Goals 2 through 11

- Continue in the same manner for Goals 2-11, having buddies or the teacher initial/date each goal as it is reviewed and mastered. These 11 Goals contain the core of the **learning-to-read** process taught in SSR&W Level 1. It is essential that each student master these 11 Goals in order to be successful in the SSR&W Level 2 program. (Directions for the individual **learning-to-read** components are found in TM pp. 40-65.)

- For students who have completed SSR&W Level 1 and have read SSR&W Level 1 Storybook Readers 1-17, this phonics review should take no longer than three weeks.

- For individual students who have not mastered these goals in the three-week time frame, continue until **EACH STUDENT MASTERS EACH GOAL**. Have students work in pairs for peer tutoring and provide additional practice as needed.

- Once a student has mastered all of the 11 Goals on page 4, remove the **Individual Skills Assessment Chart** from the *Grand Tour I* Student Book, and file it in his/her reading portfolio.

- For students unable to pass the *Quick Placement Test* (80% or better), see Quick Intervention Plan A or B, TM pp. 34-39, and continue to work with them 30 minutes a day until they master these skills.

Directions for Days 1 through 5, *Grand Tour I*, pp. 5-16

As a class, review the daily spelling words by having students take turns around the room:

- Reading the words orally.
- Using the words in oral sentences.
- Spelling the words orally.

Have students pick buddies and take turns spelling the 20 words to each other.

Have students:
- Choose five words from the daily spelling list.
- Write the five words on a paper labeled "Homework."
- Take the five words home and write them in sentences for homework.
- Send home the First Day Letter to Parents in Reproducible section, TM p. 469, asking a parent to initial the homework paper and return it to class the following morning. (**Let the students and parents know that this homework pattern will continue throughout the year, four nights each week. Beginning with Step 2 students will take ten words home to write in sentences for homework.**)

As a class, read and discuss the directions on both sides of the daily lesson in *Grand Tour I*. The daily lesson plans, which begin on page 89 of this Teacher's Manual, will provide additional information and suggestions for teaching each concept. It is important for students to fully understand the concept being taught and what is expected of them before they are asked to do any part of the lesson independently.

Teach/review correct manuscript letter formation. The teacher scripts for manuscript writing instruction are found on TM pp. 66-73. Students will practice correct letter formation on pp. 15-16 throughout the week.

Grand Tour I Step 1

Step-by-Step Detailed Lesson Plans for Step 1

Phonics Review

- Schedule 30 minutes per day for students to work on mastering Goals 1-11, listed on **Individual Skills Assessment Chart**, page 4. (See TM p. 86.)
- Sing *A-Z Phonics Song* and say ABC Echoes, CD tracks 2 and 3. (See TM pp. 40 and 43.)

***Grand Tour I*, p. 5**

Spelling Words
Phonetic Grouping: ă

- As a class, take turns reading the 20 spelling words, using the words in sentences, and spelling the words orally.
- Next, have students pick buddies and take turns spelling the words to each other.
- Have students choose five words from the list and write them on a sheet of paper labeled "Homework."
- Students will take the five words home and write them in sentences for homework.
- Parents are to initial and date the paper before the student turns it in the following day.

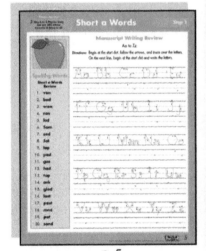

p. 5

Manuscript Writing Review

- Tell students they will review and practice the correct formation of all manuscript letters. (Teacher scripts for manuscript writing instruction are in this Teacher's Manual on pages 66-73.)
- Remind them to hold their paper and pencil correctly.
- Tell students the **dots** show where to begin writing, and the **arrows** tell them which direction to go.
- Remind students that "practice makes perfect." If they have been forming letters by starting in the wrong place and/or going in the wrong direction, **NOW** is the time to fix it. Tell them this is especially important because they will be learning cursive writing later in the year. The formation of most cursive letters is based on the manuscript letter formations. That it is why it is so important that they learn to **START AT THE DOT AND FOLLOW THE ARROWS!**
- On page 5, have students trace over the gray letters first and then write the same letters on the next line.
- Walk around the room, checking to be sure that all students are starting at the dots and following the arrows. Insisting on correct manuscript letter formation now will ensure an easy transition into cursive writing later in the year.
- **It may take considerable effort on your part to help students break any incorrect writing habits they may have already developed, but it will be time well spent in the long run.**

(Right Handed)

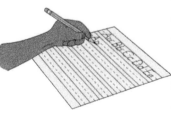

(Left Handed)

(Continued on next page)

89

Day 1 continued

Grand Tour I, p. 6

Letter Switch

- Tell students you can make a new word by changing one letter in a word.
  Example: Change bat to bad replacing **t** with **d**.

- Write **rag** on the board and ask students which letter you would change to make a word that means the same as **sack**. (**b**ag)

- Tell students to read each sentence on page 6.

- Have students look at the **word in the box** and the **underlined letter**.

- Students will change the **underlined letter** to make a new word and then write the word on the lines provided.

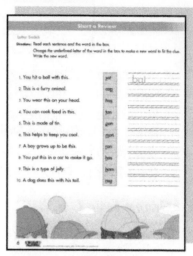

p. 6

Day 2

Getting Started

Collect homework and put stars on Homework Chart. (See TM p. 26.)

Phonics Review

- Schedule 30 minutes per day for students to work on mastering Goals 1-11, listed on **Individual Skills Assessment Chart**, page 4. (See TM p. 86.)

- Sing *Short Vowel Song*, CD track 4, and *Ferris Wheel Song*, CD track 5. (See TM pp.48 and 46.)

Grand Tour I, p. 7

Spelling Words
Phonetic Grouping: ĕ

- As a class, take turns reading the 20 spelling words, using the words in sentences, and spelling the words orally.

- Next, have students pick buddies and take turns spelling the words to each other.

- Have students choose five words from the list and write them on a sheet of paper labeled "Homework."

- Students will take the five words home and write them in sentences for homework.

- Parents are to initial and date the paper before the student turns it in the following day.

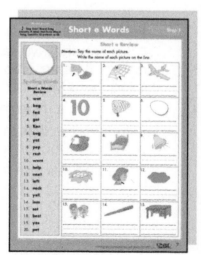

p. 7

> **Note:** Use Grand Tour I Student Book Answer Key Booklet to correct student papers. Student Book pages pictured in TM are for reference only.

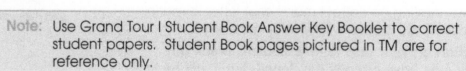

Short e Review

- To prepare students for this activity, say several **short e** words and ask students to spell each word orally.
  Examples: let, rest, bent, bet, men

- Remind students each word will have letter **e** with a **short e** sound.

- Tell students to say the name of the pictures on page 7. Have them listen for the **beginning, middle,** and **ending** sounds. Have students segment (break apart or stretch) each sound as they say the word, drawing out each sound that can be extended. Then they should say the word in the normal fashion.
  Examples: l l l l l - ĕ ĕ ĕ ĕ ĕ - g, leg
  w w w w w - ĕ ĕ ĕ ĕ ĕ - b, web

- Students will write the word (name of the picture) on the line.

- Remind students to form letters properly as shown on *Manuscript Wall Chart.*

Grand Tour I, p. 8

Rhyming

- Tell students **rhyming** words have the same ending vowel and consonant sounds.

- Write **net—bet** and **rat—fat** on the chalkboard and point out to students the underlined vowel and consonant sounds are the same in each pair of **rhyming** words.

- Say the following pairs of words and ask students to **clap** if the words **rhyme** and **remain silent** if the words do not **rhyme.**
  Examples: jet—bet (clap); lad—sad (clap); big—bag (silent); went—bent (clap)

- Tell students to read each sentence on page 8 and look at the picture next to the sentence.

- Students will change the underlined word to a word that **rhymes** and matches the picture.

- Remind students to change the first letter only.

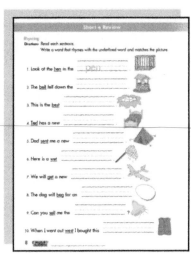

p. 8

(Continued on next page)

Day 2 *continued*

Grammar Chalkboard Lesson
Rhyming Words

Objective
- Students will hear and understand **rhyming** words.

Practice/Apply
- Write the words shown below on the board. Students will write each word and write another word that **rhymes**.

  Example: wet—set

1. pad - _____
2. sand - _____
3. van - _____
4. last - _____
5. Sal - _____

6. yell - _____
7. rest - _____
8. fed - _____
9. tent - _____
10. pet - _____

Handwriting Practice

Have students practice writing manuscript letter **Aa**. (*Grand Tour I*, p. 15)

Day 3

Getting Started

Collect homework and put stars on Homework Chart. (See TM p. 26.)

Phonics Review

- Schedule 30 minutes per day for students to work on mastering Goals 1-11, listed on **Individual Skills Assessment Chart**, page 4. (See TM p. 86.)
- Sing *Ferris Wheel Song* and *Ferris Wheel Blends Song*, CD tracks 5 and 7. (See TM p. 46.)

Day 3 *continued*

Grand Tour I, p. 9

Spelling Words
Phonetic Grouping: ĭ

- As a class, take turns reading the 20 spelling words, using the words in sentences, and spelling the words orally.
- Next, have students pick buddies and take turns spelling the words to each other.
- Have students choose five words from the list and write them on a sheet of paper labeled "Homework."
- Students will take the five words home and write them in sentences for homework.
- Parents are to initial and date the paper before the student turns it in the following day.

Short i Review

- To prepare students for this activity say **short i** words and ask students to spell each word orally.
  Examples: tin, lip, fig, fill
- Remind students each word will have **short i**.
- Have students say the names of the pictures on page 9. Have them listen for the **beginning, middle,** and **ending** sounds. Have students break apart each sound as they say the word, drawing out each sound that can be extended. Then they should say the word in the normal fashion.
  Examples: p — ĭ ĭ ĭ ĭ ĭ - nnnnn, pin
  p — ĭ ĭ ĭ ĭ ĭ - g, pig
- Students will write the name of each picture on the lines provided.
- Remind students to form letters properly as shown on *Manuscript Wall Chart*.

p. 9

Grand Tour I, p. 10

Word Fun

- Read clue #1 to the class. (It begins like **top** and ends like **can**.)
- Next, have students look at the first picture in clue #1 (**top**). **Top** begins with **t** so the word they are looking for must begin with **t**.
- Students then look at the second picture in clue #1 (**can**). **Can** ends with **n** so the word they are looking for must end with **n**.
- Have students look in the shaded box to find a word that matches the clue. The word must be **tin**.
- Students will write the word **tin** and continue in the same manner to complete the page.

Handwriting Practice

Have students practice writing manuscript letter **Bb**. (*Grand Tour I, p. 15*)

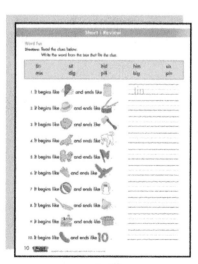

p. 10

Grand Tour I

Day 4

Getting Started

Collect homework and put stars on Homework Chart. (See TM p. 26.)

Phonics Review

* Schedule 30 minutes per day for students to work on mastering Goals 1-11, listed on **Individual Skills Assessment Chart**, page 4. (See TM p. 86.)
* Sing *Letter Cluster Phonics Song*, verses 1 and 2, CD track 8. (See TM p. 51.)

Grand Tour I, p. 11

Spelling Words
Phonetic Grouping: ŏ

* As a class, take turns reading the 20 spelling words, using the words in sentences, and spelling the words orally.
* Next, have students pick buddies and take turns spelling the words to each other.
* Have students choose five words from the list and write them on a sheet of paper labeled "Homework."
* Students will take the five words home and write them in sentences for homework.
* Parents are to initial and date the paper before the student turns it in the following day.

p. 11

Short o Review

Rhyming

* Remind students that **rhyming** words have the same ending vowel and consonant sounds.
* Say these pairs of words and ask students to **clap** if the words **rhyme** and **remain silent** if the words **do not rhyme**.
  Examples: top—pop (clap); log—dog (clap);
  stop—stick (silent); block—flock (clap)

* On page 11 students will find words from the spelling list that **rhyme** with the underlined word and write them in the spaces.
* Remind students to form letters properly as shown on *Manuscript Wall Chart*.

Grand Tour I, p. 12

Letter Switch

Have students:
* Read each sentence.
* Look at the word in the box and the underlined letter.
* Change the underlined letter to make a new word and write it.

p. 12

Day 4 *continued*

Grammar Chalkboard Lesson
Rhyming Words

Objective
- Students will hear and understand **rhyming** words.

Practice/Apply
- Write the words shown below on the board. Students will write each word and write another word that **rhymes**.
  Example: just—rust

```
  1. win - _____          6. top - _____
  2. spin - _____         7. dog - _____
  3. big - _____          8. mug - _____
  4. dip - _____          9. truck - _____
  5. block - _____        10. hut - _____
```

Handwriting Practice

Have students practice writing manuscript letter **Cc**. (*Grand Tour I*, p. 16)

Day 5

Getting Started

Collect homework and put stars on Homework Chart. (See TM p. 26.)

Phonics Review

- Schedule 30 minutes per day for students to work on mastering Goals 1-11, listed on **Individual Skills Assessment Chart**, page 4. (See TM p. 86.)
- Sing *Letter Cluster Phonics Song*, verses 1-4, CD tracks 8 and 9. (See TM p. 51.)

Grand Tour I, p. 13

Spelling Words
Phonetic Grouping: ŭ

- As a class, take turns reading the 20 spelling words, using the words in sentences, and spelling the words orally.
- Next, have students pick buddies and take turns spelling the words to each other.
- Have students choose five words from the list and write them on a sheet of paper labeled "Homework."
- Students will take the five words home and write them in sentences for homework.
- Parents are to initial and date the paper before the student turns it in the following day.

p. 13

(Continued on next page)

Grand Tour I

Short u Review

Word Clues

* Have students read the first clue, look at the spelling list, and write a word that fits the clue.

Rhyming

* Students will write spelling words that rhyme with each underlined word.

Grand Tour I, p. 14

Rhyming

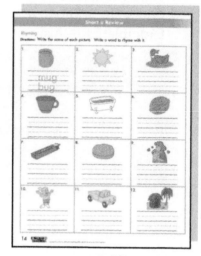

p. 14

* Ask students to say the name of the first picture. **(mug)** Have them listen for the **beginning, middle,** and **ending** sounds and say the word as before. (**m m m m m — ŭ ŭ ŭ ŭ ŭ — g**), mug
* Students will write **mug** in the first space.
* Next, have students think of a word that rhymes with **mug** and write the rhyming word in the space below **mug**.
* Remind students to only change **one letter** in each new rhyming word.
* Accept any reasonable answers.

Handwriting Practice

Have students practice writing manuscript letter **Dd**. (*Grand Tour I*, p. 16)

Additional Related Activities

Listening and Speaking

1. *Around the World* **with Rhyming Words**

Directions:

* Have a student stand beside a student seated at his/her desk.
* The teacher will say a short vowel word.
  Example: rat
* The student who first says a word to rhyme with rat moves on to the next desk.
* Continue the game in this same manner using a variety of short vowel words.

2. *Letter Switch*

* Tell students you will toss a beanbag to someone in the class.
* As that student stands up, the teacher writes a word on the board.
  Example: bed
* Ask the student to change a letter in **bed** to make it say **a color**.
  The student should change **b** to **r** to make the word **red**.

  Example:
  1. Change a letter to make **bat** mean **a small gray animal**. (rat)
  2. Change a letter to make **run** mean **something that shines in the sky**. (sun)
  3. Change a letter to make **lock** mean **something you wear on your foot**. (sock)
  4. Change a letter to make **not** mean **very warm**. (hot)
  5. Change a letter to make **dig** mean **the name of an animal**. (pig)
  6. Change a letter to make **fix** mean **a number**. (six)
  7. Change a letter to make **top** mean **to jump on one foot**. (hop)

NOTES

Grand Tour I

Overview for Step 2

Objectives

Phonics: To sing *SSR&W Phonics Songs* and play *SSR&W Phonics Games,* providing review and/or new instruction for the phonics/decoding skills taught in SSR&W Level 1 Program

Spelling: To learn to spell short vowel, multisyllable words and compound words

Grammar: To understand how to divide words into syllables between twin Consonants
To recognize and read compound words
To write a sentence by arranging words in the correct order
To know how to use verbs (**is—are; don't—doesn't**)

Writing: To write complete sentences using subject and verb agreement
To use the Five Steps of Process Writing, focusing on writing to share ideas

Handwriting: To review the correct formation of manuscript letters
Ee to **Hh**

Suggested Pacing
1 Week

Materials
Grand Tour I, pp. 17-28

Homework
Daily homework is described in TM p. 99.

Spelling
Daily spelling is described in TM p. 99.

Phonics Games
Letter Cluster Sound-O (See TM p. 52.)
Letter Cluster Pick-A-Sound (See TM p. 55.)

Phonics Songs and Charts
Letter Cluster Phonics Song, CD track 8 (See TM p. 51.)
Long Vowel Marching Song, CD track 10 (See TM p. 57.)
ABC Echoes (all sounds), CD track 12 (See TM p. 59.)
Two Vowels Get Together Song, CD track 13 (See TM p. 60.)
Silent e Song, CD track 15 (See TM p. 61.)
Gh Clown Song, CD track 17 (See TM p. 62.)

Additional Related Activities
Additional activities are found in TM p. 109.

Procedure for Step 2

Grand Tour I, p. 4

Individual Skills Assessment Chart

- Each day of the week you need to schedule 30 minutes per day for students to work on mastering Goals 1-11, listed on **Individual Skills Assessment Chart**, page 4. (See TM p. 86)

- Students must demonstrate competence and be signed off in the initial/date boxes on all 11 goals in order to successfully participate in the Level 2 Program.

Sample Schedule for using *Grand Tour I*, Step 2, Day 1

1. During the first 30 minutes, continue with the **Individual Skills Assessment Chart** as described in Step 1. (See TM p. 86.)

2. As a class, review the daily **Spelling Words** by having students take turns around the room:

    - Reading the words orally.
    - Using the words in oral sentences.
    - Spelling the words orally.

3. Have students:

    - Copy the 10 spelling words from the daily spelling list on a paper labeled "Homework."

    - Take the ten words home and write them in sentences for homework. (They may use more than one spelling word in a sentence.)

    - Have parents initial the homework paper to be returned to class the following day.

    - This related homework/parental component is designed not only to have the students practice spelling and writing skills, but it is also a key factor in helping to establish consistent, daily habits for both students and parents.

4. Go over all **Spelling Vocabulary Activities** on page 17. Read and discuss the directions for the **Grammar** lesson on page 18. (See TM p. 101 for detailed instructions.)

> - Look for the pencil icon on the student pages:
> - The pencil icon will identify important concepts as they are introduced and/or practiced.
> - The daily lesson plans in the Teacher's Manual provide the teacher with additional information and suggestions for introducing, practicing and reviewing each concept.

5. Be sure all students fully understand each new/reviewed concept before asking them to complete any activities independently.

6. During independent work time, students will complete all the activities on pages 17 and 18. This is their lesson for the day.

(Continued on next page)

Procedure for Step 2 *continued*

7. Have students work on **Handwriting Practice** on pages 27-28 throughout the week. Emphasize the correct formation of each letter. (See TM pp. 69-70.)

8. Begin Process Writing Lesson #1. (See TM p. 431.)

Sample Schedule for using *Grand Tour I*, Step 2, Day 2

1. Collect homework sentences from previous day and put stars on Homework Chart. (See TM p. 26.)

2. Distribute lined paper and give spelling test of yesterday's spelling words from page17. Say the spelling word, use the word in a sentence, and say the word again.

   Example: saddle – The cowboy put a **saddle** on his horse. – **saddle**. The student writes each word on lined, numbered paper. Dictate one sentence for students to write. (See TM p. 100.)

Teacher Tip:

The sentence dictation can provide **bonus** points for students. Errors in Sentence Dictation should never take points away. If the student spells each word in the sentence correctly, uses a capital letter, and places a period at the end of the sentence, this can count as 10 points towards a misspelled word on the spelling test.

Example: A student spells 9 out of 10 spelling words correctly on the test to make 90%. He/She writes the dictated sentence correctly so the grade is scored as 100%. (90% + 10% bonus points = 100%)

The maximum score for a spelling test remains at 100%, even if the student spells the sentence and all 10 spelling words correctly.

---

3. During the next 30 minutes, continue with the **Individual Skills Assessment Chart** as described in Step 1. (See TM p. 86.)

4. As a class read, use in sentences, and practice spelling orally the new spelling words on page 19.

5. Have students copy the 10 spelling words on page 19 on a separate sheet of paper to take home, study, and write in sentences. (Parents are to initial and date the homework page before the student hands in the page the following day.)

6. Teach and discuss the Spelling Vocabulary Activities on page 19. As a class, read and discuss the directions.

7. Teach and discuss the Grammar Lesson on page 20. As a class, read and discuss the directions. Be sure each student understands what is expected before being asked to complete pages 19 and 20 independently.

8. During independent work time, students will complete all the activities on pages 19-20. This is their lesson for the day. Teacher may choose to have students tear out, complete, and hand in each page, or the pages can remain in each student book.

9. Review handwriting on pages 27-28 throughout the week. Emphasize the correct formation of each letter.

Teacher Tip:

As you establish and follow these routines throughout the school year, you will find you need to spend less time giving directions and more time instructing.

Grand Tour I

Step-By-Step Detailed Lesson Plans for Step 2

Day 1

Phonics Review

Schedule 30 minutes per day for students to work on mastering Goals 1-11, listed on **Individual Skills Assessment Chart**, page 4. (See TM p. 86.)

Grand Tour I, p. 17

Spelling Words
Phonetic Grouping: ă

* Note that words #1-5 end in **le** and words #6-10 are **compound words**.
* As a class, read the 10 spelling words and discuss the meanings.
* Have students copy the 10 spelling words to take home, study, and write in sentences for homework.

Spelling Vocabulary Activities

Compound Words
* Tell students **compound words** are two words put together to make one word and are often related in some way.
Example: hatbox. **Hat** and **box** are related because you place a **hat** in a **box**.

* Students will write five spelling words that are compound words.

Syllables
* Explain to students that syllables are the **parts** you hear in a word and there are rules for dividing words into syllables. For example, when you hear two parts in a word and the word has twin consonants, you usually divide the word between the twin consonants.
Example: fiddle – fid • dle

* You can also divide words into syllables between the two words in a compound word.
Example: football – foot • ball

* Students will write the 10 spelling words and divide them into syllables.

Grand Tour I, p. 18

Grammar

Sentence Scramble
* Tell students a sentence is a group of words that expresses a complete thought.
* Students will unscramble a group of words and write each sentence.

p. 17

p. 18

(Continued on next page)

Day 1 continued

Handwriting Practice

Have students practice writing manuscript letter **Ee**. (*Grand Tour I*, page 27)

Process Writing

Process Writing Lesson #1 for Steps 2 and 3 is found in TM p. 431.

Day 2

Getting Started

* Collect homework and put stars on Homework Chart. (See TM p. 26.)
* Administer spelling test with Day 1 spelling words in *Grand Tour I*, p. 17. Sentence for dictation: This man <u>cannot</u> hop. (See TM p. 100.)

Phonics Review

* Schedule 30 minutes per day for students to work on mastering Goals 1-11, listed on **Individual Skills Assessment Chart**, page 4. (See TM p. 86.)
* Sing *Long Vowel Marching Song*, CD track 10 and ABC Echoes (all sounds), CD track 12. (See TM pp. 57 and 59.)

Grand Tour I, p. 19

Spelling Words
Phonetic Grouping: ĕ

* Note that all the words have twin consonants. Have students mark words as indicated: **peb • ble**
* As a class, read the 10 spelling words and discuss the meanings.
* Have students copy the 10 spelling words to take home, study, and write in sentences for homework.

Spelling Vocabulary Activities

Syllables
* Explain to students that syllables are the parts you hear in a word. When you hear two parts in a word with twin consonants, you usually divide the word between the twin consonants.
  Example: yel • low

* Students will write each spelling word in syllables.

Riddles
* Students will write a spelling word to answer each riddle.

p. 27

p. 19

Day 2 continued

Grand Tour I, p. 20

Grammar

Using is and are

- Tell students to use **is** in a sentence when you are talking about **one** person, place or thing, and use **are** when you are talking about **two or more.**
- Write 10 singular and plural nouns on the board and ask students if **is** or **are** should be used with each word.

  Examples: dog—is; dogs—are
  friend—is; friends—are

- Students will fill in the blanks with **is** or **are**.

p. 20

The Writing Connection

Writing Complete Sentences

- Students will write one sentence using **is** and one sentence using **are**.

Grammar Chalkboard Lesson

is and are Review

Objective

- Students will understand subject-verb agreement. (**is—are**).

Practice/Apply

- Write the sentences on the board. Students will copy each sentence and write **is** or **are** in each blank.

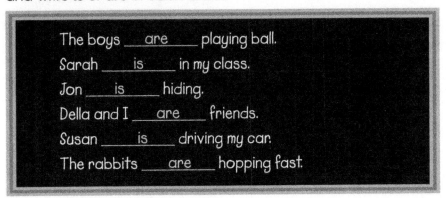

The boys ___are___ playing ball.
Sarah ___is___ in my class.
Jon ___is___ hiding.
Della and I ___are___ friends.
Susan ___is___ driving my car.
The rabbits ___are___ hopping fast.

Handwriting Practice

Have students practice writing manuscript letter **Ff**. (*Grand Tour I*, page 27)

Process Writing

Process Writing Lesson #1 for Steps 2 and 3 is found in TM p. 431.

p. 27

Day 3

Getting Started

- Collect homework and put stars on Homework Chart. (See TM p. 26.)
- Administer spelling test with Day 2 spelling words in *Grand Tour I*, p. 19. Sentence for dictation: I like to eat <u>jelly</u>. (See TM p. 100.)

Phonics Review

- Schedule 30 minutes per day for students to work on mastering Goals 1-11, listed on **Individual Skills Assessment Chart**, page 4. (See TM p. 86.)
- Sing *Two Vowels Get Together Song*, CD track 13. (See TM p. 60.)

Grand Tour I, p. 21

Spelling Words
Phonetic Grouping: ĭ

- Tell students when you hear two parts in a word with twin consonants, you usually divide the word between the twin consonants.
  Example: ripple—rip•ple

- Note that each word has twin consonants. Have students mark each word as indicated: **rip • ple**

- As a class, read the 10 spelling words and discuss the meanings.

- Have students copy the 10 spelling words to take home, study, and write in sentences for homework.

Spelling Vocabulary Activities

Syllables

- Tell students when you hear two parts in a word with twin consonants, you usually divide the word between the twin consonants.
  Example: ripple—rip•ple

- Students will write each spelling word in syllables.

Cloze

- Students will fill in the blanks with the correct spelling words.

p. 21

Day 3 *continued*

Grand Tour I, p. 22

Grammar

Using <u>is</u> and <u>are</u>

- Talk about the rule for using **is** and **are** in a sentence. You use **is** when you are talking about **one** person, place, or thing. You use **are** when you are talking about **more than one** person, place, or thing.

- Write 10 singular and plural nouns on the board and ask students if **is** or **are** should be used in the sentence.

  Examples: girl—is; girls—are
  cage—is; cages—are

- Students will fill in the blanks with **is** or **are**.

p. 22

The Writing Connection

Writing Complete Sentences

- Students will write one sentence using **is** and one sentence using **are**.

Handwriting Practice

Have students practice writing manuscript letter **Gg**. (*Grand Tour I,* page 28)

Process Writing

Process Writing Lesson #1 for Steps 2 and 3 is found in TM p. 431.

Day 4

p. 28

Getting Started

- Collect homework and put stars on Homework Chart. (See TM p. 26.)
- Administer spelling test with Day 3 spelling words in *Grand Tour I,* p. 21. Sentence for dictation: It is fun to <u>giggle</u>. (See TM p. 100.)

Phonics Review

- Schedule 30 minutes per day for students to work on mastering Goals 1-11, listed on **Individual Skills Assessment Chart**, page 4. (See TM p. 86.)
- Sing *Silent ∅ Song,* CD track 15. (See TM p. 61.)

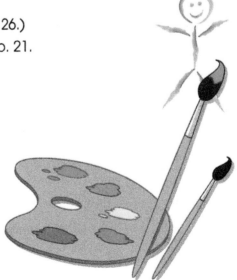

(*Continued on next page*)

Grand Tour I

Day 4 *continued*

Grand Tour I, p. 23

Spelling Words
Phonetic Grouping: ŏ

- Note that words #1-4 have **ck** and words #5-10 have twin consonants.
- As a class, read the 10 spelling words and discuss the meanings.
- Have students copy the 10 spelling words to take home, study, and write in sentences for homework.

Spelling Vocabulary Activities

Rhyming

- Talk about what makes words rhyme. (Rhyming words have the same ending vowel and consonant sounds.)
  Examples: drop—shop; sock—rock

- Think of pairs of words and say them to the class. Ask the students to clap if the words **rhyme** and to remain silent if they do not rhyme.
  Examples: boat—coat (clap); flag—day (silent)

- Students will write **pocket** and three spelling words that **rhyme** with **pocket**.

Syllables

- Review the rule for dividing words into syllables between twin consonants.
- Say words #5-10 and ask students to clap for each syllable. Model how each word would be divided between the twin consonants.
  Examples: bottle—bot • tle

- Students will write words #5-10 and divide into syllables.

Word Scramble

- Students will unscramble the letters to make a spelling word.

p. 23

Grand Tour I, p. 24

Grammar

Using <u>don't</u> and <u>doesn't</u>

- Tell students to use **don't** when you are talking about words that mean **two or more**, and **I** or **you**. Use **doesn't** when you are talking about **one** person, place, or thing in a sentence.

- Write 10 singular and plural nouns on the board and ask students if **don't** or **doesn't** should be used with each word.
  Examples: boy—doesn't; boys—don't

- Students will fill in the blanks with **doesn't** or **don't**.

p. 24

Day 4 *continued*

The Writing Connection

Writing Complete Sentences

- Students will write one sentence using **doesn't** and one sentence using **don't**.

Grammar Chalkboard Lesson
Using Don't and Doesn't

Objective

- Students will understand subject-verb agreement. (**don't–doesn't**)

Practice/Apply

- Write the sentences on the board. Students will copy each sentence and write **don't** or **doesn't** in the blank.

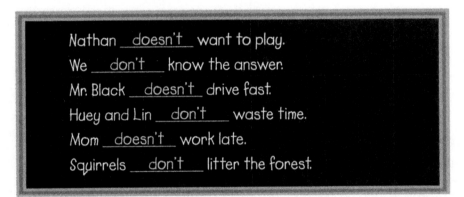

Nathan __doesn't__ want to play.

We __don't__ know the answer.

Mr. Black __doesn't__ drive fast.

Huey and Lin __don't__ waste time.

Mom __doesn't__ work late.

Squirrels __don't__ litter the forest.

Handwriting Practice

Have students practice writing manuscript letter **Hh**. (*Grand Tour I*, page 28)

Process Writing

Process Writing Lesson #1 for Steps 2 and 3 is found in TM p. 431.

p. 28

Getting Started

- Collect homework and put stars on Homework Chart. (See TM p. 26.)
- Administer spelling test with Day 4 spelling words in *Grand Tour I*, p. 23. Sentence Dictation: The red <u>bottle</u> is big. (See TM p. 100.)

Phonics Review

- Schedule 30 minutes per day for students to work on mastering Goals 1-11, listed on **Individual Skills Assessment Chart**, page 4. (See TM p. 86.)
- Sing *Gh Clown Song*, CD track 17. (See TM p. 62.)

Grand Tour I, p. 25

Spelling Words
Phonetic Grouping: ŭ

- Note that words #1-8 have twin consonants and words #9 and 10 are compound words.
- As a class, read the 10 spelling words and discuss the meanings.

Spelling Vocabulary Activities

Crossword Puzzle

- Explain to students how to work a crossword puzzle.
- Students will read the clues, find a spelling word that goes with the clue, and write the word by the number in the crossword puzzle. You may want to do this as a total group until children are familiar with working crossword puzzles.

Syllables

- Review the rule for dividing words into **syllables** between twin consonants. Another rule for dividing a word into **syllables** is divide between the two words in a **compound** word.
  Example: fishtank—fish • tank

- Write the multisyllable nonsense words below on the board and have students read the nonsense words. This is good practice for students to use their phonics skills. Remind students these are not real words.

suddle   mufpan   cuffle   dutsell   tubble   dutter

- On page 25 students will write each spelling word in syllables.

Grand Tour I, p. 26

Grammar

Using <u>don't</u> and <u>doesn't</u>

- Review the rule for using **don't** and **doesn't**.
- Write 10 singular and plural nouns on the board and ask students if **don't** or **doesn't** should be used with each word.
  Example: cars—don't; bus—doesn't

- Students will fill in the blanks on page 26 with **don't** or **doesn't**.

p. 25

p. 26

Day 5 *continued*

The Writing Connection

Writing Complete Sentences
- Students will write one sentence using **doesn't** and one sentence using **don't**.

Process Writing

Process Writing Lesson #1 for Steps 2 and 3 is found in TM p. 431.

Additional Related Activities for Step 2

Listening and Speaking

1. Syllable Clapping
- Write the poem below on chart paper. As a class, choral read the poem and clap the syllables.
- Identify the two or three syllable words by underlining the word and placing a mark between the syllables.

A <u>lit • tle</u> girl went <u>skip • ping</u>.   She saw a <u>chirp • ing</u> <u>spar • row</u>
One <u>love • ly</u> <u>sum • mer</u> day.   Fly from tree to tree.
She saw a <u>lit • tle</u> <u>rab • bit</u>   She picked a <u>pret • ty</u> <u>flow • er</u>
That <u>quick • ly</u> ran <u>a • way</u>.   Then said, "You <u>be • long</u> to me."

2. Compound Words
- Toss a beanbag to a student in the class and say a word that can have a second word added to make a compound word, **rain** for example. The student catches the beanbag and says, "**rain**coat," "**rain**bow" or any acceptable compound word using rain. The student tosses the beanbag back to the teacher and the game continues.

- Suggestions for words:

sail____ (boat)	skate____ (board)	row____ (boat)
base____ (ball)	rail____ (road)	pan____ (cake)
ear____ (ring)	foot____ (ball)	thumb____ (tack)
cow____ (boy)	day____ (time)	stomach____ (ache)
snow____ (man)	tip____ (toe)	camp____ (fire)
grand____ (mother)	play____ (time)	toe____ (nail)
note____ (book)	fire____ (house)	side____ (walk)
tooth____ (brush)	back____ (pack)	some____ (day)

- Accept any reasonable answer as fireman, firefighter, etc.

3. Rhyming Words
- Ask children which of our five senses we use to discover if a poem rhymes. (hearing)
- Read some nursery rhymes or poems that have rhyming words and ask students to identify the rhyming words.

4. Riddles
- Children will work in pairs to make riddles using spelling words from Step 2.
   Example: This is something that begins with an **r** and flies to the moon. (rocket)
- Let students share their riddles with the class.

Grand Tour I

Overview for Step 3

Objectives

Phonics: To sing *SSR&W Phonics Songs* and play *SSR&W Phonics Games*, providing review and/or new instruction for the phonics/decoding skills taught in SSR&W Level 1 Program

Spelling: To learn to spell short vowel, multisyllable, and compound words

Grammar: To know how to use verbs (**went–gone**; **came–come**; **did–done**)

Writing: To write sentences using the correct verb tense
To write a different ending for a story
To use the Five Steps of Process Writing, focusing on writing to share ideas

Handwriting: To review the correct formation of manuscript letters
Ii to **Ll**

Suggested Pacing

1 Week

Materials

Grand Tour I, pp. 29-40

Homework

Daily homework is described in TM p. 99.

Spelling

Daily spelling is described in TM p. 99.

Phonics Games

Letter Cluster Sound-O (See TM p. 52.)
Letter Cluster Pick-A-Sound (See TM p. 55.)

Phonics Songs (See TM pp. 40-65.)

Continue to sing selected *SSR&W Songs* as needed for reinforcement.

Additional Related Activities

Additional activities are found in TM p. 119.

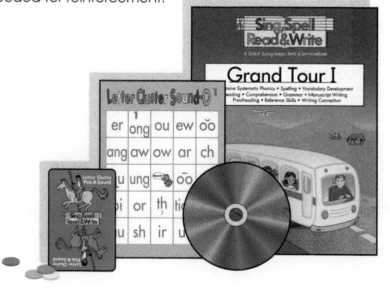

Day 1

Phonics Review

Schedule 30 minutes per day for students to work on mastering Goals 1-11, listed on **Individual Skills Assessment Chart**, page 4. (See TM p. 86.)

Grand Tour I, p. 29

Spelling Words
Phonetic Grouping: ă

- Note that each word has a **short a**.
- As a class, read the 10 spelling words and discuss the meanings.
- Have students copy the 10 spelling words to take home, study and write in sentences for homework. Continue throughout the year the homework pattern that was established during Steps 1 and 2.

p. 29

Spelling Vocabulary Activities

Rhyming
- Tell students words that **rhyme** end with the same ending vowel and consonant sounds.
- Students will write spelling words that **rhyme** and end in **le** or **et**.

Cloze
- Students will fill in each blank with the correct spelling word.

Word Scramble
- Students will unscramble the letters to make a spelling word.

Grand Tour I, p. 30

Grammar

Using <u>went</u> and <u>gone</u>
- Explain to students that **have**, **has**, and **had** are called helping words.
- Gone must have a helping word.
  Example: We **have gone** to the store.

- **Went** may be used alone.
  Example: We **went** to the store. This sentence does not have the helping word **have**, **has**, or **had**.

- Think of several sentences and say them aloud to the class, leaving out **went** or **gone**. Ask students which word would be correct.
  Examples: Mieko ____ skating. (went)
  Kevin has ____ skating. (gone)

- Students will write **went** or **gone** in each sentence on page 30.

p. 30

(Continued on next page)

Sing Spell Read & Write. 111

Grand Tour I

Day 1 continued

The Writing Connection

Writing Complete Sentences
- Students will write one sentence using **went** and one sentence using **gone**.

Handwriting Practice

Have students practice writing manuscript letter **Ii**. (*Grand Tour I*, p. 39)

Process Writing

Process Writing Lesson #1 for Steps 2 and 3 is found in TM p. 431.

Day 2

Getting Started

- Collect homework and put stars on Homework Chart. (See TM p. 26.)
- Administer spelling test with Day 1 spelling words in *Grand Tour I*, p. 29. Sentence for dictation: That is not my <u>jacket</u>. (See TM p. 100.)

Phonics Review
- Schedule 30 minutes per day for students to work on mastering Goals 1-11, listed on **Individual Skills Assessment Chart**, page 4. (See TM p. 86.)

Grand Tour I, p. 31

Spelling Words
Phonetic Grouping: ě

- Note that all the words have two syllables.
- As a class, read the 10 spelling words and discuss the meanings.
- Have students copy the 10 spelling words to take home, study, and write in sentences for homework.

Spelling Vocabulary Activities

Word Meanings
- Students will read the phrase and write a spelling word to fit each meaning.

Words ending in y
- Explain to students that when a two-syllable word ends in **y**, the **y** usually has a **long e** sound.
  Example: Billy

- Ask students to say other words that end in **y** with a **long e** sound.
  Example: curly, baby, tiny, etc.

- Students will write five spelling words that end in **y** with a **long e** sound.

p. 31

Day 2 *continued*

Word Association
- Talk about how words are associated with each other. They go together in some way.
  Example: (ball—bat) You hit a base**ball** with a **bat**.

- Give these examples of the first word and ask the class for suggestions for the second word: needle—(thread); shoes—(socks); peanut butter—(jelly); milk —(cookies); umbrella—(rain). Accept any reasonable answers.

- Ask students for other pairs of words that go together.

- Students will write a spelling word that goes with each word listed.

Grand Tour I, p. 32

Grammar

Using went and gone
- Remind students that **gone** must be used with a helping word such as **have**, **has**, or **had**.

- Think of several sentences and say them aloud to the class, leaving out **went** or **gone**. Ask students to supply the missing verb.
  Example: He _____ to the store. (went)
  He has _____ to the store. (gone)

- Ask students why the second sentence would need the word **gone**. (Because of helping word **has**.)

- Students will write **went** or **gone** in each sentence on page 32.

The Writing Connection

Writing Complete Sentences
- Students will write one sentence using **went** and one sentence using **gone**.

p. 32

Grammar Chalkboard Lesson
Using came and come

Objective
- Students will understand correct verb usage. (**came**–**come**)

Practice/Apply
- Write the sentences on the board. Students will copy each sentence and write **came** or **come** in the blank.

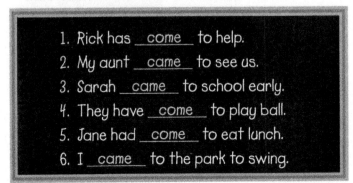

1. Rick has __come__ to help.
2. My aunt __came__ to see us.
3. Sarah __came__ to school early.
4. They have __come__ to play ball.
5. Jane had __come__ to eat lunch.
6. I __came__ to the park to swing.

(Continued on next page)

Day 2 continued

Handwriting Practice

Have students practice writing manuscript letter **Jj**. (*Grand Tour I*, p. 39)

Process Writing

Process Writing Lesson #1 for Steps 2 and 3 is found in TM p. 431.

Day 3

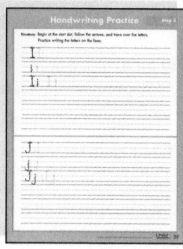

p. 39

Getting Started

- Collect homework and put stars on Homework Chart. (See TM p. 26.)
- Administer spelling test with Day 2 spelling words in *Grand Tour I*, p. 31. Sentence for dictation: I need one <u>penny</u>. (See TM p. 100.)

Phonics Review

- Schedule 30 minutes per day for students to work on mastering Goals 1-11, listed on **Individual Skills Assessment Chart**, page 4. (See TM p. 86.)

Grand Tour I, p. 33

Spelling Words
Phonetic Grouping: ĭ

- Note that words #1-5 are compound words.
- As a class, read the 10 spelling words and discuss the meanings.
- Have students copy the 10 spelling words to take home, study, and write in sentences for homework.

p. 33

Spelling Vocabulary Activities

Compound Words

- Tell students compound words are two words put together to make one word and the words are often related in some way.
  Example: suitcase – a **suit** can go in a **case**

- Give these examples of words and ask students to give the second word.

  rain - _____ (bow, coat, etc.)
  mail - _____ (box, man)
  rail - _____ (road)
  sun - _____ (shine, ray)

- Students will write five spelling words that are compound words.

Day 3 *continued*

Rhyming

- Remind students that rhyming words have the same ending vowel and consonant sounds.
- Students will write words that rhyme with **pimple** and **gripper**.

Word Meanings

- Students will write a spelling word to fit each meaning.

Cloze

- Students will fill in the blank with a spelling word.

Grand Tour I, p. 34

Sentences

Children's Literature Puzzle

- Locate a copy of *Little Red Riding Hood* in your library and read it aloud to the class.
- Talk about the sequence of the story. What happened first, next, etc?
- Students will draw a line to match the groups of words to make sentences on page 34.

The Writing Connection

Writing a New Ending for a Story

- Talk about the story, *Little Red Riding Hood*, and model how you can write a different ending for a story.
  Example: The hunter rushed into the house. The wolf said that if the hunter would let him go, he would never hurt any other person or animal.

p. 34

- Tell students to think of their own ending and write it on another sheet of paper.

Handwriting Practice

Have students practice writing manuscript letter **Kk**. (*Grand Tour I*, p. 40)

Process Writing

Process Writing Lesson #1 for Steps 2 and 3 is found in TM p. 431.

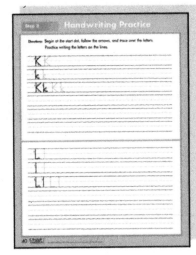
p. 40

Grand Tour I

Day 4

Getting Started

- Collect homework and put stars on Homework Chart. (See TM p. 26.)
- Administer spelling test with Day 3 spelling words in *Grand Tour I*, p. 33. Sentence for dictation: This test is <u>simple</u>. (See TM p. 100.)

Phonics Review

Schedule 30 minutes per day for students to work on mastering Goals 1-11, listed on **Individual Skills Assessment Chart**, page 4. (See TM p. 86.)

Grand Tour I, p. 35

Spelling Words
Phonetic Grouping: ŏ

- Note that words #1-8 have twin consonants.
- As a class, read the 10 spelling words and discuss the meanings.
- Have students copy the 10 spelling words to take home, study, and write in sentences for homework.

Spelling Vocabulary Activities

Syllables

- Tell students a **syllable** is a word part and each **syllable** must have a vowel.
- Think of and say several one, two, and three syllable words. Have students clap the number of syllables.
  Example: sum • mer • time = 3 claps
- Students will write the first eight spelling words and divide into **syllables**.

Cloze

- Students will fill in the blanks with a spelling word.

Rhyming
Students will write:
- Five spelling words that **rhyme** and end with **y**.
- Two spelling words that **rhyme** and end with **ow**.

Word Scramble

- Students will unscramble the letters to make spelling words.

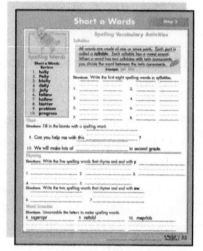

p. 35

Day 4 continued

Grand Tour I, p. 36

Grammar

Using <u>came</u> and <u>come</u>

- Explain to students that **have**, **has**, and **had** are called helping words.
- **Come** must be used with a helping word **have**, **has**, or **had** to make it mean in the past.
- He **came** home. This sentence does not have helping word **have**, **has**, or **had**.
- Think of and say several sentences aloud to the class, leaving out **came** or **come**. Ask which word would be correct.
  Example: Maria has _____ home. (come)
- Students will write **came** or **come** in each sentence on page 36.

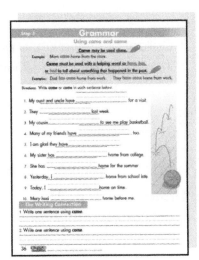

p. 36

The Writing Connection

Writing Complete Sentences

- Students will write one sentence using **came** and one sentence using **come**.

Grammar Chalkboard Lesson
Using <u>did</u> and <u>done</u>

Objective

- Students will understand correct verb usage. (**did**—**done**)

Practice/Apply

- Write the sentence on the board. Students will copy each sentence and write **did** or **done** in the blank.

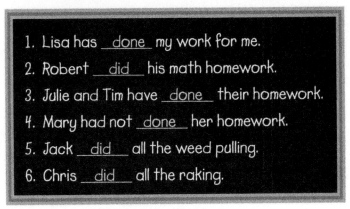

1. Lisa has _done_ my work for me.
2. Robert _did_ his math homework.
3. Julie and Tim have _done_ their homework.
4. Mary had not _done_ her homework.
5. Jack _did_ all the weed pulling.
6. Chris _did_ all the raking.

Handwriting Practice

Have students practice writing manuscript letter **Ll**. (Grand Tour I, p. 40)

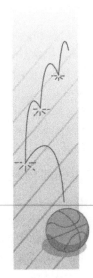

Process Writing

Process Writing Lesson #1 for Steps 2 and 3 is found in TM p. 431.

p. 40

(Continued on next page)

Day 5

Getting Started

- Collect homework and put stars on Homework Chart. (See TM p. 26.)
- Administer spelling test with Day 4 spelling words in *Grand Tour I*, p. 35. Sentence for dictation: Will you <u>follow</u> me? (See TM p. 100.)

Phonics Review

Schedule 30 minutes per day for students to work on mastering Goals 1-11, listed on **Individual Skills Assessment Chart**, page 4. (See TM p. 86.)

Grand Tour I, p. 37

Spelling Words
Phonetic Grouping: ŭ

- Note that each word has a **short u**.
- As a class, read the 10 spelling words and discuss the meanings.

Spelling Vocabulary Activities

Crossword Puzzle
- Explain to students how to work a crossword puzzle.
- Students will read the clues by the number, find a spelling word that goes with the clue, and write the word by the number. You may want to do this as a total group until children are familiar with working crossword puzzles.

Cloze
- Students will fill in the blank with the correct spelling word.

Rhyming
- Ask students why words #1-5 **rhyme**. (They all end with the same vowel and consonant sounds, **umble**.)
- Ask why **jungle** does not rhyme even though it ends in **le**. (It has the consonants **ng** instead of consonants **mb**.)
- Students will write five spelling words that **rhyme** and end with **le**.

Grand Tour I, p. 38

Grammar

Using <u>did</u> and <u>done</u>
- Explain to students **done** must be used with a helping word as **have, had, has, is, are, was,** or **were**.
  Example: We **have done** our homework.
- **Did** may be used alone.
  Example: She **did** her homework.
- Think of and say several sentences aloud to the class, leaving out **did** or **done**. Ask which word would be correct.
  Example: Todd has _____ a good job. (done)
- Students will write **did** or **done** in each sentence on page 38.

p. 37

p. 38

Day 5 continued

The Writing Connection

Writing Complete Sentences
* Students will write one sentence using **did** and one sentence using **done**.

Process Writing

Process Writing Lesson #1 for Steps 2 and 3 is found in TM p. 431.

Additional Related Activities for Step 3

Listening and Speaking

1. ***Around the World* with Rhyming Words**
   * Have a student stand beside another student seated at his/her desk.
   * The teacher will say a short vowel word.
     Example: rat
   * The first student to say a word to rhyme with **rat** moves on to the next desk and the game continues.

2. **Syllable Clapping**
   * Say these words aloud and ask the students to clap the number of syllables.

home (1)	sun (1)	suddenly (3)
animal (3)	football (2)	painted (2)
apart (2)	breakfast (2)	go (1)
beach (1)	yesterday (3)	seagull (2)
sentence (2)	rulebreaker (3)	along (2)
cost (1)	button (2)	number (2)
speak (1)	message (2)	

3. ***Around the World* with Compound Words**
   * Have a student stand beside another student seated at his/her desk.
   * The teacher will say a word that can have another word added to it to make a compound word.
     Example: sun_____
   * The student who says **shine, rays, beam, burn, set, rise, up, spot, bathe,** or any other word that is acceptable to make a compound word, moves on to the student in the next desk.
   * Continue the game in this same manner.
   * Suggestions for words the teacher will say:

moon ____	rain ____	sail ____	sea ____
base ____	air ____	snow ____	some ____
straw ____	any ____	school ___	tooth ____
book ____	cook ____	flash ____	basket ____
stair ____	door ____	out ____	over ____
pine ____	play ____	pop ____	fire ____
finger ____	eye ____	corn ____	hair ____
down ____	birth ____		

Overview for Step 4

Objectives

Phonics: To sing *Two Vowels Get Together Song* and play the phonics reinforcement games listed below, providing phonics/decoding review and/or new instruction for those who need it

Spelling: To spell two vowel words (ō¢, ē¢, ē¢, āí)

Grammar: To alphabetize words by the first letter
To recognize complete and incomplete sentences
To add **es** to a word to make a plural
To know the suffix **ing** makes a word mean "happening now"
To know compound words are two words put together to make one word

Comprehension: To read short stories and answer questions requiring higher level thinking skills

Writing: To write complete sentences
To write a story
To write a weather report
To use the Five Steps of Process Writing, focusing on narrowing the topic

Handwriting: To review the correct formation of manuscript letters **Mm** through **Pp**

Suggested Pacing
1 week

Materials
Grand Tour I, pp. 41-50
Two Vowels Get Together Song Chart

Homework
Daily homework is described in TM p. 99.

Spelling
Daily spelling is described in TM p. 99.

Phonics Games
Letter Cluster Sound-O (See TM p. 52)
Letter Cluster Pick-A-Sound (See TM p. 55)

Phonics Songs
Two Vowels Get Together Song,
    CD track 13 (See TM p. 60)

Additional Related Activities
Additional activities are found in TM p. 128.

Day 1

Phonics Review

Sing *Two Vowels Get Together Song,* CD track 13 (See TM p. 60.)

Grand Tour I, p. 41

Spelling Words
Phonetic Grouping: ōá

p. 41

- Note that each word has **oa**. Have students mark each word as indicated: **bōát**.
- As a class, read the 10 spelling words and discuss the meanings.
- Discuss the compound words: **boatramp, roadblock, soapsuds**
- Have students copy the 10 spelling words to take home, study, and write in sentences for homework.

Spelling Vocabulary Activities

Cloze
- Students will fill in the blank with the correct spelling word.

Alphabetical Order
- Tell students that arranging words in **alphabetical order** means to list them so the first letter of each word follows the order of the alphabet. Write the five words below on the chalkboard and, with students, practice arranging the words in **ABC order**. **man** (5) **big** (2) **leg** (4) **at** (1) **fast** (3)
- Discuss some uses for **ABC order**.
  Examples: telephone book, dictionary, encyclopedia
- Students will write each group of spelling words on page 41 in **ABC order**.

Grand Tour I, p. 42

Grammar

p. 42

Complete and Incomplete Sentences
- Tell students that:
  A **complete sentence** is a group of words that tells a **complete thought** and makes sense.
  A complete sentence tells **who** the sentence is about and **what** happened.

(**Continued on next page**)

Grand Tour I

Day 1 continued

- Practice this skill by saying the groups of words below. Have students clap if it is a **complete sentence**. Have them remain silent if it is **not a complete sentence**.

    1. Went to the store (Incomplete/Silent)

       This sentence is incomplete because it doesn't tell **who** went to the store.

    2. Carla went to the store. (Complete/Clap)

       This sentence is complete because it tells **who** did something and **what** they did.

    3. Fred is at the beach. (Complete/Clap)

    4. Mom baked a (Incomplete/Silent)

       Ask what is missing in this incomplete sentence.

    5. Bill and Sarah will (Incomplete/Silent)

       Ask what is missing in this incomplete sentence.

- Have students draw a line under the groups of words on page 42 that are not complete sentences.

The Writing Connection

Writing Complete Sentences

- Students will add words to each incomplete sentence on page 42 to make complete sentences.

Process Writing

Process Writing Lesson #2 for Steps 4 and 5 is found in TM pp. 433-434.

Day 2

Getting Started

- Collect homework and put stars on Homework Chart. (See TM p. 26.)
- Administer spelling test with Day 1 spelling words in *Grand Tour I*, p. 41. Sentence for dictation: We will eat the <u>toast</u>. (See TM p. 100.)

Grand Tour I, p. 43

Spelling Words
Phonetic Grouping: ēá

- Note that words #1-8 have an **ea**. Have students mark each word as indicated: **rēá̸ch**

- Introduce rulebreakers **come** and **some**. Tell students these words are in a cage because the **o** is stealing the **ŭ** sound.

- As a class, read the 10 spelling words and discuss the meanings.

- Have students copy the 10 spelling words to take home, study, and write in sentences for homework.

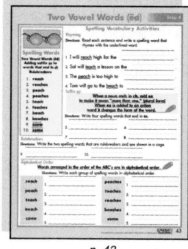

p. 43

Day 2 *continued*

Spelling Vocabulary Activities

Rhyming
* Students will write a spelling word that **rhymes** with the underlined word.

Suffix es
* Tell students that the word **plural** means **more than one**.
* Sometimes you add **s** to a word to make it **plural**. Sometimes you add **es**. If a word ends in **ch**, you add **es** to make a **plural**.
* Students will write four spelling words that end in the suffix **es**.

Rulebreakers
* Students will write the two words that are shown in cages because they do not follow the rules. In **come** and **some**, the **o** is stealing the sound of the letter **ŭ**.

Alphabetical Order
* Tell students that arranging words in **alphabetical order** means to list them so the first letter of each word follows the A to Z order of the alphabet. Write the five words below on the chalkboard and, with students, practice arranging the words in **ABC** order. **road** (5) **gas** (2) **place** (4) **doll** (1) **kick** (3)
* Discuss some uses for **ABC** order.
  Examples: dictionary, index, encyclopedia
* Students will write each group of spelling words on page 43 in **alphabetical order**.

Grand Tour I, p. 44

Story Comprehension

A Picnic at the Beach
As a group, have students:
* Underline the eight spelling words in the story.
* Read the story aloud.
* Read the questions and underline the correct answers.

The Writing Connection

Writing a Story
Have students:
* Write a story telling about what they like to do on a hot day.
* Include some sentences that tell **who, what, when, where, why,** or **how**.
* Illustrate the story.

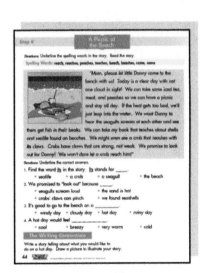

p. 44

(Continued on next page)

Grammar Chalkboard Lesson
Complete and Incomplete Sentences

Objective
- Students will know a complete sentence is a group of words that makes sense and tells a complete thought.

Practice/Apply
- Students will write each group of words and write **yes** if it is a sentence and **no** if it is not a sentence.

---

1. The little squirrels.   __no__

2. My best friend came to visit.   __yes__

3. All the children.   __no__

4. Mom and Dad went on a trip.   __yes__

5. The big oak tree.   __no__

6. The red sailboat.   __no__

Process Writing

Process Writing Lesson #2 for Steps 4 and 5 is found in TM p. 433.

Day 3

Getting Started

- Collect homework and put stars on Homework Chart. (See TM p. 26.)
- Administer spelling test with Day 2 spelling words in *Grand Tour I*, p. 43.
  Sentence for dictation: We went to the <u>beach</u>. (See TM p. 100.)

Grand Tour I, p. 45

Spelling Words
Phonetic Grouping: ēé

Spelling Words

- Note that each word has **ee**. Have students mark each word as indicated: fḗed
- Call attention to suffix **ing** on words #2, 4, 6, 8, and 10.
- As a class, read the 10 spelling words and discuss their meanings.
- Have students copy the 10 spelling words to take home, study, and write in sentences for homework.

p. 45

Spelling Vocabulary Activities

Rhyming

- Tell students that **rhyming** words have the same ending vowel and consonant sounds. Say the following pairs of words. Have students show thumbs up if the words **rhyme** and thumbs down if they do not **rhyme**.

  damp—ramp   clap—boy   fish—wish   trap—trip   boat—coat

- On page 45 students will write spelling words that rhyme with the underlined words **seed**, **beep**, and **peel**.

Suffix <u>ing</u>

- Tell students that when **ing** is added to the end of a word, the **ing** is called a **suffix**.
  Example: talk + ing = talk**ing**

- When you add the suffix **ing** to a word it makes the word mean "happening now."

- Ask students to think of other words to which you could add the suffix **ing**.

- On page 45 have students write the five spelling words that mean an "happening now."

Alphabetical Order

- On page 45 have students write the letter in the alphabet that comes before and after the letter in bold print.

  Example: **D** comes after__C__and before__E__ .

(Continued on next page)

Day 3 *continued*

Grand Tour I, p. 46

Grammar

Complete and Incomplete Sentences

- As a class, review what makes a **complete sentence**. (A complete sentence is a group of words that tells a complete thought and makes sense.)
- Say the groups of words below. Have students clap if the group of words is a **complete sentence** and remain silent if the group of words is **not a complete sentence**. If it is an **incomplete sentence**, have students tell you what part is missing.
    1. My best friend (Silent/Incomplete)
    2. We went to the store. (Clap/Complete)
    3. Rick is my best friend. (Clap/Complete)
    4. A long time ago we (Silent/Incomplete)
    5. Mr. Green is a (Silent/Incomplete)
- Have students draw a line under the groups of words on page 46 that are not complete sentences.

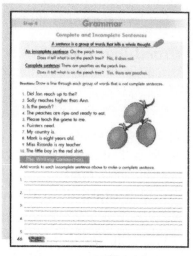

p. 46

The Writing Connection

Complete Sentences

- Students will add words to each **incomplete sentence** on page 46 to make complete sentences.
  Example: Did Jan reach up to the top of the shelf?

Process Writing

Process Writing Lesson #2 for Step 4 and 5 is found in TM p. 433.

Day 4

Getting Started

- Collect homework and put stars on Homework Chart. (See TM p. 26.)
- Administer spelling test with Day 3 spelling words in *Grand Tour I*, p. 45. Sentence for dictation: I can <u>feed</u> the cat. (See TM p. 100.)

Grand Tour I, p. 47

Spelling Words
Phonetic Grouping: āī

- Note that all words have **ai**. Have students mark each word as indicated: **māĭl**
- As a class, read the 10 spelling words and discuss the meanings.
- Have students copy the 10 spelling words to take home, study, and write in sentences for homework.

p. 47

Day 4 *continued*

Spelling Vocabulary Activities

Crossword Puzzle
- Students will read the clues, find a spelling word that goes with the clue, and write the word by the number in the crossword puzzle.

Compound Words
- Tell students **compound words** are two words put together to make one word and are often related in some way.
- Students will write five spelling words that **are** compound words and five spelling words that **are not** compound words.

Grand Tour I, p. 48

Story Comprehension

The Sailboat Kit
As a group, have students:
- Underline the eight spelling words in the story.
- Read the story aloud.
- Read the questions and underline the correct answers.

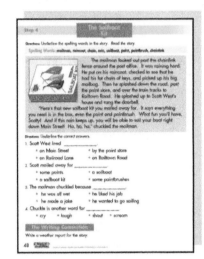

p. 48

The Writing Connection

Writing a Weather Report
- Share some newspaper weather reports with the class.
- Have students write a weather report that reflects the weather in the story *The Sailboat Kit*.

Grammar Chalkboard Lesson
Complete and Incomplete Sentences

Objective
- Students will know a complete sentence is a group of words that makes sense and tells a complete thought.

Practice/Apply
- Students will write each group of words and write **yes** if it is a sentence and **no** if it is not a sentence.

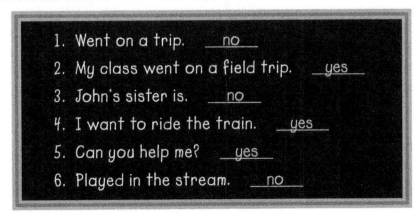

1. Went on a trip. _no_
2. My class went on a field trip. _yes_
3. John's sister is. _no_
4. I want to ride the train. _yes_
5. Can you help me? _yes_
6. Played in the stream. _no_

SAILBOAT KIT

(Continued on next page)

Grand Tour I

Process Writing

Process Writing Lesson #2 for Steps 4 and 5 is found in TM p. 433.

Day 5

Getting Started

- Collect homework and give stars on Homework Chart. (See TM p. 26.)
- Administer spelling test with Day 4 spelling words on page 47.
  Sentence for dictation: My <u>raincoat</u> is red. (See TM p. 100.)

Grand Tour I, pp. 49-50

Handwriting Practice

- Tell students the dot shows where to begin writing each letter **Mm**, **Nn**, **Oo**, and **Pp**. The arrow shows which direction to go with their pencils.
- Have students trace over the letters and practice writing the letters on the lines.

pp. 49-50

Additional Related Activities for Step 4

Listening and Speaking

1. *Tell Me What I'm Doing*

- Tell students you will pantomime an activity you enjoy doing.
  They are to tell what you are doing, using a complete sentence.
  Example: Teacher will pantomime swimming.
  Student will say, "Mrs. Jones is swimming."

- After the teacher pantomimes a few times, ask a student to volunteer pantomiming what he/she likes to do. Then, call on another student to tell about the activity using a complete sentence.

2. Rhyming

- Read aloud the nursery rhymes below. Ask students to listen and be prepared to repeat rhyming words from these nursery rhymes or other poems.

  Wee Willie Winkie runs through the **town**,
  Upstairs and downstairs in his **nightgown**.
  Rapping at the window, crying through the **lock**,
  Are the children all in bed, for now it's eight **o'clock**.

  Pat-a-cake, pat-a-cake, baker's **man**,
  Bake me a cake as fast as you **can**.
  Pat it, and roll it, and mark it with a **T**,
  And put it in the oven for Tommy and **me**.

  Georgie Porgie, pudding and **pie**,
  Kissed the girls and made them **cry**.
  When the boys came out to **play**,
  Georgie Porgie ran **away**.

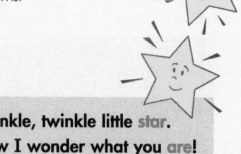

Twinkle, twinkle little star.
How I wonder what you are!
Up above the world so high,
Like a diamond in the sky.

Additional Related Activities *continued*

3. **Illustrating Compound Words**
   * Write these compound words on the chalkboard.
   * Have students choose a compound word and draw three pictures. Draw one picture for each of the two words in the compound word and one for the compound word.
     Example: rain + coat = raincoat
   * Allow students to choose several to illustrate.
   * You may want to collect all the drawings and make a class book.

campfire	dragonfly	jellyfish
basketball	earring	lipstick
blackbird	eyeball	starship
clothesline	football	pancake
cowboy	sunlight	pigtail
crosswalk	goldfish	rattlesnake
cupcake	headlight	starfish

Grand Tour I

Overview for Step 5

Objectives

Phonics: To sing *Silent e̸ Song* and play the phonics reinforcement games listed below, providing phonics/decoding review and/or new instruction for those who need it

Spelling: To spell **silent e** words; **c = s** words

Grammar: To understand the suffixes **ful** and **less**
To understand subjects and predicates

Comprehension: To read short stories and answer questions requiring higher level thinking skills

Writing: To write a new ending for a story
To use the Five Steps of Process Writing, focusing on narrowing the topic

Handwriting: To review the correct formation of manuscript letters **Qq** to **Tt**

Suggested Pacing
1 Week

Materials
Grand Tour I, pp. 51-60
Silent e̸ Song and Dance Chart

Homework
Daily homework is described in TM p. 99.

Spelling
Daily spelling is described in TM p. 99.

Phonics Games
Letter Cluster Sound-O (See TM p. 52.)
Letter Cluster Pick-A-Sound (See TM p. 55.)

Phonics Song
Silent e̸ Song, CD track 15 (See TM p. 61.)

Additional Related Activities
Additional activities are found in TM p. 139.

Day 1

Phonics Review

Silent ¢ Song, CD track 15. (See TM p. 61.)

Grand Tour I, p. 51

Spelling Words
Phonetic Grouping: ¢

* Note that words #1-8 all have **silent e**. Tell students when a word ends in **silent e**, it usually makes the first vowel say its name. Have students mark words as indicated: **nāmé**

* Words #3, 5, and 8 are compound words.

* Call attention to rulebreakers **you** and **your**.

* As a class, read the 10 spelling words and discuss the meanings.

* Have students copy the 10 spelling words to take home, study, and write in sentences for homework.

p. 51

Spelling Vocabulary Activities

Rhyming
* Students will write a spelling word that answers the question and rhymes with the underlined word.

Compound Words
* Tell students **compound words** are two words put together to make one word and are often related in some way.

   Example: A pinecone is a **cone** that grows on a **pine** tree.

* Give these examples of words and have students give the second word.

Example:	moon	(beam, light)
	cook	(book)
	book	(case, mark, bag)
	school	(house, room, bag)

* Students will write three spelling words that are compound words.

Silent e
* Tell students when a word ends in **silent e**, it usually makes the first vowel say its name. (long vowel sound)

   Example: rāké

* On page 51 students will write eight spelling words that have **silent e**.

Cloze
* Students will fill in the missing spelling words.

(Continued on next page)

Grand Tour I

Day 1 continued

Grand Tour I, p. 52

Sentences

Children's Literature Puzzle

- Locate a copy of *The Three Little Pigs* in your library and read it aloud to the class.
- Talk about the sequence of the story. What happened first, next, etc.?
- Students will draw lines to match the groups of words to make sentences on page 52.

p. 52

The Writing Connection

Writing a New Ending

- Tell students this story ends with the wolf coming down the chimney into a kettle of water. However, a story has many possibilities for endings.

  Example: The pigs opened the door and invited the wolf to come in. The wolf was surprised at how friendly the pigs were and decided to be a friend. The wolf and three pigs became lifelong friends.

- Students will write a different ending for *The Three Little Pigs*.

Process Writing

Process Writing Lesson #2 for Steps 4 and 5 is found in TM p. 433.

Getting Started

- Collect homework and put stars on Homework Chart. (See TM p. 26.)
- Administer spelling test with Day 1 spelling words in *Grand Tour I*, p. 51. Sentence for dictation: My <u>name</u> is _____. (See TM p. 100.)

Grand Tour I, p. 53

Spelling Words
Phonetic Grouping: e̸

- Note that words #1-9 all have **silent e**. Tell students when a word ends in **silent e**, it usually makes the first vowel say its name. Have students mark the words as indicated: **cāre̸**
- Note that words #1, 4, and 7 are root words. The suffixes **ful** and **less** have been added to the root words to make new words.
- Call attention to rulebreaker **any**. It is a rulebreaker because it cannot be sounded out.
- As a class, read the 10 spelling words and discuss the meanings.
- Have students copy the 10 spelling words to take home, study, and write in sentences for homework.

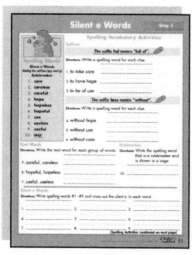

p. 53

Day 2 continued

Spelling Vocabulary Activities

Suffixes

- Explain to students that **ful** is a **suffix** or ending that can be added to the end of a root word. Write **careful**, **hopeful**, and **useful** on the board. Draw a line under **ful** in each word and show how the root words are still there even if you take off **ful**. Explain that the suffix **ful** means "full of." If you are careful, you are **full of care**. If you are hopeful, you are **full of hope**, etc. Ask students to think of other words you can add **ful** to.
  Examples: help, play, forget

- Tell students that **less** is also a **suffix** or ending that can be added to a root word. Write **careless** on the board. **Less** means "without," so care**less** means **without care**. Ask students to tell you other words to which you can add **less**.
  Examples: help, cheer, hope

- Students will write a spelling word for clues #1-6 on page 53.

Root Words

- Tell students that **root words** are words without any added prefixes or suffixes. The **root word** of **helpless** is **help**.

- Students will write the root word for each group of words on page 53.

Rule Breaker

- **Rule breakers** are words that do not follow phonetic rules and are shown in cages.
  Example: Any sounds like it could be spelled **eny**.

- Students will write the spelling word that is a **rulebreaker**.

Silent e Words

- Tell students when a word ends in **silent e**, it usually makes the first vowel say its name. (long vowel sound)
  Example: rāk̶e̶

- Students will write spelling words #1-9 and cross out the **silent e** in each word.

Cloze

- Students will fill in the missing spelling word.

Grand Tour I, p. 54

Story Comprehension

How to be a Star

- Have students underline the six spelling words in the poem.
- Teacher will read poem aloud to model the rhythm.
- Choral read the poem with the group two or three times.
- Ask students to find the five spelling words with suffixes and tell you the meaning of each word.
  Example: careless (without care)

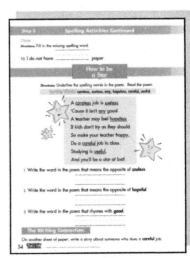

(Continued on next page)

p. 54

Day 2 *continued*

The Writing Connection

Writing a Story

● Have students write a four or five sentence story. Ask them to focus on **why** and **how** someone did a **careful** job.

Grammar Chalkboard Lesson
Subject and Predicate

Objective

● Students will understand a sentence has two parts, **subject** and **predicate**. The subject tells **who** or **what** the sentence is about.

Practice/Apply

● Students will write each sentence and draw a line under the **subject**.

> 1. The big dog barked at the car.
> 2. Samuel walked home.
> 3. My baby sister crawls on the floor.
> 4. Dorie rode her bicycle fast.
> 5. The red bird flew away.
> 6. Mrs. Brown helped me today.

Process Writing

Process Writing Lesson #2 for Steps 4 and 5 is found in TM p. 433.

Step 5

Day 3

Getting Started

- Collect homework and put stars on Homework Chart. (See TM p. 26.)
- Administer spelling test with Day 2 spelling words in *Grand Tour I*, p. 53. Sentence for dictation: I am <u>careful</u> at home. (See TM p. 100.)

Grand Tour I, p. 55

Spelling Words
Phonetic Grouping: ¢

p. 55

- Note that words #1-9 all have **silent e**. Tell students when a word ends in **silent e**, it usually makes the first vowel say its name. Have students mark words as indicated: **shīnȩ**
- Words #2, 5, 7, and 9 are compound words.
- Call attention to rulebreaker **from**.
- As a class, read the 10 spelling words and discuss the meanings.
- Have students copy the 10 spelling words to take home, study, and write in sentences for homework.

Spelling Vocabulary Activities

Cloze

- Ask students which words in the spelling list are compound words and how the two words in each compound word are related.
- Students will fill in the blanks with spelling words.

Silent e

- Students will write spelling words #1-9 and cross out the **silent e**.
  Example: shīnȩ

Rulebreakers

- Tell students a rulebreaker cannot be sounded out.
  Example: from sounds like it should be spelled **frum**.
- Students will write the spelling word that is a rulebreaker.

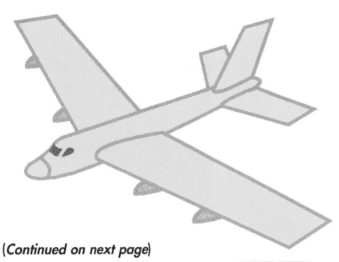

(Continued on next page)

Day 3 continued

Grand Tour I, p. 56

Grammar

Sentence Parts

- Tell students that a sentence must have a **subject** and a **predicate**. The subject is the **who** part of the sentence. It tells **who** or **what** the sentence is about.

  Example: Mary went to the store. The **subject** is Mary, because Mary is **who** the sentence is about.

- Think of several simple sentences to say to the class. Ask students to identify each **subject**. Include sentences that have subjects other than people.

  Example: The **snow** is beautiful.

- Students will draw a line under the subject in each sentence.

p. 56

Process Writing

Process Writing Lesson #2 for Steps 4 and 5 is found in TM p. 433.

Day 4

Getting Started

- Collect homework and put stars on Homework Chart. (See TM p. 26.)
- Administer spelling test with Day 3 spelling words in *Grand Tour I*, p. 55. Sentence for dictation: The <u>sunshine</u> feels good. (See TM p. 100.)

Grand Tour I, p. 57

Spelling Words
Phonetic Grouping: c = s

- Discuss the **soft c** sound. If **c** is followed with an **e, i,** or **y (ce, ci, cy)** the **c** sounds like **s**.
- Have students mark the words as indicated: spa(ce)
- Call attention to rulebreaker **many**.
- As a class, read the 10 spelling words and discuss the meanings.
- Have students copy the 10 spelling words to take home, study, and write in sentences for homework.

p. 57

Spelling Vocabulary Activities

Crossword Puzzle

- Students will read the clues by the number, find a spelling word that goes with the clue, and write the word by the number in the crossword puzzle. You may want to do this as a total group until children are familiar with working crossword puzzles.

Compound Words

- Remind students that **compound words** are two words put together to make a word.

- Students will write four spelling words that are compound words and six spelling words that are not compound words.

Grand Tour I, p. 58

Story Comprehension

Bruce and Tracy

- Have students underline the 10 spelling words in the story.

- Read the story aloud with the class.

- Discuss the questions and make sure each student understands how to arrive at the answers.

- Students will underline the correct answers.

p. 58

The Writing Connection

Writing a Story

- Brainstorm with students about favorite games they like to play and list them on the board.

- Have students write a story about their favorite game. Tell them to be sure to include **why** it is their favorite.

- Next, students will draw pictures to illustrate their stories.

- Come together in a circle to share stories and pictures. It's very important to share writings! Children love it, and it's a great learning tool.

(Continued on next page)

Day 4 continued

Grammar Chalkboard Lesson
Subject and Predicate

Objective
- Students will understand a sentence has two parts, **subject** and **predicate**. The subject tells **who** or **what** the sentence is about.

Practice/Apply
- Students will write the sentences, filling in a word of their choice for the missing subject.

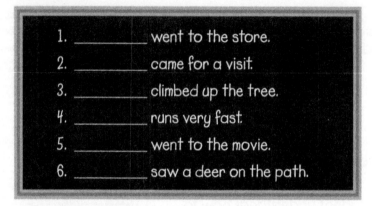

1. _____ went to the store.
2. _____ came for a visit.
3. _____ climbed up the tree.
4. _____ runs very fast.
5. _____ went to the movie.
6. _____ saw a deer on the path.

Process Writing

Process Writing Lesson #2 for Steps 4 and 5 is found in TM p. 433.

Day 5

Getting Started

- Collect homework and put stars on Homework Chart. (See TM p. 26.)
- Administer spelling test with Day 4 spelling words in *Grand Tour I*, p. 57. Sentence for dictation: It is fun to run a <u>race</u>. (See TM p. 100.)

Grand Tour I, pp. 59-60

Handwriting Practice

Students will practice writing manuscript letters **Qq** to **Tt**. Encourage them to begin at the start dot and follow the arrows.

Process Writing

Process Writing Lesson #2 for Steps 4 and 5 is found in TM p. 433.

p. 59

p. 60

Additional Related Activities for Step 5

Listening and Speaking

1. Rhyming Word Families

* Write the following words on the board: **hill**, **take**, **pine**, **sake**, and **mail**.
* Ask students to come to the board and add words that rhyme by changing the first consonant only.

  Example: hill
  pill
  fill
  will
  sill

2. *Hot Potato* with Suffixes <u>ing</u>, <u>ful</u>, and <u>less</u>

* Sit in a circle. Toss a beanbag to a student and say:
  1. Make help mean "without help." (helpless)
  2. Make run mean "happening now." (running)
  3. Make care mean "full of care." (careful)
  4. Make hope mean "full of hope." (hopeful)
  5. Make play mean "happening now" (playing)
  6. Make use mean "without use." (useless)
  7. Make care mean "without care." (careless)
  8. Make sweep mean "happening now." (sweeping)
  9. Make beauty mean "full of beauty." (beautiful)
  10. Make help mean "full of help." (helpful)
* Continue in this manner with other words.

3. *Hang an Apple* with Suffixes

* Draw three large trees, one each on three different sheets of chart paper.
* Label the trees "Words with **less**," "Words with **ful**," and "Words with **ing**."
* Write words with the suffixes **less**, **ful**, and **ing** on cut-out apples.
* Give each child a cut-out apple and ask him/her to come hang his/her apple on the appropriate tree.

4. *Alphabet Rummy*

* Write the 26 letters of the alphabet on index cards, one letter to a card.
* With a group of three children, deal five cards to each child.
* Place the remaining cards face down in a pile in the center of the table. Each child in turn draws and discards one card at a time.
* The object of the game is to get five letters in alphabetical sequence. If no one has five letters in ABC order at the end of the deck, turn the discard pile over and continue drawing until there is a winner.

Grand Tour I

Overview for Step 6

Objectives

Spelling: To spell **ay** words; **y = i** words; **ge**, **gi**, and **gy** words; and **y = e** words

Grammar: To understand subjects, predicates, nouns, and syllables

Comprehension: To read short stories and answer questions requiring higher level thinking skills

Writing: To write a title for a story
To use the Five Steps of Process Writing, focusing on sequencing

Handwriting: To review the correct formation of manuscript letters **Uu** to **Xx**

Suggested Pacing
1 week

Materials
Grand Tour I, pp. 61-70

Homework
Daily homework is described in TM p. 99.

Spelling
Daily spelling is described in TM p. 99.

Phonics Games
Letter Cluster Sound-O (See TM p. 52.)
Letter Cluster Pick-A-Sound (See TM p. 55.)

Phonics Songs (See TM pp. 40-65.)
Continue to sing selected songs as needed for reinforcement.

Additional Related Activities
Additional activities are found in TM p. 147.

Sing,Spell
Read&Write

Step 6

Day 1

Grand Tour I, p. 61

Spelling Words
Phonetic Grouping: ay

- Note that words #1-8 have **ay**. In words with **ay**, **y** is silent and **a** is long. Have students mark each word as indicated: **pay**

- Call attention to rulebreakers **one** and **once**.

- As a class, read the 10 spelling words and discuss the meanings.

- Have students copy the 10 spelling words to take home, study, and write in sentences for homework.

Spelling Vocabulary Activities

Rhyming
- Students will write four spelling words that rhyme with **say**.

Word Meanings
- Students will read the clues and write a spelling word for each clue.

Cloze
- Students will fill in each blank with a spelling word.

p. 61

The Writing Connection

Writing a Title for a Story
- Ask students to think of what the story on page 61 is **mostly** about. Discuss their ideas.

- Tell students a **title** is often like the **main idea** of the story.

- Brainstorm some possible titles for the story.
  Example: *A Fun Day*

- Students will write a title for the story on page 61.

Grand Tour I, p. 62

Grammar

Sentence Parts
- Tell students a complete sentence must have a **subject** and a **predicate**. The subject tells **who** or **what** the sentence is about.

  Example: <u>The boxes</u> are full of paper. The subject is <u>The boxes</u>, because that is **what** you are talking about.

- Think of simple sentences and say them to the class. Ask students to identify the subjects.
  Examples: <u>The boy</u> ran fast. <u>My school</u> is big. <u>The bicycle</u> has a flat tire.

- Continue in this manner, including sentences that have persons, places, or things for the subject.

- Students will draw a line under the subject in each sentence on page 62.

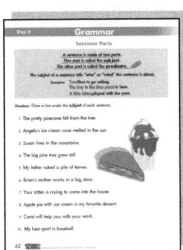

p. 62

(Continued on next page)

Grand Tour I

Day 1 continued

Process Writing

Process Writing Lesson #3 for Steps 6 and 7 is found in TM p. 435.

Day 2

Getting Started

- Collect homework and put stars on Homework Chart. (See TM p. 26.)
- Administer spelling test with Day 1 spelling words in *Grand Tour I*, p. 61. Sentence for dictation: Today is <u>payday</u>. (See TM p. 100.)

Grand Tour I, p. 63

Spelling Words
Phonetic Grouping: y = ī

- Note that all words have **y** that sounds like **long i**. If the **y** follows a consonant in a one-syllable word, the **y** sounds like **long i**.
- As a class, read the 10 spelling words and discuss the meanings.
- Have students copy the 10 spelling words to take home, study, and write in sentences for homework.

Spelling Vocabulary Activities

Cloze
- Students will fill in the blanks with spelling words.

Word Scramble
- Students will unscramble the letters to make a spelling word.

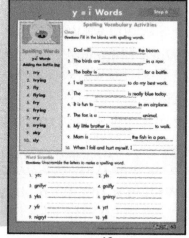

p. 63

Grand Tour I, p. 64

Story Comprehension

The Family Picnic
Students will:

- Draw a line under the eight spelling words in the story.
- Read the story silently.

The Writing Connection

Drawing a Picture
- Tell students the story does not tell exactly what happened to the cake, but they are to use the information they have and draw a conclusion about what happened.

  Example: We know the fly landed on top of the cake. We know the little brother went "smack," got the fly, and Mom started to cry. We can draw a conclusion that the cake was smashed.

- Have students draw a picture showing what they think happened to the cake.

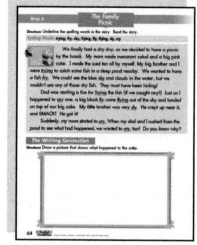

p. 64

Day 2 *continued*

Grammar Chalkboard Lesson
Nouns in the Subject

Practice/Apply

Students will:

- Know a noun is a **person**, **place**, or **thing**.
- Identify nouns in the **subject** of a **sentence**.

Objective

- Write the sentences on the board and draw a line under the **subject**.
- Students will copy the sentences and circle the **noun** in each **subject**.

  Example: The little (kitten) drank milk.

1. The brown (dog) ran fast.
2. A little (kitten) ran away.
3. The big (bus) goes fast.
4. The green (grass) is pretty.
5. The red (fox) is hiding.
6. The nice (lady) will help me.

Process Writing

Process Writing Lesson #3 for Steps 6 and 7 is found in TM p. 435.

(Continued on next page)

Day 3

Getting Started

- Collect homework and put stars on Homework Chart. (See TM p. 26.)
- Administer spelling test with Day 2 spelling words in *Grand Tour I*, p. 63. Sentence for dictation: I see a bird <u>flying</u>. (See TM p. 100.)

Grand Tour I, p. 65

Spelling Words
Phonetic Grouping: ge, gi, gy

- Discuss the **soft g** sound. If **g** is followed by **e**, **i**, or **y** (**ge**, **gi**, or **gy**), the **g** may sound like a **j**.
- Note that words #1-8 all have a **soft g**. Have students mark each word as indicated: (germ)
- Call attention to rulebreakers **was** and **who**.
- As a class, read the 10 spelling words and discuss the meanings.
- Have students copy the 10 spelling words to take home, study, and write in sentences for homework.

Spelling Vocabulary Activities

ABC Order

- Tell students to look at the beginning letters of the four words in the shaded box. Which letter comes first in the alphabet? (**e** in **edge**) The first word in **ABC order** should be **edge**. The **g** in **giant** comes next, etc.
- Students will write words in **ABC order**.

Word Association

- Tell students to read the words listed and find a spelling word that can be associated with each word.
  Example: Basketball and gym can be associated because **basketball** is played in a **gym**.
- Students will write the spelling word that goes with each word listed.

Word Meanings

- Tell students the words **was** and **who** cannot be spelled correctly by listening to the way they sound. Because of this, they are called rulebreakers. Some of the letters make a different sound.
- Students will write a spelling word that fits each meaning.

p. 65

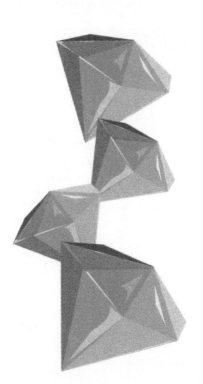

Grand Tour I, p. 66

Grammar

Sentence Parts

- Tell students a complete sentence must have a **subject** and a **predicate**. The subject is the **who** part of the sentence. It tells **who** or **what** the sentence is about.
- Think of simple sentences and say them to the class. Ask students to identify the **subjects**.
- Students will draw a line under the **subject** of each sentence on page 66.

p. 66

Process Writing

Process Writing Lesson #3 for Step 6 and 7 is found in TM p. 435.

Day 4

Getting Started

- Collect homework and put stars on Homework Chart. (See TM p. 26.)
- Administer spelling test with Day 3 spelling words in *Grand Tour I*, p. 65. Sentence for dictation: The <u>giant</u> is big. (See TM p.100.)

Grand Tour I, p. 67

Spelling Words
Phonetic Grouping: y = ē

- Usually, if a two-syllable word ends in **y**, the **y** will sound like a **long e**.
- Note that all words end in **y** that sounds like **long e**. Have students mark words as indicated: **pretty**, **lady**
- As a class, read the 10 spelling words and discuss the meanings.
- Have students copy the 10 spelling words to take home, study, and write in sentences for homework.

p. 67

Spelling Vocabulary Activities

Word Search

- Tell students all the spelling words can be found in the word search. The words go across or down.
- Students will draw a ring around each word as they find it.

(Continued on next page)

Day 4 *continued*

Syllables

- Explain to students that a **syllable** is a word part and each **syllable** must have a vowel sound.

- Say each spelling word and have students clap when they hear each **syllable**.

- Write the following **multisyllable nonsense words** on the board and have students read the nonsense words. This allows students to practice applying their phonics skills. Remind students these are not real words.

boffy	junny	bikky	leddy
zummy	rilly	suggy	wappy

- Have students write each spelling word and divide it into **syllables** between the twin consonants.

Grand Tour I, p. 68

Story Comprehension

Fussy Tommy Penny

Students will:

- Underline the spelling words in the story.

- Read the story silently and underline the correct answer.

p. 68

The Writing Connection

Writing a Story

- Tell students they will write a story about a time they spilled something and made a mess.

- Brainstorm with students about things they should include in their story.

- Focus on **what** was spilled, **where** it was spilled, and **how** the spill made a mess.

Grammar Chalkboard Lesson
Nouns in the Subject

Objective

Students will:

- Know a noun is a **person**, **place**, or **thing**.

- Identify **nouns** in the **subject** of a **sentence**.

Practice/Apply

- Write the sentences on the board and draw a line under the **subject**.

- Students will copy the sentences and circle the **noun** in each **subject**.
  Example: The young man ran the race.

1. Many ants are on the plant.
2. The TV is too loud.
3. The big school is crowded.
4. Lots of kites are in the air.
5. The jellybeans are sweet.
6. The desk is very old.

Day 4 continued

Process Writing

Process Writing Lesson #3 for Steps 6 and 7 is found in TM p. 435.

Day 5

Getting Started

- Collect homework and put stars on Homework Chart. (See TM p. 26.)
- Administer spelling test with Day 4 spelling words in *Grand Tour I,* p. 67. Sentence for dictation: Sally is a <u>happy</u> girl. (See TM p. 100.)

Grand Tour I, pp. 69-70

Handwriting Practice

- Students will practice writing manuscript letters **Uu** to **Xx**.
- Encourage them to begin at the start dot and follow the arrows.

Process Writing

Process Writing Lesson #3 for Steps 6 and 7 is found in TM p. 435.

p. 69-70

Additional Related Activities for Step 6

Listening and Speaking

1. *Around the World* with ABC Order

- Have a student stand beside another student seated at his/her desk.
- The teacher will say a letter of the alphabet.
  Example: g
- The student who says **f** first (the letter that comes in front of **g**) moves on to the next desk, and the game continues.

2. *Riddle Time*

- Have children write a riddle for one of the spelling words in Step 6.
- Next, have them draw the answer on a separate sheet of paper and write the spelling word under the picture.
- Teacher will collect and display the pictures.
- Have one child ask a riddle.
  Example: This is the day I get paid. What word am I?
- Have another student find the picture that answers the riddle.
  (payday)

> This is the day I get paid. What word am I?

payday

Grand Tour I

Overview for Step 7

Objectives

Spelling: To spell **y = e** words; **ed** says "**t**" words; **ed** says "**d**" words

Grammar: To learn how to look at the second letter to alphabetize words
To understand subjects and predicates
To know **ed** added to a root word is a suffix

Comprehension: To read short stories and answer questions requiring higher level thinking skills

Writing: To write a story about a rainy day
To use the Five Steps of Process Writing, focusing on sequencing

Proofreading: To find spelling and capital letter errors

Reference Skills: To understand guide words and entry words

Handwriting: To review the correct formation of manuscript letters **Yy** and **Zz**

Suggested Pacing
1 Week

Materials
Grand Tour I, pp. 71-80

Homework
Daily homework is described in TM p. 99.

Spelling
Daily spelling is described in TM p. 99.

Phonics Games (See TM pp. 40-65.)
Continue to play selected games as needed for reinforcement.

Phonics Songs (See TM pp. 40-65.)
Continue to sing selected songs as needed for reinforcement.

Additional Related Activities
Additional activities are found in TM p. 155.

Grand Tour I, p. 71

Spelling Words
Phonetic Grouping: y = ē

- Note that all words end in a **y** that sounds like **long e**. Tell students when a two-syllable word ends in **y**, the **y** usually has a **long e** sound. Have students mark words as indicated: **windy**

- As a class, read the 10 spelling words and discuss the meanings.

- Have students copy the 10 spelling words to take home, study, and write in sentences for homework.

Spelling Vocabulary Activities

Word Scramble
- Students will unscramble letters to make spelling words.

p. 71

Alphabetical Order
- Tell students if two words in a group begin with the same letter they must look at the second letter to alphabetize.

- Write this group of words on the board:

flag	**apple**
ball	**bus**

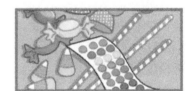

- Explain that **a** comes first in the alphabet so **apple** is #1. However, **ball** and **bus** both begin with a **b** so they must look at the second letter in each word which is **a** in **ball** and **u** in **bus**. Which letter comes first in the alphabet? Letter **a** comes first so **ball** is #2, **bus** is #3, and **flag** is #4.

- Students will write each group of words on page 71 in ABC order.

Grand Tour I, p. 72

Grammar

Sentence Parts

- Tell students a complete sentence must have a **subject** and a **predicate**. Remind students they have learned that the **subject** of a sentence is **who** or **what** you are talking about. The **predicate** tells what the subject is doing. The **predicate** is the action part of the sentence.

- Think of simple sentences and say them to the class. Ask students to tell what the **predicate** is.

  Example: Martin ran home. Who are we talking about? (Martin) What did Martin do? (ran home) **Ran home** is the **predicate** of the sentence.

- Students will draw a line under the **predicate** in each sentence.

Process Writing

Process Writing Lesson #3 for Steps 6 and 7 is found in TM p. 435.

p. 72

Grand Tour I

Getting Started

- Collect homework and put stars on Homework Chart. (See TM p. 26.)
- Administer spelling test with Day 1 spelling words in *Grand Tour I*, p. 71. Sentence for dictation: The <u>candy</u> is good. (See TM p. 100.)

Grand Tour I, p. 73

Spelling Words
Phonetic Grouping: ed = t

- Note that all the words end in **ed** but sound like a **t**.
- As a class, read the 10 spelling words and discuss the meanings.
- Tell students when **ed** is added to the end of a word, the **ed** is a suffix and makes the word mean "it happened in the past."
- Have students copy the 10 spelling words to take home, study, and write in sentences for homework.

p. 73

Spelling Vocabulary Activities

Root Words
- Tell students a **root word** is the spelling word without the **ed** ending.
- Students will underline the **root word** in each spelling word.
- Next, students will fill in the blanks with spelling words.

Suffix <u>ed</u>
- Students will write each spelling word and the root word.

Example: locked—lock

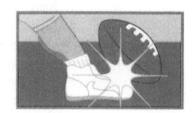

Grand Tour I, p. 74

Story Comprehension

Camping at Wildwood
Students will:
- Draw a line under the nine spelling words in the story.
- Read the story silently and underline the correct answer to each question.

The Writing Connection

Building Pictures in Your Mind (Visualizing)
Students will:
- Visualize in their minds the scenes from the story *Camping at Wildwood*.
- Draw a picture of Dave, Patty, and Little Joe hiking up the trail.
- Write a sentence that tells about the picture.

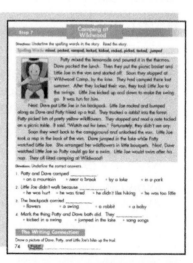

p. 74

Day 2 *continued*

Grammar Chalkboard Lesson
Subjects and Predicates

Objective
- Students will understand a sentence has two parts, **subject** and **predicate**, and the **predicate** tells what is happening in the sentence.

Practice/Apply
- Students will write each sentence and draw a line under the **predicate**.

> Mr. Smith <u>plays golf each week.</u>   My little kitten <u>runs fast.</u>
>
> Tom and Ann <u>swam in the lake.</u>   Tanya <u>sang a funny song.</u>
>
> All the sheep <u>jumped the fence.</u>   The geese <u>flew away.</u>

Process Writing

Process Writing Lesson #3 for Steps 6 and 7 is found in TM p. 435.

Day 3

Getting Started

- Collect homework and put stars on Homework Chart. (See TM p. 26.)
- Administer spelling test with Day 2 spelling words in *Grand Tour I*, p. 73. Sentence for dictation: Mom and Dad <u>camped</u> in the woods. (See TM p. 100.)

Grand Tour I, p. 75

Spelling Words
Phonetic Grouping: ed = t

- Note that each word ends in **ed** and sounds like **t**.
- As a class, read the 10 spelling words and discuss the meanings.
- Have students copy the 10 spelling words to take home, study, and write in sentences for homework.

Spelling Vocabulary Activities

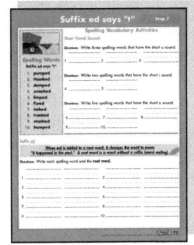

p. 75

Short Vowel Sounds
- Students will write three spelling words with a **short u**, two words with **short i**, and five words with **short a**.

(Continued on next page)

Day 3 *continued*

Suffix <u>ed</u>
- Tell students a root word is the word without the **ed** ending.
- Students will write each spelling word and the root word.
  Example: pumped—pump

Grand Tour I, p. 76

Grammar

Sentence Parts
- Review **subjects** and **predicates** with students. The subject tells **who** or **what** the sentence is about and the **predicate** tells **what is happening** in the sentence.
- Students will draw a line under the **predicate** in each sentence.

p. 76

Process Writing

Process Writing Lesson #3 for Steps 6 and 7 is found in TM p. 435.

Getting Started
- Collect homework and put stars on Homework Chart. (See TM p. 26.)
- Administer spelling test with Day 3 spelling words in *Grand Tour I,* p. 75. Sentence for dictation: I <u>pumped</u> the gas for the car. (See TM p. 100.)

Grand Tour I, p. 77

Spelling Words
Phonetic Grouping: ed = d

- Note that all words end in **ed** and sound like **d**.
- As a class, read the 10 spelling words and discuss the meanings.
- Have students copy the 10 spelling words to take home, study, and write in sentences for homework.

Spelling Vocabulary Activities

Crossword Puzzle
- Students will read the clues by the number, find a spelling word that goes with the clue, and write the word by the number in the crossword puzzle. You may want to do this as a total group until children are familiar with working crossword puzzles.

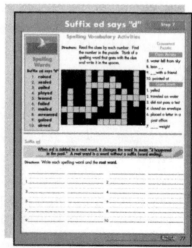

p. 77

Day 4 *continued*

Suffix ed

- Tell students **ed** added to the end of a root word makes it mean **it happened in the past.**
- Students will write each spelling word and the root word.

Grand Tour I, p. 78

Story Comprehension

A Rainy Day
Students will:

- Underline the seven spelling words in the story.
- Read the story silently and underline the correct answers.

p. 78

The Writing Connection

Writing a Story

- Brainstorm with students about things they have done on rainy days.
- Tell students they will write a story about something they did on a rainy day.
- Suggest they include in their story:
    - **What** they did on a rainy day.
    - **How** they did it.
    - **Where** they did it.
    - **Why** they chose to do that particular thing.
- Next, students will draw a picture to illustrate their story.

Grammar Chalkboard Lesson
Subjects and Predicates

Objective
- Students will understand a sentence has two parts, **subject** and **predicate.** The **predicate** tells what is happening in the sentence.

Practice/Apply
- Students will write each sentence and draw a line under the **predicate**.

> 1. Jerome and Kate <u>unlocked the door.</u>
> 2. Lucy <u>smiled at me.</u>
> 3. We <u>ate our lunch outside.</u>
> 4. The jogger <u>jogs on the path.</u>
> 5. The little birds <u>chirped loudly.</u>
> 6. Eric <u>hit the ball hard.</u>

Process Writing

Process Writing Lesson #3 for Steps 6 and 7 is found in TM p. 435.

Grand Tour I

Getting Started

- Collect homework and put stars on Homework Chart. (See TM p. 26.)
- Administer spelling test with Day 4 spelling words in *Grand Tour I*, p. 77. Sentence for dictation: It <u>rained</u> at my home. (See TM p. 100.)

Grand Tour I, p. 79

Handwriting Practice

- Students will practice writing manuscript letters **Yy** and **Zz**.
- Encourage students to begin at the start dot and follow the arrows.

Grand Tour I, p. 80

Proofreading

- Discuss with students the proofreading marks. Make sure everyone understands what each mark means, as these are the marks that will be used throughout the year for proofreading.
- Have students look at the example closely to observe the marks.
- Next, students will read the paragraph and mark three spelling mistakes and three capital letter mistakes with the proofreading marks.

Reference Skill

Dictionary Guide Words

- Have students look in a dictionary to find the **guide words** at the top of the page.
- Tell students that the words listed in ABC order on that page are called **entry words**.
- Tell students the first **guide word** is the first **entry word** on that page and the second **guide word** is the last **entry word** on that page.
- Tell students all entry words must be in ABC order between the two **guide words**.

p. 79

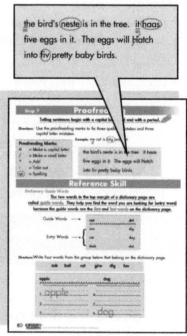

p. 80

Day 5 *continued*

- Draw this sample dictionary page on the board and write **ball** and **desk** on it for **guide words**.
- Next, write **apple**, **cat**, **bus**, **day**, **cup**, and **fish** on the board.
- Have students tell you which four words listed above will fit between **ball** and **desk** on the sample dictionary page.

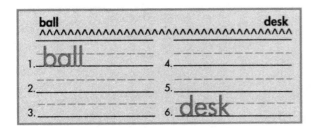
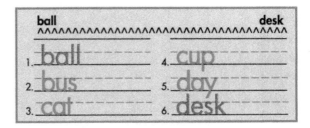

- Discuss with students why **apple** and **fish** will not fit on this page.
- Students will write four words in *Grand Tour I* p.80 that belong on the sample dictionary page.

Process Writing

Process Writing Lesson #3 for Steps 6 and 7 is found in TM p. 435.

Additional Related Activities for Step 7

Listening and Speaking

1. *Beanbag Toss* with Discriminating Ending Sounds

- Have students sit in a circle.
- Toss a beanbag to a student.
- Say any word from this week's lesson that ends in **ed**.
  Example: locked
- Next, ask the student who caught the beanbag to tell you if **ed** sounds like **d** or **t**.
- The student then tosses the beanbag back to teacher and game continues.

2. *Beanbag Toss* with Subjects and Predicates

- Play same as above except say either the subject part of a sentence or the predicate part.
  Example: walked to the store.
- Student will say "predicate."
- A variation of this game is for the teacher to say "subject" and the student who has the beanbag must give a subject for a sentence.
  Example: The little boy

3. *Alphabet Rummy* (Refer to TM p. 139, Step 5.)

4. *Alphabet Lineup*

- Have children get up out of their seats and line up in ABC order by first name. Time them to see how long it takes.

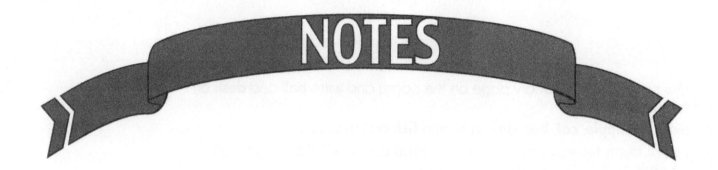

NOTES

Overview for Step 8

Objectives

Phonics: To sing *Silent ¢ Song*, providing phonics review and/or new instruction for those who need it

Spelling: To spell words that end in **ed**, and words that end in **silent e**
To double the last consonant before adding a suffix

Grammar: To understand subjects and predicates; verb usage; suffixes **ed, er, ing**

Comprehension: To read short stories and answer questions requiring higher level thinking skills

Writing: To use the Five Steps of Process Writing, focusing on writing a good beginning

Proofreading: To find spelling and capital letter errors

Reference Skills: To understand guide words and entry words

Handwriting: To review writing manuscript letters **Aa** to **Ff**

Suggested Pacing

1 week

Materials

Grand Tour I, pp. 81-90
Silent ¢ Song and Dance Chart

Homework

Daily homework is described in TM p. 99.

Spelling

Daily spelling is described in TM p. 99.

Phonics Games (See TM pp. 40-65.)

Continue to play selected games as needed for reinforcement.

Phonics Song

Silent ¢ Song, CD track 15 (See TM p. 61.)

Additional Related Activities

Additional activities are found in TM p. 165.

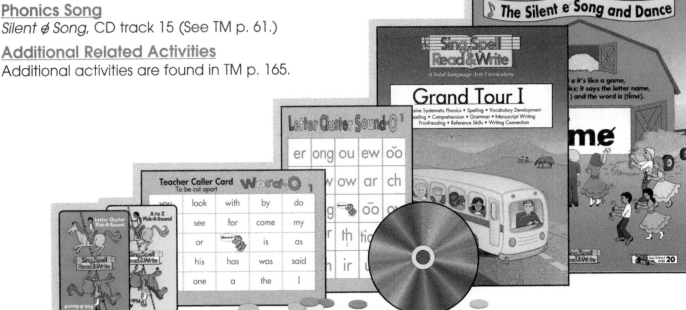

Grand Tour I

Day 1

Grand Tour I, p. 81

Spelling Words
Phonetic Grouping: suffix ed

- Note that all spelling words end in **ed** and the **ed** adds a syllable to these words. Have students mark the words as indicated: **hunted**

- As a class, read the 10 spelling words and discuss the meanings.

- Say each word and have students clap for each syllable.

- Have students copy the 10 spelling words to take home, study, and write in sentences for homework.

p. 81

Spelling Vocabulary Activities

Verb Usage

- Tell students **ed** added to a word makes the word mean **it happened in the past**.

- Students should read each sentence and write the correct form of the word to complete the sentence.

Suffix ed

- Tell students that the root word is the spelling word without the **ed** ending.

- Students will write each spelling word and the root word.
  Example: hunted—hunt

Grand Tour I, p. 82

Grammar

Sentence Parts

- Tell students a complete sentence must have a **subject** and a **predicate**. The **subject** tells **who** or **what** the sentence is about and the **predicate** tells us something about the **subject** of the sentence. It can tell **what is happening** in the sentence.

- Students will draw one line under the **subject** and two lines under the **predicate** in each sentence.

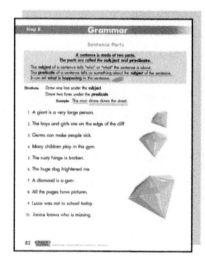

p. 82

Process Writing

Process Writing Lesson #4 for Steps 8 and 9 is in TM p. 438.

Day 2

Getting Started

- Collect homework and put stars on Homework Chart. (See TM p. 26.)
- Administer spelling test with Day 1 spelling words in *Grand Tour I*, p. 81. Sentence for dictation: My dog <u>wanted</u> to go home. (See TM p. 100.)

Phonics Review

Sing *Silent e̸ Song*, CD track 15. (See TM p. 61.)

Grand Tour I, p. 83

Spelling Words
Phonetic Grouping: e̸

- Note that each word has **silent e** at the end which makes the vowel long. Have students mark words as indicated: sāve̸
- For words that end in **silent e**, you only add **d** for the **ed** ending.
- As a class, read the 10 spelling words and discuss the meanings.
- Have students copy the 10 spelling words to take home, study, and write in sentences for homework.

Silent e̸ Song and Dance Chart

Spelling Vocabulary Activities

Suffix <u>ed</u>
- Students will write five spelling words that end in **ed** and mean **in the past**.

Synonyms
- Tell students **synonyms** are two or more words that mean the same thing or nearly the same.

  Example: coat—jacket
- Say the following words and ask students to give you the synonym:

big	(huge)
tiny	(little)
beautiful	(pretty)
house	(home)

- Students will write spelling words to answer the questions on page 83.

Rhyming
- Students will write spelling words to answer the questions.

Breaking the Code
- Explain to students that there are many different kinds of codes. In this code each number represents a letter of the alphabet.
- Students will use the code to decode the spelling words and write them on the lines.

p. 83

(Continued on next page)

Day 2 *continued*

Grand Tour I, p. 84

Story Comprehension

Steve Helped

* Have students underline the seven spelling words in the story.
* Students will read the story silently and answer the questions.
* Tell students they will have to think hard about the questions today, because the answers are not directly in the story. They will need to use the information given and draw conclusions.

The Writing Connection

Writing Sentences

* Students will write a sentence to tell what they think Steve might do. Remind them to begin it with a capital letter and end with a period.

Grammar Chalkboard Lesson
Verbs in the Predicate

Objectives

* To learn that a **verb** often shows action such as **hop**, **sing**, **walk**, **run**
* To identify the **verb** in the **predicate** part of the sentence

Practice/Apply

* Write the sentences on the board and draw a line under the **predicate**.
* Students will copy the sentences and circle the **verb** in each **predicate**.
  Example: The little bird (flew) away.

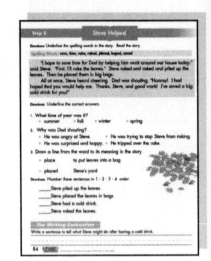

p. 84

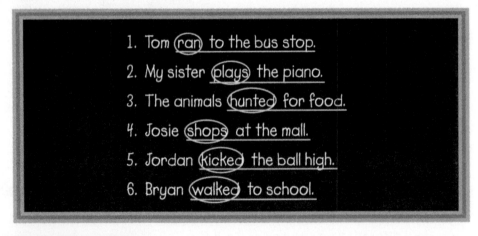

1. Tom (ran) to the bus stop.
2. My sister (plays) the piano.
3. The animals (hunted) for food.
4. Josie (shops) at the mall.
5. Jordan (kicked) the ball high.
6. Bryan (walked) to school.

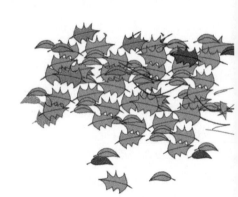

Process Writing

Process Writing Lesson #4 for Steps 8 and 9 is in TM p. 438.

Getting Started

- Collect homework and put stars on Homework Chart. (See TM p. 26.)
- Administer spelling test with Day 3 spelling words in *Grand Tour I*, p. 83. Sentence for dictation: She <u>hoped</u> to win the race. (See TM p. 100.)

Grand Tour I, p. 85

Spelling Words
Phonetic Grouping: ¢

- Note that each word has **silent e** at the end that makes the vowel long. Have students mark words as indicated: **pīl¢**
- For words that end in **silent e** you only add **d** for the **ed** ending.
- As a class, read the 10 spelling words and discuss the meanings.
- Have students copy the 10 spelling words to take home, study, and write in sentences for homework.

Spelling Vocabulary Activities

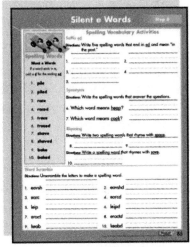

p. 85

Suffix <u>ed</u>
- Students will write five spelling words that end in **ed** and mean **in the past**.

Synonyms
- Tell students **synonyms** are two or more words that mean the same or nearly the same.
- Say the following words and ask a student to give a **synonym** for the word called.

  Examples:
car	(automobile)
infant	(baby)
adore	(love)
sack	(bag)

- Students will write the spelling words that answer the questions on page 85.

Rhyming
- Students will write two spelling words that rhyme with **space** and one word that rhymes with **save**.

Word Scramble
- Students will unscramble the letters to make spelling words.

Grand Tour I, p. 86

Grammar

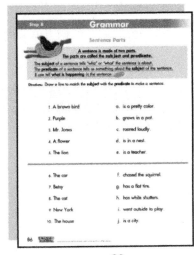

Sentence Parts
- Tell students each complete sentence must have a **subject** and **predicate**.
- Students will draw a line to match the **subject** with the **predicate** to make a sentence.

p. 86

Process Writing

Process Writing Lesson #4 for Steps 8 and 9 is in TM p. 438.

Getting Started

- Collect homework and put stars on Homework Chart. (See TM p. 26.)
- Administer spelling test with Day 3 spelling words in *Grand Tour I*, p. 85. Sentence for dictation: Mom <u>baked</u> a cake. (See TM p. 100.)

Grand Tour I, p. 87

Spelling Words
Phonetic Grouping: vc pattern

- Note that if a word ends in one vowel and one consonant (**vc**), double the last letter before adding **ed**, **er**, and **ing**. Have students mark each root word as indicated: **hop**
- As a class, read the 10 spelling words and discuss the meanings.
- Talk about the suffixes **ed**, **er**, and **ing** and how they change the meaning of the root word.
- The suffix **ed** means **in the past**; **er** changes it to a **person**; **ing** means **it's happening now**.
- Ask which two words in the spelling list mean a person. (**batter, hopper**)
- Have students copy the 10 spelling words to take home, study, and write in sentences for homework.

p. 87

Spelling Vocabulary Activities

Word Search

- Tell students all the spelling words are found in the word search. The words go across or down.
- Students will draw a ring around each word as they find it.

Suffixes

- Tell students if a word ends in one vowel and one consonant (**vc** pattern), they must double the last consonant before adding a suffix.
  Example: get—getting
- Students will add the suffixes **ed**, **er**, and **ing** to each root word.

Grand Tour I, p. 88

Story Comprehension

Mr. Grasshopper

Students will:
- Underline the seven spelling words in the story.
- Read the story silently.

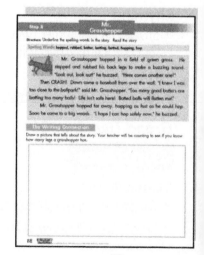

p. 88

Day 4 *continued*

The Writing Connection

Doing Research and Illustrating a Story

• Encourage students to look in an encyclopedia, dictionary, or website to find out how many legs a grasshopper has.

• Next, students will draw a picture that tells about the story.

Grammar Chalkboard Lesson
Verbs in the Predicate

Objectives

• To learn that a **verb** often shows action such as **hop**, **sing**, **walk**, **run**

• To identify the **verb** in the **predicate** part of the sentence

Practice/Apply

• Write the sentences on the board and draw a line under the **predicate**.

• Students will copy the sentences and circle the **verb** in each **predicate**.

Example: Mr. Jones (wrote) a letter to me.

1. Dorrie (ate) lunch with me.
2. The little bird (chirped) loudly.
3. An airplane (flew) over the house.
4. My pet rabbit (eats) lettuce.
5. A red fox (runs) fast.
6. Dad (drove) the truck.

Process Writing

Process Writing Lesson #4 for Steps 8 and 9 is in TM p. 438.

Day 5

Getting Started

• Collect homework and put stars on Homework Chart. (See TM p. 26.)

• Administer spelling test with Day 4 spelling words in *Grand Tour I*, p. 87.
  Sentence for dictation: Tom <u>hopped</u> on one foot. (See TM p. 100.)

(Continued on next page)

Day 5 *continued*

Grand Tour I, p. 89

Proofreading

- Discuss with students the proofreading marks.
- Have students look at the example closely to observe the marks.
- Students will read the paragraph and mark three spelling mistakes, two capital letter mistakes, and change one capital letter to a small letter.

Reference Skill

Dictionary Guide Words

- Have students look in a dictionary to find the **guide words** at the top of the page.
- Tell students that the words listed in ABC order on that page are called **entry words**.
- Tell students the first **guide word** is the first **entry word** on that page and the second **guide word** is the last **entry word** on that page.
- Tell students all **entry words** must be in ABC order between the two **guide words**.
- Draw this sample dictionary page on the board and write **gas** and **jump** on it for **guide words**.

gas	jump
1. gas	4.
2.	5.
3.	6. jump

- Next, write **goat**, **ran**, **hand**, **get**, **jam**, and **man** on the board.
- Have students tell you which four words listed above will fit on the sample dictionary page.

gas	jump
1. gas	4. hand
2. get	5. jam
3. goat	6. jump

- Discuss with students why **ran** and **man** will not fit on this page.
- Students will write four words on page 89 that belong on the sample dictionary page.

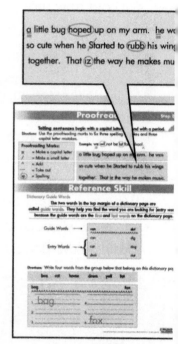

p. 89

Day 5 *continued*

Grand Tour I, p. 90

Handwriting Practice

* Students will practice writing manuscript letters **Aa** to **Ff**.
* Encourage students to start at the start dot.

Process Writing

Process Writing Lesson #4 for Steps 8 and 9 is in TM p. 438.

p. 90

Additional Related Activities for Step 8

Listening and Speaking

1. *Around the World* with Synonyms

* Have a student stand beside another student seated at his/her desk.
* The teacher will say a word that has a synonym.
  Example: pretty
* The student who first says a synonym (beautiful, gorgeous, lovely) moves on to the next desk.
* Suggested words to say:

1. big (large)	9. look (see)	17. cure (heal)
2. woman (lady)	10. begin (start)	18. finish (complete)
3. car (automobile)	11. question (ask)	19. error (mistake)
4. scream (yell)	12. below (under)	20. fix (repair)
5. nice (good)	13. annoy (bother)	21. frequent (often)
6. pretty (lovely)	14. city (town)	22. happy (glad)
7. hope (wish)	15. shut (close)	23. high (tall)
8. save (keep)	16. country (nation)	24. job (occupation)

* Accept any reasonable answers.

2. *Spelling Baseball*

* Divide the class into two teams.
* "Pitch" words to a team by calling out a word to spell from Week 8 lists.
* A team gets a **hit** for each word spelled correctly, and an **out** for each misspelled word.
* After **three outs** the next team comes to bat and the teacher begins "pitching" words to the new team.

3. Rhyming Word Families

* Write words on the board and have students come up and change the first consonant to make as many rhyming words as possible.

  Examples: hop   mop   top

  pop   stop   shop

Overview for Step 9

Objectives

Spelling: To spell words by doubling the last consonant before adding **ed**, **er**, or **ing**

Grammar: To know how to use the correct form of **ed**, **er**, and **ing** words

To know how the suffixes **ed**, **er**, and **ing** change the meaning of a word

To hear parts of a word and divide into syllables

To understand telling and asking sentences

Comprehension: To read short stories and answer questions requiring higher level thinking skills

Proofreading: To find spelling, capital letter, and end mark errors

Reference Skill: To understand some words in the dictionary have more than one meaning

Writing: To write an informational paragraph

To write a title for a story

To use the Five Steps of Process Writing, focusing on writing a good beginning

Handwriting: To review writing manuscript letters **Gg** to **Ll**

Suggested Pacing
1 week

Materials
Grand Tour I, pp. 91-100

Homework
Daily homework is described in TM p. 99.

Spelling
Daily Spelling is described in TM p. 99.

Phonics Game
Word-O (See TM p. 58.)

Phonics Songs (See TM pp. 40-65.)
Continue to sing selected songs as needed for reinforcement.

Additional Related Activities
Additional activities are found in TM p. 174.

Day 1

Grand Tour I, p. 91

Spelling Words
Vowel Consonant (vc) Pattern

• Note that the last consonant has been doubled before adding the suffix **ed**, **er**, or **ing** to words #2, 3, 4, 6, 7, 9, and 10. If a word ends in one vowel and one consonant (**vc**), double the last letter before adding **ed**, **er**, or **ing**. Have students mark words as indicated: st**ŏp**—st**ŏpped**

• As a class, read the 10 spelling words and discuss the meanings.

• Have students copy the 10 spelling words to take home, study, and write in sentences for homework.

Spelling Vocabulary Activities

Verb Usage
• Students will fill in the blank with the correct spelling word.

Suffixes
• Teach the vowel consonant (**vc**) pattern in a word.

• If the word ends in a **vc** pattern, you double the last consonant before adding the suffix **ed**, **er**, or **ing**.
Example: st**ŏp**—st**ŏpping**.

• Students will add the suffix **ed**, **er**, or **ing** to the root words listed.

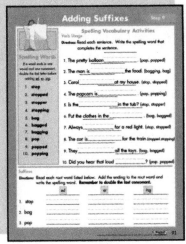

p. 91

Grand Tour I, p. 92

Grammar

Telling and Asking Sentences
• Tell students sentences may **tell** or **ask**.

• If a sentence **tells**, it does not need a response. It has a period at the end and is called a **telling sentence**.
Example: I will help you.

• If a sentence **asks**, it does need a response. It has a question mark at the end and is called a **question**.
Example: May I help you?

• Think of several simple **telling** and **asking** sentences and say them aloud to class. Tell students to clap one time if it is telling and twice if it is asking.

• Students will read the sentences on page 92, place a period or question mark at the end, and write **telling** or **asking** to tell what kind of sentence it is.

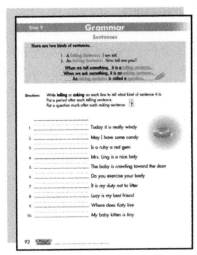

p. 92

Process Writing

Process Writing Lesson #4 for Steps 8 and 9 is found in TM p. 438.

Grand Tour I

Getting Started

- Collect homework and put stars on Homework Chart. (See TM p. 26.)
- Administer spelling test with Day 1 spelling words in *Grand Tour I*, p. 91. Sentence for dictation: Dan <u>popped</u> the bag. (See TM p. 100.)

Grand Tour I, p. 93

Spelling Words
Vowel Consonant (vc) Pattern

- Note that if a word ends in one vowel and one consonant (**vc**), double the last letter before adding **ed**, **er**, or **ing**. Have students mark words as indicated: jŏg— jŏgger
- As a class, read the 10 spelling words and discuss the meanings.
- Have students copy the 10 spelling words to take home, study, and write in sentences for homework.

Spelling Vocabulary Activities

Suffixes

- Tell students **ed** added to a word changes it to mean **in the past**; **ing** added to a word means it's **happening now**; **er** added to a word changes it to mean **a person**.
- Students will write two spelling words with an **ed** ending; three with an **ing** ending; two with an **er** ending.

Root Words

- Students will write three spelling words that are root words.

Syllables

- As a class, read the spelling words and clap for each syllable.
- Write these **multisyllable nonsense words** on the board and have students read the nonsense words. Have students clap for each syllable. This is good practice and allows students to use their phonics skills. Remind students these are not real words.

| sogger | jummer | bipper | dopping |
| zilling | lummed | gammed | bapping |

- On page 93, students will write each spelling word and the number of syllables in each word.

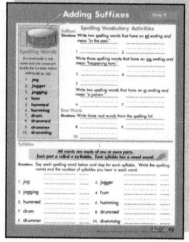

p. 93

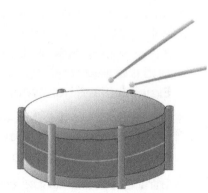

Day 2 continued

Grand Tour I, p. 94

Story Comprehension

A Morning Jogger

Have students:

- Underline the eight spelling words in the story.
- Read the story silently.
- Read the questions and underline the answers.

The Writing Connection

Researching a Topic and Writing a Paragraph

- Brainstorm with students about different types of birds: hummingbirds, robins, bluebirds, cardinals, crows, mockingbirds, etc.
- Let each student choose a bird to gather information about. Students may use an encyclopedia, bird books, or other sources.
- Students will write a paragraph about his/her bird.

p. 94

Grammar Chalkboard Lesson
Telling and Asking Sentences

Objective

- Students will unscramble the group of words to make an **asking** or **telling** sentence.

Practice/Apply

- Write the groups of words on the board. Students will unscramble the words to make a **sentence** and then place a **period** or **question mark** at the end of each sentence.

  Example: friend Mary is good my
  Is Mary my good friend? **or** Mary is my good friend.

1. name is what your   What is your name?

2. little Joanie my sister is
   Little Joanie is my sister. or Is Joanie my little sister?

3. sarah store to went the   Sarah went to the store.

4. happy brother always my is
   My brother is always happy. or Is my brother always happy?

5. will today the shine sun
   Will the sun shine today? or The sun will shine today.

6. me my please with help homework   Please help me with my homework.

Process Writing

Process Writing Lesson #4 for Steps 8 and 9 is found in TM p. 438.

Grand Tour I

Day 3

Getting Started

- Collect homework and put stars on Homework Chart. (See TM p. 26.)
- Administer spelling test with Day 2 spelling words in *Grand Tour I*, p. 93. Sentence for dictation: Can you <u>jog</u> fast? (See TM p. 100.)

Grand Tour I, p. 95

Spelling Words
Vowel Consonant (vc) Pattern

- Note that if a word ends in one vowel and one consonant (**vc**), double the last letter before adding **ed**, **er**, or **ing**. Have students mark words as indicated: **pet—petted**
- As a class, read the 10 spelling words and discuss the meanings.
- Have students copy the 10 spelling words to take home, study, and write in sentences for homework.

Spelling Vocabulary Activities

Suffixes
- Discuss how adding **ed**, **er**, or **ing** to the end of a word changes the meaning.
- Students will write three spelling words with an **ed** ending, three spelling words with an **ing** ending, and one with an **er** ending.

Root Words
- Students will write three spelling words that are root words.

Syllables
- As a class, read the spelling words and clap for each syllable.
- Students will write each spelling word and the number of syllables in each word.

p. 95

Grand Tour I, p. 96

Grammar

Telling and Asking Sentences
- Think of and say several **telling** and **asking** sentences aloud to class. Tell students to clap one time if the sentence is **telling** and twice if it is **asking**.
- Students will read the sentences, place a period or question mark at the end, and write **telling** or **asking** to describe the sentence.

Process Writing

Process Writing Lesson #4 for Steps 8 and 9 is found in TM p. 438.

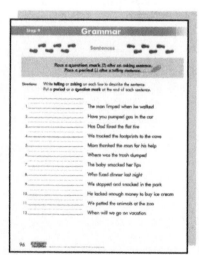

p. 96

Day 4

Getting Started

- Collect homework and put stars on Homework Chart. (See TM p. 26.)
- Administer spelling test with Day 3 spelling words in *Grand Tour I*, p. 95. Sentence for dictation: She is <u>petting</u> my dog. (See TM p. 100.)

Grand Tour I, p. 97

Spelling Words
Vowel Consonant (vc) Pattern

- Note that if a word ends in one vowel and one consonant (**vc**), double the last letter before adding **ed**, **er**, or **ing**. Have students mark words as indicated: **scrub—scrubbed**
- As a class, read the 10 spelling words and discuss the meanings.
- Have students copy the 10 spelling words to take home, study, and write in sentences for homework.

Spelling Vocabulary Activities

Word Search

- Tell students all the spelling words in this lesson are hidden in the puzzle.
- All words are written across or down.
- Students will draw a ring around each word as they find it.

Syllables

- As a class, read the spelling words and clap for each syllable.
- Students will write each spelling word and the number of syllables in each word.

p. 97

Grand Tour I, p. 98

Story Comprehension

Jill's Messy Kitchen

Have students:
- Underline the eight spelling words in the story.
- Read the story silently.
- Read the questions and underline the answers.

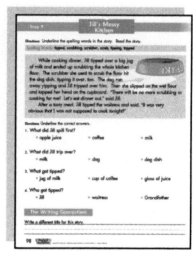

p. 98

(Continued on next page)

Day 4 *continued*

The Writing Connection

Writing a Story Title
- Read aloud the story *The Morning Jogger* in *Grand Tour I,* page 94.
- As a class, brainstorm different titles for this story.
    Examples: *A Jog in the Park*
                Sounds of Birds
                Special Things About Jogging
- Next, tell students they will write a different title for the story *Jill's Messy Kitchen* on page 98.

Grammar Chalkboard Lesson
Telling and Asking Sentences

Objective
- Students will unscramble the group of words to make an **asking** or **telling** sentence.

Practice/Apply
- Write these groups of words on the board. Students will unscramble the words to make a **sentence** and place a **period** or **question mark** at the end of each sentence.
    Example: home time be will you on
                Will you be home on time? **or** You will be home on time.

1. red a the robin nest built   The red robin built a nest.
2. many are how in eggs nest the   How many eggs are in the nest?
3. there eggs four are
   There are four eggs. or Are there four eggs?
4. little hatched four robins   Four little robins hatched.
5. the fed who birds baby   Who fed the baby birds?
6. robin the babies mama fed   Mama robin fed the babies.

Process Writing

Process Writing Lesson #4 for Steps 8 and 9 is found in TM p. 438.

Day 5

Getting Started

- Collect homework and put stars on Homework Chart. (See TM p. 26.)
- Administer spelling test with Day 4 spelling words in *Grand Tour I*, p. 97. Sentence for dictation: Can you <u>scrub</u> the floor? (See TM p. 100.)

Grand Tour I, p. 99

Proofreading

- Talk about the **proofreading** marks.
- Tell students to read the paragraph and correct two spelling mistakes, insert two capital letters, and two end marks.

Reference Skill

Finding the Right Meaning in the Dictionary

- Tell students some words have more than one meaning.
  Example: run can mean (1) to run a race, (2) an engine will run, (3) to run a business.
- Have students look at entry words in a dictionary to see how some words have more than one meaning. Point out that the definitions are numbered.
- Have them look at the word **bark** on page 99 in *Grand Tour I*. It has two definitions and a sentence for each definition.
- Help students identify which is the **meaning** and which is the **sentence**.
- Next, students will read the sentences and write **1** or **2** by each sentence at the bottom of the page to tell which meaning of **bark** is used.

Grand Tour I, p. 100

Handwriting Practice

Students will trace over the letter first and then practice writing **Gg** to **Ll**.

Process Writing

Process Writing Lesson #4 for Steps 8 and 9 is found in TM p. 438.

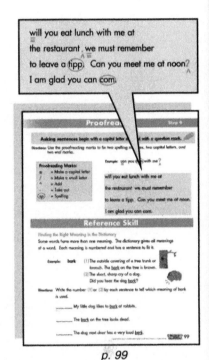
p. 99

p. 100

Additional Related Activities for Step 9

Listening and Speaking

1. Spelling Word Riddles

- Divide the students into pairs and have each pair write a riddle for one of the spelling words in Step 9.
- The riddle should first say the letter the answer begins with.
  Example: I begin with a **b**. I am an animal that can fly. (**bird**)
- After students have written their riddles, ask them to share with the class.
- Each student should have his or her *Grand Tour I* book open to pages 91-100 to look for a spelling word that will answer a riddle.

2. Changing Sentences from Asking to Telling

- Have students stand in a circle. Tell them you will toss the beanbag to a student and say an **asking** sentence.
- The student who catches the beanbag will answer with a **telling** sentence using almost the same words.
- Sentences to ask:
  Did you go to a movie? (I did go to a movie.)
  Can Mary help me? (Mary can help me.)
  Is Stella at the store? (Stella is at the store.)
- Continue the game with similar sentences.
- **Variation**: Reverse the sentences. The teacher will say a **telling** sentence and the student will answer back with an **asking** sentence.
  Example: Fernando can fly to Miami. (Can Fernando fly to Miami?)

3. Using Suffixes

- Tell students all the spelling words this week are root words with **ed**, **er**, or **ing** added.
- Tell students you will say a root word and what you want it to mean.
  Example: The root word is scrub. I want it to mean it is **happening now**. What is the spelling word? (**scrubbing**)
- Continue in this manner using the terms **in the past**, **happening now**, or **means a person**.

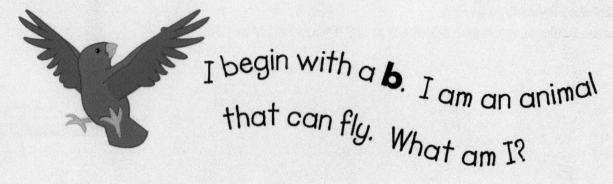

I begin with a **b**. I am an animal that can fly. What am I?

NOTES

Overview for Step 10

Objectives

Phonics: To sing *Letter Cluster Phonics Song*, verses 1 and 2, providing phonics review and/or new instruction for those who need it

Spelling: To spell words with letter cluster **or**

Grammar: To understand asking and telling sentences

Comprehension: To read short stories and answer questions requiring higher level thinking skills

Writing: To write a headline for a news report

To use the Five Steps of Process Writing, focusing on story elements

Proofreading: To find spelling and punctuation errors

Reference Skills: To understand an entry word may have more than one definition

Handwriting: To review writing manuscript letters **Mm** to **Rr**

Suggested Pacing
1 week

Materials
Grand Tour I, pp. 101-110
Letter Cluster Phonics Song Charts 1 and 2

Homework
Daily homework is described in TM p. 99.

Spelling
Daily spelling is described in TM p. 99.

Phonics Games (See TM pp. 40-65.)
Continue to play selected games as needed for reinforcement.

Phonics Song
Letter Cluster Phonics Song, verses 1-2,
  CD track 8 (See TM p. 51.)

Additional Related Activities
Additional activities are found in TM p. 184.

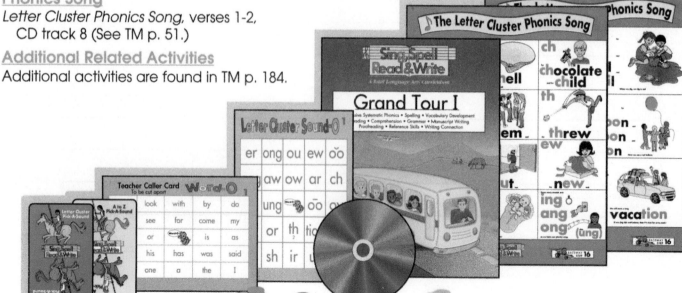

Phonics Review

Sing *Letter Cluster Phonics Song*, verses 1 - 2, CD track 8. (See TM p. 51.)

Grand Tour I, p. 101

Spelling Words
Phonetic Grouping: or

* Note that words #1-9 all have **or**. Have students mark each word as indicated: **born**
* Call attention to rulebreakers **you** and **your**.
* As a class, read the 10 spelling words and discuss the meanings.
* Have students copy the 10 spelling words to take home, study, and write in sentences for homework.

Spelling Vocabulary Activities

Compound Words
* Students will write two spelling words that are **compound words**.

Rhyming
* Students will write three spelling words that **rhyme** with **corn**.

Word Meanings
* Students will write a spelling word for each meaning.

Rulebreaker
* Remind students that **rulebreakers** do not follow phonetic rules and have to be memorized. For example, **all** sounds like it would be spelled **awl**.
* Students will write one spelling word that is a rulebreaker.

Antonyms
* Tell students **antonyms** are words that mean the opposite.
  Examples: good—bad; hot—cold; boy—girl; angry—happy
* Students will write **antonyms** for the words listed.

Cloze
* Students will fill in the missing spelling words.

Letter Cluster Phonics Song Charts

p. 101

Grand Tour I, p. 102

Grammar

Asking Sentences
* Review **telling** and **asking** sentences with students.
* Tell students they will change a **telling** sentence into an **asking** sentence by rearranging the words.
  Example: It is cold outside. Is it cold outside?
* Students will rewrite the eight sentences into **asking** sentences.

Process Writing

Process Writing Lesson #5 for Steps 10 and 11 is found in TM p. 440.

p. 102

Grand Tour I

Day 2

Getting Started

- Collect homework and put stars on Homework Chart. (See TM p. 26.)
- Administer spelling test with Day 1 spelling words in *Grand Tour I*, p. 101. Sentence for dictation: Do not <u>forget</u> the book. (See TM p. 100.)

Grand Tour I, p. 103

Spelling Words
Phonetic Grouping: or

- Note that words #1-9 have letter cluster **or**. The **or** may be at the **beginning** or **middle** of the word. Have students mark each word as indicated: st**or**k
- Have students close their books as the teacher says each spelling word. Students will say if the **or** comes at the **beginning** or **middle** of each word.
- Ask which word is a **compound** word and which word means **it's happening now**.
- How does it sound like you should spell the rulebreaker **said**? (**sĕd**)
- As a class, read the 10 spelling words and discuss the meanings.
- Have students copy the 10 spelling words to take home, study, and write in sentences for homework.

Spelling Vocabulary Activities

Cloze
- Students will fill in the blanks with spelling words.

Word Clues
- Tell students to write a spelling word for each clue.

Grand Tour I, p. 104

Story Comprehension

Norman in Orbit
Students will:

- Underline all the **or** words in the story.
- Read the story and underline the correct answers.

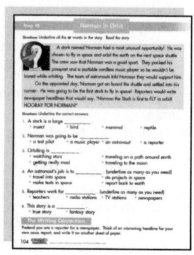

p. 103

p. 104

The Writing Connection

Writing a Newspaper Headline

- Tell students to refer back to the story, *Norman in Orbit*, and read what the newspaper would write in headlines for that story.

- Brainstorm some possibilities for other headlines for newspaper articles.

    Examples: *Hubble Telescope Repaired*
    Hurricane Hits North Carolina
    Tampa Bay Buccaneers Win
    Super Bowl Comes to St. Louis
    Circus Comes to Town

- Ask what each one of these headlines would be about. Talk about some things that would be included in the article.

- Tell students to think of an interesting headline for a story and write it on another sheet of paper.

Grammar Chalkboard Lesson
Telling and Asking Sentences

Objective

- Students will understand the difference between a **telling** and **asking** sentence.

Practice/Apply

- Write the **telling** sentences on the board. Students will change each **telling** sentence into an **asking** sentence.

    Example: Brian will sail the boat.
    Will Brian sail the boat?

A bat can fly fast.	Can a bat fly fast?
Anita will run the errand.	Will Anita run the errand?
Jacob is my best friend.	Is Jacob my best friend?
The movie will play tonight.	Will the movie play tonight?
The waves are very rough.	Are the waves very rough?
A storm is coming this way.	Is a storm coming this way?

Process Writing

Process Writing Lesson #5 for Steps 10 and 11 is found in TM p. 440.

Grand Tour I

Day 3

Getting Started

- Collect homework and put stars on Homework Chart. (See TM p. 26.)
- Administer spelling test with Day 2 spelling words in *Grand Tour I*, p. 103. Sentence for dictation: Baseball is my best <u>sport</u>. (See TM p. 100.)

Grand Tour I, p. 105

Spelling Words
Phonetic Grouping: or

- Note that words #1-9 have letter cluster **or**. Have students mark each word as indicated: **thȯrn**
- Ask which two words are compound words.
- How does it sound like you should spell the rulebreaker **would**? (**woŏd**)
- As a class, read the 10 spelling words and discuss the meanings.
- Have students copy the 10 spelling words to take home, study, and write in sentences for homework.

Spelling Vocabulary Activities

Breaking the Code

- Tell students there are many different kinds of codes. This code has a number to represent a letter.
  Example: 1 = a
- Students will use the code to decode the spelling words.

Word Association

- Tell students to write a spelling word that is associated in some way with each word listed.
  Examples: jacket—cold; gasoline—car; shoe—sock

Cloze

- Students will fill in the missing spelling words.

Grand Tour I, p. 106

Grammar

Telling Sentences

- Review **telling** and **asking** sentences with students.
- Tell students they will change an **asking** sentence into a **telling** sentence by rearranging the words.
  Example: Will we go on vacation? (We will go on vacation.)
- Students will rewrite the eight sentences into **telling** sentences.

Process Writing

Process Writing Lesson #5 for Steps 10 and 11 is found in TM p. 440.

p. 105

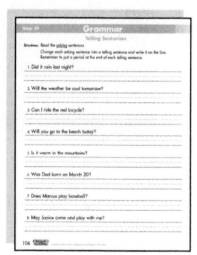

p. 106

Day 4

Getting Started

- Collect homework and put stars on Homework Chart. (See TM p. 26.)
- Administer spelling test with Day 3 spelling words in *Grand Tour I*, p. 105. Sentence for dictation: I like to eat <u>shortcake</u>. (See TM p. 100.)

Grand Tour I, p. 107

Spelling Words
Phonetic Grouping: or

- Note that all words have letter cluster **or**. Have students mark each word as indicated: **sort**
- As a class, read the 10 spelling words and discuss the meanings.
- Have students copy the 10 spelling words to take home, study, and write in sentences for homework.

Spelling Vocabulary Activities

Word Search

- Tell students all the spelling words in this lesson are hidden in the puzzle.
- All words are written across or down.
- Students will draw a ring around each word as they find it.

Rhyming

- Remind students that **rhyming** words have the same ending vowel and consonant sounds. Students will write spelling words that **rhyme** with the words listed.

Cloze

- Students will write the missing spelling words.

p. 107

(Continued on next page)

Day 4 *continued*

Grand Tour I, p. 108

Story Comprehension

The Food Store

- Before reading the story, discuss with students where different foods come from.

        bread – wheat   eggs – chickens
        milk – cows   pork – pigs

Students will:

- Underline the nine spelling words in the story.

- Read the story silently and underline the correct answers.

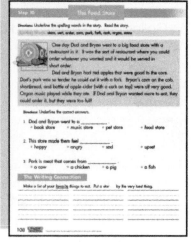

p. 108

The Writing Connection

Listing Favorite Foods

Students will make a list of their favorite foods and put a ☆ by their very favorite.

Grammar Chalkboard Lesson
Telling and Asking Sentences

Objective

- Students will understand the difference between a **telling** and **asking** sentence.

Practice/Apply

- Write the **asking** sentences on the board. Students will change the **asking** sentences into **telling** sentences.

    Example: Will John go to the store?
                   John will go to the store.

Did Trina sleep late?	Trina did sleep late.
Will Maria help with lunch?	Maria will help with lunch.
Can Tom sweep the porch?	Tom can sweep the porch.
Is Daniel waiting outside?	Daniel is waiting outside.
Are Nate and Jacob in the park?	Nate and Jacob are in the park.
Do I have enough money?	I do have enough money.

Process Writing

Process Writing Lesson #5 for Steps 10 and 11 is found in TM p. 440.

Day 5

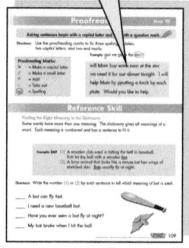

Getting Started

- Collect homework and put stars on Homework Chart. (See TM p. 26.)
- Administer spelling test with Day 4 spelling words in *Grand Tour I*, p. 107. Sentence for dictation: I use a <u>fork</u> to eat. (See TM p. 100.)

Grand Tour I, p. 109

Proofreading

- Review the proofreading marks and have students look at the example to see how it is marked.
- Next, students will read the paragraph and mark three spelling mistakes, two capital letters, and two end marks.

Reference Skill

Finding the Right Meaning in the Dictionary

- Have students look in a dictionary to find words that have more than one meaning.
- On page 109 students will read the two definitions for the word **bat**.
- Next, they will write number **1** or **2** by each sentence to tell which meaning of **bat** is used.

p. 109

Grand Tour I, p. 110

Handwriting Practice

Students will practice writing manuscript letters **Mm** to **Rr**.

Process Writing

Process Writing Lesson #5 for Steps 10 and 11 is found in TM p. 440.

p. 110

Additional Related Activities for Step 10

Listening and Speaking

1. Word Box

box

- Make a box like the one shown.

- Cut a slit in the cover of the box. On a 3 x 5 index card write a word to be used in a sentence. On the reverse side write **telling** or **asking**. Make enough cards for each child to have one.

- Ask students to pick a card and say the appropriate kind of sentence using the word.

- Student may say, "What color is the boat?"

- When all the cards have been used, invite students to make cards to go in the box for the next time you play the game.

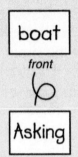

front

back

2. Illustrating Things That Fly

- Brainstorm with children things that can fly. List them on the board.
  Examples: airplanes, rockets, helicopters, kites, birds (list by name)

- Next, have students choose one item to illustrate and write a complete **telling** or **asking** sentence about it.

3. *Around the World* with Antonyms

- Have a student stand beside another student seated at his/her desk.

- The teacher will say a word that has an antonym.
  Example: hot

- The student who says the antonym **cold** first moves on to the next desk and the game continues.

Words to call:

above – below	black – white	dark – light
absent – present	top – bottom	night – day
add – subtract	short – long	easy – difficult
love – hate	boy – girl	after – before
sell – buy	earth – sky	open – shut
answer – question	expensive – cheap	begin – end
arrive – depart	adult – child	evening – morning
awake – asleep	chilly – warm	true – false
back – front	dirty – clean	fast – slow
good – bad	open – close	thin – fat
ugly – beautiful	hot – cold	finish – start
little – big	cry – laugh	lead – follow

- Accept any reasonable answer.

NOTES

Grand Tour I

Overview for Step 11

Objectives

Phonics: To sing *Letter Cluster Phonics Song*, verses 1-2, providing phonics review and/or new instruction for those who need it

Spelling: To spell words with letter cluster **sh**

Grammar: To begin each sentence with a capital letter

To understand compound words, root words, syllables, and making plurals by adding **es**

Comprehension: To read short stories

Writing: To write a paragraph

To use the Five Steps of Process Writing, focusing on story elements

Proofreading: To find spelling, capital letters, and end mark errors

Reference Skill: To understand guide words

Handwriting: To review writing manuscript letters **Ss** to **Zz**

Suggested Pacing

1 week

Materials

Grand Tour I, pp. 111-120
Letter Cluster Phonics Song Charts 1 and 2

Homework

Daily homework is described in TM p. 99.

Spelling

Daily spelling is described in TM p. 99.

Phonics Games (See TM pp. 40-65.)

Continue to play selected games as needed for reinforcement.

Phonics Song

Letter Cluster Phonics Song, verses 1-2, CD track 8 (See TM p. 51.)

Additional Related Activities

Additional activities are found in TM p. 194.

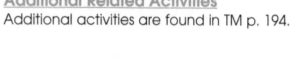

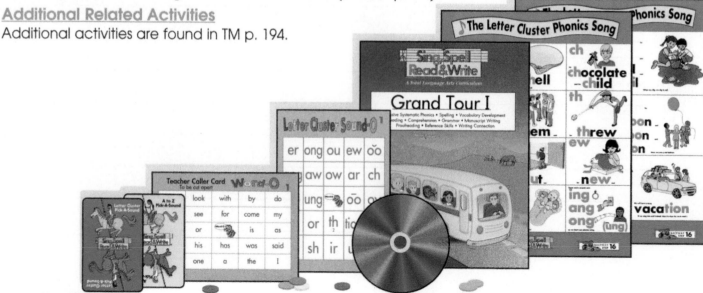

Phonics Review

Sing *Letter Cluster Phonics Song*, verses 1-2, CD track 8. (See TM p. 51.)

Grand Tour I, p. 111

Spelling Words
Phonetic Grouping: sh

- Each spelling word contains the letter cluster **sh**. Have students mark words as indicated: ⓢhore
- Note that there are four root words and six words that are a form of the root words.
- As a class, read the 10 spelling words and discuss the meanings.
- Have students copy the 10 spelling words to take home, study, and write in sentences for homework.

p. 111

Spelling Vocabulary Activities

Cloze
- Student will fill in the blanks with the correct spelling word.

Compound Words
- Students will write four spelling words that are compound words.

Root Words
- Students will write four spelling words that are root words.

Word Meanings
- Students will write spelling words to fit the meanings.

Grand Tour I, p. 112

Grammar

Capital Letters
- Tell students all sentences begin with a capital letter.
- Students will write the missing capital letter in each sentence and rewrite the sentences in the spaces provided.

Process Writing

Process Writing Lesson #5 for Steps 10 and 11 is found in TM p. 440.

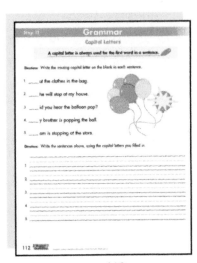

p. 112

Grand Tour I

Getting Started

- Collect homework and put stars on Homework Chart. (See TM p. 26.)
- Administer spelling test with Day 1 spelling words in *Grand Tour I*, p. 111. Sentence for dictation: We went to the <u>seashore</u>. (See TM p. 100.)

Grand Tour I, p. 113

Spelling Words
Phonetic Grouping: sh

- Each spelling word contains the letter cluster **sh**. Have students mark words as indicated: ⓈＨeep
- Note that there are four root words and five compound words made from the root words.
- Call attention to rulebreaker **been**.
- As a class, read the 10 spelling words and discuss the meanings.
- Have students copy the 10 spelling words to take home, study, and write in sentences for homework.

Spelling Vocabulary Activities

Word Scramble
- Students will unscramble the letters to make a spelling word.

Syllables
- Tell students all words are made of one or more parts. Each part is called a **syllable**. A compound word is divided into syllables between the two words. **Example:** sheep•dog

- Have students say each spelling word and clap for each syllable.
- Write the following multisyllable nonsense words on the board and have students read them aloud. This is good practice for students to use their phonics skills. Remind students these are not real words.

  steepbog   shapdot   bishbook   whetsig

- Students will write the one-syllable spelling words in one box and the two-syllable spelling words in another box.

Grand Tour I, p. 114

Story Comprehension

Fernando's Snapshots
Have students:
- Underline the nine spelling words in the story.
- Read the story silently.

p. 113

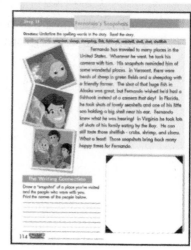

p. 114

Day 2 *continued*

The Writing Connection

Drawing a Snapshot
- Brainstorm with students about places they have visited and have them think about who was with them.
- Tell students to visualize a scene at one of their favorite places with their favorite people.
- Students will draw a snapshot including people and background.

Grammar Chalkboard Lesson
Add suffix <u>ed</u>

Objective
Students will know how to add **ed** to a word:

- If a word ends in vowel, consonant (**vc**), double the last consonant before adding **ed**.
  Example: stop—stopped

- If a word ends in a silent **e**, drop the silent **e** before adding **ed**.
  Example: save—saved

- If a word ends in consonant, consonant (**cc**), just add the **ed**.
  Example: push—pushed

Practice/Apply
- Write the words below on the board.
- Students will write the word and the word with the suffix **ed**.
  Example: rake—raked

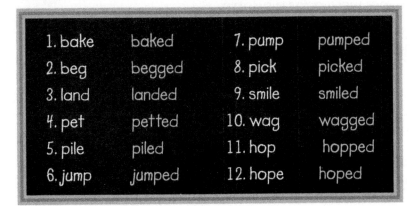

1. bake	baked	7. pump	pumped
2. beg	begged	8. pick	picked
3. land	landed	9. smile	smiled
4. pet	petted	10. wag	wagged
5. pile	piled	11. hop	hopped
6. jump	jumped	12. hope	hoped

Process Writing

Process Writing Lesson #5 for Steps 10 and 11 is found in TM p. 440.

Grand Tour I

Day 3

Getting Started

- Collect homework and put stars on Homework Chart. (See TM p. 26.)
- Administer spelling test with Day 2 spelling words in *Grand Tour I*, p. 113. Sentence for dictation: The <u>sheep</u> are running fast. (See TM p. 100.)

Grand Tour I, p. 115

Spelling Words
Phonetic Grouping: sh

- Note that words #1, 3, 5, 7, and 9 are root words that end in the letter cluster **sh**. Have students mark each word as indicated: **cra(sh)**
- Note that words #2, 4, 6, 8, and 10 are the same root words with **es** added.
- **Rule:** When a word ends in **s**, **sh**, **ch**, **x**, or **zz**, the plural is formed by adding **es**.
- As a class, read the 10 spelling words and discuss the meanings.
- Have students copy the 10 spelling words to take home, study, and write in sentences for homework.

p. 115

Spelling Vocabulary Activities

Word Usage
- Students will complete the sentence with the correct form of the word.

Plurals
- Plurals are words that mean more than one. When a word ends in **sh**, add **es** to make it mean **more than one**.
- Tell students **es** added to the end of the root word adds a syllable.

Root Words
- Students will write five spelling words that are root words.

Grand Tour I, p. 116

Grammar

Capital Letters
- Tell students the first word in each sentence is missing.
- Brainstorm with students words that help ask questions and list them on the board.
  Examples: will, can, do, what, etc.

- Remind students to look at the end punctuation. If it is an asking sentence, they need to use a word that helps ask a question.
- Students will read the phrases and write a word to begin each sentence.

Process Writing

Process Writing Lesson #5 for Steps 10 and 11 is found in TM p. 440.

p. 116

Day 4

Getting Started

- Collect homework and put stars on Homework Chart. (See TM p. 26.)
- Administer spelling test with Day 3 spelling words in *Grand Tour I*, p. 115. Sentence for dictation: I help with the <u>dishes</u>. (See TM p. 100.)

Grand Tour I, p. 117

Spelling Words
Phonetic Grouping: sh

- Note that words #1–9 have the **sh** letter cluster. Have students mark each word as indicated: (sh)oe, (sh)ine, (sh)oe(sh)ine
- Call attention to rulebreakers **shoe** and **very** and the four compound words.
- As a class, read the 10 spelling words and discuss the meanings.
- Have students copy the 10 spelling words to take home, study, and write in sentences for homework.

Spelling Vocabulary Activities

p. 117

Crossword Puzzle
- Students will read the clues by the number, find a spelling word that goes with the clue, and write the word by the number in the crossword puzzle.

Compound Words
- Students will write four spelling words that are **compound words**.

Plurals
- Tell students plural means **more than one**, and if a word ends in **sh**, add **es** to make a plural.
- Students will change two spelling words to plurals by adding **es**.

Rhyming
- Students will write spelling words that rhyme with **chin** and **nine**.

Rulebreakers
- Rulebreakers are words that do not follow phonetic rules.
- Have students tell you how **shoe** sounds like it should be spelled. (shoo)
- Ask what the **y** sounds like in ve**ry**. (long e)

(*Continued on next page*)

Grand Tour I

Day 4 *continued*

Grand Tour I, p. 118

Story Comprehension

Little Joe's Checkup

- Have students underline the six spelling words in the story.
- Read story aloud in class and discuss.
- Be sure to include in your discussion the meanings of **funnybone**, **wishbone**, and **shinbone**.

The Writing Connection

Writing a Paragraph

- Explain to students that a paragraph is a group of sentences that tell about the same thing.
- Have students write a two to four sentence paragraph about what they would wish for if they had a wishbone.

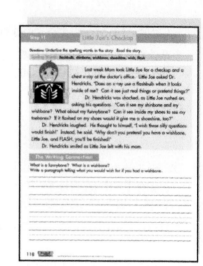

p. 118

Grammar Lesson
Nouns and Verbs

Objective
- Students will recognize **nouns** and **verbs**.

Practice/Apply
- Give each student a 3 x 5 index card with **noun** written on one side and **verb** written on the other side. (Students could write these words.)
- Teacher will call words that are either a **noun** or a **verb**. As the teacher calls the word, students will hold up card for appropriate answer.

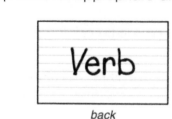

Noun	Verb
front	back

Process Writing

Process Writing Lesson #5 for Steps 10 and 11 is found in TM p. 440.

Getting Started

- Collect homework and put stars on Homework Chart. (See TM p. 26.)
- Administer spelling test with Day 4 spelling words in *Grand Tour I,* p. 117. Sentence for dictation: Did you get the <u>wishbone</u>? (See TM p. 100.)

Grand Tour I, p. 119

Proofreading

- Review the **proofreading marks** and have students look at the example to see how it is marked.
- Next, students will read the paragraph and mark the spelling mistakes, two capital letters, and two end marks.

Dictionary Guide Words

- Have students look in a dictionary to find the guide words at the top of the page.
- Point out to students that the words listed and described on the dictionary page are called **entry words** and that they are listed in ABC order.
- Tell students the **first guide word**, located at the top left of the page, is the **first entry word** on that dictionary page. The **second guide word**, located at the top right of the page, is the **last entry** word on that page.
- Tell students all entry words must be in ABC order between the two guide words.
- Draw this sample dictionary page on the board and write **dog** and **lamb** on it for guide words.
- Next, write **desk, egg, zoo, gas, lad,** and **fall** on the board.
- Have students tell you which four words will fit on the sample dictionary page.

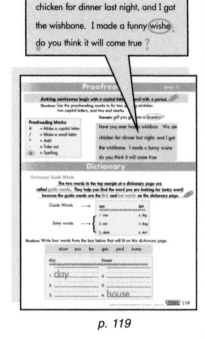

p. 119

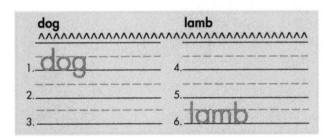

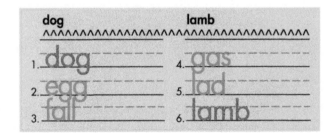

- Discuss why **desk** and **zoo** do not belong on this page.
- Students will write four words that belong on the sample dictionary page printed on page 119.

(Continued on next page)

Grand Tour I

Day 5 continued

Grand Tour I, p. 120

Handwriting Practice

Students will practice writing manuscript letters **Ss** to **Zz**.

Process Writing

Process Writing Lesson #5 for Steps 10 and 11 is found in TM p. 440.

p. 120

Additional Related Activities for Step 11

Listening and Speaking

1. Syllable Clapping

* Say the spelling words from each spelling list for Step 11.
* Ask students to clap for the number of syllables they hear in each word.

2. *What's the Word*

* On 3x5 index cards, write the spelling words written in parentheses below.
* Hand out the cards to students.
* Say a definition and student will hold up the correct card to match the definition.

A word that could be a person (shopkeeper, shopper)
A big boat (ship)
To close (shut)
To shop now (shopping)
A store (shop)
A picture (snapshot)
You catch a fish with this (fishhook)
An animal that has fur (sheep, sheepdog)
A home for some sea animals (seashell)

The front part of your leg (shin)
To hurry (rush, rushes)
To not talk (hush, hushes)
You eat from this (dish, dishes)
To fall with great force (crash, crashes)
To polish shoes (shoeshine)
To want something (wish)
A bright light (flash)
A bone in the leg (shinbone)
Something you wear on your foot (shoe)

3. *Guess the Animal*

* Have children work in pairs to describe an animal. Ask them to describe the animal in complete sentences. As one partner describes the animal, the other partner listens and guesses the animal.

    Example: This animal is often gray.
    It has four feet.
    It has a long tail.
    It is small and can climb trees very fast.
    It sits on its hind legs to eat and loves to eat acorns.
    (squirrel)

Additional Related Activities *continued*

4. Matching and Drawing Compound Words

- Write these columns of words on the chalkboard.

butter	fold
pan	cat
bill	melon
tooth	fly
wild	brush
water	cake
cup	plane
air	cake

butterfly

- Give each student one sheet of 12" x 18" newsprint paper and fold as illustrated.

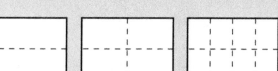

cupcake

- Now, open the paper. Using the words above, students will write a compound word in each box and illustrate it.

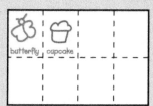

5. *Place the Sound in the Train*

- Make a train consisting of three parts, an engine, a boxcar, and a caboose.

  Materials: Three shoeboxes
  Construction paper
  Markers
  Scissors
  Glue
  Reproducibles TM pp. 472-474

- Discard the lids from the boxes. Cover the shoeboxes with construction paper. Make a copy of the reproducible train patterns. Cut and color the patterns. Glue them to the sides of the boxes. It is important that the engine be on the left end.

- Give each student a strip of paper with **sh** written on it.

- Call a student's name and a spelling word from Week 11 list. If the **sh** comes at the beginning of the word as in **ship,** the student places the **sh** strip in the engine. If the **sh** comes in the middle of the word as in **seashore,** the student places the strip in the middle car. If the **sh** comes at the end of the word, as in **rush**, the child places the strip in the caboose.

- Keep the train for future use!

Grand Tour I

Overview for Step 12

Objectives

Phonics: To sing *Letter Cluster Phonics Song*, verses 1-2, providing phonics review and/or new instruction for those who need it

Spelling: To spell words with letter cluster **sh** and **ch**

Grammar: To learn how to write complete sentences
To begin each sentence with a capital letter
To know the word **I** is always a capital letter

Comprehension: To read short stories and answer questions requiring higher level thinking skills

Writing: To write a paragraph about a sport
To use the Five Steps of Process Writing, focusing on writing story endings

Suggested Pacing
1 week

Materials
Grand Tour I, pp. 121-128
Letter Cluster Phonics Song Charts 1 and 2

Homework
Daily homework is described in TM p. 99.

Spelling
Daily spelling is described in TM p. 99.

Phonics Games (See TM pp. 40-65.)
Continue to play selected games as needed for reinforcement.

Phonics Song
Letter Cluster Phonics Song, verses 1-2,
CD track 8 (See TM p. 51.)

Additional Related Activities
Additional activities are found in TM p. 204.

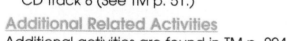

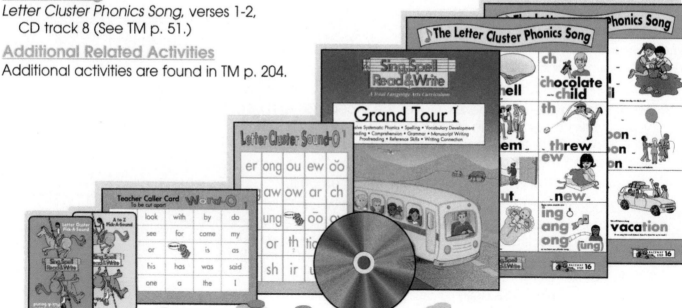

Day 1

Phonics Review

Sing *Letter Cluster Phonics Song*, verses 1-2, CD track 8. (See TM p. 51.)

Grand Tour I, p. 121

Spelling Words
Phonetic Grouping: sh

p. 121

- Note that each word has **sh**. The **sh** may be at the **beginning** or **end** of the word. Have students mark each word as indicated: ra(sh)
- As a class, read the 10 spelling words and discuss the meanings.
- Have students close their books, and teacher will say each spelling word. Students will say if the **sh** is at the **beginning** or **end** of each word.
- Have students copy the 10 spelling words to take home, study, and write in sentences for homework.

Spelling Vocabulary Activities

Word Scramble
- Students will unscramble the letters to make a spelling word.

Suffix es
- When a word ends in **s**, **sh**, **ch**, **x**, or **zz**, the plural is formed by adding **es**. Write the words **box**, **car**, **dress**, **ship**, and **bush** on the board and change each word into a plural by adding **s** or **es**.
- Students will add **es** to the words and write the new words on page 121.

Word Clues
- Students will write the spelling word that fits each clue.

Rhyming
- Students will write a spelling word that rhymes with **rave** and **boot**.

Grand Tour I, p. 122

Grammar

Capital Letters
Students will write sentences. Remind them to begin each sentence with a capital letter. Tell them the sentences may be asking or telling.

Process Writing

Process Writing Lesson #6 for Steps 12 and 13 is found in TM p. 442.

p. 122

Grand Tour I

Getting Started

- Collect homework and put stars on Homework Chart. (See TM p. 26.)
- Administer spelling test with Day 1 spelling words in *Grand Tour I*, p. 121. Sentence for dictation: Dad has to <u>shave</u> each day. (See TM p. 100.)

Grand Tour I, p. 123

Spelling Words
Phonetic Grouping: ch

- Note that words #1, 3, 5, 7, and 9 are root words with **ch** at the beginning or end. Spelling words #2, 4, 6, 8, and 10 are the same root words with **es** added to make a plural. Have students mark words as indicated: **inch**

- As a class, read the 10 spelling words and discuss the meanings.

- Next, have students close their books, and teacher will say each spelling word. Students will say if the **ch** comes at the **beginning**, **middle**, or **end** of the word.

- Have students copy the 10 spelling words to take home, study, and write in sentences for homework.

p. 123

Spelling Vocabulary Activities

Plurals and Singulars

- Tell students if a word means **more than one**, it is **plural**.
  Examples: girls, boys, churches, etc.

- For most words, you add an **s** to make a plural. However, if a word ends in **s**, **ch**, **sh**, **x**, or **zz**, you add **es** to make a plural. The **es** also adds a syllable to a word.

- Students will write five **plural** spelling words and five **singular** spelling words.

Word Usage

- Students will write the correct form of the word to complete the sentence.

Step 12

Grand Tour I, p. 124

Story Comprehension

The Olympic Games

* Students will underline the seven spelling words in the story.
* Students will read the story silently.

The Writing Connection

Writing a Paragraph

* Tell students a paragraph is two or more sentences telling about the same subject.
* The subject they will write about today is a favorite sport.
* Talk about the two different meanings of the word **sport**:
  (1) A kind of game such as football
  (2) A person who plays fair
* Have students write a paragraph that tells which **sport** is their favorite and how they can be a good **sport**.

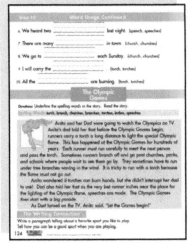

p. 124

Grammar Chalkboard Lesson
Capital Letters

Objective

* Students will know to begin a sentence with a capital letter and know the word **I** is always a capital letter.

Practice/Apply

* Write the sentences on the board. Students will write the sentences correctly.

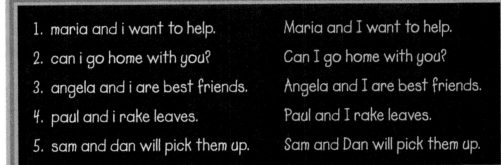

1. maria and i want to help.	Maria and I want to help.
2. can i go home with you?	Can I go home with you?
3. angela and i are best friends.	Angela and I are best friends.
4. paul and i rake leaves.	Paul and I rake leaves.
5. sam and dan will pick them up.	Sam and Dan will pick them up.

Process Writing

Process Writing Lesson #6 for Steps 12 and 13 is found in TM p. 442.

Grand Tour I

Day 3

Getting Started

- Collect homework and put stars on Homework Chart. (See TM p. 26.)
- Administer spelling test with Day 2 spelling words in *Grand Tour I*, p. 123. Sentence for dictation: My dad made a <u>speech</u>. (See TM p. 100.)

Grand Tour I, p. 125

Spelling Words
Phonetic Grouping: ch

- Note that words #1, 3, 5, 7, and 9 are root words with **ch** at the end. Words #2, 4, 6, 8, and 10 are the same root words with **es** added to make a plural. Have students mark words as indicated: **ranch**
- As a class, read the 10 spelling words and discuss their meanings.
- Have students copy the 10 spelling words to take home, study, and write in sentences for homework.

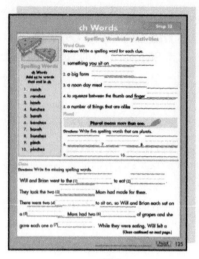

p. 125

Spelling Vocabulary Activities

Word Clues
- Students will write the spelling word that fits each clue.

Plurals
- Remind students that **plural** means **more than one**. If a word ends in **s**, **sh**, **ch**, **x**, or **zz**, you add **es** to make a plural.
- Students will write five spelling words that are plurals.

Cloze
- Students will write the missing spelling words to complete the sentence.

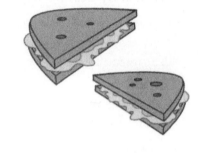

Grand Tour I, p. 126

Grammar

Capital Letters: I
- Tell students the word **I** is always a capital letter.
- Students will read the sentence and fill in the blank with the word **I** for sentences #1-8. For #9-10, students will write sentences using the word **I**.

Process Writing

Process Writing Lesson #6 for Steps 12 and 13 is found in TM p. 442.

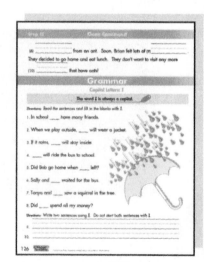

p. 126

Grand Tour I

Day 4

Getting Started

- Collect homework and put stars on Homework Chart. (See TM p. 26.)
- Administer spelling test with Day 3 spelling words in *Grand Tour I*, p. 125. Sentence for dictation: We will eat <u>lunch</u> at noon. (See TM p. 100.)

Grand Tour I, p. 127

Spelling Words
Phonetic Grouping: ch

- Note that all words have **ch** at the **beginning** or **end**. Have students mark words as indicated: (ch)illy
- As a class, read the 10 spelling words and discuss the meanings.
- Have students close their books, and teacher will say each spelling word. Students will say if **ch** is at the **beginning** or **end** of the spelling word.
- Have students copy the 10 spelling words to take home, study, and write in sentences for homework.

Spelling Vocabulary Activities

Crossword Puzzle

- Students will read the clues by the number, find a spelling word that goes with the clue, and write the word by the number.

Word Pairs

- Tell students you will say some sentences, and students will fill in the blank in the second sentence. The sentences are related in some way.

  Sentences to say:

  1. Bees live in a hive.
     Fish live in _____. (water)

  2. When it is night, it is dark.
     When it is day, it is _____. (light)

  3. If you are old, you are an adult.
     If you are very young, you are a _____. (child)

  4. If you are very warm, you are hot.
     If you are very cool, you are _____. (cold)

  5. A carpenter uses a hammer and nails.
     A baseball player uses a ball and _____. (bat)

- Have student read the pairs of sentences and complete the second sentence with a spelling word on page 127.

Rhyming

- Students will write spelling words that rhyme with **best, damp,** and **bunch.**

p. 127

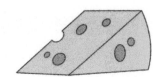

(*Continued on next page*)

Grand Tour I

Day 4 *continued*

p. 128

Grand Tour I, p. 128

Story Comprehension

Healthy Lunches

Have students:

* Underline the 10 spelling words in the story.
* Read the story silently.
* Answer the questions and underline the correct answers.

The Writing Connection

Eating healthy foods is good for you.

*Treasure Chest
Reproducible*

Writing Sentences

* Brainstorm with students a list of healthy foods.
* Have each student draw a treasure chest or give each student a copy of the Treasure Chest Reproducible, TM page 475.
* Students will draw healthy foods inside the treasure chest and write a sentence telling why it is important to eat healthy foods.

Grammar Chalkboard Lesson
Capital Letters

Objective

* Students will know to begin a sentence with a capital letter and know the word **I** is always a capital letter.

Practice/Apply

* Write the sentences on the board. Students will write the sentences correctly.

1. tony and i like to ride bicycles.	Tony and I like to ride bicycles.
2. jerry and i want to play football.	Jerry and I want to play football.
3. am i late for the party?	Am I late for the party?
4. may i walk home with you?	May I walk home with you?
5. tyrone and bill will come, too.	Tyrone and Bill will come, too.

Process Writing

Process Writing Lesson #6 for Steps 12 and 13 is found in TM p. 442.

Day 5

Getting Started

- Collect homework and put stars on Homework Chart. (See TM p. 26.)
- Administer spelling test with Day 4 spelling words in *Grand Tour I*, p. 127. Sentence for dictation: It is a <u>chilly</u> day. (See TM p. 100.)

Just for Fun

- **Figurative language** and **proverbs** are common sayings that are short and can apply to different situations. Here are just a few you and your students can enjoy.

  1. Don't count your chickens until they're hatched.
     (Don't be 100% sure of anything until it has really happened.)
  2. The early bird catches the worm.
     (People who get some place first get the best choices.)
  3. Don't cry over spilt milk.
     (No need to worry and fret about what has already happened.)
  4. An apple a day keeps the doctor away.
     (Eat healthy and stay well.)
  5. Money burns a hole in your pocket.
     (You spend money as fast as you earn it.)

- Write the proverbs on chart paper and keep the chart to add more sayings to it.
- Discuss the proverbs with the students.
- A fun activity is to have each child choose a proverb to illustrate.

Money burns a hole in your pocket.

- There will be proverbs given on Day 5, Steps #12-15. You may want to save some of the drawings to make a class book titled *Figurative Language* or *Proverbs.*

Process Writing

Process Writing Lesson #6 for Steps 12 and 13 is found in TM p. 442.

Grand Tour I

Additional Related Activities for Step 12

Listening and Speaking

1. Comparing with Antonyms

- Read aloud the following comparisons. Ask a student to give an antonym for the underlined word.

    Win is to lose as <u>stop</u> is to _____. (start)
    Much is to little as <u>early</u> is to _____. (late)
    Evening is to morning as <u>good</u> is to _____. (bad)
    Hot is to cold as <u>warm</u> is to _____. (chilly)
    Him is to her as <u>father</u> is to _____. (mother)
    North is to south as <u>no</u> is to _____. (yes)
    New is to old as <u>big</u> is to _____. (little)
    Above is to below as <u>up</u> is to _____. (down)
    Beautiful is to ugly as <u>forward</u> is to _____. (backward)

2. *Around the World* with Nouns and Verbs

- Remind students a **noun** is a **person**, **place**, or **thing**.
    Examples: boy, school, desk

- Remind students a **verb** shows action and is something you can do.
    Examples: running, reading, swimming

- Have a student stand beside another student. The teacher will say a word that is either a noun or a verb.
    Example: apple

- The student who says **noun** first, moves on to the student in the next desk, and the other student sits down in his/her desk.

- Continue the game with the teacher alternating between nouns and verbs.

3. Drawing Pictures with Nouns and Verbs

- Write the lists of nouns and verbs below on the board.

    <u>Nouns</u>

    cat   boy   girl   teacher   baby   sailboat   dog

    <u>Verbs</u>

    drinking   jumping   swinging   hiding   climbing   crying   floating

- Give each student a sheet of drawing paper.
- Have students choose one noun and one verb to illustrate in one picture and write a sentence about the picture.

My <u>cat</u> is <u>climbing</u>
the tree.

4. *Place the Sound in the Train*

- Write Step 12 spelling words on strips of paper for students to place in the train.
- Refer to TM p. 195 for directions for this activity.

NOTES

Overview for Step 13

Objectives

Phonics: To sing *Letter Cluster Phonics Song*, verses 1-2, providing phonics review and/or new instruction for those who need it

Spelling: To spell words with letter clusters **ch**, **er**, **ir**, and **ur**

Grammar: To use a capital letter for first word in sentences, the word **I**, and the months of the year.
To understand synonyms, antonyms, suffix **ly**

Comprehension: To read short stories and answer questions requiring higher level thinking skills

Writing: To write a paragraph
To use the Five Steps of Process Writing, focusing on writing story endings

Suggested Pacing
1 week

Materials
Grand Tour I, pp. 129-136
Letter Cluster Phonics Song Charts 1 and 2

Homework
Daily homework is described in TM p. 99.

Spelling
Daily spelling is described in TM p. 99.

Phonics Games (See TM pp. 40-65.)
Continue to play selected games as needed for reinforcement.

Phonics Song
Letter Cluster Phonics Song, verses 1-2,
     CD track 8 (See TM p. 51.)

Additional Related Activities
Additional activities are found in TM p. 214.

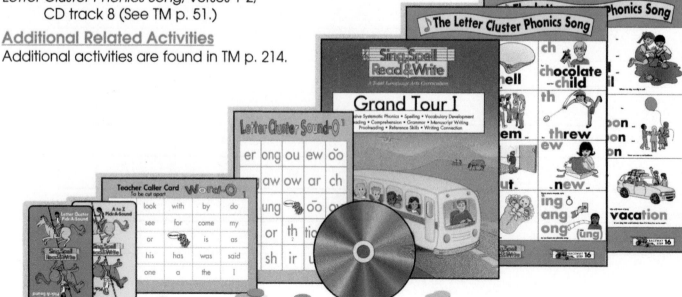

Day 1

Phonics Review

Sing *Letter Cluster Phonics Song*, verses 1-2, CD track 8. (See TM p. 51.)

Grand Tour I, p. 129

Spelling Words
Phonetic Grouping: ch

- Note that each spelling word has the letter cluster **ch** at the **beginning** or **end**. Have students mark each word as indicated: (ch)in
- As a class, read the 10 spelling words and discuss the meanings.
- Have students close their books, and teacher will say each spelling word. Students will say if the **ch** sound is at the **beginning** or **end** of the word.
- Have students copy the 10 spelling words to take home, study, and write in sentences for homework.

Spelling Vocabulary Activities

Synonyms
- Tell students synonyms are words that have nearly the same meaning. **Examples:** gift—present; high—tall; tiny—small
- Students will write a spelling word that means nearly the same as the word in dark print.

Rhyming
- Students will write the two spelling words that **rhyme**.

Word Clues
- Students will write a spelling word for each clue.

Breaking the Code
- Tell students there are many different kinds of codes. This code has a number to represent a letter. **Example:** 1 = C
- Students will use the code to decode the spelling words.

Grand Tour I, p. 130

Grammar

Capital Letters
- Remind students sentences always begin with a capital letter and end with a punctuation mark.
- Students will write the eight sentences correctly.

Process Writing

Process Writing Lesson #6 for Steps 12 and 13 is found in TM p. 442.

p. 129

p. 130

Getting Started

- Collect homework and put stars on Homework Chart. (See TM p. 26.)
- Administer spelling test with Day 1 spelling words in *Grand Tour I*, p. 129. Sentence for dictation: Will you help me <u>chop</u> the wood? (See TM p. 100.)

Grand Tour I, p. 131

Spelling Words
Phonetic Grouping: er

p. 131

- Note that all the spelling words have the letter cluster **er**. The **er** may come at the **beginning**, in the **middle**, or at the **end** of the word. Have students mark each word as indicated: h(er)
- As a class, read the 10 spelling words and discuss the meanings.
- With students, clap the syllables in each word.
- Have students close their books, and teacher will say each word. Students will say if the **er** sound comes in the **beginning**, **middle** or **end** of the word.
- Ask which three words are compound words. (**herself, overcoat, buttercup**)
- Have students copy the 10 spelling words to take home, study, and write in sentences for homework.

Spelling Vocabulary Activities

Cloze
- Students will fill in the blanks with spelling words.

Compound Words
- Students will write three spelling words that are compound words.

Antonyms
- Tell students antonyms are words that mean the **opposite**.
  Examples: find—lose; forget—remember; none—all
- Students will write spelling words that are **opposites** of the words listed.

Word Association
- Students will write the spelling word that is associated with each word listed.

Grand Tour I, p. 132

Story Comprehension

The Field Trip

Students will:

* Underline the seven words in the story.
* Read the story silently.
* Underline the correct answers.

The Writing Connection

Writing a Paragraph

* Brainstorm with students about places they have gone on a school trip.
* Make a list of the places they have visited.
* Tell students a **paragraph** is a group of sentences (two or more) that tells about one thing. That one thing is called a **subject**.

Students will:

* Write a paragraph about a school trip they have taken.
* Tell **where** they went on the trip, **when** they went on the trip, **what** they saw, and **how** they liked the trip.
* Illustrate the paragraph.

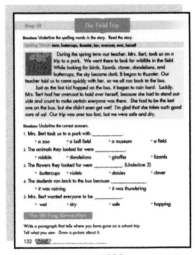

p. 132

Grammar Chalkboard Lesson
Capital Letters

Objective

* Students will know a sentence begins with a capital letter and the word **I** is always written with a capital letter.

Practice/Apply

* Write the sentences on the board. Students will write the sentences correctly.

1. my friend and i walked to the store   My friend and I walked to the store.

2. can i help you with your work   Can I help you with your work?

3. al and i ran a race   Al and I ran a race.

4. kris and i will be late   Kris and I will be late.

5. am i on this team   Am I on this team?

Process Writing

Process Writing Lesson #6 for Steps 12 and 13 is found in TM p. 442.

Day 3

Getting Started

- Collect homework and put stars on Homework Chart. (See TM p. 26.)
- Administer spelling test with Day 2 spelling words in *Grand Tour I*, p. 131. Sentence for dictation: Do you hear <u>thunder</u> outside? (See TM p. 100.)

Grand Tour I, p. 133

Spelling Words
Phonetic Grouping: ir

- Note that each spelling word has the letter cluster **ir**. Tell students you cannot hear any difference between **er** and **ir**. Have students mark each word as indicated: **di̅rt**
- As a class, read the 10 spelling words and discuss the meanings.
- Ask students which words have a suffix added to a root word. (dir**ty**, firm**ly**, swirl**ing**, chirp**ing**)
- Have students copy the 10 spelling words to take home, study, and write in sentences for homework.

Spelling Vocabulary Activities

p. 133

Silly Questions
- Have students read the silly questions, write the underlined spelling word on the line, and write **yes** or **no** to answer the question.

Word Meanings
- Tell students **ly** is a suffix and means **in that way**.
  Examples: Firmly means in a firm way.
  Slowly means in a slow way.

- Students will write a spelling word for each word clue.

Syllables
- Say each spelling word and have students clap the number of syllables.
- Students will write each spelling word in the correct box.

Grand Tour I, p. 134

Grammar

Capital Letters: Months

- Introduce the months of the year by reading the months in consecutive order.
- Point out that each month begins with a capital letter.
- Discuss with students the symbol by each month and what the symbols mean. Discuss other appropriate holidays or activities such as Saint Patrick's Day, etc.
- Show students how to write a date in number only.
  Example: January 6, 2000 is 01-06-00.

- Students will write the name of the month to answer each question and then write the months in order.

The Writing Connection

Writing a Paragraph

- Remind students a paragraph is two or more sentences telling about the same subject.
- Brainstorm with students about favorite things they like to do for their birthday.

  Have students:

  - Write a paragraph telling about their favorite birthday activity.
  - Tell **what** the activity is.
  - Tell **when** they have done this special activity.
  - Tell **why** it is a favorite activity.
  - Illustrate the paragraph.

Process Writing

Process Writing Lesson #6 for Steps 12 and 13 is found in TM p. 442.

p. 134

Day 4

Getting Started

- Collect homework and put stars on Homework Chart. (See TM p. 26.)
- Administer spelling test with Day 3 spelling words in *Grand Tour I*, p. 133. Sentence for dictation: My <u>shirt</u> is wet. (See TM p. 100.)

Grand Tour I, p. 135

Spelling Words
Phonetic Grouping: ur

- Note that all the words have letter cluster **ur**. Have students mark each word as indicated: c(ur)b
- As a class, read the 10 spelling words and discuss the meanings.
- Ask students which word is a compound word. (**curbside**)
- Have students copy the 10 spelling words to take home, study, and write in sentences for homework.

Spelling Vocabulary Activities

Word Search

- Tell students all the spelling words for this lesson are hidden in this puzzle. The words go across or down.
- Have students circle each word as they find it.

Riddles

- Have students write a spelling word to answer each riddle.

The Writing Connection

Writing Riddles

- Have students write their own riddles.
- Schedule a time for each child to share his or her riddle.

Grand Tour I, p. 136

Story Comprehension

The Purple Car

Students will:

- Underline the eight spelling words in the story.
- Read the story silently.
- Read the questions and underline the correct answers.

The Writing Connection

Students will:

- Visualize a funny-looking car.
- Write a list of words that could be used to describe the funny-looking car.
- Draw a picture of the car.

p. 135

p. 136

Grammar Chalkboard Lesson
Capital Letters: Months

Objective
Students will:

• Know the sequence of the months.

• Know the names of the months begin with capital letters.

Practice/Apply

• Write the sentences on the board. Students will write each sentence and fill in the blank with the correct month. Have students refer to the chart of months and pictures in *Grand Tour I*, page 134.

> 1. <u>December</u> is the last month of the year.
>
> 2. October comes after <u>September</u>.
>
> 3. <u>July</u> comes before August.
>
> 4. May comes after <u>April</u>.
>
> 5. <u>March</u> is the third month of the year.

Process Writing

Process Writing Lesson #6 for Steps 12 and 13 is found in TM p. 442.

Day 5

Getting Started

• Collect homework and put stars on Homework Chart. (See TM p. 26.)

• Administer spelling test with Day 4 spelling words in *Grand Tour I*, p. 135. Sentence for dictation: Park the car at the <u>curbside</u>. (See TM p. 100.)

Just for Fun

• **Figurative language** and **proverbs** are common sayings that are short and can apply to different situations.

• Here are a few more proverbs for you and your students to enjoy:

1. A penny saved is a penny earned. (Use your money wisely.)
2. If the shoe fits, wear it. (If the message is for you, listen to it and make changes.)
3. Two heads are better than one. (Two people's thoughts and input is more valuable than one alone.)
4. A quitter never wins and a winner never quits. (You have to be diligent and dedicated to whatever you do to be a winner.)
5. Make hay while the sun shines. (Take advantage of each moment.)

• See TM p. 203 for directions for illustrating and making a book.

(Continued on next page)

Grand Tour I

Process Writing

Process Writing Lesson #6 for Steps 12 and 13 is found in TM p. 442.

Additional Related Activities for Step 13

Listening and Speaking

1. Synonym Challenge

- Divide the class into two teams.
- Have each team stand in a line facing each other as in a spelling bee.
- Say a word to the first player on Team 1.
- The player must respond with a synonym in order to continue standing. If the player cannot respond with a synonym, the player must sit down and the game continues with Team 2.
- Rotate between saying a word to Team 1, Team 2, Team 1, etc.

Synonyms to call: (Accept any reasonable answers.)

1. entire — (all)	16. go — (leave)
2. anger — (mad)	17. happy — (glad)
3. behind — (back)	18. difficult — (hard)
4. under — (below)	19. help — (assist)
5. begin — (start)	20. high — (tall)
6. call — (shout)	21. rush — (hurry)
7. car — (automobile)	22. idea — (thought)
8. city — (town)	23. ill — (sick)
9. close — (shut)	24. injure — (hurt)
10. country — (nation)	25. job — (work)
11. cure — (heal)	26. right — (correct)
12. separate — (split)	27. kind — (nice)
13. end — (complete)	28. large — (big)
14. fix — (repair)	29. leave — (go)
15. gift — (present)	30. listen — (hear)

2. Synonym Pictures

- Give each student a 9" x 12" sheet of drawing paper.
- Have students fold the paper in half.
- Students will write a pair of synonyms in each block of paper and draw a picture to illustrate each pair.
- It's fun to put these together into a class book.

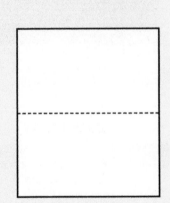

car-automobile

circle-round

NOTES

Grand Tour I

Overview for Step 14

Objectives

Phonics: To sing *Letter Cluster Phonics Song*, verses 1-2, providing phonics review and/or new instruction for those who need it

Spelling: To spell words with letter clusters **th** (voiced); **th** (unvoiced); **tch**

Grammar: To write the names of months with capital letters

To know when to add **s** or **es** to make a plural

Comprehension: To read short stories and answer questions requiring higher level thinking skills

Writing: To write a title for a story

To use the Five Steps of Process Writing, focusing on strategies to use for correcting spelling mistakes

Suggested Pacing
1 Week

Materials
Grand Tour I, pp. 137-144
Letter Cluster Phonics Song Charts 1 and 2

Homework
Daily homework is described in TM p. 99.

Spelling
Daily spelling is described in TM p. 99.

Phonics Games (See TM pp. 40-65.)
Continue to play selected games as needed for reinforcement.

Phonics Song
Letter Cluster Phonics Song, verses 1-2,
CD track 8 (See TM p. 51.)

Additional Related Activities
Additional activities are found in TM p. 224.

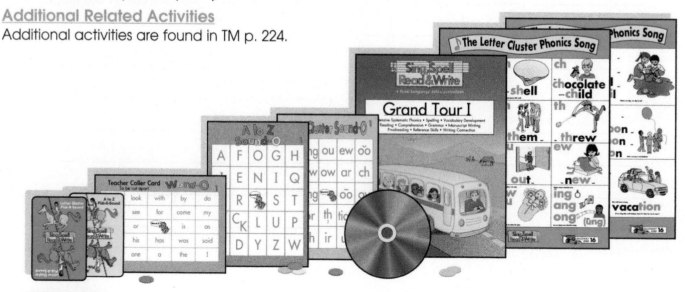

Day 1

Phonics Review

Sing *Letter Cluster Phonics Song*, verses 1-2, CD track 8. (See TM p. 51.)

Grand Tour I, p. 137

Spelling Words
Phonetic Grouping: th (voiced)

- Note that all words begin with **th** and #8-10 are **homophones**. Have students mark each word as indicated: (t)hen

- Tell students **homophones** are words that sound alike, but are spelled differently and have different meanings. Call attention to **they're, their,** and **there.**

- As a class, read the 10 spelling words and discuss the meanings.

- Have students copy the 10 spelling words to take home, study, and write in sentences for homework.

Spelling Vocabulary Activities

Word Scramble
- Students will unscramble the letters to make a spelling word.

Cloze
- Student will fill in the blanks with spelling words.

Rhyming
- Students will write a spelling word that rhymes with each word.

Homophones
- Tell students **homophones** are words that sound the same but have different meanings and usually different spellings.
  Example: aunt—ant, hear—here, be—bee

- Talk about the **homophone** spelling words: **their, there, they're.** Discuss the clues given on page 137 to help students remember the meaning for each **homophone.**

- Students will write the correct **homophone** in each blank.

Grand Tour I, p. 138

Grammar

Capital Letters: Months
- Remind students the months of the year always begin with a capital letter.

Students will:

- Circle the names of the months in the word search and print a capital letter on top of the first letter of the month.

- Write the names of the months on the lines provided as the words are found.

Process Writing

Process Writing Lesson #7 for Steps 14 and 15 is found in TM p. 444.

p. 137

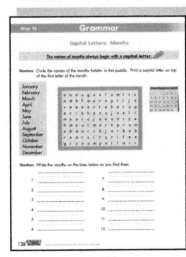
p. 138

Grand Tour I

Getting Started

- Collect homework and put stars on Homework Chart. (See TM p. 26.)
- Administer spelling test with Day 1 spelling words in *Grand Tour I*, p. 137. Sentence for dictation: <u>They</u> will be late. (See TM p. 100.)

Grand Tour I, p. 139

Spelling Words
Phonetic Grouping: th (unvoiced)

- Note that each word has the letter cluster **th (unvoiced)** at the beginning or end. Have students mark each word as indicated: (th)anks
- As a class, read the 10 spelling words and discuss the meanings.
- Have students copy the 10 spelling words to take home, study, and write in sentences for homework.

Spelling Vocabulary Activities

Word Meanings
- Students will write a spelling word for each meaning.

Rhyming
- Students will write a spelling word that rhymes with each word listed.
- Students will write a spelling word that rhymes with each underlined word.

Cloze
- Students will fill in the blanks with spelling words.

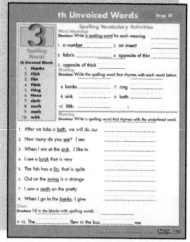

p. 139

Grand Tour I, p. 140

Story Comprehension

Mr. Dragonfly and Miss Luna Moth
Students will:

- Underline the eight spelling words in the story.
- Read the story silently.
- Underline the correct answers.

The Writing Connection

Illustrating a Story
- Have students draw a picture of Miss Luna Moth dressed for the ball.

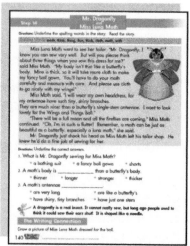

p. 140

Day 2 *continued*

Grammar Chalkboard Lesson
Homophones: their, they're, there

Objective
- Students will know how to use **their**, **they're**, and **there** correctly.

Practice/Apply
- Write sentences on the board. Students will write the sentences with the correct **homophone**.

> they're   there   their
>
> 1. __They're__ coming to visit us.
> 2. I like __their__ new car.
> 3. __They're__ going to be here later.
> 4. Do you live __there__?
> 5. Put the box over __there__.
> 6. We will go to __their__ house.

Process Writing

Process Writing Lesson #7 for Steps 14 and 15 is found in TM p. 444.

Grand Tour I

Getting Started

- Collect homework and put stars on Homework Chart. (See TM p. 26.)
- Administer spelling test with Day 2 spelling words in *Grand Tour I*, p. 139. Sentence for dictation: I like my <u>math</u> class. (See TM p. 100.)

Grand Tour I, p. 141

Spelling Words
Phonetic Grouping: tch

- Note that words #1, 3, 5, 7, 9 are root words ending in the letter cluster **tch**. Words #2, 4, 6, 8, 10 are the same root words made into plurals by adding **es**. Have students mark each word as indicated: **ma(tch)**
- As a class, read the 10 spelling words and discuss the meanings.
- Have students copy the 10 spelling words to take home, study, and write in sentences for homework.

Spelling Vocabulary Activities

Word Usage
- Students will read each sentence and write the correct form of the word to complete the sentence.

Singular and Plural
- Tell students singular means one and plural means more than one.
- Most plural words end in **s** or **es**.
- If a word ends in **ch**, add an **es** to make a plural.
- Tell students **es** added to the end of a root word adds a syllable.
- Say each spelling word and have students clap the number of syllables.
- Students will write five spelling words that are plurals and five spelling words that are singular.

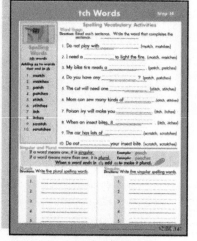

p. 141

Grand Tour I, p. 142

Grammar

Plurals
- Tell students if a word ends in **sh**, **ch**, **s**, **x**, or **zz**, add an **es** to change it to a **plural** to mean **more than one**.
- If the word does not end in any of the letters listed above, add **s** to change it to a **plural**.
- Have students read the words and add **s** or **es** to each word to make a plural. Write the plural word in the space.

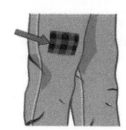

Process Writing

Process Writing Lesson #7 for Steps 14 and 15 is found in TM p. 444.

p. 142

Day 4

Getting Started

- Collect homework and put stars on Homework Chart. (See TM p. 26.)
- Administer spelling test with Day 3 spelling words in *Grand Tour I*, p. 141. Sentence for dictation: Do not play with <u>matches</u>. (See TM p. 100.)

Grand Tour I, p. 143

Spelling Words
Phonetic Grouping: tch

- Note that words #1, 3, 5, 7, 9 end in **tch** and #2, 4, 6, 8, 10 are the same root words made into plurals by adding **es**. Have students mark each word as indicated: **latch**
- When a word ends in **ch**, add **es** to make a plural.
- As a class, read the 10 spelling words and discuss the meanings.
- Have students copy the 10 spelling words to take home, study, and write in sentences for homework.

Spelling Vocabulary Activities

Crossword Puzzle
- Students will read the clues by the number, find a spelling word that goes with the clue, and write the word by the number in the crossword puzzle.

Singular and Plural
- Tell students **singular** means **one** and **plural** means **more than one**. Most plurals end in **s** or **es**.
- Have students write five spelling words that are plural and five spelling words that are singular.

Grand Tour I, p. 144

Story Comprehension

Students will:

- Underline all the **ch** words in the story.
- Read story silently.
- Answer the questions.

p. 143

p. 144

(Continued on next page)

Grand Tour I

The Writing Connection

Writing a Story Title

- Discuss the difference between the main idea of a story and a story detail.
- A main idea is like an umbrella that tells what the whole story is about.
  Example: *A Day at the Fair* could be a main idea.
- A story detail tells one thing you did at the fair.
  Example: Ride the roller coaster.
- Tell students the title of a story is more like the main idea and not a story detail.
- Have students write a story title at the top of page 144.

Main Idea

Grammar Chalkboard Lesson
Plurals

Objective

- Students will know if a word ends in **sh**, **ch**, **s**, **x**, or **zz**, add **es** to change it to a **plural**.

Practice/Apply

- Write the sentences on the board. Students will write the sentences with the **plural** form of the word.

1. Will you wash the (dish)?	Will you wash the dishes?
2. My dad has two (car).	My dad has two cars.
3. We visited lots of (farm).	We visited lots of farms.
4. Tommy picked the (peach).	Tommy picked the peaches.
5. The (box) are too small.	The boxes are too small.

Process Writing

Process Writing Lesson #7 for Steps 14 and 15 is found in TM p. 444.

Mon Tues Wed Thurs Fri

Day 5

Getting Started

- Collect homework and put stars on Homework Chart. (See TM p. 26.)
- Administer spelling test with Day 4 spelling words in *Grand Tour I*, p. 143.
  Sentence for dictation: The man dug a <u>ditch</u>. (See TM p. 100.)

Just for Fun

- **Figurative language** and **proverbs** are common sayings that are short and
  can apply to different situations. Here are a few for you and your students
  to enjoy.

1. Early to bed, early to rise, makes a man healthy, wealthy, and wise.
   (Get a good night's sleep, get up early and work hard and you will
   be a better person.)
2. Every cloud has a silver lining.
   (Everything has some good to it.)
3. Two wrongs don't make a right.
   (If someone does you wrong, it still isn't right for you to do that
   person wrong.)
4. Actions speak louder than words.
   (People will pay more attention to what you do than the words you speak.)
5. Out of the frying pan into the fire.
   (Getting out of a bad situation into a worse situation.)

- See Step 12, TM p. 203, for directions for making and illustrating a book.

Process Writing

Process Writing Lesson #7 for Steps 14 and 15 is found in TM p. 444.

Additional Related Activities for Step 14

Listening and Speaking

1. *Words in the Hopper*

- To reinforce **homophones**, **synonyms**, and **antonyms**, make a large kangaroo (directions below) and dress it in a carpenter's apron of paper using a contrasting color. Add three pockets to the apron and attach them so they stand out. Label them **homophones**, **synonyms**, and **antonyms**.

Directions for kangaroo:

- Make a transparency of the Reproducible TM p. 476.
- Use an overhead projector to trace the kangaroo on a large piece of tagboard or poster board.
- Complete the kangaroo with apron and pockets.

Write these pairs of words on the chalkboard.

their – there	south – north	cut – chop
cook – bake	rich – wealthy	run – walk
hear – here	adult – child	follow – lead
heap – pile	pick – choose	rest – work
remember – forget	him – her	none – all
ate – eight	beat – beet	I – eye
call – yell	high – tall	ill – sick
for – four	close – shut	happy – glad

- Give each child a strip of white paper on which to write a pair of **homophones**, **synonyms**, or **antonyms**.

- Have each child read his/her pair of words to the class and place them in the appropriate pocket.

NOTES

Grand Tour I

Overview for Step 15

Objectives

Phonics: To sing *Letter Cluster Phonics Song*, verses 1-2, providing phonics review and/or new instruction to those who need it

Spelling: To spell words with letter clusters **ow** and **ou**

Grammar: To write the days of the week with capital letters
To learn antonyms and synonyms
To understand suffixes **ed**, **less**, **ly**, and **ing**

Comprehension: To read short stories and answer questions requiring higher level thinking skills

Writing: To use the Five Steps of Process Writing, focusing on strategies to use for correcting spelling mistakes

Suggested Pacing
1 week

Materials
Grand Tour I, pp. 145-152
Letter Cluster Phonics Song Charts 1 and 2

Homework
Daily homework is described in TM p. 99.

Spelling
Daily spelling is described in TM p. 99.

Phonics Games (See TM pp. 40-65.)
Continue to play selected games as needed for reinforcement.

Phonics Song
Letter Cluster Phonics Song, verses 1-2,
  CD track 8 (See TM p. 51.)

Additional Related Activities
Additional activities are found in TM p. 234.

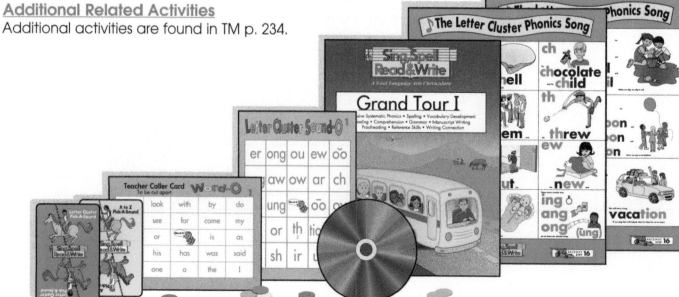

Day 1

Phonics Review

Sing *Letter Cluster Phonics Song*, verses 1-2, CD track 8. (See TM p. 51.)

Grand Tour I, p. 145

Spelling Words
Phonetic Grouping: ow

- Note that each word has the letter cluster **ow**. Have students mark each word as indicated: **h(ow)**
- As a class, read the 10 spelling words and discuss the meanings.
- Have students copy the 10 spelling words to take home, study, and write in sentences for homework.

Spelling Vocabulary Activities

Antonyms

- Remind students that **antonyms** are **opposites**.
  Examples: big—little; day—night

- Have students write a spelling word that is the **opposite** of the words listed.

Compound Word

- Tell students a **compound word** is two words put together to make one word.
- Students will write the spelling word that is a compound word.

Word Clue

- Students will write a spelling word for each clue.

Synonyms

- Remind students that synonyms are words that are spelled differently but mean almost the same.
  Examples: big—huge

- Students will write the spelling word that means the same as **permission**.

Cloze

- Students will write the missing spelling words.

Syllables

- Remind students that **syllables** are the number of word parts you hear in a word.
- As a class, say each spelling word and clap for each **syllable**.
- Students will write each spelling word and the number of **syllables** they hear in each word.

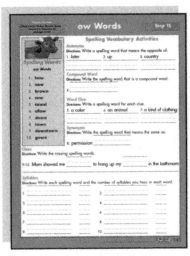

p. 145

(Continued on next page)

Grand Tour I

Day 1 *continued*

Grand Tour I, p. 146

Grammar

Capital Letters: Days of the Week

- Point out to students that the first day of the week is Sunday, not Monday.

- With students, read the names of the days of the week and tell them each day should beginning with a capital letter.

- Students will read and complete each sentence with a day of the week.

- Next, students will write the days of the week in order.

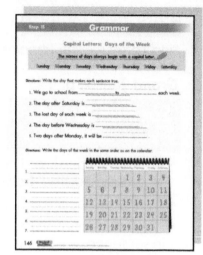

p. 146

Process Writing

Process Writing Lesson #7 for Steps 14 and 15 is found in TM p. 444.

Day 2

Getting Started

- Collect homework and put stars on Homework Chart. (See TM p. 26.)

- Administer spelling test with Day 1 spelling words in *Grand Tour I*, p. 145. Sentence for dictation: The red <u>towel</u> is wet. (See TM p. 100.)

Grand Tour I, p. 147

Spelling Words

Phonetic Grouping: ow

- Note that each word has letter cluster **ow**. Have students mark each word as indicated: **clown**

- As a class, read the 10 spelling words and discuss the meanings.

- Have students copy the 10 spelling words to take home, study, and write in sentences for homework.

p. 147

Day 2 *continued*

Spelling Vocabulary Activities

Cloze

* Students will fill in the blanks with spelling words.

Rhyming

* Tell students rhyming words are words that end in the same vowel and consonant sounds. Ask students to listen as you say two words. If the two words rhyme, children will stamp their feet. If the two words do not rhyme, they will remain silent.

  Words to call:

      drown—brown (stamp feet)   shower—tower (stamp feet)
      red—black (silent)   bike—like (stamp feet)
      growl—howl (stamp feet)   note—flute (silent)
      coat—goat (stamp feet)   feed—cake (silent)
      run—hop (silent)   late—date (stamp feet)

* Students will write four spelling words that rhyme with **brown**; three spelling words that rhyme with **fowl**; one spelling word that rhymes with **tower**.

Suffixes

* Tell students a **suffix** is added to the end of a root word and a **suffix** changes the meaning of a word.

* The suffix **ed** means **in the past** and changes a word to mean it has already happened.
  Example: wash—washed

* Students will write the spelling words that have the suffix **ed** or **ing**.

Grand Tour I, p. 148

Story Comprehension

The Clown's Flowers

Students will:

* Underline the six spelling words in the story.

* Read the story silently and answer the questions.

The Writing Connection

Students will draw a picture of the clown's bathtub with flowers in it.

p. 148

(Continued on next page)

Grand Tour I

Grammar Chalkboard Lesson
Capital Letters: Days of the Week

Objective

Students will:
- Know the days of the week begin with capital letters.
- Learn the sequence of the days of the week.

Practice/Apply

- Write the scrambled spelling of the days of the week on the board. Students will unscramble the letters to write the days of the week, beginning each with a capital letter. Then, students will write the days of the week in sequence.

1. aydonm	Monday	Sunday
2. seutayd	Tuesday	Monday
3. dyafir	Friday	Tuesday
4. seweddnya	Wednesday	Wednesday
5. tasruayd	Saturday	Thursday
6. rusthyad	Thursday	Friday
7. dysuna	Sunday	Saturday

Process Writing

Process Writing Lesson #7 for Steps 14 and 15 is found in TM p. 444.

Day 3

Getting Started

- Collect homework and put stars on Homework Chart. (See TM p. 26.)
- Administer spelling test with Day 2 spelling words in *Grand Tour I*, p. 147. Sentence for dictation: Did you hear the dog <u>howl</u>? (See TM p. 100.)

Grand Tour I, pp. 149-150

Spelling Words
Phonetic Grouping: ou

- Note that all words have the letter cluster **ou**. Have students mark each word as indicated: **gro͝und**
- As a class, read the 10 spelling words and discuss the meanings.
- Have students copy the 10 spelling words to take home, study, and write in sentences for homework.

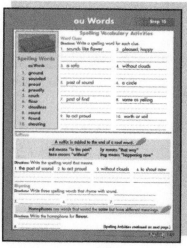

p. 149

Day 3 continued

Spelling Vocabulary Activities

Word Clues
- Students will write a spelling word for each clue.

Suffixes
- Tell students a **suffix** is added to the end of a root word.
- Tell students **ed** added to the end of a root word makes the word mean **in the past**.
  Example: cook—cooked
- Ask students to volunteer words with the suffix **ed** and write them on the board.
- Continue in this same manner with **less**, **ly**, and **ing**.
- Students will write the spelling word that fits each definition listed.

Rhyming
- Students will write three spelling words that rhyme with **sound**.

Homophones
- Tell students **homophones** are words that sound the same, but are spelled differently and have different meanings.
  Example: pair—pear
- Say these riddles and ask students to answer with a pair of homophones.

    1) Name two words that sound the same, but one is another name for a rabbit and the other grows on your head. (hare—hair)
    2) Name two words that sound the same, but one is a bloom on a plant and the other is used to make bread. (flower—flour)
    3) Name two words that sound the same, but one is a big furry animal and the other means to be without clothes or a cover. (bear—bare)

- Students will write the homophone for **flower**.

Cloze
- Students will write the missing spelling words on page 150.

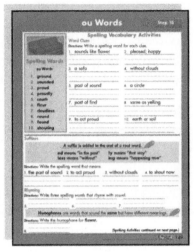

p. 149

Grand Tour I, p. 150

Grammar

Capital Letters: Days of the Week
- Tell students the days of the week always begin with a capital letter.
- Students will write the day that makes each sentence true.

Process Writing

Process Writing Lesson #7 for Steps 14 and 15 is found in TM p. 444.

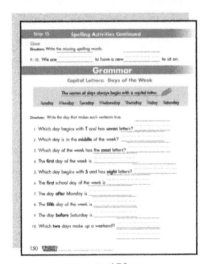

p. 150

Grand Tour I

Day 4

Getting Started

- Collect homework and put stars on Homework Chart. (See TM p. 26.)
- Administer spelling test with Day 3 spelling words in *Grand Tour I*, p. 151. Sentence for dictation: The <u>ground</u> is wet. (See TM p. 100.)

Grand Tour I, p. 151

Spelling Words
Phonetic Grouping: ou

- Note that each word has the letter cluster **ou**. Have students mark each word as indicated: **about**
- As a class, read the 10 spelling words and discuss the meanings.
- Have students copy the 10 spelling words to take home, study, and write in sentences for homework.

Spelling Vocabulary Activities

Crossword Puzzle

- Students will read the clues by the number, find a spelling word that goes with the clue, and write the word by the number in the crossword puzzle.

Word Fun

- Students will write the missing spelling word.

Grand Tour I, p. 152

Story Comprehension

The Scout Trip

- Have students underline the nine spelling words in the story.
- Tell them today's story is about farm animals.
- Talk about different names for adult and baby animals.

hog or pig—piglet	goose—gosling
cat—kitten	sheep—lamb
dog—puppy	deer—fawn
duck—duckling	hen—chick
horse—colt	cow—calf
goat—kid	bear—cub

- Students will read the story and fill in the correct answer word from the box.

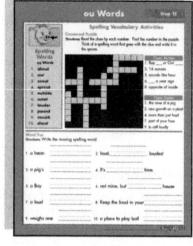

p. 151

p. 152

- Tell students that they will play a detective game with word pairs. They will need to use clues and find missing words. Every time the class finds a missing word, they get a point. Ten points end the game. Remind students to think how the first pair of words go together. Make the second pair go together in the same way. Accept any reasonable answers.

> apple—red; banana—(yellow)
> up—down; hot—(cold)
> finger—hand; toe—(foot)
> small—little; big—(large, huge)
> stove—hot; refrigerator—(cold)
> fast—quick; happy—(glad, joyful)
> old—new; in—(out)
> shoe—foot; glove—(hand)
> pencil—write; brush—(paint)
> unhappy—sad; pretty—(beautiful)
> sour—sweet; dirty—(clean)
> talk—talking; walk—(walking)
> read—book; sing—(song)
> high—up; low—(down)

- If necessary, repeat the list if the class has not earned 10 points. Help the students to think through the analogies by asking leading questions and prompting.
Example: The words given are pencil—write; brush—_____. Ask "How do pencil and write go together?" (You use a pencil to write.) Ask "What is missing from the second pair?" (You use a brush to _____?) (paint)

Process Writing

Process Writing Lesson #8 for Steps 16 and 17 is found in TM p. 447.

Additional Related Activities for Step 17

Listening and Speaking

1. *Toss Out* Game

- Name sets of objects slowly. Select students to say which object does not belong with the rest and should be tossed out. Some suggested groups:

> pizza, hot dog, <u>truck</u>, hamburger
> green, <u>globe</u>, yellow, blue
> apple, grape, strawberry, <u>pencil</u>
> under, <u>telephone</u>, over, above
> whisper, whisker, why, <u>chair</u>
> eye, ear, <u>tree</u>, nose

(Continued on next page)

Additional Related Activities *continued*

2. Analogy Detective

- Tell the students that today they will make **analogies**. They won't need paper, paste, or crayons. They will just need brainpower. Explain that an **analogy** is a special kind of sentence that shows how words go together. Write the following sentence on the chalkboard:

  <u>Apple</u> is to <u>red</u> as <u>banana</u> is to _____.

- Ask the students to think how **apple** and **red** go together. What word goes with **banana** in the same way? **(yellow)** Call on a student to provide the missing word. Fill in the blank with the word **yellow**. Tell the students that they have just made their first **analogy**. Write an **analogy frame** on the chalkboard as follows:

_____ is to _____ as _____ is to _____.

- Explain that **analogies** always use these words. Read the following analogy while pointing to the corresponding spaces and words on the chalkboard:

  <u>Kitten</u> is to <u>cat</u> as <u>puppy</u> is to _____. **(dog)**

- Tell the class they will earn points for completing analogies, just as they did in the earlier detective game. Some suggested analogies:

  Hot is to **cold** as **big** is to **(little)**.
  Pretty is to **ugly** as **out** is to **(in)**.
  Bird is to **nest** as **spider** is to **(web)**.
  Go is to **leave** as **gift** is to **(present)**.
  All is to **every** as **finish** is to **(end)**.
  Begin is to **start** as **shut** is to **(close)**.
  Run is to **fast** as **crawl** is to **(slow)**.
  Pizza is to **eat** as **book** is to **(read)**.
  Rose is to **flower** as **peach** is to **(fruit)**.
  Man is to **walk** as **airplane** is to **(fly)**.

- You may also use word pairs from the spelling vocabulary activities.

3. A Paper Quilt

Materials: crayons and a piece of 6" x 6" white drawing paper for each student.

- Tell the students about quilts and quilt patterns. Explain that quilts are used on beds, just as blankets are. Quilts are made of small pieces of colorful cloth sewn together to make a design. There are many different quilt patterns. If possible, bring in pictures or a real quilt for students to examine.

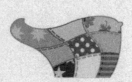

- Give each student a square of white drawing paper. Students will make a crayon design that fills their square completely.

- Arrange the completed designs into a "quilt" on bulletin board paper. Hang the finished project for an attractive display.

NOTES

Grand Tour I

Overview for Step 18

Objectives

Spelling: To spell words with letter cluster **ar**

Grammar: To know that names of schools, streets, towns, states, and countries begin with a capital letter

To know that compound words are two words put together to make one word

Comprehension: To read short stories and answer questions requiring higher level thinking skills

Writing: To write silly sentences and riddles

To use the Five Steps of Process Writing, focusing on editing run-on sentences

Suggested Pacing

1 week

Materials

Grand Tour I, pp. 169-176

Homework

Daily homework is described in TM p. 99.

Spelling

Daily spelling is described in TM p. 99.

Phonics Game

Word-O (See TM p. 58.)

Phonics Songs (See TM pp. 40-65.)

Continue to sing selected songs as needed for reinforcement.

Additional Related Activities

Additional activities are found in TM p. 265.

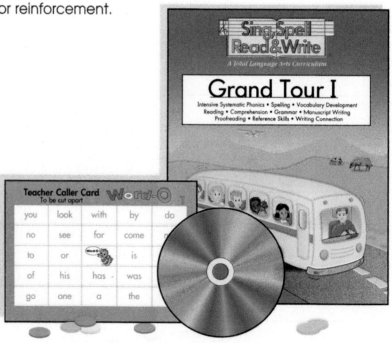

Day 1

Grand Tour I, p. 169

Spelling Words
Phonetic Grouping: ar

- Note that each word has letter cluster **ar**. Have students mark each word as indicated: a̲r̲t̲

- Have students close their books and the teacher will say each spelling word. Students will say if the **ar** is at the **beginning**, **middle**, or **end** of the word.

- As a class, read the 10 spelling words and discuss the meanings.

- Have students copy the 10 spelling words to take home, study, and write in sentences for homework.

p. 169

Spelling Vocabulary Activities

Silly Questions
- Ask the silly question, "Can a tree run?"
- The answer is **no** because a tree is planted and cannot move.
- Students will read each sentence, write the underlined spelling word, and answer the question **yes** or **no**.

Word Meanings
- Students will write spelling words to fit the meanings.

The Writing Connection

Writing Silly Sentences
- Students will write two silly sentences and share them with the class.

Grand Tour I, p. 170

Grammar

Capital Letters: Names
- Ask a volunteer to tell you the name of the street he/she lives on. Write the name of the street on the chalkboard, modeling the proper way to write the names of streets.

- Model writing the names of the city and state in which your school is located.

- Model the proper way to write the name of your school.

- Students will write the names of the streets, cities, states, and schools with capital letters.

p. 170

Process Writing

Process Writing Lesson #9 for Steps 18 and 19 is found in TM p. 449.

Grand Tour I

Day 2

Getting Started

- Collect homework and put stars on Homework Chart. (See TM p.26.)
- Administer spelling test with Day 1 spelling words in *Grand Tour I*, p. 169. Sentence for dictation: We live on a <u>farm</u>. (See TM p. 100.)

Grand Tour I, p. 171

Spelling Words
Phonetic Grouping: ar

- Note that all words have letter cluster **ar**. Have students mark each word as indicated: (ar)my
- Have students close their books and the teacher will say each spelling word. Students will say if the **ar** is at the **beginning** or **middle** of the word.
- As a class, read the 10 spelling words and discuss the meanings.
- Have students copy the 10 spelling words to take home, study, and write in sentences for homework.

p. 171

Spelling Vocabulary Activities

Cloze
- Students will fill in the blanks with spelling words.

<u>ar</u> Words
- Students will write the ten spelling words and circle the **vowel + r** sound in each word.

Grand Tour I, p. 172

Story Comprehension

Mark's Trip to the Farm
Have students:
- Underline the 10 spelling words in the story.
- Read the story silently.
- Underline the correct answer and write the word on the line.
- In words #1-7 students will fill in the blank with a word from the shaded box.

p. 172

Grammar Chalkboard Lesson
Capital Letters

Objective
- Students will know that names of schools, streets, towns, states, and countries begin with a capital letter.

Practice/Apply
- Write the words below on the board. Students will write the words with correct capital letters.

1. washington elementary school	Washington Elementary School
2. bayview avenue	Bayview Avenue
3. tarpon springs, florida	Tarpon Springs, Florida
4. canada	Canada
5. oak park high school	Oak Park High School

Process Writing

Process Writing Lesson #9 for Steps 18 and 19 is found in TM p. 449.

Day 3

Getting Started

- Collect homework and put stars on Homework Chart. (See TM p. 26.)
- Administer spelling test with Day 2 spelling words in *Grand Tour I*, p. 171. Sentence for dictation: The hen is in the <u>barnyard</u>. (See TM p. 100.)

Grand Tour I, p. 173

Spelling Words
Phonetic Grouping: ar

- Note that each word has letter cluster **ar**. Have students mark each word as indicated: **Mar̄s**
- Tell students Mars is written with a capital letter because Mars is the name of a planet.
- Note that words #3, 6, and 9 are compound words. Discuss how the two words within compound words #6 and 9 are related.
  Example: A starfish is shaped like a star.
- Point out that sometimes the two words within a compound are not related.
  Example: outsmart

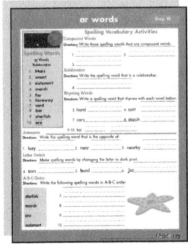

p. 173

(Continued on next page)

Grand Tour I

Day 3 continued

- Call attention to rulebreaker **are**.
- As a class, read the 10 spelling words and discuss the meanings.
- Have students copy the 10 spelling words to take home, study, and write in sentences for homework.

Spelling Vocabulary Activities

Compound Words
- Students will write three spelling words that are compound words.

Rulebreaker
- Students will write the spelling word that is a rulebreaker.

Rhyming Words
- Ask students to name pairs of rhyming words and tell why the words **rhyme**.
  Example: Rag and **bag** rhyme because they both end in the same vowel and consonant (**ag**).
- Students will write a spelling word that rhymes with each word listed.

Antonyms
- Students will write a spelling word that is the opposite of the words listed.

Letter Switch
- Write **t**ent, **p**ark, and **s**oon on the board. Invite a student to change the underlined letter to another letter to make a new word.
- On page 173 students will make spelling words by changing the letter in dark print.

ABC Order
- Students will write the four spelling words in **ABC order**.

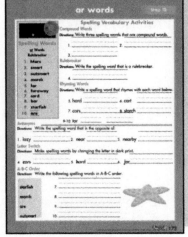

p. 173

Grand Tour I, p. 174

Grammar

Compound Words
- Students will read each riddle and choose a compound word from the shaded box to answer each riddle.

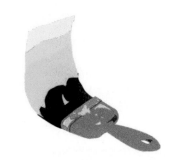

The Writing Connection

Writing Riddles for Compound Words
- Students will write a riddle for a compound word.
- Allow time for students to share riddles with the class.

Process Writing

Process Writing Lesson #9 for Steps 18 and 19 is found in TM p. 449.

p. 174

Day 4

Getting Started

- Collect homework and put stars on Homework Chart. (See TM p. 26.)
- Administer spelling test with Day 3 spelling words in *Grand Tour I*, p. 173. Sentence for dictation: The <u>starfish</u> is on the rock. (See TM p. 100.)

Grand Tour I, p. 175

Spelling Words
Phonetic Grouping: ar

- Note that all words have the letter cluster **ar** in the **middle** of the word. Have students mark each word as indicated: **ga͡rden**
- Ask which three spelling words have the suffix **er** added to it. (**gardener, marker, charmer**)
- As a class, read the 10 spelling words and discuss the meanings.
- Have students copy the 10 spelling words to take home, study, and write in sentences for homework.

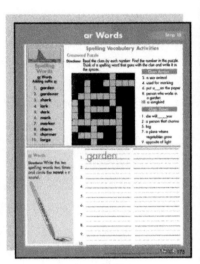

p. 175

Spelling Vocabulary Activities

Crossword Puzzle
- Students will read the clues by the number, think of a spelling word that fits the clue, and write the word by the number in the crossword puzzle.

<u>ar</u> Words
- Students will write the 10 spelling words two times and circle the **vowel + r** sound.

Grand Tour I, p. 176

Story Comprehension

Marvin From Mars
Have students:
- Underline all the **ar** words in the story.
- Read the story silently.
- Underline the correct answers.

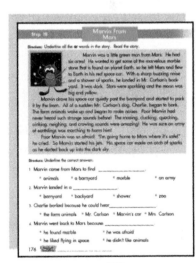

p. 176

(Continued on next page)

Grammar Chalkboard Lesson
Capital Letters

Objective
- Students will know that names of schools, streets, towns, states, and countries begin with a capital letter.

Practice/Apply
- Write the sentences on the board. Students will write the sentences correctly.

> 1. My sister lives in austin, texas.
>   My sister lives in Austin, Texas.
>
> 2. My house is on brentwood street.
>   My house is on Brentwood Street.
>
> 3. When I visit new york, it will be fun.
>   When I visit New York, it will be fun.
>
> 4. The students at clearview elementary school are happy.
>   The students at Clearview Elementary School are happy.
>
> 5. When will you visit mexico and california?
>   When will you visit Mexico and California?

Process Writing

Process Writing Lesson #9 for Steps 18 and 19 is found in TM p. 449.

Day 5

Getting Started

- Collect homework and put stars on Homework Chart. (See TM p. 26.)
- Administer spelling test with Day 4 spelling words in *Grand Tour I*, p. 175. Sentence for dictation: Mom will work in her <u>garden</u>. (See TM p. 100.)

Just for Fun

Completing Analogies

- Remind students that an **analogy** is a special kind of sentence that shows how words go together.
- Words may go together for various reasons.
  Examples: big—little (opposites); pretty—beautiful (synonyms);
  red—yellow (colors); square—rectangle (shapes)

- Write the following analogies on the board and have students fill in the missing word:

Paw is to dog as fin is to _____ .	(fish)
Princess is to queen as prince is to _____ .	(king)
Hot dog is to eat as song is to _____.	(sing)
Mom is to Dad as Grandma is to _____.	(Grandpa)
Snow is to cold as sun is to _____.	(hot)

- Have students illustrate one analogy.

Process Writing

Process Writing Lesson #9 for Steps 18 and 19 is found in TM p. 449.

Additional Related Activities for Step 18

Listening and Speaking

1. *Beanbag Toss* with Compound Words

- Toss a beanbag to a student in the class and say a word that can have a second word added to make a compound word.

  Example: base

  The student catches the beanbag and says, "**baseball**," or any acceptable compound word using **base**. The student tosses the beanbag back to the teacher and the game continues.

- Suggestions for words:

cup (cake)	rail (road)	tooth (pick, brush)
birth (day)	side (walk)	week (end)
camp (fire)	sun (rise, set)	air (port)
day (time, dream)	star (fish, light)	hay (stack)
down (town, stairs)	skate (board)	pop (corn)
drive (way)	wash (cloth)	jelly (fish)
some (one, place, where)	fish (hook)	sea (shell)

Accept any reasonable answers.

2. *Stand Up and Say the Word*

- Write Step 18 spelling words on 3 x 5 index cards. (one word per card)
- Pass out cards to students.
- Teacher says a definition for a spelling word.

  Example: This is a covering for the floor in your house.

- The child who has the card with **carpet** written on it stands up and says, "**carpet**."
- The teacher may also want to ask the student to spell the word or use the word in a sentence.

NOTES

Grand Tour II

Overview for Step 19

Objectives

Phonics: To sing *Letter Cluster Phonics Song*, verses 1-4, providing phonics review and/or new instruction for those who need it

Spelling: To spell **aw** and **au** words

Grammar: To proofread a story and circle all the words that need capital letters

Comprehension: To read short stories and answer questions requiring higher level thinking skills

Writing: To write riddles

To write a short story telling about what friends like to do together

To use the Five Steps of Process Writing, focusing on editing run-on sentences

Handwriting: To learn how to write cursive letters *Aa* and *Bb*

Suggested Pacing
1 week

Materials
Grand Tour II, pp. 5-14
Letter Cluster Phonics Song Charts 1-4
Cursive Wall Chart

Homework
Daily homework is described in TM p. 99.

Spelling
Daily spelling is described in TM p. 99.

Phonics Games
Letter Cluster Sound-O (See TM p. 52.)
Letter Cluster Pick-A-Sound (See TM p. 55.)

Phonics Song
Letter Cluster Phonics Song, verses 1-4,
   CD tracks 8 - 9 (See TM p. 51.)

Additional Related Activities
Additional activities are found in TM p. 274.

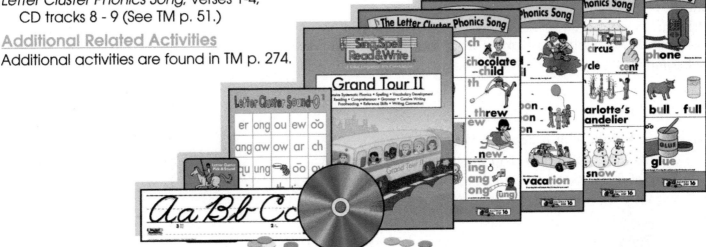

Grand Tour II

Phonics Review

Sing *Letter Cluster Phonics Song*, verses 1-4, CD tracks 8 - 9.

Grand Tour II, p. 5

Spelling Words
Phonetic Grouping: aw

- Note that each word has letter cluster **aw**. Have students mark each word as indicated: **straw**
- Call attention to the four compound words (**strawberries, rawhide, seesaw, jawbone**).
- As a class, read the 10 spelling words and discuss the meanings.
- Have students copy the 10 spelling words to take home, study, and write in sentences for homework.

p. 5

Spelling Vocabulary Activities

Compound Words
- Remind students **compound words** are two words put together and are often related in some way.
- Ask if **straw** and **berries** are related in the word **strawberries**. (**no**)
- How are **jaw** and **bone** related? (**Jawbone is a bone in the jaw.**)
- Students will write four spelling words that are **compound words**.

Rhyming
- Students will write four spelling words that rhyme with **paw**.

Antonyms
- Students will write a spelling word that is the opposite of **good** and **laugh**.

Word Scrambles
- Students will unscramble the letters to make a spelling word.

Grand Tour II, p. 6

Grammar

Riddles
- Students will read the riddle and the word in the box. Have them change the underlined letter to make a word that answers the riddle.
  Example: This is a kind of tree. [nine] should be changed to [pine]

The Writing Connection

Writing a Riddle with a Spelling Word
- Students will choose a spelling word and write a riddle.
  Example: This is found on a playground and goes up and down. (**seesaw**)

p. 6

Process Writing

Process Writing Lesson #9 for Steps 18 and 19 is found in TM p. 449.

Day 2

Getting Started

- Collect homework and put stars on Homework Chart. (See TM p. 26.)
- Administer spelling test with Day 1 spelling words in *Grand Tour II*, p. 5. Sentence for dictation: This was an <u>awful</u> plan. (See TM p. 100.)

Grand Tour II, pp. 7-8

Spelling Words
Phonetic Grouping: aw

p. 7

- Note that each word has letter cluster **aw**. Have students mark each word as indicated: **crȃwl**
- Call attention to the two compound words (**withdraw, lawnmower**).
- As a class, read the 10 spelling words and discuss their meanings.
- Identify the two words that have the suffix **ed** meaning **in the past**. (**crawled, yawned**)
- Identify the word that has the suffix **ed** meaning **happening now**. (**crawling**)
- Have students copy the 10 spelling words to take home, study, and write in sentences for homework.

Spelling Vocabulary Activities

Cloze
- Students will fill in the blanks with spelling words.

Compound Words
- Students will write the two spelling words that are **compound words**.

Synonyms
- Remind students that **synonyms** are words that mean almost the same thing. Ask students to give you a **synonym** for begin (**start**) and gift (**present**).
- Have students write **synonyms** for **daybreak** and **creep**.

Rhyming
Students will write two spelling words that rhyme with **dawn**.

Suffixes <u>ed</u> and <u>ing</u>
Students will write two spelling words that have the suffix **ed** and one spelling word with the suffix **ing** on p. 8

Grand Tour II, p. 8

Story Comprehension

A Hawk at Dawn
Students will:
- Underline the spelling words in the story.
- Read the story.

p. 8

(Continued on next page)

Day 2 continued

Grammar Chalkboard Lesson
Sensible Sentences

Objective
* Students will change the first letter in the underlined word to make a sensible sentence.

Practice/Apply
* Copy the sentences on the board. Students will change the first letter of the underlined word to make a word that makes sense in the sentence.

> Paul will mow the <u>fawn</u>.   lawn
>
> Strawberries <u>paste</u> good to me.   taste
>
> It is not safe to eat <u>saw</u> meat.   raw
>
> The man <u>barks</u> his automobile.   parks
>
> Please put applesauce in this <u>fish</u>.   dish

Process Writing

Process Writing Lesson #9 for Steps 18 and 19 is found in TM pp. 449.

Day 3

Getting Started

* Collect homework and put stars on Homework Chart. (See TM p. 26.)
* Administer spelling test with Day 2 spelling words in *Grand Tour II*, p. 7. Sentence for dictation: I saw a <u>hawk</u> fly away. (See TM p. 100.)

Grand Tour II, pp. 9-10

Spelling Words
Phonetic Grouping: au

* Note that words #1-8 have letter cluster **au** and that **au** has the same sound as **aw**. Have students mark each word as indicated: **s͜au͜ce**
* As a class, read the 10 spelling words and discuss their meanings.
* Tell students **homophones** are words that **sound alike** but have **different meanings**. **Hear** and **here** are homophones. They sound the same but **hear** means **to listen**, and here means **a place**.
* Have students copy the 10 spelling words to take home, study, and write in sentences for homework.

p. 9

Day 3 *continued*

Spelling Vocabulary Activities

Homophones
- Students will fill in the blank with correct homophones.

Synonyms
- Remind students **synonyms** are words that mean almost the **same thing**.
- Students will write spelling words that mean the same as the words in bold print.

Word Scrambles
- Students will unscramble the letters to make a word.

Word Clues
- Students will write a spelling word to fit each clue.

Grand Tour II, p. 10

Grammar

Capital Letters
- Review with students the rules for **capitalizing** a word: beginning of a sentence; names of people, places and pets; days of the week; months; streets; cities and states.

- Students will read the story and circle 23 words that should begin with a capital letter.

The Writing Connection

Writing a Story
- Brainstorm with students about favorite things they like to do with a friend.

- Tell students their story should tell **what** they like to do with a friend and **why** it is a favorite thing to do.

- Students will draw a picture that shows the activity.

Process Writing

Process Writing Lesson #9 for Steps 18 and 19 is found in TM p. 449.

p. 9

p. 10

Grand Tour II

Day 4

Getting Started

- Collect homework and put stars on Homework Chart. (See TM p. 26.)
- Administer spelling test with Day 3 spelling words in *Grand Tour II*, p. 9. Sentence for dictation: I like to eat <u>applesauce</u>. (See TM p.100.)

Grand Tour II, p. 11

Spelling Words
Phonetic Grouping: au

- Note that words #1-7 have the **au** sound. Have students mark each word as indicated: h(au)l
- Point out that words #8-10 are **homophones**. (The meanings of **to**, **too**, and **two** will be discussed later on this same page.)
- As a class, read the 10 spelling words and discuss the meanings.
- Have students copy the 10 spelling words to take home, study, and write in sentences for homework.

Spelling Vocabulary Activities

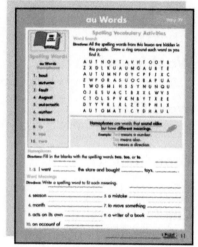

p. 11

Word Search

- Tell students all the spelling words for this lesson are hidden in this puzzle. The words go across or down.
- Have students draw a ring around each word as they find it.

Homophones

- Tell students homophones are words that **sound alike** but have **different meanings**.
- Today's spelling list has the homophones **to**, **too**, and **two**.
- Tell students **to** means a **direction**.
  Example: In the sentence "I will go **to** the store," **to** means **in the direction** of the store.

- **Too** means **also** and often comes at the end of the word.
  Example: : In the sentence "I would like to go, **too**," **too** means I would like to go **also**.

- **Two** means a **number**, as in "I have **two** pencils."
- Think of several sentences using **to**, **too**, or **two** and ask students to orally spell the correct word.
  Example: You may come with me, ____. **(too)**
    I need ____ new pencils. **(two)**
    Will you go ____ the beach? **(to)**

- Continue in this manner for more practice.
- On page 11, students will fill in the blanks with the correct spelling words.

Word Meanings

- Students will write a spelling word to fit each meaning.

Day 4 continued

Grand Tour II, p. 12

Story Comprehension

The Automatic Sweeper
Students will:
* Underline the six spelling words in the story.
* Read the story.
* Underline the correct answers.

The Writing Connection

Writing a Story
* Discuss with students what it means to invent something.
* Brainstorm with students things they would like to invent.
* Students will:
  * Write a story about something they would like to invent.
  * Include a name for the invention.
  * Tell what the invention will do.
  * Draw a picture of the invention.

p. 12

Grammar Chalkboard Lesson
Capital Letters

Objective
* Students will know that names of people, pets, schools, streets, towns, states, and countries begin with a capital letter.

Practice/Apply
* Write the sentences on the board. Students will identify 11 words that need capital letters and will write the sentences correctly.

1. Please give this food to amy for her dog, bozo.
   Please give this food to Amy for her dog, Bozo.

2. I think that melrose elementary school is beautiful.
   I think that Melrose Elementary School is beautiful.

3. Dad went to a baseball game in cleveland, ohio.
   Dad went to a baseball game in Cleveland, Ohio.

4. Someone is building a new house on woodlands drive.
   Someone is building a new house on Woodlands Drive.

5. My best friend lives in toronto, canada.
   My best friend lives in Toronto, Canada.

Process Writing

Process Writing Lesson #9 for Steps 18 and 19 is found in TM p. 449.

Day 5

Getting Started

- Collect homework and put stars on Homework Chart. (See TM p. 26.)
- Administer spelling test with Day 4 spelling words in *Grand Tour II*, p. 11. Sentence for dictation: Lita was born in <u>August</u>. (See TM p. 100.)

Grand Tour II, pp. 13-14

Learning Cursive Writing

- To introduce cursive letters $\mathcal{A}a$ and $\mathcal{B}b$, refer to TM p. 75.
- Students will trace over the letters and/or letter combinations and practice writing them on the lines.

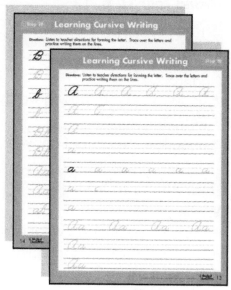

pp. 13-14

Process Writing

Process Writing Lesson #9 for Steps 18 and 19 is found in TM p. 449.

Additional Related Activities for Step 19

Listening and Speaking

1. Homophone Fun

- Write pairs of homophones on 3 x 5 index cards, one **homophone** per card.
- Give each child two cards, making sure the two cards contain matching **homophones**.

Example:
 Blue ● Blew

- Students will illustrate each word on the opposite side of the card.

  Teacher will collect the cards and use them in a variety of activities:

  Place all cards in a learning center and have students arrange cards into pairs.

  Teacher may hold up a card with word displayed and ask a student to use the **homonym** in a sentence.

  Example: blue – Student says, "The sky is blue."

  Teacher shows a card with the picture displayed and says the name of the homonym the picture illustrates. Next, teacher asks a student to spell the correct homophone.

  Example: Student spells **b – l – e – w.**

2. Play *Hot Potato* with Suffixes <u>ed</u> and <u>ing</u>

Sit in a circle. Toss a beanbag to a student and say:

Make **work** mean "in the past." (worked)

Make **crawl** mean "happening now" (crawling)

Make **haul** mean "happening now." (hauling)

Make **play** mean "in the past." (played)

Make **play** mean "happening now." (playing)

- Continue in this manner with other words.

NOTES

Grand Tour II

Overview for Step 20

Objectives:

Phonics: To sing *Letter Cluster Phonics Song*, verses 1-4, providing phonics review and/or new instruction for those who need it

Spelling: To spell words with letter clusters **ing; ang; ong; ung; oy; oi**

Grammar: To know that names of holidays and initials begin with capital letters

To know an initial must be followed by a period

To know that all words are made up of one or more parts called syllables

Comprehension: To read short stories and answer questions requiring higher level thinking skills

Writing: To write a descriptive paragraph

To use the Five Steps of Process Writing, focusing on using descriptive words

Handwriting: To learn how to write cursive letters *Cc* and *Dd*

Suggested Pacing

1 week

Materials

Grand Tour II, pp. 15-24
Letter Cluster Phonics Song Charts 1-4
Cursive Wall Chart

Homework

Daily homework is described in TM p. 99.

Spelling

Daily spelling is described in TM p. 99.

Phonics Games (See TM pp. 40-65.)

Continue to play selected games as needed for reinforcement.

Phonics Song

Letter Cluster Phonics Song, verses 1-4,
    CD tracks 8 - 9 (See TM p. 51.)

Additional Related Activities

Additional activities are found in TM p. 283.

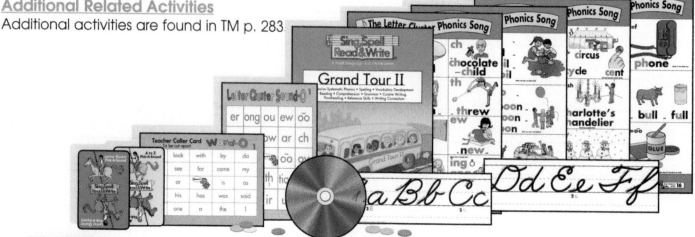

Day 1

Phonics Review

Sing *Letter Cluster Phonics Song*, verses 1-4, CD tracks 8 - 9.

Grand Tour II, pp. 15-16

Spelling Words
Phonetic Groupings: ing, ang

* Note that words #1-7 have **ing** and words #8-10 have **ang**. Have students mark each word as indicated: **thing hang**
* As a class, read the 10 spelling words and discuss the meanings.
* Have students copy the 10 spelling words to take home, study, and write in sentences for homework.

Spelling Vocabulary Activities

Letter Switch
* Students will change the letters in dark print to make spelling words.

Compound Words
* Remind the students that **compound words** are two words put together to make one word. Students will fill in the blanks with the **compound** spelling words.

Word Scramble
* Students will unscramble the letters and fill in the blank with the correct spelling word.

Silly Questions
* Students will read questions, write the spelling word found in each sentence, and answer the question by writing **yes** or **no**.

Cloze
* Students will fill in the blanks with the correct spelling words.

p. 15

Grand Tour II, p. 16

Grammar

Capital Letters: Holidays
* Remind students that names of **holidays** always begin with a **capital letter**.
* As a class, read the names of the **holidays**.
* Discuss the **holidays** and the symbols shown representing each **holiday**.
* Students will fill in the blanks with the correct holidays.

The Writing Connection

Writing a Paragraph
* Have students write a paragraph identifying their favorite holidays and telling what they like to do to celebrate it.

p. 16

Process Writing

Process Writing Lesson #10 for Steps 20 and 21 is found in TM p. 451.

Grand Tour II

Getting Started

- Collect homework and put stars on the Homework Chart. (See TM p. 26.)
- Administer spelling test with Day 1 spelling words in *Grand Tour II*, p. 15. Sentence for dictation: He likes <u>springtime</u> days. (See TM p. 100.)

Grand Tour II, pp. 17-18

Spelling Words
Phonetic Groupings: ong, ung

- Note that words #1-8 contain **ong** and words #9-10 contain **ung**. Have students mark each word as indicated: st(ong), s(ung)
- As a class, read the 10 spelling words and discuss the meanings.
- Have students copy the 10 spelling words to take home, study, and write in sentences for homework.

p. 17

Spelling Vocabulary Activities

Cloze
- Students will fill in the blanks with the correct spelling words.

Superlatives
- Remind students that the suffix **er** is sometimes added to a root word when you want to compare two things. It means **more**.
- **Est** is added when you want to compare three or more things. It **means the most**.
- Hold up two pencils of different lengths. Ask students which one is **longer**. Then hold up three pencils. Have students tell which one is **longest**.
- On page 17 students will fill in the blanks with the correct words.

Follow the Pattern
- Students will fill in the blanks to complete the pattern.

Word Clues
- Students will write a spelling word to fit each clue.

Word Scrambles
- Students will unscramble the letters to make a spelling word.

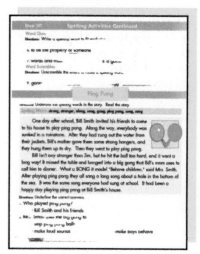

p. 18

Day 2 continued

Grand Tour II, p. 18

Story Comprehension

Ping Pong

- Have students underline the eight spelling words in the story.
- Read the story aloud with students.
- Students will complete the activity by underlining the correct answers.

Grammar Chalkboard Lesson
Capital Letters

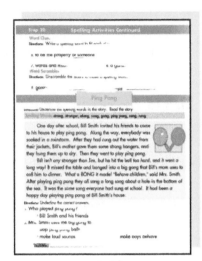

p. 18

Objective

- Students will know that names of **holidays** begin with a **capital letter**.

Practice/Apply

- Write the sentences on the board. Students will write the sentences correctly.

> 1. On valentine's day I will give cards to my friends.
>   On Valentine's day I will give cards to my friends.
>
> 2. The children sang christmas songs.
>   The children sang Christmas songs.
>
> 3. Potato pancakes are a special hanukkah treat.
>   Potato pancakes are a special Hanukkah treat.
>
> 4. Mom will bake pumpkin pie for our thanksgiving dinner.
>   Mom will bake pumpkin pie for our Thanksgiving dinner.
>
> 5. The band marches in the fourth of july parade.
>   The band marches in the Fourth of July parade.

Process Writing

Process Writing Lesson #10 for Steps 20 and 21 is found in TM p. 451.

Grand Tour II

Day 3

Getting Started

- Collect homework and put stars on the Homework Chart. (See TM p. 26.)
- Administer spelling test with Day 2 spelling words in *Grand Tour II*, p. 17. Sentence for dictation: The tall man is <u>strong</u>. (See TM p. 100.)

Grand Tour II, p. 19

Spelling Words
Phonetic Grouping: oy

- Note that all of the words have **oy**. Have students mark each word as indicated: **Roy**
- As a class, read the 10 spelling words and discuss the meanings.
- Have students copy the 10 spelling words to take home, study, and write in sentences for homework.

Spelling Vocabulary Activities

Synonyms
- Students will write a spelling word that means the same as each word listed.

Word Clues
- Students will write a spelling word to fit each clue.

Syllables
- Remind students that all words are made up of one or more parts called **syllables**.
- Have students say each spelling word and clap for each **syllable**. Students will write spelling words in the correct boxes.

Grand Tour II, p. 20

Grammar

Capital Letters: Initials
- Tell students that the first letter in each part of a person's name is called an **initial**. Initials are always written with a **capital letter** and must be followed by a **period**.
- Call on several students to write their **initials** on the chalkboard.
- On page 20 students will write **initials** and write each sentence correctly.
- Students will draw lines connecting names with the correct **initials**.

The Writing Connection

Writing Initials
- Students will write the names of family members and write their initials correctly.

Process Writing

Process Writing Lesson #10 for Steps 20 and 21 is found in TM p. 451.

p. 19

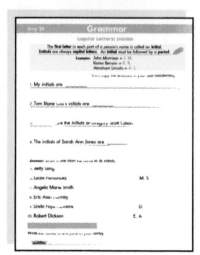

p. 20

Day 4

Getting Started

- Collect homework and put stars on the Homework Chart. (See TM p. 26.)
- Administer spelling test with Day 3 spelling words in *Grand Tour II*, p. 19. Sentence for dictation: The king is a <u>royal</u> man. (See TM p. 100.)

Grand Tour II, pp. 21-22

Spelling Words
Phonetic Grouping: oi

- Note that all words have **oi**. Have students mark each word as indicated: p<u>oi</u>nt
- As a class, read the 10 spelling words and discuss the meanings.
- Have students copy the 10 spelling words to take home, study, and write in sentences for homework.

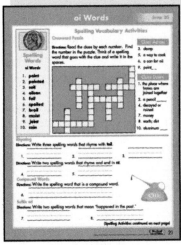

p. 21

Spelling Vocabulary Activities

Crossword Puzzle
- Students will read the clues by the number, find a spelling word that goes with the clue, and write the word by the number in the crossword puzzle.

Rhyming
- Students will fill in the blanks with the correct **rhyming** words.

Compound Words
- Students will fill in the blank with the correct **compound** word.

Suffix <u>ed</u>
- Remind students that **ed** added to a root word means "happened in the past."
- Students will fill in the blanks with the correct spelling words.

Antonyms
- Remind students that **antonyms** are **opposites**.
- Students will fill in the blanks with the correct spelling words.

Story Comprehension

Roy Gets a Coin
- Have students underline the five spelling words in the story.
- As a group, read the story aloud.
- Students will read the questions and underline the correct answers.

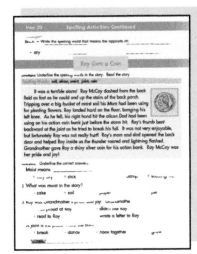

p. 22

(Continued on next page)

Day 4 *continued*

Grammar Chalkboard Lesson
Capital Letters

Objective
• The students will know that initials for a person's name are always **capital letters** and that **initials** are always followed by **periods**.

Practice/Apply
• Write the names on the board. Students will write the initials for the names correctly.

1. Melanie Jean Knapp	(M. J. K.)	6. Kayley Marie Johnson	(K. M. J.)
2. Darla Sue Jones	(D. S. J.)	7. Patrick David Ryan	(P. D. R.)
3. Sarah Ellen Bennett	(S. E. B.)	8. Tyrone Howard Taft	(T. H. T.)
4. Jose William Mendez	(J. W. M.)	9. John Fitzgerald Kennedy	(J. F. K.)
5. Joshua James Bui	(J. J. B.)	10. Maria Grace Garcia	(M. G. G.)

Process Writing

Process Writing Lesson #10 for Steps 20 and 21 is found in TM p. 451.

Day 5

Getting Started

• Collect homework and put stars on the Homework Chart. (See TM p. 26.)
• Administer spelling test with Day 4 spelling words in *Grand Tour II*, p. 21. Sentence for dictation: Put a <u>coin</u> in the box. (See TM p. 100.)

Grand Tour II, pp. 23-24

Learning Cursive Writing

• To introduce cursive letters Cc and Dd, refer to TM pp. 75-76.
• Students will trace over the letters, letter combinations, and/or words and practice writing them on the lines.

Process Writing

Process Writing Lesson #10 for Steps 20 and 21 is found in TM p. 451.

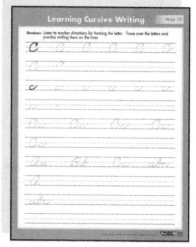

p. 23

p. 24

Additional Related Activities for Step 20

Listening and Speaking

1. *Forty Ways to Get There*

- Give each student a 3 x 5 index card. Have them write their initials in large letters on the card. Check the cards to make sure the initials are written with capital letters followed by periods.

- Collect the cards. Use them in random order to select players for the game.

- Select a card from the stack and read the initials. The student whose initials are called is to travel across the room in some manner.
  Examples: run, crawl, hop, or skip

  Each student must cross the room in a manner different from any of the other students.

- Continue calling initials until all students have had a chance to play.

2. Writing Couplets

- Explain that a **couplet** is a two-line poem with rhyming words at the end of each line.
  Example: I saw a <u>bee</u>.
                  It stung <u>me</u>.

- Have children write at least 2 couplets using rhyming words from the Step 20 word lists.

Overview for Step 21

Objectives

Phonics: To sing *Letter Cluster Phonics Song,* verses 1-4, providing phonics review and/or new instruction for those who need it

Spelling: To spell words with letter cluster o͞o

Grammar: To know that an abbreviation of a person's title begins with a capital letter and ends with a period
To know that initials are always capital letters and must be followed by a period

Comprehension: To read short stories and answer questions requiring higher level thinking skills

Writing: To write a descriptive paragraph
To use the Five Steps of Process Writing, focusing on using descriptive words

Handwriting: To learn how to write cursive letters *Ee* and *Ff*

Suggested Pacing
1 week

Materials
Grand Tour II, pp. 25-34
Letter Cluster Charts, 1-4
Cursive Wall Chart

Homework
Daily homework is described in TM p. 99.

Spelling
Daily spelling is described in TM p. 99.

Phonics Games (See TM pp. 40-65.)
Continue to play selected games as needed for reinforcement.

Phonics Song
Letter Cluster Phonics Song, verses 1-4,
      CD tracks 8 - 9 (See TM p. 51.)

Additional Related Activities
Additional activities are found in TM p. 291.

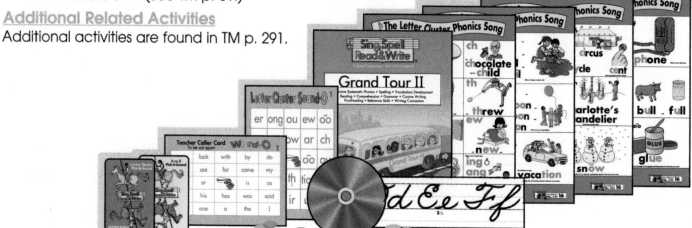

Day 1

Phonics Review

Sing *Letter Cluster Phonics Song*, verses 1-4, CD tracks 8 - 9.

Grand Tour II, pp. 25-26

Spelling Words
Phonetic Grouping: o͞o

- Note that all words have letter cluster **o͞o**. Have students mark each word as indicated: **bro͞om**
- As a class, read the 10 spelling words and discuss the meanings.
- Have students copy the 10 spelling words to take home, study, and write in sentences for homework.

Spelling Vocabulary Activities

Compound Words
- Students will name the pictures and words. Then they will write the **compound words** represented by the pictures and words.

Plurals
- Remind students **plurals** are words that mean **more than one**.
- Students will make **plurals** by adding **s** to each word. Then they will write the **plural**.

Silly Questions
- Students will read questions, write the spelling word found in each sentence, and answer the question by writing **yes** or **no**.

p. 25

Grand Tour II, p. 26

Grammar

Capital Letters: Titles of People
- Tell students an **abbreviation** of a person's **title** is a shorter way to write the title. A title always begins with a **capital letter** and ends with a **period**.
- Note that **Miss** is not an abbreviation and does not need a period.
- As a class, read the **titles** in the shaded box and discuss the meanings.
- The students will read the sentences and fill in the blanks with the correct titles.

Process Writing

Process Writing Lesson #10 for Steps 20 and 21 is found in TM p. 451.

p. 26

Day 2

Getting Started

- Collect homework and put stars on Homework Chart. (See TM p. 26.)
- Administer spelling test with Day 1 spelling words in *Grand Tour II*, p. 25. Sentence for dictation: This is my <u>schoolroom</u>. (See TM p. 100.)

Grand Tour II, pp. 27-28

Spelling Words
Phonetic Grouping: o͞o

- Note that all words have letter cluster **o͞o**. Have students mark each word as indicated: **to͞oth**
- As a class, read the 10 spelling words and discuss the meanings.
- Have students copy the 10 spelling words to take home, study, and write in sentences for homework.

Spelling Vocabulary Activities

Word Fun
- Students will cross out every other letter, starting with the second letter, to make a spelling word. Demonstrate this procedure on the board.
  Example: b ¢ i ⫽ g ⫽   **big**
- Students will cross out the letters and fill in the blanks with the correct spelling words.

Plurals
- Remind students that **plurals** are words that mean **more than one**. Explain that most of the time you form a **plural** by adding **s** to the root word.
- When a word ends in **sh**, you must add **es** to make a **plural**.
- Tell students that some **plurals** do not follow these rules. Some words are made **plural** by changing the spelling.
- Have the students read the examples in the shaded box.
- Students will fill in the blanks with the correct words.

Antonyms
- Students will write the spelling word that means the **opposite** of each word listed.

Grand Tour II, p. 28

Story Comprehension

The Goose and the Loose Tooth
Have students:
- Underline the six spelling words in the story.
- Read the story aloud with the students.
- Complete the activity by underlining the correct answers.

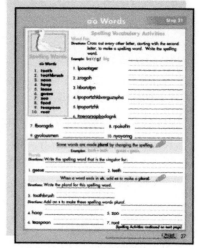

p. 27

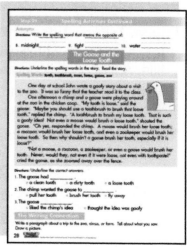

p. 28

Day 2 *continued*

The Writing Connection

Writing a Descriptive Paragraph

- Students will write a paragraph about a trip to the zoo, circus, or farm. They will write to **describe** what they saw.

- If some students have not had any of these experiences, suggest they write about what they saw on a class field trip.

- Students will draw a picture of what they saw on their trip.

Grammar Chalkboard Lesson
Capital Letters

Objective

- The students will know that an **abbreviation** of a person's **title** begins with a **capital letter** and ends with a **period**.

Practice/Apply

- Write the sentences on the board. Students will write the sentences correctly.

---

1. My teachers are miss Jones and mrs Fulton.
   My teachers are Miss Jones and Mrs. Fulton.

2. Sammy went to see dr West.
   Sammy went to see Dr. West.

3. Our next door neighbor is mr Jim Smith.
   Our next door neighbor is Mr. Jim Smith.

4. Tim's mother is mrs Tina Taylor.
   Tim's mother is Mrs. Tina Taylor.

5. I saw ms Jane Carman at the store.
   I saw Ms. Jane Carman at the store.

Process Writing

Process Writing Lesson #10 for Steps 20 and 21 is found in TM p. 451.

Grand Tour II

Day 3

Getting Started

- Collect homework and put stars on Homework Chart. (See TM p. 26.)
- Administer spelling test with Day 2 spelling words in *Grand Tour II*, p. 27. Sentence for dictation: Bill has a red <u>toothbrush</u>. (See TM p. 100.)

Grand Tour II, p. 29

Spelling Words
Phonetic Grouping: o͞o

- Note that all words have letter cluster **o͞o**. Have students mark each word as indicated: **no͞on**
- As a class, read the 10 spelling words and discuss the meanings.
- Have students copy the 10 spelling words to take home, study, and write in sentences for homework.

Spelling Vocabulary Activities

Cloze
- Students will fill in the blanks with spelling words.

Word Clues
- Students will write the spelling words that match the clues.

Syllables
- Students will write the words and fill in the blanks with the number of syllables in each word.

p. 29

Grand Tour II, p. 30

Grammar

Capital Letters: Titles and Initials
- Remind students that an **abbreviation** of a person's **title** begins with a **capital letter** and ends with a **period**. **Initials** are always **capital letters** followed by a **period**.
- Review the **titles** and the **initials** in the shaded boxes.
- The students will write the sentences correctly by adding capital letters and punctuation.

Process Writing

Process Writing Lesson #10 for Steps 20 and 21 is found in TM p. 451.

p. 30

Day 4

Getting Started

- Collect homework and put stars on Homework Chart. (See TM p. 26.)
- Administer spelling test with Day 3 spelling words in *Grand Tour II*, p. 29. Sentence for dictation: We eat lunch at <u>noontime</u>. (See TM p. 100.)

Grand Tour II, pp. 31-32

Spelling Words
Phonetic Grouping: ōō

p. 31

- Note that words #1-9 have letter cluster **ōō**. Have students mark each word as indicated: **lōōp**
- Discuss rulebreaker **poor**.
- As a class, read the 10 spelling words and discuss the meanings.
- Have students copy the 10 spelling words to take home, study, and write sentences for homework.

Spelling Vocabulary Activities

Word Search

- Tell students that all ten spelling words are found in the word search. The words go across and down.
- Students will draw a ring around each word as they find it.

Suffix <u>ish</u>

- Remind students that a **suffix** is added at the end of a root word. The suffix **ish** means "that way." Write the words **childish**, **brownish**, and **greenish** on the board. Have a student underline the suffix in each word and circle the root word.
- On page 31 students will fill in the blank with the correct spelling word.

Root Words

- Students will fill in the blank with the correct spelling word.

Word Meanings

- Write the words **fast**, **faster**, and **fastest** on the board. Ask the students to tell which word means "more than fast"? **(faster)** Which word means "the most fast"? **(fastest)**
- Students will fill in the blanks with words that fit the meanings.

Silly Questions

- Students will read questions, write the spelling word found in each sentence, and answer the question by writing **yes** or **no**.

(Continued on next page)

Day 4 *continued*

Grand Tour II, p. 32

Story Comprehension

A Smooth, Cool Treat

* Have students underline the 10 spelling words in the story.
* As a group, read the story aloud.
* Have students draw a picture of the "smooth, cool treats" that Uncle Kevin, Donna, and Angela had at the street fair. Then make a picture of their own favorite smooth, cool treat.

The Writing Connection

Writing a Paragraph

* Discuss video arcades with the students.
* Have students write a paragraph about a game they would like to play in a video arcade.
* If a student is not familiar with the video arcades, they might write about home video games, computer games, or board games they would like to play.

Grammar Chalkboard Lesson
Capital Letters

Objective

* The students will know that an **abbreviation** of a person's **title** begins with a **capital letter** and ends with a **period** and that **initials** are always **capital letters** followed by a **period**.

Practice/Apply

* Write the sentences on the board. Students will write the sentences correctly.

> 1. the best cookie baker is mrs b j cockrell.
>   The best cookie baker is Mrs. B. J. Cockrell.
>
> 2. i will go to see dr r e finley.
>   I will go to see Dr. R. E. Finley.
>
> 3. my dad's friend is mr w k patton.
>   My dad's friend is Mr. W. K. Patton.
>
> 4. the author is ms t m cromwell.
>   The author is Ms. T. M. Cromwell.
>
> 5. who is riding with miss evans?
>   Who is riding with Miss Evans?

p. 32

Process Writing

Process Writing Lesson #10 for Steps 20 and 21 is found in TM p. 451.

Day 5

Getting Started

- Collect homework and put stars on Homework Chart. (See TM p. 26.)
- Administer spelling test with Day 4 spelling words in *Grand Tour II*, p. 31. Sentence for dictation: I like to play <u>stoop</u> tag. (See TM p. 100.)

Grand Tour II, pp. 33-34

Learning Cursive Writing

- To introduce cursive letters *Ee* and *Ff*, refer to TM p. 76.
- Students will trace over the letters, letter combinations, and/or words and practice writing them on the lines.

Process Writing

Process Writing Lesson #10 for Steps 20 and 21 is found in TM p. 451.

Additional Related Activities for Step 21

Listening and Speaking

1. *I Am Thinking of a Word*

- The teacher will choose a spelling word from one of the Step 21 lessons and say, "I am thinking of a word." The teacher then calls on students to ask **yes** or **no** questions about the word. Questions might be ones such as, "Is it in the Day 2 spelling list?" "Is it a compound word?" "Does it have 8 letters?" "Is the word teaspoon?"
- The student continues asking questions as long as the teacher answers **yes**, but when the teacher answers **no**, the turn passes to another student.
- The student who identifies the correct word is the next caller.

2. *Climbing the Ladder*

- Teacher will draw a ladder with 10 steps on the board and write a compound word on the first step. Students then climb the ladder by putting compound words on the other steps.
- Variation: Begin with a word containing a letter cluster. Students climb the ladder by writing other words with that cluster.

classroom

Overview for Step 22

Objectives

Phonics: To sing *Letter Cluster Phonics Song*, verses 1-4, providing phonics review and/or new instruction for those who need it

Spelling: To spell ŏŏ words; **tion** words; and homophones

Grammar: To know that the first word and all important words in the title of a book, story, movie, play, or song begin with a capital letter

To know that homophones are words that sound alike but have different meanings

Comprehension: To read a poem and a short story and answer questions requiring higher level thinking skills

Writing: To use the Five Steps of Process Writing, focusing on developing a list of self-selected story ideas

Proofreading: To learn proofreading marks

To find spelling and capital letter errors

Reference Skills: To understand Guide Words

Handwriting: To learn how to write cursive letter *Gg*

Suggested Pacing

1 week

Materials

Grand Tour II, pp. 35-44
Letter Cluster Phonics Song Charts 1-4
Cursive Wall Chart

Homework

Daily homework is described in TM p. 99.

Spelling

Daily spelling is described in TM p. 99.

Phonics Games (See TM pp. 40-65.)

Continue to play selected games as needed for reinforcement.

Phonics Song

Letter Cluster Phonics Song, verses 1-4,
   CD tracks 8 - 9 (See TM p. 51.)

Additional Related Activities

Additional activities are
   found in TM p. 301.

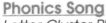

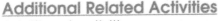

Day 1

Phonics Review

Sing *Letter Cluster Phonics Song*, verses 1-4, CD tracks 8 - 9.

Grand Tour II, pp. 35-36

Spelling Words
Phonetic Grouping: o̽o

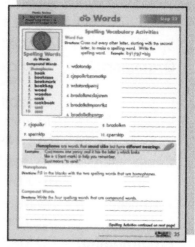

p. 35

- Note that words #1-8 have letter cluster **o̽o**. Have students mark the words as indicated: **bo̽ok**
- Call attention to the homophones **cent** and **sent**.
- As a class, read the 10 spelling words and discuss the meanings.
- Have students copy the 10 spelling words to take home, study, and write in sentences for homework.

Spelling Vocabulary Activities

Word Fun
- Students will cross out every other letter, starting with the second letter, to make a spelling word.
- Demonstrate this procedure on the chalkboard.

Homophones
- Tell the students **homophones** are words that **sound alike** but have **different meanings** and **different spellings**.
- Write these examples on the board: **blue—blew**; **hi—high**; **grown—groan**
- As a class, read the words and discuss the meanings.
- Discuss the meanings of **sent** and **cent**.
- On page 35 students will fill in the blanks with the correct words.

Compound Words
- Students will fill in the blanks with the correct words.

Letter Switch
- Students will change the underlined letters to make spelling words and then write the new words.

Word Meanings
- Students will write the word to fit the meaning.

Grand Tour II, p. 36

Grammar

Capital Letters: Titles
- Remind students that the **first word** and all the **important words** in the **title** of a **book**, **story**, **movie**, **play**, or **song** begin with a **capital letter**.
- Students will circle the letters that should be capital letters and then write the titles correctly.

p. 36

Day 1 continued

Process Writing

Process Writing Lesson #11 for Steps 22 and 23 is found in TM p. 453.

Day 2

Getting Started

- Collect homework and put stars on Homework Chart. (See TM p. 26.)
- Administer spelling test with Day 1 spelling words in *Grand Tour II*, p. 35. Sentence for dictation: Mom made a big <u>bookcase</u>. (See TM p. 100.)

Grand Tour II, pp. 37-38

Spelling Words
Phonetic Grouping: o͝o

- Note that spelling words #1-8 have letter cluster **o͝o**. Have students mark words as indicated: **ho͝ok**
- Call attention to the homophones **cents** and **sense**.
- As a class, read the 10 spelling words and discuss the meanings.
- Have students copy the 10 spelling words to take home, study, and write in sentences for homework.

p. 37

Spelling Vocabulary Activities

Cloze
- Students will fill in the blanks with spelling words.

Synonyms
- Remind students *synonyms* are two or more words that mean nearly the same thing.
- Students will fill in the blanks with the correct spelling words.

Compound Words
- Students will fill in the blank with the correct spelling word.

Silly Questions
- Students will read questions, write the spelling word found in each sentence, and answer the question **yes** or **no**.

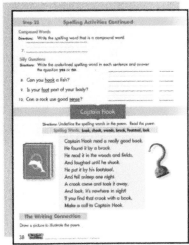

p. 38

(*Continued on next page*)

Grand Tour II, p. 38

Story Comprehension

Captain Hook

* Have students underline the six spelling words in the poem.
* Read the poem aloud with the students.

The Writing Connection

Illustrating a Poem

* Brainstorm with the students, thinking of what book Captain Hook might have been reading.
* Provide drawing paper. Students will draw a picture to illustrate the poem.

Grammar Chalkboard Lesson
Titles

Objective

* The students will know that the **first word** and all **important words** in the **title** of a **book, story, movie, play,** or **song** begin with a **capital letter**.

Practice/Apply

* Write the titles on the board. Students will write them correctly.

p. 38

1. the star spangled banner   The Star Spangled Banner
2. i love lucy   I Love Lucy
3. home on the range   Home on the Range
4. make way for ducklings   Make Way for Ducklings
5. green eggs and ham   Green Eggs and Ham
6. amelia bedelia and the baby   Amelia Bedelia and the Baby

Process Writing

Process Writing Lesson #11 for Steps 22 and 23 is found in TM p. 453.

Day 3

Getting Started

- Collect homework and put stars on Homework Chart. (See TM p. 26.)
- Administer spelling test with Day 2 spelling words in *Grand Tour II*, p. 37. Sentence for dictation: This is a <u>good</u> book. (See TM p. 100.)

Grand Tour II, p. 39

Spelling Words
Phonetic Grouping: oŏ

- Note that words #1-7 have letter cluster **oŏ**. Have the students mark the words as indicated: **coŏkie**
- Call attention to synonyms **start** and **begin** and rulebreaker **should**.
- As a class, read the 10 spelling words and discuss the meanings.
- Have the students copy the 10 spelling words to take home, study, and write in sentences for homework.

Spelling Vocabulary Activities

Word Clues
- Students will write a spelling word for each clue.

Synonyms
- Students will write the two spelling words that mean nearly the same thing.

Word Scrambles
- Students will unscramble the letters and fill in the blank with the correct spelling word.

p. 39

Grand Tour II, p. 40

Grammar

Capital Letters: Titles
- Remind students that the **first word** and all **important words** in the **title** of a **book**, **story**, **movie**, **play**, or **song** begin with a **capital letter**.
- Students will circle the letters that should be **capital letters** and write the **titles** correctly on the lines.

Process Writing

Process Writing Lesson #11 for Step 22 and 23 is found in TM p. 453.

p. 40

Day 4

Getting Started

- Collect homework and put stars on Homework Chart. (See TM p. 26.)
- Administer spelling test with Day 3 spelling words in *Grand Tour II*, p. 39. Sentence for dictation: This is a <u>woolen</u> hat. (See TM p. 100.)

Grand Tour II, p. 41

Spelling Words
Phonetic Grouping: tion

- Note that all words have **tion**. Tell students that **tion** usually sounds like **shun**. Words #1-9 follow this rule. Have students mark words as indicated: **na̩tio̩n**
- Call attention to rulebreaker word #10, **question**. The **tion** sounds like **chun**.
- As a class, read the 10 spelling words and discuss the meanings.
- Have students copy the 10 spelling words to take home, study, and write in sentences for homework.

Spelling Vocabulary Activities

Crossword Puzzle
- Students will read the clues by the number, find a spelling word that goes with the clue, and write the word by the number in the crossword puzzle.

Antonyms
- Students will fill in the blanks with the correct spelling words.

Rhyming
- Students will write three spelling words that **rhyme** and have a **long a** in the first syllable.

Cloze
- Students will fill in the blanks with the correct spelling words.

Grand Tour II, p. 42

Story Comprehension

A Vacation at Our Grandparents' House
Have students:

- Read the story silently and underline the eight spelling words.
- Read the questions and underline the correct answers.

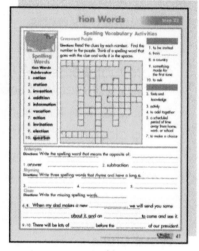

p. 41

p. 42

Day 4 continued

The Writing Connection

Writing Questions

- Remind students that **questions** are **asking sentences**. They **always** end with a **question mark**.
- Ask students to name some words that are often used in **questions**.
  Examples: who, what, where, when, why, how many
- Write these examples on the board: **who**, **what**, **where**, **when**, **why**, **how many**
- Each student will write three questions about horses and share them with the class.

Grammar Chalkboard Lesson
Titles

Objective

- The students will know that the **first word** and **all important** words in the **title** of a **book**, **story**, **movie**, **play**, or **song** begin with a capital letter.

Practice/Apply

- Write the titles on the board. Students will write them correctly.

> 1. harry the dirty dog   Harry the Dirty Dog
> 2. where the wild things are   Where the Wild Things Are
> 3. may i bring a friend?   May I Bring a Friend?
> 4. the stars and stripes forever   The Stars and Stripes Forever
> 5. i'm a little teapot   I'm a Little Teapot
> 6. toy story   Toy Story

Process Writing

Process Writing Lesson #11 for Steps 22 and 23 is found in TM p. 453.

Day 5

Getting Started

- Collect homework and put stars on Homework Chart. (See TM p. 26.)
- Administer spelling test with Day 4 spelling words in *Grand Tour II,* p. 41. Sentence for dictation: A <u>vacation</u> is fun. (See TM p. 100.)

Grand Tour II, p. 43

Proofreading

- Discuss the use of the **proofreading marks** printed in the shaded box.
- Students will use the **proofreading marks** to correct two spelling mistakes, insert three capital letters, and take out a word.

Reference Skill

Dictionary Guide Words

- Have students look in a dictionary to find the **guide words** at the top of the page.
- Next, tell students the words listed in ABC order on that page are called **entry words**.
- Tell students the first **guide word** is the first **entry word** on that page and the second **guide word** is the last **entry word** on that page.
- Tell students all **entry words** must be in ABC order between the two **guide words**.
- Draw this sample dictionary page on the board and write **cent** and **hook** on it for guide words.
- Next, write **color, dig, ball, farm, send,** and **gem** for entry words.
- Have students tell you which four words listed above will fit on this sample dictionary page.

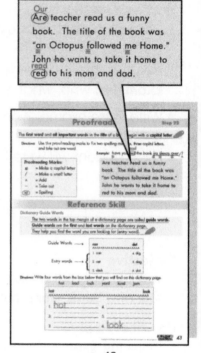

p. 43

cent	hook
1. cent	4.
2.	5.
3.	6. hook

cent	hook
1. cent	4. farm
2. color	5. gem
3. dig	6. hook

- Discuss why **ball** and **send** do not belong on this page.
- Students will write four words on page 43 that belong on the sample dictionary page.

Day 5 continued

Grand Tour II, p. 44

Learning Cursive Writing

- To introduce cursive letter *Gg*, refer to TM p. 77.
- Students will trace over the letters, letter combinations and/or words and practice writing them on the lines.

Process Writing

Process Writing Lesson #11 for Steps 22 and 23 is found in TM p. 453.

p. 44

Additional Related Activities for Step 22

Listening and Speaking

1. Word Sort

- Prepare copies of the Flowers and Fish Reproducibles, one per child. (See TM pp. 481-482.)
- On the board, draw and label the key words **blo͞om** and **hoŏk**.
- Write the following words on the board:

book	spoon
wood	stood
noon	fool
cook	hood
moon	boot

- Have students read the words, then write one **o͞o** word on each flower and one **oŏ** word on each fish.
- Students will cut out the flowers and fish and glue them in the appropriate place on the reproducible.

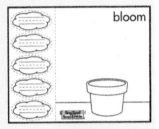

2. *Simon Says* with Synonyms

- The teacher says two words.
- If the words are synonyms, the students stand or remain standing.
- If the words are <u>not</u> synonyms, the students sit or remain seated.
- Students who do not stand for synonyms are eliminated from the game.
- Continue to play until all students are eliminated.
- Some synonyms:

children—youngsters	heal—mend
high—tall	danger—hazard
car—auto	border—edge
all—every	go—leave
shout—yell	start—begin
hurry—rush	thin—slender
vacant—empty	turn—revolve

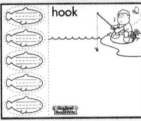

NOTES

Grand Tour II

Overview for Step 23

Objectives

Phonics: To sing *Gh Clown Song*, providing phonics review and/or new instruction for those who need it

Spelling: To spell words with **silent gh**

Grammar: To know how to use commas in the greeting and closing of a friendly note
To know a period is used at the end of a telling sentence

Comprehension: To read short stories and answer questions requiring higher level thinking skills

Writing: To use the Five Steps of Process Writing, focusing on developing a list of self-selected story ideas

Handwriting: To learn how to write cursive letters *Hh* and *Ii*

Suggested Pacing
1 week

Materials
Grand Tour II, pp. 45-54
Gh Clown Chart
Cursive Wall Chart

Homework
Daily homework is described in TM p. 99.

Spelling
Daily spelling is described in TM p. 99.

Phonics Games (See TM pp. 40-65.)
Continue to play selected games as needed for reinforcement.

Phonics Song
Gh Clown Song, CD track 17 (See TM p. 62.)

Additional Related Activities
Additional activities are found in TM p. 311.

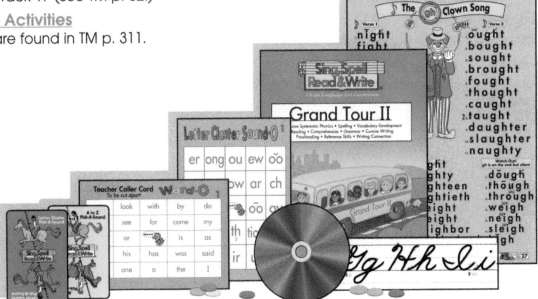

Grand Tour II

Day 1

Phonics Review

Sing *Gh Clown Song*, CD track 17.

Grand Tour II, p. 45

Spelling Words
Phonetic Grouping: gh

- Note that each word has **silent gh**. Have students mark each word as indicated: **fright**
- As a class, read the 10 spelling words and discuss the meanings.
- Have students identify the compound words. (**flashlight, lighthouse**)
- Have students copy the 10 spelling words to take home, study, and write in
  sentences for homework.

Spelling Vocabulary Activities

Homophones

- Tell students **homophones** are words that **sound alike** but have **different meanings** and **different spellings**.
- Ask them to use their imagination to think of clues to help remember how a word is spelled.
  Example: A <u>k</u>night is a person who works for a <u>k</u>ing. Use the **k** in <u>k</u>ing to help you remember how to spell <u>k</u>night correctly.
- Students will fill in the blanks with spelling words.

Compound Words

- Students will write two spelling words that are **compound words**.

Antonyms

- On page 45 students will write the spelling words that are the opposite of **dim** and **left**.

Word Meanings

- Students will write a spelling word that fits each meaning.

Syllables

- Students will write each spelling word and the number of syllables in each word.

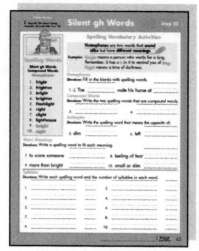

p. 45

Grand Tour II, p. 46

Grammar

Punctuation: Comma

- Tell students a **comma** is used after the **greeting** in a note or letter.
  Example: Dear Sam,

- Also, a comma is used after the **closing** in a note or letter.
  Example: With love,

- Students will place a **comma** after the **greeting** and **closing** in the note and write the note on the lines provided.

Process Writing

Process Writing Lesson #11 for Steps 22 and 23 is found in TM p. 453.

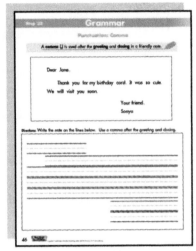

p. 46

Day 2

Getting Started

- Collect homework and put stars on Homework Chart. (See TM p. 26.)
- Administer spelling test with Day 1 spelling words in *Grand Tour II*, p. 45.
  Sentence for dictation: Tom has a <u>bright</u> <u>flashlight</u>. (See TM p. 100.)

Phonics Review

Sing *Gh Clown Song*, CD track 17.

Grand Tour II, p. 47

Spelling Words
Phonetic Grouping: gh

- Note that all words have **silent gh**. Have students mark each word as indicated: **ought**

- Note that words #1-6 have **ought** and words #7-10 have **aught**. **Ought** and **aught** have the same sound in these words.

- As a class, read the 10 spelling words and discuss the meanings.

- Have students copy the 10 spelling words to take home, study, and write in sentences for homework.

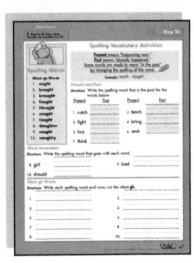

p. 47

(Continued on next page)

Grand Tour II

Spelling Vocabulary Activities

Present and Past

- Tell students **present** means "now." It is "happening at the present" or it is "happening now."

- **Past** means it has "already happened." Maybe it happened years ago, yesterday, or just a moment ago.

- Often you add **ed** to a word to change it to mean "in the past."
  Example: look—looked

- Tell students some words are made to mean "in the past" by changing the spelling of the word.
  Example: teach—taught. It would be incorrect to add **ed** and say teach**ed**.

- Ask students the past of:

sell	(sold)
sleep	(slept)
ring	(rang)
eat	(ate)

- On page 47 students will write the spelling word that is the **past** for the words listed.

Word Association

- Students will write the spelling word that goes with each word.

Silent <u>gh</u> Words

- Students will write each spelling word and cross out the **silent gh**.

p. 47

Grand Tour II, p. 48

Story Comprehension

Sometimes Naughty, Sometimes Nice

Have students:

- Underline the spelling words in the story.
- Read the story.
- Read the questions and underline the correct answers.

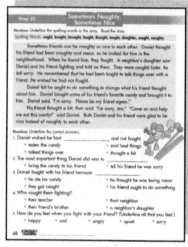

p. 48

Day 2 *continued*

Grammar Chalkboard Lesson
Punctuation

Objective
- The students will know that a **comma** is used after the **greeting** and **closing** in a friendly letter.

Practice/Apply
- Write the letter on the board. Students will copy it correctly.

Dear Nita,

      Thank you for the new baseball. I really like to play ball. I hope you can come to my next game.

                       Your friend,
                       Ramon

Process Writing

Process Writing Lesson #11 for Steps 22 and 23 is found in TM p. 453.

Day 3

Getting Started

- Collect homework and put stars on Homework Chart. (See TM p. 26.)
- Administer spelling test with Day 2 spelling words in *Grand Tour II*, p. 47. Sentence for dictation: Mom <u>bought</u> me a toy. (See TM p. 100.)

Phonics Review

Sing *Gh Clown Song*, CD track 17.

(Continued on next page)

Grand Tour II, pp. 49-50

Spelling Words
Phonetic Grouping: gh

- Note that all words have **silent gh**. Have students mark each word as indicated: **eig̸h̸t**

- As a class, read the 10 spelling words and discuss the meanings.

- Have students copy the 10 spelling words to take home, study, and write in sentences for homework.

p. 49

Spelling Vocabulary Activities

Homophones

- Tell students **homophones** are words that **sound alike** but have **different meanings** and **different spellings**.
  Example: blue—blew

- Students will write the spelling words that sound the same as the words listed on page 49.

Compound Words

- Students will write the spelling word that is a **compound word**.

Word Clues

- Students will write the spelling word that fits the clues.

Silent <u>gh</u> Words

- Students will write each spelling word and cross out the **silent gh**.

Grand Tour II, p. 50

Grammar

Punctuation: Period

- Tell students a **telling sentence** is a sentence that **tells** something. A **period** is always placed at the end of this kind of sentence.
  Example: Yesterday was a windy day.
  This sentence tells **when** and **what**.

- Students will read each sentence and place a period at the end.

- Next, students will write five of their own **telling sentences** and place a **period** at the end.

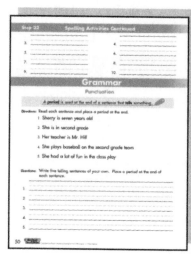

p. 50

Process Writing

Process Writing Lesson #11 for Steps 22 and 23 is found in TM p. 453.

Day 4

Getting Started

- Collect homework and put stars on Homework Chart. (See TM p. 26.)
- Administer spelling test with Day 3 spelling words in *Grand Tour II*, p. 49. Sentence for dictation: I like my <u>neighbor</u>. (See TM p. 100.)

Phonics Review

Sing *Gh Clown Song*, CD track 17.

Grand Tour II, p. 51

Spelling Words
Phonetic Grouping: gh (fff)

- Note that words #1-7 have **gh** that sounds like **fff**.
- As a class, read the 10 spelling words and discuss the meanings.
- Have students copy the 10 spelling words to take home, study, and write in sentences for homework.

Spelling Vocabulary Activities

Crossword Puzzle
- Students will read the clues by the number, find a spelling word that goes with the clue, and write the word by the number in the crossword puzzle.

p. 51

Homophones
- Remind students that **homophones** are words that **sound alike** but have **different meanings** and **different spellings**.
- Discuss the meanings for: **right—write; see—sea**
- Say the following sentences and ask a student to spell the correct **homophone**.

        Can you (**see**) me?
        We will sail on the (**sea**).
        I try to (**write**) neatly.
        Your answer is (**right**).

- Students will fill in each blank with the correct **homophone** on page 51.

Cloze
- Students will fill in each blank with a spelling word.

(**Continued on next page**)

Day 4 *continued*

Grand Tour II, p. 52

Story Comprehension

A Trough for Harry the Hippo

Have students:

- Underline the nine spelling words in the story.
- Read the story silently.
- Underline the correct answers.

The Writing Connection

Using a Reference Source

- Have students look in an encyclopedia, dictionary or picture book to see the difference between a rhinoceros and hippopotamus. (The rhino has one or two horns on its head, the hippo does not have horns.)
- Have students write a couple of sentences to tell how they are different.
- Next, students will draw a picture to show the difference.

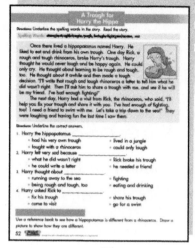

p. 52

Grammar Chalkboard Lesson
Punctuation

Objective

- The students will know that a **comma** is used after the **greeting** and **closing** in a friendly letter and that a **period** is used at the end of a sentence that **tells something**.

Practice/Apply

- Write the letter on the board. Students will copy it correctly.

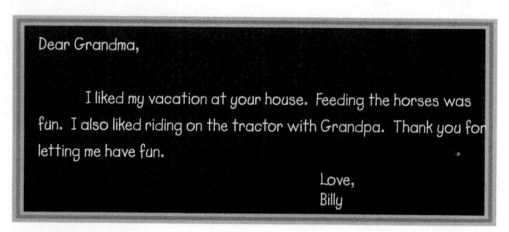

Dear Grandma,

   I liked my vacation at your house. Feeding the horses was fun. I also liked riding on the tractor with Grandpa. Thank you for letting me have fun.

                                        Love,
                                        Billy

Process Writing

Process Writing Lesson #11 for Steps 22 and 23 is found in TM p. 453.

Day 5

Getting Started

- Collect homework and put stars on Homework Chart. (See TM p. 26.)
- Administer spelling test with Day 4 spelling words in *Grand Tour II*, p. 51. Sentence for dictation: Fish swim in the <u>sea</u>. (See TM p. 100.)

Grand Tour II, pp. 53–54

Learning Cursive Writing

- To introduce cursive letters *Hh* and *Ii*, refer to TM p. 77.
- Students will trace over the letters, letter combinations, and/or words and practice writing them on the lines.

pp. 53-54

Process Writing

Process Writing Lesson #11 for Steps 22 and 23 is found in TM p. 453.

Additional Related Activities for Step 23

Listening and Speaking

1. ***Around the World* with Irregular Verb Forms**
   - Have a student stand beside another student seated at his/her desk.
   - The teacher will say the present form of a **verb** that changes its spelling to mean it **happened in the past**.
   - The student who is the first to say the correct verb moves on to the next desk, and the game continues.
   - Verbs to be called:

bite	(bit)	go	(went)	catch	(caught)
blow	(blew)	see	(saw)	teach	(taught)
break	(broke)	sit	(sat)	speak	(spoke)
fall	(fell)	sell	(sold)	write	(wrote)
eat	(ate)	ride	(rode)	win	(won)
drive	(drove)	make	(made)	wear	(wore)
get	(got)	know	(knew)	take	(took)
give	(gave)	hide	(hid)	sing	(sang)

2. ***Spelling Baseball***
   - Divide the class into two teams.
   - "Pitch" words to a team by calling out a word to spell from Step 23 spelling word lists.
   - A team gets a **hit** for each word spelled correctly and an **out** for each misspelled word. After three **outs** the next team comes to bat and the teacher begins "pitching" words to the new team.

NOTES

Overview for Step 24

Objectives

Phonics: To sing *Gh Clown Song*, providing phonics review and/or new instruction for those who need it

Spelling: To spell words with **gh**; **all**; **ar** = **or**; **dge** = **j**

Grammar: To know an abbreviation is a shorter way to write a word
To know a period is used after an abbreviation
To know that some months have abbreviations

Comprehension: To read short stories and answer questions requiring higher level thinking skills

Writing: To write sentences using homophones
To use the Five Steps of Process Writing, focusing on supporting ideas and specific details

Handwriting: To learn how to write cursive letters *Jj* and *Kk*

Suggested Pacing
1 week

Materials
Grand Tour II, pp. 55-64
Gh Clown Chart
Cursive Wall Chart

Homework
Daily homework is described in TM p. 99.

Spelling
Daily spelling is described in TM p. 99.

Phonics Games (See TM pp. 40-65.)
Continue to play selected games as needed for reinforcement.

Phonics Song
Gh Clown Song, CD track 17 (See TM p. 62.)

Additional Related Activities
Additional activities are found in TM p. 320.

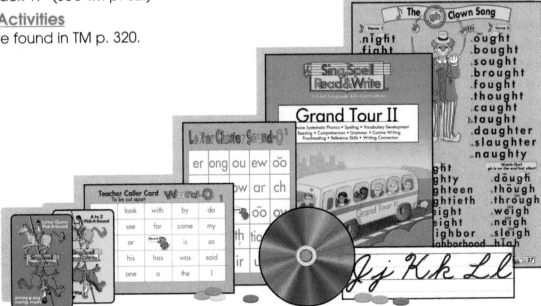

Grand Tour II

Day 1

Phonics Review

Sing *Gh Clown Song*, CD track 17.

Grand Tour II, p. 55

Spelling Words
Phonetic Grouping: gh

- Note that words #1-6 have **silent gh**. Have students mark each word as indicated: **dough**
- As a class, read the 10 spelling words and discuss the meanings.
- Introduce the homophone pairs: **led—lead** and **herd—heard**.
- Have students copy the 10 spelling words to take home, study, and write in sentences for homework.

Spelling Vocabulary Activities

Cloze
- Students will fill in the blanks with the correct words.

Break the Code
- Explain to students there are many different kinds of codes. In this code, each number represents a letter.
- Students will use the code to decode the spelling words and write them on the lines.

Grand Tour II, p. 56

Grammar

Abbreviations
- Remind students an **abbreviation** is a shorter way of writing a word. A **period** is used after an **abbreviation**.
- Have students read the **abbreviations** for the months and draw a line from the **abbreviation** to its matching month.
- Have students name the months that do not have abbreviations. **(May, June, July)**

p. 55

p. 56

Day 1 continued

Homophones

- Tell students **homophones** are words that **sound alike** but have **different meanings**.
  Example: cent—sent

- Write these pairs of **homophones** on the chalkboard: **I—eye; ad—add; chilly—chile; burro—burrow; flour—flower**

- Discuss the meanings and have students give one sentence using both words.
  Examples: ate—eight: We **ate** at **eight**.
  ant—aunt: My **aunt** found an **ant** in her soup.

- On page 56 students will draw lines to match the **homophones**.

The Writing Connection

Writing Sentences

- Have students choose three pairs of homophones from the lists on page 56 and write three sentences using a pair of homophones in each sentence.

Process Writing

Process Writing Lesson #12 for Steps 24 and 25 is found in TM p. 455.

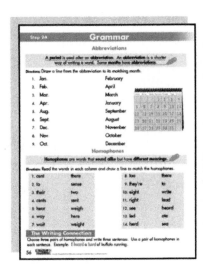

p. 56

Day 2

Getting Started

- Collect homework and put stars on the Homework Chart. (See TM p. 26.)
- Administer spelling test with Day 1 spelling words in *Grand Tour II*, p. 55. Sentence for dictation: The baker will make the <u>dough</u>. (See TM p. 100.)

Grand Tour II, p. 57

Spelling Words
Phonetic Grouping: all

- Note that words #1-8 have **all**. Have students mark words as indicated: ◯ **ball**
- Discuss homophones **flour** and **flower**.
- As a class, read the 10 spelling words and discuss the meanings.
- Have students copy the 10 spelling words to take home, study, and write in sentences for homework.

p. 57

(Continued on next page)

Grand Tour II

Day 2 *continued*

Spelling Vocabulary Activities

Word Clues
- Students will write a spelling word for each clue.

Rhyming
- Students will write the eight spelling words that **rhyme**.

Homophones
- Remind students **homophones** are words that **sound alike** but have **different meanings**.

- Students will fill in the blank with the name for each picture.

Grand Tour II, **p. 58**

p. 57

Story Comprehension

All Is Well
- Have students underline the eight spelling words in the story.

- Read the story aloud with the students.

- Students will complete the activity by underlining the correct answers.

Grammar Chalkboard Lesson
Abbreviations

Objective
- The students will know the **abbreviations** for the months of the year and that a **period** is used after **abbreviations**.

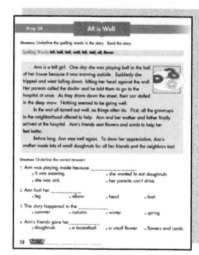

p. 58

Practice/Apply
- Write the names of the months on the board. Students will write the abbreviations correctly.

January	(Jan.)
February	(Feb.)
March	(Mar.)
April	(Apr.)
August	(Aug.)
September	(Sept.)
October	(Oct.)
November	(Nov.)
December	(Dec.)

Process Writing

Process Writing Lesson #12 for Steps 24 and 25 is found in TM p. 455.

Day 3

Getting Started

- Collect homework and put stars on the Homework Chart. (See TM p. 26.)
- Administer spelling test with Day 2 spelling words in *Grand Tour II*, p. 57. Sentence for dictation: <u>All</u> the boys went camping. (See TM p. 100.)

Grand Tour II, pp. 59-60

Spelling Words
Phonetic Grouping: ar = or

- Note that words #1-8 have **ar**. Explain that some words are exceptions to the phonics rules. In these words **ar = or**. They do not have the **ar** sound as in **car**. Have students mark words as indicated: **war**
- As a class, read the 10 spelling words and discuss the meanings.
- Have students copy the 10 spelling words to take home, study, and write in sentences for homework.

Spelling Vocabulary Activities

Cloze
- Students will fill in the blanks with the correct words.

Suffix <u>ed</u>
- Remind students a **suffix** is an ending added to a root word. The suffix **ed** changes the root word to mean "happened in the past."
- Students will change the spelling words to mean "happened in the past" by adding **ed**.

Silly Questions
- Have students read the silly questions, write the underlined spelling word in the blank, and write **yes** or **no** to answer the question.

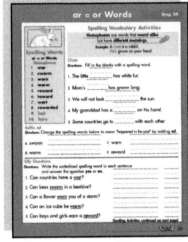

p. 59

Grand Tour II, p. 60

Grammar

Punctuation
- Remind students an **abbreviation** is a **shorter** way of writing a word. A **period** is used after an **abbreviation**.
- Have students read the **abbreviations**. Next, students will write the correct **abbreviation** for each day.
- Remind students to place a **period** after each **abbreviation** as they write the sentences correctly.

Process Writing

Process Writing Lesson #12 for Steps 24 and 25 is found in TM p. 455.

p. 60

Grand Tour II

Day 4

Getting Started

- Collect homework and put stars on Homework Chart. (See TM p. 26.)
- Administer spelling test with Day 3 spelling words in *Grand Tour II*, p. 59. Sentence for dictation: We saw a <u>swarm</u> of bees. (See TM p. 100.)

Grand Tour II, p. 61

Spelling Words
Phonetic Grouping: dge = j

- Note that all words have **dge**, making the **j** sound.
- As a class, read the 10 spelling words and discuss the meanings.
- Have students copy the 10 spelling words to take home, study, and write in sentences for homework.

Spelling Vocabulary Activities

Crossword Puzzle
- Students will read the clues by the number, find a spelling word that goes with the clue, and write the word by the number in the crossword puzzle.

Compound Words
- Students will fill in the blanks with the correct words.

Rhyming
- Students will write three spelling words that rhyme with **wedge** and three spelling words that rhyme with **budge**.

Word Scrambles
- Students will unscramble the letters and fill in the blanks with the correct spelling words.

Grand Tour II, p. 62

Story Comprehension

The Dodgeball Game
- Have students underline the seven spelling words in the story.
- As a group, read the story aloud.
- Students will read the questions and underline the correct answers.

The Writing Connection

Answering Questions
- Students will read the questions and fill in the blanks with appropriate answers.

p. 61

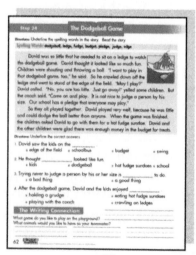

p. 62

Day 4 *continued*

Grammar Chalkboard Lesson
Abbreviations

Objective
* The students will know how to write the **abbreviations** for the days of the week.

Practice/Apply
* Write the names of the days on the board. Students will write the abbreviations correctly.

Sunday	(Sun.)
Monday	(Mon.)
Tuesday	(Tue.)
Wednesday	(Wed.)
Thursday	(Thu.)
Friday	(Fri.)
Saturday	(Sat.)

Process Writing

Process Writing Lesson #12 for Steps 24 and 25 is found in TM p. 455.

 Day 5

Getting Started

* Collect homework and put stars on the Homework Chart. (See TM p. 26.)
* Administer spelling test with Day 4 spelling words in *Grand Tour II*, p. 61. Sentence for dictation: The cat sat on the <u>ledge</u>. (See TM p. 100.)

Grand Tour II, pp. 63-64

Learning Cursive Writing

* To introduce cursive letters *Jj* and *Kk*, refer to TM p. 70.
* Students will trace over the letters, letter combinations, and/or words and practice writing them on the lines.

Process Writing

Process Writing Lesson #12 for Steps 24 and 25 is found in TM p. 455.

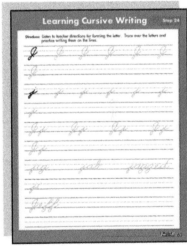

p. 63

p. 64

Additional Related Activities for Step 24

Listening and Speaking

1. Secret Messages

- Prepare a secret code chart as follows: Write the alphabet in a column. Next to each letter write the corresponding number 1 through 26. (A=1, B=2, C=3, etc.)
- Demonstrate the use of the chart by writing a short coded message to the students.
- Have students use the code to write a message naming their favorite food.
- Have students sign their name in the same code.
- Collect the coded messages and place them in a container.
- Have each student take a message from the container and decode it.
- Give each student an opportunity to read the decoded message to the class.

2. Rhyme Time

- As a class, look for pairs of rhyming words in the spelling word lists, Step 24, Days 1 through 4.
- Write the pairs of rhyming words on the chalkboard.
- Have each student write a couplet using a pair of rhyming words.

  Example: You are the **judge**.
  Is this the best **fudge**?

- Have students illustrate their couplets and share them with the class. You may want to collect these to make a class book.

NOTES

Grand Tour II

Overview for Step 25

Objectives

Spelling: To spell **ue** words; **x = cks** words; **ie = e** words; **ea = a** words

Grammar: To know how to write an asking sentence and place a question mark at the end

To know that when a word ends in **x**, add **es** to make it plural

To know a comma is used between the name of a city and state

Comprehension: To read short stories and answer questions requiring higher level thinking skills

Writing: To write a paragraph telling about the place you live

To use the Five Steps of Process Writing, focusing on supporting ideas and specific details

Handwriting: To learn how to write cursive letters *Ll* and *Mm*

Suggested Pacing
1 week

Materials
Grand Tour II, pp. 65-74
Cursive Wall Chart

Homework
Daily homework is described in TM p. 99.

Spelling
Daily spelling is described in TM p. 99.

Phonics Games (See TM pp. 40-65.)
Continue to play selected games as needed for reinforcement.

Phonics Songs (See TM pp. 40-65.)
Continue to sing selected songs as needed for reinforcement.

Additional Related Activities
Additional activities are found in TM p. 329.

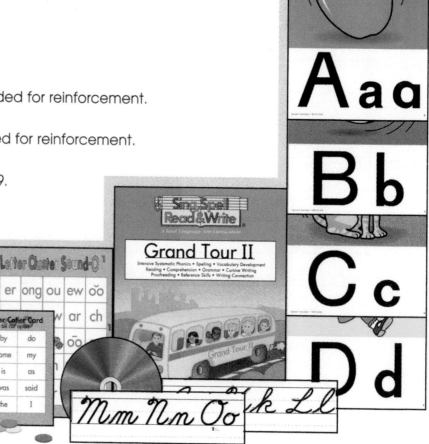

Day 1

Grand Tour II, pp. 65-66

Spelling Words
Phonetic Grouping: ue

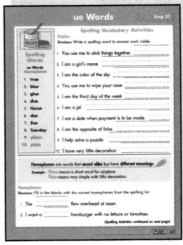

p. 65

- Note that words #1-8 have **ue** that sounds like $\overline{oo}$. Have students mark each word as indicated: true

- Point out homophones **plane** and **plain**.

- As a class, read the 10 spelling words and discuss the meanings.

- Have students copy the 10 spelling words to take home, study, and write in sentences for homework.

Spelling Vocabulary Activities

Riddles
- Students will write a spelling word to answer each **riddle**.

Homophones
- Remind students **homophones** are words that **sound alike** but have **different meanings**.

- Read and discuss the meaning of the homophones **plane** and **plain**.

- Say the following sentences and ask a student to spell the correct **homophone**.

        Dad will fly the small _____. (plane)
        I need _____ paper for the project. (plain)
        The shirt is _____ and simple. (plain)
        We saw a _____ overhead. (plane)

- On page 65 students will fill in the blanks with the correct **homophone**.

Syllables
- Students will write two spelling words that have two **syllables**.

Rhyming
- Students will write six spelling words that **rhyme**.

Grand Tour II, p. 66

Grammar

Punctuation: Question Mark
- Tell students sentences that begin with **what, when, why, where, who,** or **how** ask a **question**.

- Say the following sentences and ask students to identify the word that makes the sentence ask a **question**:

    What is your name? (what)   Why are you late? (why)
    Who will be with you? (who)   Where is your coat? (where)
    How late will you be? (how)

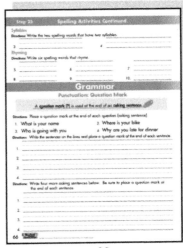

p. 66

- On page 66 students will place a **question mark** at the end of each **question** and then write the sentences on the lines.

- Next, students will write four more **asking sentences** of their own.

(**Continued on next page**)

Grand Tour II

Day 1 *continued*

Process Writing

Process Writing Lesson #12 for Steps 24 and 25 is found in TM p. 475.

Day 2

Getting Started

- Collect homework and put stars on Homework Chart. (See TM p. 26.)
- Administer spelling test with Day 1 spelling words in *Grand Tour II*, p. 65. Sentence for dictation: Can you give me a <u>clue</u>? (See TM p. 100.)

Grand Tour II, p. 67

Spelling Words
Phonetic Grouping: x = cks

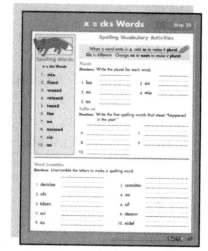

- Note that **x** at the end of a word sounds like **cks**.
- Have students sing the *A to Z Phonics Song* to hear the sound of **x** as in bo**x**.
- Note that all words have **x = cks**. Have students mark each word as indicated: mi**x**
- As a class, read the 10 spelling words and discuss the meanings.
- Have students copy the 10 spelling words to take home, study, and write in sentences for homework.

Spelling Vocabulary Activities

Plurals

- Tell students when a word means **more than one**, it is a **plural**. When a word ends in **s**, **sh**, **ch**, **x**, or **zz**, add **es** to make it **plural**.
  Example: box—boxes

- Tell students some words are **irregular plurals**. These words change their spelling and you don't add **s** or **es** to make the word plural. **Ox** to **oxen** is an **irregular plural**.
- Students will write plurals for the words listed.

Suffix <u>ed</u>

- Remind students that **ed** added to the end of a word is a **suffix** and makes the word mean "happened in the past."
- Students will write five spelling words that mean "happened in the past."

Word Scrambles

- Students will unscramble the letters to make a spelling word.

p. 67

Day 2 *continued*

Grand Tour II, p. 68

Story Comprehension

Taxes, Foxes, and Axes

Students will:

- Underline the ten spelling words in the story.
- Read the story.
- Underline the correct answers.

Grammar Chalkboard Lesson
Punctuation

Objective

- Students will know that a **period** is used at the end of a **telling sentence** and a **question mark** is used at the end of an **asking sentence**.

Practice/Apply

- Write the sentences on the board. Students will write and punctuate the sentences correctly.

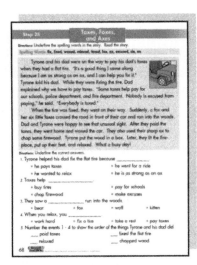

p. 68

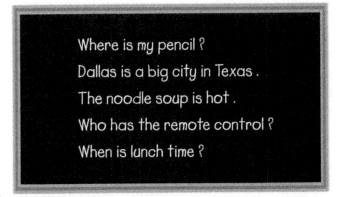

Where is my pencil ?

Dallas is a big city in Texas .

The noodle soup is hot .

Who has the remote control ?

When is lunch time ?

Process Writing

Process Writing Lesson #12 for Steps 24 and 25 is found in TM p. 475.

Day 3

Getting Started

- Collect homework and put stars on Homework Chart. (See TM p. 26.)
- Administer spelling test with Day 2 spelling words in *Grand Tour II*, p. 67. Sentence for dictation: Dad and I <u>waxed</u> our car. (See TM p. 100.)

(Continued on next page)

Grand Tour II

Grand Tour II, p. 69

Spelling Words
Phonetic Grouping: /ē = ē

- Tell students that some words are exceptions to the phonetic rules and today's list of words are all exceptions. The **ie** in each word sounds like a **long e**.

- Have students mark each spelling word as indicated: **bel/ēve**

- As a class, read the 10 spelling words and discuss the meanings.

- Have students copy the 10 spelling words to take home, study, and write in sentences for homework.

Spelling Vocabulary Activities

Break the Code

- Tell students they will be learning a new skill today. They will be using symbols to find the mystery letters. Have students look at the grid at the top right corner of page 69. Have them point to and repeat the name of each symbol as you say them (**star, heart, square, circle, flower, triangle, rectangle,** and **x**).

- Have students put one finger on the star and one finger on the **triangle**. Then have them trace one finger **straight across** from the **star** and the other finger **straight up** from the **triangle**. Ask them to tell what letter they found when their fingers bumped together. The letter **b** is found where the triangle and star **intersect**. Help students understand that **intersect** means to **meet** or **bump into**.

- It may help students if you describe the concept in this way: "Pretend the **triangle** is a car traveling **up** the row of letters, and the **star** is a car traveling **across** the row of letters. The two cars will meet at the letter b. Letter b is the point where the triangle and the **star intersect.**"

- This is not an easy concept for students to grasp, but an important one; so take the time to teach it and give assistance as long as needed.

- Students will use the code to write spelling words.

Silent i and Long e Words

- Students will write each spelling word, cross out the **silent i**, and mark the **long e**.
  Example: y/ēld

p. 69

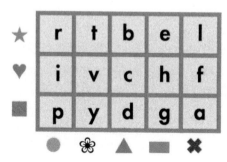

Sing, Spell Read & Write

Grand Tour II, p. 70

Grammar

Punctuation: Comma

- Tell students a **comma** is used to separate a **city** and **state**. Write the following cities and states on the board to model using **commas**.

    Clearwater, Florida
    Irvine, California
    Chicago, Illinois
    Nashville, Tennessee

- Students will place a **comma** between the **city** and **state** in the sentences on page 70. Next, they will write the sentences on the lines provided.

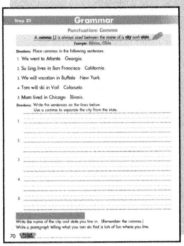

p. 70

The Writing Connection

Writing a Paragraph

- Brainstorm with students several fun activities in which they can participate in the city or town where they live.

- Have each student choose one activity he/she enjoys most and write a three to four sentence paragraph telling about the activity.

Process Writing

Process Writing Lesson #12 for Steps 24 and 25 is found in TM p. 475.

Day 4

Getting Started

- Collect homework and put stars on Homework Chart. (See TM p. 26.)

- Administer spelling test with Day 3 spelling words in *Grand Tour II*, p. 69. Sentence for dictation: It's not good to be a <u>thief</u>. (See TM p. 100.)

Grand Tour II, p. 71

Spelling Words
Phonetic Grouping: ẹ̶ā = ā

- Tell students words #1-8 have **ea**. The **e** is **silent** and the **a** is **long**.

- Have students mark the spelling words as indicated: **b r ẹ̶ā k**

- As a class, read the 10 spelling words and discuss the meanings.

- Have students copy the 10 spelling words to take home, study, and write in sentences for homework.

p. 71

(*Continued on next page*)

Grand Tour II

Spelling Vocabulary Activities

Crossword Puzzle
- Students will read the clue by the number, think of a spelling word that fits the clue, and write the word in the crossword puzzle.

Homophones
- Students will write a spelling word that is a **homophone** for each word listed.

Rhyming
- Students will write three spelling words that **rhyme** with **pear**.

Compound Words
- Students will write a spelling word that is a **compound word**.

Cloze
- Students will fill in the blanks with spelling words.

Grand Tour II, p. 72

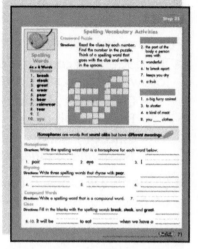

p. 71

Story Comprehension

The Bear and the Pear
Students will:
- Underline the nine spelling words in the story.
- Read the story.

The Writing Connection

- After reading *The Bear and the Pear*, students will draw two pictures.
- Have students write a sentence for each picture that tells what is happening.

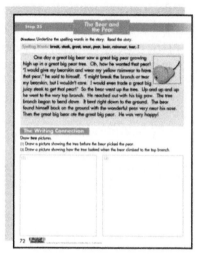

p. 72

Grammar Chalkboard Lesson
Punctuation

Objective
- The students will know that a **comma** is always used between the name of a **city** and **state**.

Practice/Apply
- Write the sentences on the board. Students will write and punctuate them correctly.

> Let's visit San Francisco, California.
>
> My friend moved to Nashville, Tennessee.
>
> There are big cactus plants in Phoenix, Arizona.
>
> We will fly to Denver, Colorado.
>
> Have you ever been to Waterloo, Iowa?

Process Writing

Process Writing Lesson #12 for Steps 24 and 25 is found in TM p. 475.

Getting Started

- Collect homework and put stars on Homework Chart. (See TM p. 26.)
- Administer spelling test with Day 4 spelling words in *Grand Tour II*, p. 71. Sentence for dictation: The <u>bear</u> went up the tree. (See TM p. 100.)

Grand Tour II, pp. 73-74

Handwriting Practice

- To introduce cursive letters *Ll* and *Mm*, refer to TM pp. 78-79.
- Students will trace over the letters, letter combinations, and/or words and practice writing them on the lines.

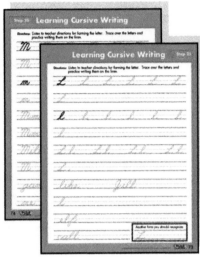

pp. 73-74

Process Writing

Process Writing Lesson #12 for Steps 24 and 25 is found in TM p. 475.

Additional Related Activities for Step 25

Listening and Speaking

1. *I Am Thinking of a Word*

- The teacher will choose a spelling word from one of the Step 25 lessons and say, "I am thinking of a word." The teacher calls on students to ask **yes** or **no** questions about the word. Questions might be ones such as, "Is it in the Day 3 list?" "Is it a word with a suffix?" "Does it have five letters?"
- The student continues asking questions as long as the teacher answers **yes**, but when the teacher answers **no**, the turn passes to another student.
- The student who identifies the correct word is the next caller.

I'm thinking of a word

2. Secret Messages

- Prepare a secret code chart as follows:
- Write the alphabet in a column. Next to each letter, write the corresponding numbers 26 to 1. A = 26, B = 25, C = 24, etc.
- Demonstrate the use of the chart by writing a short coded message to the students.
- Have each student use the code to write a message, naming his/her favorite TV program.
- Have students sign their names in the same code.
- Collect the coded messages and place them in a container.
- Have each student take a message from the container and decode it.
- Give each student an opportunity to read the decoded message to the class.

NOTES

Step 26

Overview for Step 26

Objectives

Spelling: To spell ĕđ = ĕ words; eđr = er words; f to ves words

Grammar: To know a comma is used between the day and year
To know the greeting of a letter and the first word in the closing of a letter should begin with a capital letter

Comprehension: To read short stories and answer questions requiring higher level thinking skills

Writing: To write a paragraph
To use the Five Steps of Process Writing, focusing on using varied sentence structure

Handwriting: To learn to recognize cursive letters written in sequence
To learn how to write cursive letter *Nn*

Suggested Pacing
1 week

Materials
Grand Tour II, pp. 75-84
Cursive Wall Chart

Homework
Daily homework is described in TM p. 99.

Spelling
Daily spelling is described in TM p. 99.

Phonics Games (See TM pp. 40-65.)
Continue to play selected games as needed for reinforcement.

Phonics Songs (See TM pp. 40-65.)
Continue to sing selected songs as needed for reinforcement.

Additional Related Activities
Additional activities are found in TM p. 338.

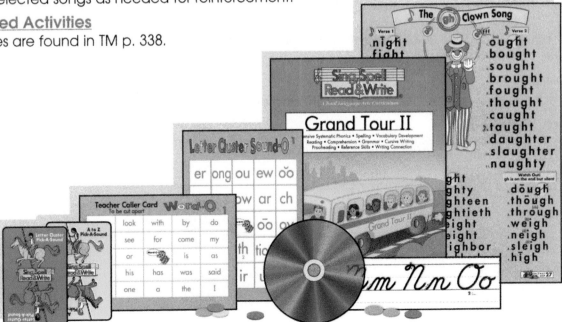

Grand Tour II

Day 1

Grand Tour II, pp. 75-76

Spelling Words
Phonetic Grouping: ĕá̸ = ĕ

- Note that each word has **ĕá̸ = ĕ**. Have students mark the words as indicated: **drĕá̸d**

- As a class, read the 10 spelling words and discuss the meanings.

- Have students copy the 10 spelling words to take home, study, and write in sentences for homework.

Spelling Vocabulary Activities

Cloze
- Students will fill in the blanks with spelling words.

Prefix un
- Remind students a **prefix** comes **at the beginning** of a **root word**. The prefix **un** means "not" and changes the word to mean the **opposite**.

- Have students give oral answers to the following questions:
  What is a shoe called when it's not tied? (**un**tied)
  What is a team called when it has not been defeated? (**un**defeated)
  How do you feel when you are not comfortable? (**un**comfortable)

- Students will write the prefix **un** at the beginning of each **root word** and draw a line from the new word to its meaning.

Word Association
- Remind students words go together for many reasons. Sometimes they go together because they mean the **same thing** or are the **same color**. Sometimes words go together because they are **used together**.

- Have students tell what word would finish these phrases:
  peanut butter and _____ (jelly)
  shoes and _____ (socks)
  in and _____ (out)

- On page 76 students will fill in the blanks with the spelling word that goes with each word listed.

Antonyms
- Students will write the opposites for **light** and **alive**.

Word Meanings
- Students will fill in the blanks with the correct words.

p. 75

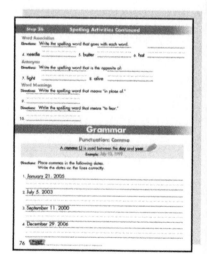

p. 76

Day 1 *continued*

Grand Tour II, p. 76

Grammar

Punctuation: Comma

- Write today's date on the board, omitting the **comma** and writing the day and year numerals fairly close together. (May 262000)

- Have students read the date. Insert the **comma** and have them read the date again. (May 26, 2000)

- Comment that the date is easier to read and understand when the **comma** is in place. Always use the **comma** between the **day** and **year**.

- Students will write the dates correctly on the lines provided.

Process Writing

Process Writing Lesson #13 for Steps 26 and 27 is found in TM p. 457.

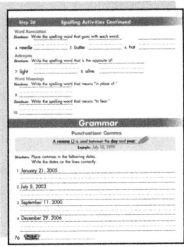

p. 76

Getting Started

- Collect homework and put stars on Homework Chart. (See TM p. 26.)

- Administer spelling test with Day 3 spelling words in *Grand Tour II*, p. 75. Sentence for dictation: We are <u>ready</u> for bed. (See TM p. 100.)

Grand Tour II, p. 77

Spelling Words
Phonetic Grouping: ĕa̸ = ĕ

- Note that words #1-8 have **ĕa̸ = e**. Have students mark the words as indicated: **wĕa̸ther**

- Note that words #9 and 10 are antonyms. (**awake, asleep**)

- As a class, read the 10 spelling words and discuss the meanings.

- Have students copy the 10 spelling words to take home, study, and write in sentences for homework.

Spelling Vocabulary Activities

Word Clues

- Students will write the spelling words that match the clues.

Silent a Words

- Tell students the first eight spelling words today are exceptions to the "two vowels go together" rule. In these words, the **ea** sounds like **ĕ**. Students will write the eight words and cross out the **silent a**.

Antonyms

- Students will fill in the blanks with the correct words.

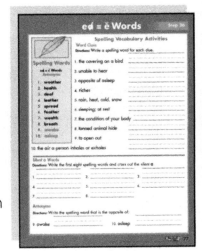

p. 77

(Continued on next page)

***Grand Tour II*, p. 78**

Story Comprehension

A Healthy Day Outdoors

Have students:

- Underline the nine spelling words in the story.
- Read the story silently.
- Underline the correct answers.

The Writing Connection

Writing a Paragraph

- Brainstorm with students, thinking of what it would be like to take a hike in the woods.
- Have students write a paragraph telling about the clothes and equipment needed for the hike.

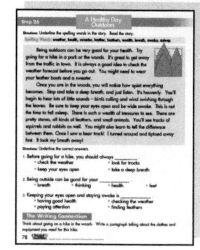

p. 78

Grammar Chalkboard Lesson
Punctuation

Objective

- The students will know that a **comma** is used between the **day** and **year**.

Practice/Apply

- Write the sentences on the board. Students will write the sentences correctly.

> Our country began on July 4, 1776.
>
> Su Lee was born on April 6, 1997.
>
> Where were you on January 1, 2000?
>
> My mom moved to Mexico City on June 17, 2000.
>
> The first men landed on the moon on July 20, 1969.

Process Writing

Process Writing Lesson #13 for Steps 26 and 27 is found in TM p. 457.

Day 3

Getting Started

- Collect homework and put stars on Homework Chart. (See TM p. 26.)
- Administer spelling test with Day 2 spelling words in *Grand Tour II*, p. 77. Sentence for dictation: The king has much <u>wealth</u>. (See TM p. 100.)

Grand Tour II, p. 79

Spelling Words
Phonetic Grouping: eǿr = er

- Note that words #1-8 have **eǿr = er**. Have students mark words as indicated: **leǿrn**
- Discuss homophones **won** and **one**.
- As a class, read the 10 spelling words and discuss the meanings.
- Have students copy the 10 spelling words to take home, study, and write in sentences for homework.

Spelling Vocabulary Activities

Homophones
- Tell students **homophones** are words that **sound alike** but have **different meanings**.
  Example: read—red

- Students will fill in the blanks with the correct words.

Word Meanings
- The students will write a spelling word to fit each meaning.

Break the Code
- Students will use the code to decode and write the spelling words.

p. 79

Grand Tour II, p. 80

Grammar

Capital Letters
- Have students locate the **heading, greeting, body, closing,** and **signature** of the letter.
- Remind students the **greeting** of a letter and the **first word** in the **closing** of a letter should begin with a **capital letter**.
- As a class, read the letter aloud.
- Have students circle the letters that should be **capitals**.
- Students will write the letter correctly on the lines provided, using **capitals** for the circled letters.

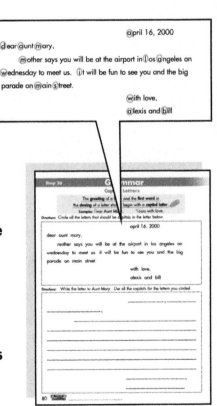

p. 80

Process Writing

Process Writing Lesson #13 for Steps 26 and 27 is found in TM p. 457.

Grand Tour II

Day 4

Getting Started

- Collect homework and put stars on Homework Chart. (See TM p. 26.)
- Administer spelling test with Day 3 spelling words in *Grand Tour II*, p. 79. Sentence for dictation: Mom has a <u>pearl</u> ring. (See TM p. 100.)

Grand Tour II, p. 81

Spelling Words
Phonetic Grouping: f to ves

- Note that words #1, 3, 5, 7, and 9 are **singular** words ending in **f**. Words #2, 4, 6, 8, and 10 are the **plural** forms of these words and the **f** has been changed to **v** and **es** has been added.
- As a class, read the 10 spelling words and discuss the meanings.
- Have students copy the 10 spelling words to take home, study, and write sentences for homework.

Spelling Vocabulary Activities

Word Search

- Tell students all the spelling words are found in the word search. The words go across or down.
- Students will draw a ring around each word as they find it.

Plurals

- Explain that the words in today's lesson are **exceptions**. They form their **plurals** in a special way, changing **f** to **v** and then adding **es**.
- Have the students touch each picture and say the picture name.
- Students will write the correct spelling words by the pictures.

Grand Tour II, p. 82

Story Comprehension

The Loaves

- Have students underline the eight spelling words in the story.
- As a group, read the story aloud.
- Students will read the sentences and fill in the blanks with the correct words.

p. 81

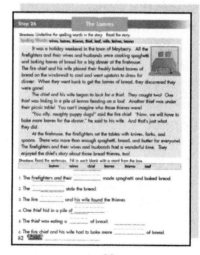

p. 82

Day 4 continued

Grammar Chalkboard Lesson
Capital Letters

Objective
- The students will know that the **greeting** of a letter and the **first word** in the **closing** of a letter should begin with a **capital letter**.

Practice/Apply
- Write the letter on the board. The students will write the letter correctly.

> august 6, 2001
>
> dear tasha,
>
>   you are invited to my birthday party on thursday afternoon
> right after school. it will be at my house. i hope you can come.
>
>   your friend,
>   natalie

Process Writing

Process Writing Lesson #13 for Steps 26 and 27 is found in TM p. 457.

Day 5

Getting Started

- Collect homework and put stars on Homework Chart. (See TM p. 26.)
- Administer spelling test with Day 4 spelling words in *Grand Tour II*, p. 81. Sentence for dictation: I saw two <u>leaves</u> fall. (See TM p. 100.)

Grand Tour II, p. 83

Recognizing Cursive Letters in Sequence

- Prepare a set of cursive alphabet flash cards, letters $a-m$ and $a-m$.
- Scramble the cards and flash them to the class.
- As a class, have students say the letter names.
- On page 83 have students connect the dots in alphabetical sequence.
- Have students practice writing the letter Mm in the space provided.
- Students will fill in the missing letter in the sentence and trace over the words.

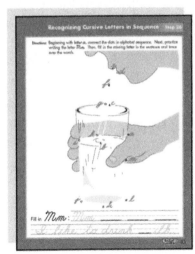

p. 83

(Continued on next page)

Grand Tour II

Grand Tour II, p. 84

Learning Cursive Writing

* To introduce cursive letter $\mathcal{Nn}$, refer to TM p. 79.
* Students will trace over the letters and/or words and practice writing them on the lines.

Process Writing

Process Writing Lesson #13 for Steps 26 and 27 is found in TM p. 457.

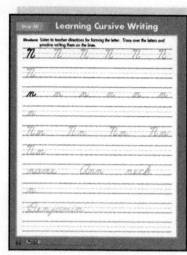

p. 84

Additional Related Activities for Step 26

Listening and Speaking

1. *Antonym Stumper*

* To prepare for the game, write the following antonym pairs on the board: **above—below; add—subtract; alone—together; answer—question; back—front; big—little; clean—dirty; day—night; dull—sharp; high—low; more—less; near—far; last—first**

* Provide each student with six cards (three 3 x 5 index cards cut in half). Have the students choose and write one word from a pair of antonyms on the front of the card and the second word on the back. Each student continues choosing and writing various antonym pairs until he/she has completed six cards.

* Erase the board.

* To demonstrate the game, hold up a card and show the word on one side to a student. Have the student say the word shown and guess the antonym on the other side. If they are "stumped," the teacher keeps the card and shows another. If the student says the word and its antonym correctly, they get the card. Then they show one of their cards to the teacher.

* To play the game, pair the students. They will proceed to play as demonstrated.

* When one partner gets all the cards, each takes their original cards and moves to a new partner.

2. Cursive Alphabet Book

* Provide a supply of plain paper for the students to use in making cursive alphabet books.

* Have students write the cursive letters $\mathcal{Aa}$ through $\mathcal{Mm}$ in their best writing on separate pages of plain paper.

* Students will illustrate each page with an object that begins with the appropriate letter.

* Continue this project, with students making additional pages as more cursive letters are learned.

* Have students make a cover and fasten the pages together to make a book when the project is complete.

NOTES

Grand Tour II

Overview for Step 27

Objectives

Spelling: To spell words with **long i**; **long o**; **u = ŏŏ**; **air**

Grammar: To know the prefix **re** means "do again"

To know a comma is used to separate things in a list

To know the suffix **er** means "more than"

To know the suffix **est** means "the most"

To know the suffix **ed** means "in the past"

To know the prefix **un** makes the new word mean the opposite

To know irregular plurals

Comprehension: To read short stories and answer questions requiring higher level thinking skills

Writing: To write a sentence using comparative words

To use the Five Steps of Process Writing, focusing on using varied sentence structure

Proofreading: To correct mistakes in a paragraph and use proofreading marks

Handwriting: To learn how to write cursive letters Oo, Pp, and $2q$

Suggested Pacing

1 week

Materials

Grand Tour II, pp. 85-96
Cursive Wall Chart

Homework

Daily homework is described in TM p. 99.

Spelling

Daily spelling is described in TM p. 99.

Phonics Games (See TM pp. 40-65.)

Continue to play selected games as needed for reinforcement.

Phonics Songs (See TM pp. 40-65.)

Continue to play selected songs as needed for reinforcement.

Additional Related Activities

Additional activities are found in TM p. 348.

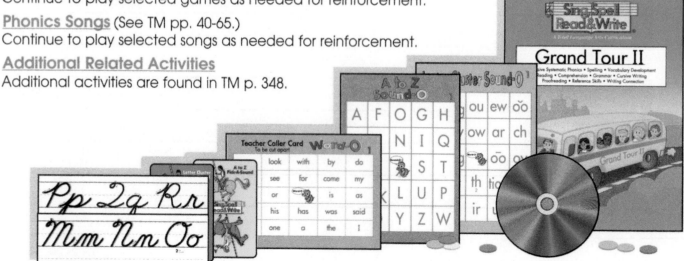

Day 1

Grand Tour II, pp. 85-86

Spelling Words
Phonetic Grouping: ī

p. 85

- Note that each word has **ind** with a **long i**. Have students mark each word as indicated: **grīnd**
- As a class, read the 10 spelling words and discuss the meanings. Point out the two pronunciations for **wind**.
- Have students copy the 10 spelling words to take home, study, and write in sentences for homework.

Spelling Vocabulary Activities

Silly Questions
Students will:
- Read the silly questions.
- Write the underlined spelling words.
- Answer each question **yes** or **no**.

Prefix re
- Tell students a **prefix** is a syllable added to the front of a word. The prefix **re** means "do again."
  Example: retell means to **tell again**.
- Ask students to think of words to which the prefix **re** could be added. Suggestions: **work, tie, read, place, count**
- On page 85, students will add **re** to the spelling words listed.

Suffixes er and ness
- Tell students **er** and **ness** are suffixes added to the end of a word.
- Students will write the spelling words that have the suffix **er** or **ness**.

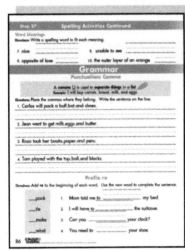

p. 86

Word Meanings
- Students will write a spelling word to fit each meaning on page 86.

(Continued on next page)

Day 1 continued

Grand Tour II, p. 86

Grammar

Punctuation: Comma

- Tell students when you have three or more items listed in a sentence, a **comma** is used to **separate the items**.

- Model the use of **commas** in a **list** by writing these sentences on the board:
  1. John, Martha, and Bob will be late.
  2. We bought paper, pencils, notebooks, and crayons at the store.
  3. Nate and Alexis are my friends.

- Discuss how sentence (1) has **three** items and has commas after the first two items. Sentence (2) has **four** items and has commas after the first three items. Sentence (3) has only **two** items and has no commas.

- On page 86 students will place **commas** where they are needed in each sentence and write the sentence on the line.

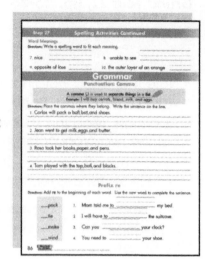

p. 86

Prefix <u>re</u>

Students will:

- Add the prefix **re** to each word in the box.
- Use the new words to complete the sentences.

Process Writing

Process Writing Lesson #13 for Steps 26 and 27 is found in TM p. 457.

Day 2

Getting Started

- Collect homework and put stars on Homework Chart. (See TM p. 26.)
- Administer spelling test with Day 1 spelling words in *Grand Tour II*, p. 85. Sentence for dictation: Did you <u>find</u> my ring? (See TM p. 100.)

Grand Tour II, p. 87

Spelling Words
Phonetic Grouping: ō

- Note that each word has **old** with a **long o**.
- Have students mark each word as indicated: **ōld**
- As a class, read the 10 spelling words and discuss the meanings.
- Have students copy the 10 spelling words to take home, study, and write in sentences for homework.

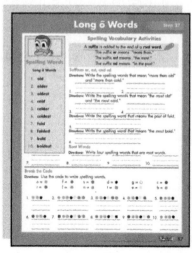

p. 87

Day 2 continued

Spelling Vocabulary Activities

Suffixes er, est, and ed

- Read and discuss the meanings of suffixes **er**, **est**, and **ed** listed in the shaded box.

- Tell students the prefix **er** can also mean "a person."

- Write the following words on the board and ask students to tell whether the suffix **er** changed the word to a person or a comparison word meaning "more than."

teacher (person)	richer (more than rich)
warmer (more than warm)	worker (person)
brighter (more than bright)	singer (person)

- Students will write spelling words with suffixes on page 87 that will fit the definitions.

Root Words

- Students will write four spelling words that are root words.

Break the Code

- Students will use the color code to write the spelling words.

p. 87

Grand Tour II, p. 88

Story Comprehension

Old, Older, Oldest

Students will:

- Underline the nine spelling words in the story.

- Read the story.

- Underline the correct answers.

The Writing Connection

Writing Sentences with Comparative Words

- Students will write a sentence that includes the comparative words **young**, **younger**, and **youngest**.

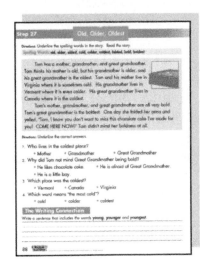

p. 88

(Continued on next page)

Day 2 continued

Grammar Chalkboard Lesson
Punctuation

Objective
- The students will know that a **comma** is used to **separate things** in a **list**.

Practice/Apply
- Write the sentences on the board. The students will write the sentences correctly.

---

1. Tony has a sandwich, a cookie, and an apple in his lunch.

2. There are cars, trucks, and vans in the parking lot.

3. My friends are Jenna, Tommy, and Mike.

4. Macon, Atlanta, and Columbus are cities in Georgia.

5. Nick lost his red, green, and yellow markers.

Process Writing

Process Writing Lesson #13 for Steps 26 and 27 is found in TM p. 457.

Mon Tues Wed Thurs Fri

Day 3

Getting Started

- Collect homework and put stars on Homework Chart. (See TM p. 26.)
- Administer spelling test with Day 2 spelling words in *Grand Tour II*, p. 87. Sentence for dictation: This day is the <u>coldest</u>. (See TM p. 100.)

Grand Tour II, pp. 89-90

Spelling Words
Phonetic Grouping: u = ŏŏ

- Tell students each word has **u** which sounds like letter cluster **ŏŏ**.
- As a class, read the 10 spelling words and discuss the meanings.
- Have students copy the 10 spelling words to take home, study, and write in sentences for homework.

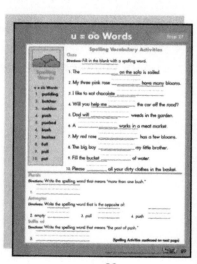

p. 89

Spelling Vocabulary Activities

Cloze
* Students will fill in the blanks with spelling words.

Plurals
* Students will write the spelling word that means "more than one bush."

Antonyms
* Remind students antonyms are opposites.
   Examples: day—night; hot—cold

* Students will write a spelling word that is the opposite of each word listed.

Suffix __ed__
* Write the spelling word that means "the past of push."

Word Meanings
* On page 90 students will write a spelling word to fit each meaning.

Grand Tour II, p. 90

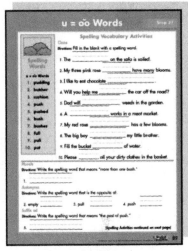

p. 89

Grammar

Punctuation: Comma
* Tell students when you have three or more items listed in a sentence, a **comma** is used to separate the items.
   Example: I ate cereal, bacon, and toast for breakfast.
   Model placement of commas in this sentence and other similar sentences on the board.

* On page 90 students will place **commas** where they belong and write the sentences on the lines.

Prefix __un__
* Tell students when the prefix **un** is added to a word, it makes the new word mean the **opposite**.
   Example: tie—untie
* Students will add **un** to each word in the box and use the new words to complete the sentences.

Process Writing

Process Writing Lesson #13 for Steps 26 and 27 is found in TM p. 457.

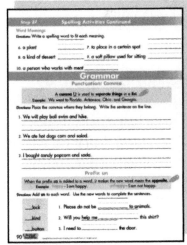

p. 90

(Continued on next page)

Grand Tour II

Day 4

Getting Started

- Collect homework and put stars on Homework Chart. (See TM p. 26.)
- Administer spelling test with Day 3 spelling words in *Grand Tour II*, p. 89. Sentence for dictation: <u>Pudding</u> is fun to eat. (See TM p. 100.)

Grand Tour II, pp. 91-92

Spelling Words
Phonetic Grouping: air

- Note that each word has **air**. Have students mark each word as indicated: st**air**
- As a class, read the 10 spelling words and discuss the meanings.
- Have students copy the 10 spelling words to take home, study, and write in sentences for homework.

Spelling Vocabulary Activities

Crossword Puzzle
- Students will read the clues by the number, find a spelling word that goes with the clue, and write the word by the number in the crossword puzzle.

Compound Words / Rhyming / Prefix / Synonyms / Antonyms
- Students will read the directions for each section and write the correct spelling words.

Word Pairs
- Students will read each pair of sentences and write a spelling word to complete the second sentence in the pair.

Grand Tour II, p. 92

Story Comprehension

The Tooth Fairy on the Stairway
- Students will underline the spelling words and read the story.
- Teach students how to take words from a question and use those words to answer the question in a complete sentence. Write the following questions on the board and have students write the answers in complete sentences:

    1. Where did Maria put her teeth for the tooth fairy?
       (Maria put her teeth under a pillow for the tooth fairy.)
    2. What did the tooth fairy leave for Maria?
       (The tooth fairy left money for Maria.)

p. 91

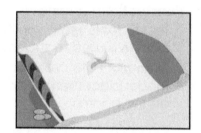

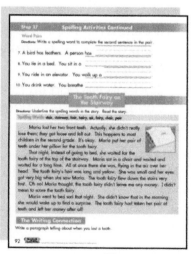

p. 92

The Writing Connection

Writing a Paragraph

- Have students share their experiences about losing a tooth. Have students write a paragraph telling:
  - How they lost a tooth.
  - Which tooth they lost.
  - What they did with the tooth.
  - If they received a gift.

Grammar Chalkboard Lesson
Punctuation

Objective

- The students will know that a **comma** is used to separate things in a series.

Practice/Apply

- Write the sentences on the board. The students will write the sentences correctly.

> 1. Ryan, Maria, and Teresa will ride with Mrs. Gomez.
> 2. At school we play baseball, basketball, and tag.
> 3. Dad put tacos, salsa, and salad on the table.
> 4. Do you like cheese, mushrooms, and ham on your pizza?
> 5. I have books, paper, and pencils in my desk.

Process Writing

Process Writing Lesson #13 for Steps 26 and 27 is found in TM p. 457.

Day 5

Getting Started

- Collect homework and put stars on Homework Chart. (See TM p. 26.)
- Administer spelling test with Day 4 spelling words in *Grand Tour II*, p. 91. Sentence for dictation: Do not run up the <u>stairs</u>. (See TM p. 100.)

Grand Tour II, p. 93

Proofreading

- Review the use of **commas** to **separate things** in a **list**.
- Review the **proofreading marks** and have students look at the example to see how it is marked.
- Students will read the paragraph and use the **proofreading marks** to correct one spelling mistake, insert three capital letters, and add four commas.

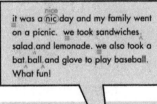

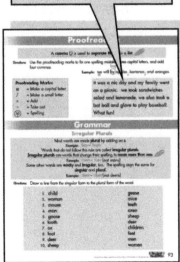

p. 93

(Continued on next page)

Grand Tour II

Grammar

Irregular Plurals

- Tell students most words are made plural by adding **s**.
  Examples: girl—girls; boy—boys

- Words that do not follow this rule are called **irregular plurals**. **Irregular plurals** change their spelling.
  Example: tooth—teeth

- Tell students there are a few words that stay the same for both **singular** and **plural**.
  Examples: deer—deer; sheep—sheep

- On page 93 students will draw a line from the **singular** form to the **plural** form of the word.

Grand Tour II, pp. 94-96

Learning Cursive Writing

- To introduce cursive letters Oo, Pp, and Qq refer to TM pp. 79-80.
- Students will trace over the letters and/or words and practice writing them on the lines.

Process Writing

Process Writing Lesson #13 for Steps 26 and 27 is found in TM p. 457.

pp. 94-96

Additional Related Activities for Step 27

Listening and Speaking

1. Riddles

- Children will work in pairs to make up **riddles** using spelling words from Step 27.
  Example: What do we call a person who cuts meat? (**butcher**)

- Let students share their riddles and ask for a volunteer to answer.

2. *Hot Potato* with Suffixes <u>er</u>, <u>est</u>, <u>ed</u>, and Prefixes <u>un</u> and <u>re</u>

- Sit in a circle.
- Toss a beanbag to a student and say:
  1. Make help mean **a person**. (help**er**)
  2. Make help mean **in the past**. (help**ed**)
  3. Make play mean **play again**. (**re**play)
  4. Make cold mean **the most cold**. (cold**est**)
  5. Make happy mean **not happy**. (**un**happy)
  6. Make tie mean **tie again**. (**re**tie)
  7. Make warm mean **more than warm**. (warm**er**)
- Continue in this manner with other words.

NOTES

Grand Tour II

Overview for Step 28

Objectives

Spelling: To spell **ui** = **ōō** words; **or** = **er** words

Grammar: To know an apostrophe is used to show ownership
To know homophones are words that sound alike but have different meanings
To know irregular plurals

Comprehension: To read a short story and a poem

Writing: To write an explanatory paragraph
To use the five steps of Process Writing, focusing on interesting word choice

Handwriting: To learn how to write cursive letter $\mathcal{R}r$

Suggested Pacing
1 week

Materials
Grand Tour II, pp. 97-106
Cursive Wall Chart

Homework
Daily homework is described in TM p. 99.

Spelling
Daily spelling is described in TM p. 99.

Phonics Games (See TM pp. 40-65.)
Continue to play selected games as needed for reinforcement.

Phonics Songs (See TM pp. 40-65.)
Continue to sing selected songs as needed for reinforcement.

Additional Related Activities
Additional activities are found in TM p. 358.

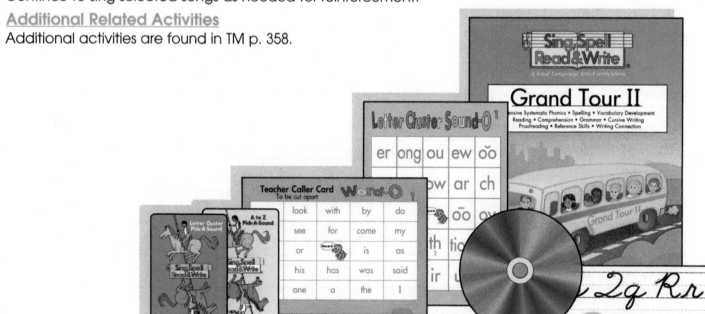

Day 1

Grand Tour II, p. 97

Spelling Words
Phonetic Grouping: ui = o͞o

- Note that words #1-6 are **ui = o͞o** words. Have students mark each word as indicated: **nuisance**

- Note that words #7-8 and #9-10 are homophones (two words that sound alike but have different meanings).

- As a class, read the 10 spelling words and discuss the meanings.

- Have students copy the 10 spelling words to take home, study, and write in sentences for homework.

Spelling Vocabulary Activities

Long o͞o Words

- Students will write six spelling words that have the **long o͞o** sound.

Long e Words

- Students will write four spelling words that have the **long e** sound.

Homophones

- As a review, have a student read the homophone examples and definitions in the shaded box.

- Students will fill in the blanks with the correct homophones.

Riddles

- Students will read the riddles and fill in the blanks with the correct spelling words.

p. 97

Grand Tour II, p. 98

Grammar

Punctuation: Apostrophe

- Write this sentence on the chalkboard: **The book belongs to Bob**. Ask the students to tell what Bob owns. **(the book)**

- Next, write: **This is Bob's book**. Ask the students to tell what Bob owns. **(the book)**

- Circle the word **Bob's**. Point to the apostrophe in **Bob's**. Explain that the mark is called an **apostrophe**, and it shows ownership.

- On the chalkboard write these sentences containing singular possessive nouns:

    This is **Levon's** desk.
    This is **Tara's** pencil.

- Point out that an **apostrophe** and **s** have been added to each name to show ownership.

- As a class, read sentences #1-8 on page 98.

- Have students add an **apostrophe** and **s** to each underlined word.

p. 98

(Continued on next page)

Grand Tour II

Homophones

- Students will read the words and draw lines to match the homophones with the pictures.

Process Writing

Process Writing Lesson #14 for Steps 28 and 29 is found in TM p. 459.

Day 2

Getting Started

- Collect homework and put stars on Homework Chart. (See TM p. 26.)
- Administer spelling test with Day 1 spelling words in *Grand Tour II*, p. 97. Sentence for dictation: I like to eat <u>fruit</u>. (See TM p. 100.)

Grand Tour II, pp. 99–100

Spelling Words
Phonetic Grouping: or = er

- Note that each word has **or** = **er**. Tell students that when **or** comes after **w** or when it is at the end of a word, it sounds like **er**. Have students mark each word as indicated: w⊙rry
- As a class, read the 10 spelling words and discuss the meanings.
- Have students copy the 10 spelling words to take home, study, and write in sentences for homework.

Spelling Vocabulary Activities

Break the Code

- Review using a grid to locate the mystery letters. (See TM p. 326.)
- Students will use the symbols to decode letters and fill in the blanks with the correct spelling words.

Cloze

- Students will fill in the blanks with the correct spelling words.

Story Comprehension

Working at the Harbor

- Have students underline the seven spelling words in the story.
- Students will read the story silently.
- Discuss the story. Ask students to tell how Mr. Stevens felt about boats. What clues helped them to think that? Why was his boss happy that Mr. Stevens worked for him? How did Mr. Stevens get his own boat?

p. 98

p. 99

p. 100

Day 2 *continued*

Grammar Chalkboard Lesson
Punctuation

Objective
• The students will know that an apostrophe is used to show ownership.

Practice/Apply
• Write the sentences on the board. The students will rewrite the sentences using an **apostrophe** and **s** to show ownership.
  Example: The book belongs to Carla. (It is Carla's book.)

1. The bike belongs to Joseph.   It is Joseph's bike.
2. The lunch belongs to Shantel.   It is Shantel's lunch.
3. The house belongs to Mr. Amman.   It is Mr. Amman's house.
4. The dish belongs to Ginger.   It is Ginger's dish.
5. The car belongs to Juan.   It is Juan's car.

Process Writing

Process Writing Lesson #14 for Steps 28 and 29 is found in TM p. 459.

Day 3

Getting Started

• Collect homework and put stars on Homework Chart. (See TM p. 26.)
• Administer spelling test with Day 2 spelling words in *Grand Tour II*, p. 99. Sentence for dictation: We ride in the <u>motorboat</u>. (See TM p. 100.)

Grand Tour II, p. 101

Spelling Words
Phonetic Grouping: or = er

• Note that each word has **or** = **er**. When **or** comes after **w** or at the end of a word, it sounds like **er**. Have students mark each word as indicated: **mirror**
• As a class, read the 10 spelling words and discuss the meanings.
• Have students copy the 10 spelling words to take home, study, and write in sentences for homework.

p. 101

(*Continued on next page*)

Day 3 *continued*

Spelling Vocabulary Activities

Suffixes ful and less

- Tell students that the suffix **ful** means **full of**.
- Write examples of **ful** words (**thankful, peaceful, careful**) on the chalkboard. Discuss the meanings: **full of thanks, full of peace, full of care**.
- Students will fill in the blanks on page 101 with two spelling words that mean **full of**.
- Tell students that the suffix **less** means **without**. Write examples of **less** words (**fearless, tasteless, careless**) on the chalkboard. Discuss the meanings: **without fear, without taste, without care**.
- Students will fill in the blanks with two spelling words that mean **less**.

Root Words

- Students will fill in the blank with the spelling word that is the root word for **colorful**.

Word Clues

- Students will write a spelling word to fit the clue.

Syllables

- Review syllables with students. Remind them that all words are made of one or more parts. Each part is called a **syllable**. Say words and have students clap for each **syllable** and tell how many **syllables** they hear in each word. Suggested words: **motorboat, worker, worrying, worm, work**
- Students will write each spelling word and the number of syllables heard in each word on page 101.

p. 101

Grand Tour II, p. 102

Grammar

Punctuation: Apostrophe

- Review the use of an **apostrophe** to show ownership. Write the following phrases on the chalkboard:

    Joshua's coat
    Kara's pencil
    Juan's book
    Lee's house

- Ask students to identify the owners of each item. Point out that an **apostrophe** and **s** have been added to each name to show **ownership**.
- Students will read the sentences and add **apostrophe** and **s** to each underlined word.

Homophones

- Students will read the words and draw lines to match the homophones with the pictures.

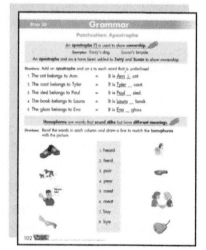

p. 102

Process Writing

Process Writing Lesson #14 for Steps 28 and 29 is found in TM p. 459.

Day 4

Getting Started

- Collect homework and put stars on the Homework Chart. (See TM p. 26).
- Administer spelling test with Day 3 Spelling words in *Grand Tour II*, p. 101. Sentence for dictation: This cake is <u>flavorful</u>. (See TM p. 100).

Grand Tour II, pp. 103–104

Spelling Words
Phonetic Grouping: or = er

- Note that all words have **or** = **er**. Remind students that when **or** comes after **w** or when it is at the end of a word, it sounds like **er**. Have students mark each word as indicated: **visitor**
- As a class, read the 10 spelling words and discuss the meanings.
- Have students copy the 10 spelling words to take home, study, and write in sentences for homework.

Spelling Vocabulary Activities

Crossword Puzzle
- Students will read the clues by the number, think of a spelling word that fits the clue, and write the words in the crossword puzzle.

Possessives
- Review the use of **apostrophe** and **s** to show ownership.
- Students will fill in the blank with the possessive form of the word.

Word Scrambles
- Students will unscramble the letters and fill in the blanks with the correct spelling words.

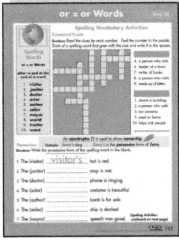

p. 103

Grand Tour II, p. 104

Story Comprehension

Doctor? Sailor? Or Actor?
- Have the students underline the six spelling words in the poem.
- As a group, read the poem aloud.
- Discuss the poem. What are the jobs named in the poem?

The Writing Connection

Writing a Paragraph
- Have students write a paragraph telling **what** they want to be when they grow up. Encourage students to write about **what** they will do and **why** they made that choice.

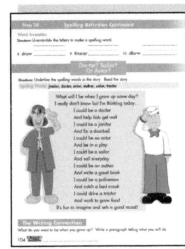

p. 104

(Continued on next page)

Grammar Chalkboard Lesson
Punctuation

Objective

* The students will know that an **apostrophe** and **s** show ownership.

Practice/Apply

* Write the sentences on the board. The students will rewrite the sentences using an **apostrophe** and **s** to show ownership.

   Example: The book belongs to Carla. It is Carla's book.

1. The dog belongs to Bert	It is Bert's dog.
2. The foot belongs to the bird.	It is the bird's foot.
3. The game belongs to Donna.	It is Donna's game.
4. The shoe belongs to Jim.	It is Jim's shoe.
5. The dress belongs to Mother.	It is Mother's dress.

Process Writing

Process Writing Lesson #14 for Steps 28 and 29 is found in TM p. 459.

Day 5

Getting Started

- Collect homework and put stars on the Homework Chart. (See TM p. 26).
- Administer spelling test with Day 4 spelling words in *Grand Tour II*, p. 103. Sentence for dictation: The <u>sailor</u> was on the ship. (See TM p. 100).

Grand Tour II, p. 105

Proofreading

- Review the **proofreading marks** and have students look at the example to see how it is marked. Call attention to the apostrophe used to show ownership in the word **Bill's**.
- Students will read the paragraph and use **proofreading marks** to correct one spelling mistake, insert two capital letters, and add two apostrophes to show ownership.

Grammar

Irregular Plurals

- Tell students that most words are made plural by adding **s** or **es**.
  Examples: cat—cats; wish—wishes
- Words that do not follow the rule are called **irregular plurals**. **Irregular plurals** change their spelling.
  Examples: ox—oxen
- Tell students that there are a few words that stay the same for both singular and plural.
  Examples: fish—fish; sheep—sheep
- Students will read the sentences on page 105 and fill in each blank with a word from the shaded box.

Grand Tour II, p. 106

Learning Cursive Writing

- To introduce the cursive letter $\mathcal{Rr}$, refer to TM p. 80.
- Students will trace over the cursive letters and words and practice writing them on the lines.

Process Writing

Process Writing Lesson #14 for Steps 28 and 29 is found in TM p. 459.

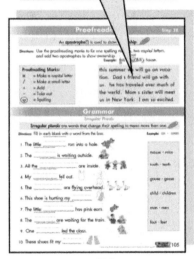

p. 105

p. 106

Grand Tour II

Additional Related Activities for Step 28

Listening and Speaking

1. *"What am I?"* Charades

- Prepare cards with occupations ending in **er** or **or**. Suggested words: **baker, sailor, doctor, janitor, author, writer, mayor, thinker, painter, actor, digger, singer, conductor, driver, flyer, builder, batter, pitcher, catcher, shopper, farmer, operator, teacher**.

- Explain to students that many words naming jobs or things people do end in **er** or **or** = **er**.

- Distribute cards, one to each student.

- Ask for a volunteer to be the leader and act out the occupation on his/her card.

- Call on students to guess the occupation word.

- The person who guesses correctly is the next leader.

- If the word has not been guessed after three tries, have the leader show the card. Call on a student to read the card and be the next leader.

2. *Bingo*

- Provide each student with one sheet of 8½″ x 11″ copy paper. Direct students to fold the paper in half, two times vertically and two times horizontally, making 16 boxes.

- Have students unfold the paper and choose 16 spelling words from the lists on pages 97, 99, 101 and 103. The students then write the 16 words, one in each box. Each Bingo sheet should have a different selection of words arranged in a different order.

- The game is played like regular Bingo except that the cards have 16 **words** instead of numbers. Students may use SSR&W see-through game markers.

- The teacher acts as the caller. Randomly call words from the four spelling lists. Write the words on the chalkboard as they are called in order to verify the winning card.

suit	meet	be	worry
worm	razor	mirror	color
worker	worth	flavor	visitor
tractor	word	actor	world

NOTES

Grand Tour II

Overview for Step 29

Objectives

Spelling: To spell contractions using are, is, will, and not; **are** = **air** words; **a** = **o** words

Grammar: To write sentences with contractions

Comprehension: To read short stories and answer questions requiring higher level thinking skills

Writing: To write a descriptive story
To use the five steps of Process Writing, focusing on interesting word choice

Proofreading: To use proofreading marks to correct mistakes in a paragraph

Reference Skill: To know how entry words are alphabetized in the dictionary

Handwriting: To learn how to write the cursive letter _Ss_

Suggested Pacing
1 week

Materials
Grand Tour II, pp. 107-116
Cursive Wall Chart

Homework
Daily homework is described in TM p. 99.

Spelling
Daily spelling is described in TM p. 99.

Phonics Games (See TM pp. 40-65.)
Continue to play selected games as needed for reinforcement.

Phonics Songs (See TM pp. 40-65.)
Continue to sing selected songs as needed for reinforcement.

Additional Related Activities
Additional activities are found in TM p. 368.

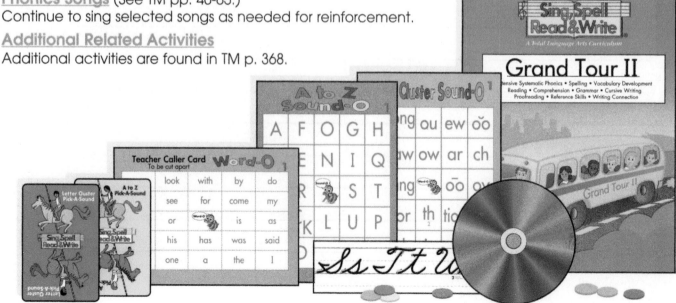

Day 1

Grand Tour II, p. 107

Spelling Words
Phonetic Grouping: Contractions

* Note that each word is a **contraction**.

* As a class, read the 10 spelling words and discuss how each contraction is made from two words:

  1. If a word is an "**are**" contraction as in **they're**, leave out the **a** in **are** and use an apostrophe.
     Example: they + are = they're

  2. If a word is an "**is**" contraction as in **he's**, you leave out the **i** in **is** and use an apostrophe.
     Example: he + is = he's

  3. If a word is a "**will**" contraction as in **he'll**, you leave out the **wi** and use an apostrophe.
     Example: he + will = he'll

* Have students copy the 10 spelling words to take home, study, and write in sentences for homework.

p. 107

Spelling Vocabulary Activities

Contractions
* Students will write the contraction for each set of words.
* Students will write the two words for each contraction.

Grand Tour II, p. 108

Grammar

Contractions
* Think of some simple sentences with two words that can be replaced with a contraction.
  Example: We will be coming late.

* Ask a student to replace **we will** with a contraction and repeat the sentence.
  Example: We'll be coming late.

* Continue in this manner for several sentences.

* Students will write each sentence and replace the underlined words with a contraction on page 108.

Process Writing

p. 108

Process Writing Lesson #14 for Steps 28 and 29 is found in TM p. 459.

Getting Started

- Collect homework and put stars on Homework Chart. (See TM p. 26.)
- Administer spelling test with Day 1 spelling words in *Grand Tour II*, p. 107. Sentence for dictation: <u>We're</u> going to the park. (See TM p. 100.)

Grand Tour II, p. 109

Spelling Words
Phonetic Grouping: Contractions

- Note that each word is a **contraction**.
- As a class, read the 10 spelling words and discuss how each **contraction** is formed.
- Tell students if it is a "**not**" contraction as in **don't**, leave out the **o** in **not** and replace it with an apostrophe.
  Example: has + not = hasn't

Spelling Vocabulary Activities

Contractions
- Students will write a contraction for each set of two words.
- Students will write two words for each contraction.

Grand Tour II, p. 110

Story Comprehension

Never Say, "I Can't"
Students will:
- Underline the 10 spelling words in the story.
- Read the story.
- Underline the correct answers.

The Writing Connection

Writing a Story
- Brainstorm with the students about trying to do something that was difficult for them to do.
- Write the list on the board.
- Talk about times they gave up and times they did not give up.
- Ask what made them continue to work at something, even when it was very difficult.
- Students will write a story that tells about something that was hard to do, but they continued to work on it.
- Have students include:
  <u>What</u> they did that was difficult.
  <u>Why</u> it was difficult.
  <u>Why</u> they continued to work on the project.

p. 109

p. 110

Day 2 *continued*

Grammar Chalkboard Lesson
Punctuation

Objective
- The students will know that in a contraction, an apostrophe is used to show that one or more letters have been left out.

Practice/Apply
- Write the groups of words on the board. The students will write the contraction for each set of words correctly.

1.	they will	they'll	6.	has not	hasn't
2.	do not	don't	7.	did not	didn't
3.	we are	we're	8.	are not	aren't
4.	would not	wouldn't	9.	she will	she'll
5.	have not	haven't	10.	he is	he's

Process Writing

Process Writing Lesson #14 for Steps 28 and 29 is found in TM p. 459.

Day 3

Getting Started

- Collect homework and put stars on Homework Chart. (See TM p. 26.)
- Administer spelling test with Day 2 spelling words in *Grand Tour II*, p. 109. Sentence for dictation: Bob <u>didn't</u> want to run the race. (See TM p. 100.)

Grand Tour II, p. 111

Spelling Words
Phonetic Grouping: ār¢ = air

- Note that each word has **ār¢ = air**.
- Tell students that the **are** in today's words sounds like **air**. Have students mark each word as indicated: **hār¢**
- As a class, read the 10 spelling words and discuss their meanings.
- Have students copy the 10 spelling words to take home, study, and write in sentences for homework.

p. 111

(Continued on next page)

Day 3 *continued*

Spelling Vocabulary Activities

Cloze
* Have students fill in each blank with a spelling word.

Word Fun
* Tell students if they use the right code they will find a spelling word inside these funny looking words.
* Students will cross out every other letter starting with the second letter to make a spelling word.

  Example: b ¢ i ł g ł = big

Grand Tour II, p.112

Grammar

Contractions
* Think of simple sentences with two words that can be replaced with a **contraction**.

  Example: Mom **did not** drive me to school.

* Ask a student to replace **did not** with a contraction and repeat the sentence.

  Example: Mom **didn't** drive me to school.

* Continue in this manner for several sentences.
* Students will write each sentence and replace the underlined words with a contraction.

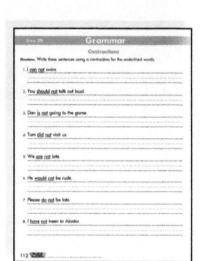

p. 112

Process Writing

Process Writing Lesson #14 for Steps 28 and 29 is found in TM p. 459.

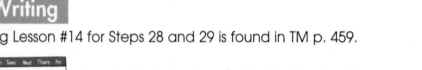

Day 4

Getting Started

* Collect homework and put stars on Homework Chart. (See TM p. 26.)
* Administer spelling test with Day 3 spelling words in *Grand Tour II*, p. 111. Sentence for dictation: We need to <u>share</u> our lunch. (See TM p. 100.)

Grand Tour II, p. 113

Spelling Words
Phonetic Grouping: a = ŏ

* Tell students each spelling word has **a** in it and the **a** sounds like **short o**.
* As a class, read the 10 spelling words and discuss their meanings.
* Have students copy the 10 spelling words to take home, study, and write in sentences for homework.

p. 113

Day 4 *continued*

Spelling Vocabulary Activities

Crossword Puzzle
- Students will read the clues by the number, think of a spelling word that fits the clue, and write the words in the crossword puzzle.

Antonyms
- Remind students that antonyms are opposites.
  Examples: big—little; up—down

- Students will write a spelling word that is the opposite of the words listed
  on page 113.

Riddles
- Students will write a spelling word to answer each riddle.

Grand Tour II, p. 114

p. 113

Story Comprehension

The Scavenger Hunt
Students will:
- Underline the 10 spelling words in the story.
- Read the story.
- Underline the correct answers.

The Writing Connection

Writing a Paragraph
- Talk about a swamp. What is it like? What kinds of animals live in a swamp? What kinds of trees grow in a swamp? Where would you find a swamp?

- If possible, show some pictures of a swamp.

- Students will write a paragraph about a swamp. Tell them to focus on **one thing** about a swamp.

- Students will illustrate the paragraph.

p. 114

(Continued on next page)

Day 4 continued

Grammar Chalkboard Lesson
Punctuation

Objective
- The students will know that in a contraction, an apostrophe is used to show that one or more letters have been left out.

Practice/Apply
- Write the sentences on the board. The students will write the sentences correctly, using a contraction for the underlined words.

> 1. Mary <u>did not</u> clean her room.   didn't
>
> 2. <u>We are</u> going to Mexico.   We're
>
> 3. <u>She is</u> baking apple pie.   She's
>
> 4. I think that <u>you are</u> a fast runner.   you're
>
> 5. This <u>is not</u> a sunny day.   isn't

Process Writing

Process Writing Lesson #14 for Steps 28 and 29 is found in TM p. 459.

Day 5

Getting Started

- Collect homework and put stars on Homework Chart. (See TM p. 26.)
- Administer spelling test with Day 4 spelling words in *Grand Tour II*, p. 113. Sentence for dictation: We saw a <u>wasp</u> nest. (See TM p. 100.)

Grand Tour II, p. 115

Proofreading

- Review the proofreading marks and have students look at the example to see how it is marked. Call attention to the word **he** in the example. This word is not needed so it has been marked with a "take out" mark.
- Students will read the paragraph and use proofreading marks to correct six mistakes.

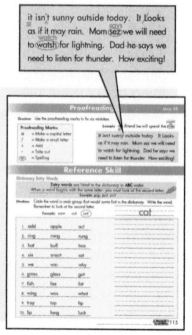

p. 115

Day 5 *continued*

Reference Skill

Dictionary Entry Words

- Remind students **entry words** are the words listed in ABC order in the dictionary.
- When words begin with the same letter, you must look at the second letter in order to place the words in ABC order.
- Write the following words on the board: **top**, **ten**, **tug**
- Ask students to look at the second letter in each word and tell which letter comes first in ABC order.
- The **e** in **ten** comes first in ABC order, so circle the word **ten**.
  Example: top, ⟨ten⟩, tug
- On page 115 students will circle the word in each group that would come first in the dictionary and write the word in the space.

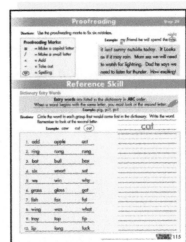

p. 115

Grand Tour II, p. 116

Learning Cursive Writing

- To introduce the cursive letter *Ss*, refer to TM p. 81.
- Students will trace over the letters and words and practice writing them on the lines.

Process Writing

Process Writing Lesson #14 for Steps 28 and 29 is found in TM p. 459.

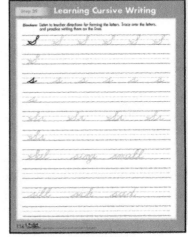

p. 116

Grand Tour II

Additional Related Activities for Step 29

Listening and Speaking

1. *Concentration* with Contractions

- Write the following phrases and contractions on the board.

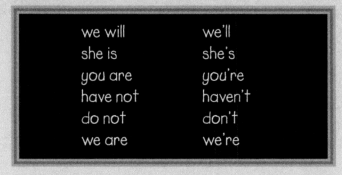

we will	we'll
she is	she's
you are	you're
have not	haven't
do not	don't
we are	we're

- Give each student six cards. (three 3 x 5 index cards cut in half)
- Have children work with partners.
- One partner will copy the **phrases** from the board onto separate cards and the other partner will copy the **contractions** onto separate cards.
- Combine the cards into a stack of 12.
- Place the cards face down into a pattern on a table.

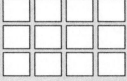

- Partner number one turns over two cards and, if the cards match, he/she keeps the pair. If they do not match, the child returns the cards to their original face down position.
- Next, partner number two turns over two cards. If they match, he/she keeps the pair; if not, he/she places the cards back in the original position.

- Have children play until all cards are matched. When all cards have been matched, the winner is the student with the most cards.
- Point out to students that they need to concentrate on remembering what was written on the card and the position of the card. This will help them to make pairs.

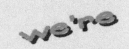

- **Note:** Play this game with other contractions, homophones, synonyms, antonyms, or anything that can be paired.

2. *Around the World* with Contractions

- Have a student stand beside a student seated at his/her desk.
- The teacher will say a contraction.
  Example: isn't
- The student who first says **is not** moves on to the next desk.
- Reverse the activity by saying the two words and having the student say the contraction.

Overview for Step 30

Objectives

Spelling: To spell **c** = **s** before **e**, **i**, or **y** words; **silent w** words

Grammar: To know an apostrophe is used to show ownership

To know when a word ends in **y** after a consonant, change the **y** to **i** and add **es** to make it plural

To know a noun is a person, place, or thing

Comprehension: To read short stories and answer questions requiring higher level thinking skills

Writing: To use the Five Steps of Process Writing, focusing on the use of similes

Handwriting: To learn how to write cursive letter 𝒯𝓉

Suggested Pacing
1 week

Materials
Grand Tour II, pp. 117-126
Cursive Wall Chart

Homework
Daily homework is described in TM p. 99.

Spelling
Daily spelling is described in TM p. 99.

Phonics Games (See TM pp. 40-65.)
Continue to play selected games as needed for reinforcement.

Phonics Songs (See TM pp. 40-65.)
Continue to sing selected songs as needed for reinforcement.

Additional Related Activities
Additional activities are found in TM p. 378.

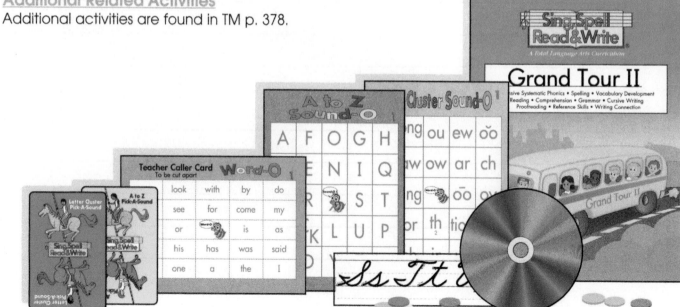

Day 1

Grand Tour II, pp. 117-118

- Note that each word contains **ce**, **ci**, or **cy**. Explain to the students that if a word has **ce**, **ci**, or **cy**, the **c** sounds like **s**.
- Have students circle the (**ce**) (**ci**) or (**cy**) in each word. Make sure they do not circle the **cu** in **circus**, the **co** in **concert**, the **ch** in **choice**, or the **cl** in **circle**.
- As a class, read the 10 spelling words and discuss their meanings.
- Have students copy the 10 spelling words to take home, study, and write in sentences for homework.

p. 117

Spelling Vocabulary Activities

Riddles
- Students will write a spelling word to answer each riddle.

Synonyms
- Students will write the spelling words that mean the same as **penny** and **selection**.

Compound Words
- Students will write the spelling word that is a compound word.

Singulars
- Remind students that **singular** means **just one**.
- Explain that when you change a plural word to a singular, you must change it back to its original spelling.
  Examples: cities—city; glasses—glass; cakes—cake
- Students will write the singular spelling words for the plural words given on pages 117-118.

Grand Tour II, p. 118

Punctuation: Apostrophe
- Remind students that an **apostrophe** makes a word possessive to show **ownership**.
- Have students read sentence #1. Have them name the object that is underlined (**nest**). Ask, "Who owns the nest?" (**The bird**). Call attention to the **apostrophe** in the word **bird's** and that **bird** has been written in the space.
- Students will complete sentences #2-10, writing the word that tells **who** owns the object that is underlined.

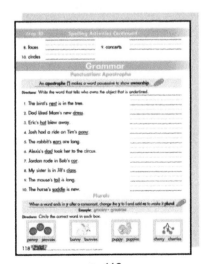

p. 118

(Continued on next page)

Grand Tour II

Plurals

* When a word ends in **y** after a consonant, change the **y** to **i** and add **es** to make it plural. Have students read the rule and look at the example.
* Students will circle the correct word in each box.

penny (pennies)

Process Writing

Process Writing Lesson #15 for Steps 30 and 31 is found in TM p. 461.

Day 2

Getting Started

* Collect homework and put stars on Homework Chart. (See TM p. 26.)
* Administer spelling test with Day 1 spelling words in *Grand Tour II*, p. 117. Sentence for dictation: I can draw a <u>circle</u>. (See TM p. 100.)

Grand Tour II, pp. 119-120

Spelling Words
Phonetic Grouping: c = s

* Note that each word contains **ce**, **ci**, or **cy**. Review with the students that if a word has a **ce**, **ci**, or **cy**, the **c** sounds like **s**. Have students circle the (ce) (ci) or (cy) in the words. Make sure they do not circle the **cl** in **bicycle** or **tricycle**.
* As a class, read the 10 spelling words and discuss the meanings.
* Have students copy the 10 spelling words to take home, study, and write in sentences for homework.

Spelling Vocabulary Activities

Cloze
* Students will fill in the blanks with the correct spelling words.

Plurals
* Students will write the spelling word that is the plural of **mouse**.

Singulars
* Remind students that **singulars** are words that mean **just one**. When you change a plural to a singular, you change the word back to its original spelling.
* Students will fill in the blanks with the singular of the words given.

Word Meanings
* Have students name several types of transportation. (**car, boat, train**)
* Students will write two spelling words that are types of transportation.

p. 119

Day 2 *continued*

Homophones
- Students will fill in the spelling word that sounds like **piece**.

Word Scramble
- Students will unscramble the letters to make a spelling word.

Grand Tour II, p. 120

Story Comprehension

The Bicycle Ride to the Office
- Have students underline the seven spelling words in the story.
- Students will read the story silently and underline the correct answers.

Grammar Chalkboard Lesson
Plurals

Objective
- The students will know common irregular plurals.

Practice/Apply
- Write the words on the board. Students will write the plurals correctly.

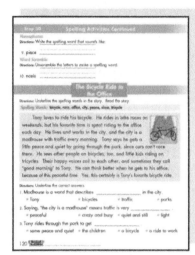

p. 120

mouse	mice
tooth	teeth
goose	geese
child	children
man	men
foot	feet

Process Writing

Process Writing Lesson #15 for Steps 30 and 31 is found in TM p. 461.

Getting Started

- Collect homework and put stars on Homework Chart. (See TM p. 26.)
- Administer spelling test with Day 2 spelling words in *Grand Tour II*, p. 119. Sentence for dictation: I rode my <u>bicycle</u> today. (See TM p. 100.)

Grand Tour II, p. 121

Spelling Words
Phonetic Grouping: w̶

p. 121

- Tell students the letter **w** is sometimes **silent**, and this week's words all have **silent w**. Have students mark each word as indicated: w̶ren
- As a class, read the 10 spelling words and discuss their meanings.
- Have students copy the 10 spelling words to take home, study, and write in sentences for homework.

Spelling Vocabulary Activities

Syllables
- As a review, tell students that all words are made of one or more parts called **syllables**.
- Say the first name of each student and have the class clap the **syllables** for each name.
- Students will write four spelling words that have two syllables.

Synonyms
- Students will write the spelling words that mean the same as **crash** and **complete**.

Homophones
- Students will fill in the blank with the word that sounds like **rung**.

Word Clues
- Students will write a spelling word for each clue.

Silent w Words
- Remind students that sometimes the letter **w** is silent.
- Students will write each spelling word and cross out the **silent w** as shown.
  Example: w̶ren

Day 3 continued

Grand Tour II, p. 122

Grammar

Nouns

- Tell students there are different kinds of words. Some words are names; some are actions; some tell what kind, how many or where. Words that tell the name of a **person**, **place**, or **thing** are called **nouns**.

- Have students say some names of people. Write them on the chalkboard. Include both common and proper nouns.
  Examples: Ruth, Fred, teacher, artist

- Follow the same procedure with names of places and things.

- As a class, read and discuss the definition and directions at the top of page 122.

- Students will write each noun under the correct picture and then write **person**, **place**, or **thing**.

p. 122

Process Writing

Process Writing Lesson #15 for Steps 30 and 31 is found in TM p. 461.

Day 4

Getting Started

- Collect homework and put stars on Homework Chart. (See TM p. 26.)

- Administer spelling test with Day 3 spelling words in *Grand Tour II*, p. 121. Sentence for dictation: The rabbit jumped <u>toward</u> me. (See TM p. 100.)

Grand Tour II, pp. 123-124

Spelling Words
Phonetic Grouping: w

- Note that each word has **silent w**. Have students mark each word as indicated: **w̶rite**

- Tell students the second **w** in **wristwatch** is not silent.

- As a class, read the 10 spelling words and discuss their meanings.

- Have students copy the 10 spelling words to take home, study, and write in sentences for homework.

Spelling Vocabulary Activities

p. 123

Crossword Puzzle

- Students will read the clues by the number, think of a spelling word that fits the clue, and write the words in the crossword puzzle.

(Continued on next page)

Grand Tour II

Day 4 *continued*

Compound Words

- Students will write a spelling word that is a compound word.

Past

- Tell students that words can tell something is **happening now**. Words can also tell something **has already happened**. That is called **in the past**. **Example:** Today I **sing**. Yesterday I **sang**.

- Students will write the spelling word that is the **past** of **write**.

Present

- Tell students that things **happening now** are in the **present**. **Example:** We jump. Birds fly.

- Students will write the spelling words that are the present of **wrote**, **wrapped**, and **wrung**.

Suffix <u>er</u>

- Students will fill in the blank with a spelling word that is a **person**.

Antonyms

- Tell students that antonyms are words that mean the opposite. **Example:** up—down; in—out

- On page 124, students will write antonyms for the words listed.

Word Scrambles

- On page 124, students will unscramble the letters and fill in the blanks with the correct spelling words.

Grand Tour II, p. 124

Story Comprehension

Hurt Wrists

- Have students underline the seven spelling words in the story.

- As a group, read the story aloud.

- Students will read the questions and underline the correct answers.

p. 123

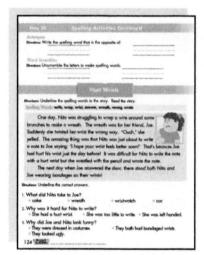

p. 124

Step 30

Day 4 *continued*

Grammar Chalkboard Lesson
Nouns

Objective
* The students will identify a noun as a person, place, or thing.

Practice/Apply
* Write the words on the board. The students will write the words and label them as **person**, **place**, or **thing**.
  Example: school (place)

1. tiger	thing	6. car	thing
2. library	place	7. pilot	person
3. man	person	8. store	place
4. pancake	thing	9. singer	person
5. wreath	thing	10. beach	place

Process Writing
Process Writing Lesson #15 for Steps 30 and 31 is found in TM p. 461.

Day 5

Getting Started
* Collect homework and put stars on Homework Chart. (See TM p. 26.)
* Administer spelling test with Day 4 spelling words in *Grand Tour II*, p. 123. Sentence for dictation: We hung a <u>wreath</u> on the door. (See TM p. 100.)

Grand Tour II, p. 125
Recognizing Cursive Letters in Sequence
* Prepare a set of cursive alphabet flash cards, letters **A** through **T** and **a** through **t**.
* Scramble the cards and flash them to the class.
* As a class, have students say the letter names.
* Distribute the cards.
* Have students holding capital letters stand and arrange themselves in ABC order.
* Repeat the procedure with lower case letters.
* On page 125 students will connect the dots in alphabet sequence.

p. 125

(Continued on next page)

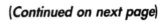 **377**

Grand Tour II

Grand Tour II, p. 126

Learning Cursive Writing

- To introduce the cursive letter $\mathcal{T}t$, refer to TM p. 81.
- Students will trace over the letters and practice writing them on the lines.

Process Writing

Process Writing Lesson #15 for Steps 30 and 31 is found in TM p. 461.

p. 126

Additional Related Activities for Step 30

Listening and Speaking

1. Plural Pictures

- Give each student a sheet of 12" x 18" newsprint.
- Have students fold the paper to make eight boxes.

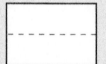 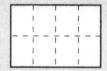

- Write eight singular nouns on the chalkboard. Suggestions: **bunny, clown, cent, mouse, child, foot, leaf, dish**
- Have students unfold the paper, write the plural form of one word in each box, and illustrate each word.

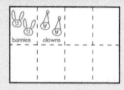

bunnies

clowns

2. Collections

- Name a set of three objects slowly. Select students to say another object that could belong with the set and to tell why the object could be in that collection. Accept any reasonable answers.
  Examples: red, blue, yellow, green • They are all colors.
    jump, walk, run, leap • They are all actions.

Suggested sets:

boy, girl, man, _____ (people)
cat, dog, fish, _____ (pets)
table, chair, desk, _____ (furniture)
monkey, giraffe, bear, _____ (zoo animals)
pig, chicken, cow, _____ (farm animals)
farmer, doctor, teacher, _____ (workers)
ball, doll, skateboard, _____ (toys)
stars, moon, clouds, _____ (sky things)
bird, butterfly, mosquito, _____ (flying things)
river, lake, pond, _____ (bodies of water)

NOTES

Grand Tour II

Overview for Step 31

Objectives

Spelling: To spell **silent k** and **silent l** words

Grammar: To know a noun is a **person**, **place**, or **thing**
To make a word plural by changing the **y** to **i** and adding **es**
To know when prefix **un** is added to a word, it means the **opposite**

Comprehension: To read short stories and answer questions requiring higher level thinking skills

Writing: To write a paragraph
To use the Five Steps of Process Writing, focusing on the use of similes

Handwriting: To learn how to write cursive letters *Uu* and *Vv*

Suggested Pacing
1 week

Materials
Grand Tour II, pp. 127-136
Cursive Wall Chart

Homework
Daily homework is described in TM p. 99.

Spelling
Daily spelling is described in TM p. 99.

Phonics Games (See TM pp. 40-65.)
Continue to play selected games as needed for reinforcement.

Phonics Songs (See TM pp. 40-65.)
Continue to sing selected songs as needed for reinforcement.

Additional Related Activities
Additional activities are found in TM p. 388.

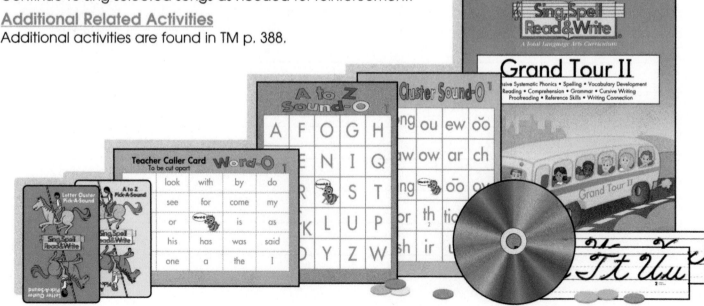

Day 1

Grand Tour II, p. 127

Spelling Words
Phonetic Grouping: k̸

- Tell students when **n** follows **k** in a word (as in **knew**) the **k** is **silent**. Have students mark each word as indicated: k̸**not**
- As a class, read the 10 spelling words and discuss the meanings.
- Have students copy the 10 spelling words to take home, study, and write in sentences for homework.

Spelling Vocabulary Activities

p. 127

Silent k Words
- Have students write each spelling word and cross out the **silent k**.

Homophones
- Remind students homophones are words that sound alike but do not mean the same thing.
  Example: hear—here
- Students will write the spelling words that sound the same as **not** and **need**.

Compound Words
- Students will write the spelling word that is a compound word.

Plurals
- Students will write the spelling word that is the plural of **knife**.

Past
- Tell students you usually add **ed** to make a word mean **in the past**.
  Example: play—played

- However, some words change their spelling. These are called irregular verbs.
  Example: run—ran

- Students will write the spelling word that is the **past** of **kneel**.

Singulars
- Students will write the spelling word that is the singular of **knives**.

Present
- Students will write the spelling word on p. 128 that means **to kneel now**.

Synonyms
- Write the spelling word on p. 128 that means the same as **handle**.

Cloze
- Students will fill in the blanks with the correct spelling words on p. 128.

(Continued on next page)

Grand Tour II

Grand Tour II, p. 128

Grammar

Nouns

- Tell students a **noun** is a word that is a **person**, **place**, or **thing**.
- Tell students you will say a word that is a **noun**.
  Example: boy

- Ask students to tell you if a boy is a **person**, **place**, or **thing**. (person)
- A suggested list of words to say:

yard	(place)	town	(place)	girl	(person)
man	(person)	baby	(person)	bank	(place)
cat	(thing)	chair	(thing)	toy	(thing)

- Reverse the procedure and say the word **person**, **place**, or **thing**. Students will name a noun to fit.
  Example: Teacher says **thing** and the student may reply **bicycle**.

- On page 128, students will read the sentence, underline the noun in each sentence, and write the noun on the line.

Plurals

- Tell students most words are made **plural** by adding **s** or **es**.
- Some words are different. If a word ends in **y** after a consonant, you change the **y** to **i** and add **es** to make a **plural**.
  Example: cherry—cherries

- Students will change the word in each box to a **plural** and complete the sentences with the new words.

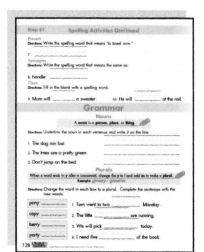

p. 128

Process Writing

Process Writing Lesson #15 for Steps 30 and 31 is found in TM p. 461.

Day 2

Getting Started

- Collect homework and put stars on Homework Chart. (See TM p. 26)
- Administer spelling test with Day 1 spelling words in *Grand Tour II*, p. 127. Sentence for dictation: I hurt my <u>kneecap</u>. (See TM p. 100.)

Day 2 *continued*

Grand Tour II, p. 129

Spelling Words
Phonetic Grouping: k̸

- Tell students when **n** follows **k** in a word (as in **know**) the **k** is always **silent**. Have students mark each word as indicated: **k̸napsack**

- Tell students they do not mark the **k** after the **c** in **knuckles**, **knocked**, **knack**, or **knapsack**.

- As a class, read the 10 spelling words and discuss the meanings.

- Have students copy the 10 spelling words to take home, study, and write in sentences for homework.

Spelling Vocabulary Activities

Silent k Words
- Students will write each spelling word and cross out the **silent k**.

Compound Words
- Students will write the spelling word that is a **compound word**.

Homophones
- Remind students that **homophones** are words that sound the same but are not spelled the same.
  Example: know—no

- Ask students to think of pairs of words that are **homophones**.

- Students will write spelling words that sound the same as the words listed on page 129.

Word Association
- Tell students words can be associated with each other in many ways.
  Example: man, boy, and **dad** can be associated with each other because they are all male people. **Back, sack**, and **tack** can be associated because they all rhyme.

- Tell students they are to read each group of words on page 129, think of how they are associated, and write the spelling word that fits in the group.

Cloze
- Students will fill in the blank with a spelling word.

Grand Tour II, p. 130

Story Comprehension

The Knight Who Could Knit
Students will:
- Underline the spelling words in the story.
- Read the story silently.
- Read the sentences and underline the correct answer.

p. 129

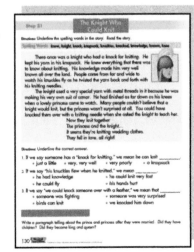

p. 130

(Continued on next page)

Day 2 *continued*

The Writing Connection

Writing a Paragraph

- Students will write a paragraph that tells what they think may have happened to the prince and princess after they were married.

Grammar Chalkboard Lesson
Nouns

Objective

- Students will know that a **noun** is a **person**, **place**, or **thing**.

Practice/Apply

- Write the sentences on the board. The students will write the sentences and underline the nouns.

> 1. <u>Julia</u> has a new <u>coat</u>.
> 2. The <u>dog</u> barked at <u>Taylor</u>.
> 3. <u>Mr. Woo</u> drove his <u>car</u> to the <u>city</u>.
> 4. The <u>teacher</u> read a <u>book</u> to the <u>class</u>.
> 5. The <u>cow</u> is in the <u>barn</u>.

Process Writing

Process Writing Lesson #15 for Steps 30 and 31 is found in TM p. 461.

Day 3

Getting Started

- Collect homework and put stars on Homework Chart. (See TM p. 26.)
- Administer spelling test with Day 2 spelling words in *Grand Tour II*, p. 129. Sentence for dictation: A <u>knight</u> will help the king. (See TM p. 100.)

Grand Tour II, p. 131

Spelling Words
Phonetic Grouping: *l*

- Tell students the letter **l** in the middle of a word is sometimes **silent**, and the **l** is **silent** in each word in today's list. Have students mark each word as indicated: **sta/lk**
- As a class, read the 10 spelling words and discuss the meanings.
- Have students copy the 10 spelling words, take home, study, and write in sentences for homework.

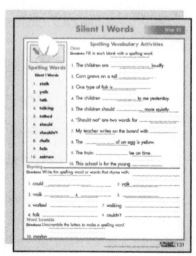

p. 131

Spelling Vocabulary Activities

Cloze
- Have students read each sentence and fill in the blank with a spelling word.

Rhyming
- Students will write the spelling word or words that rhyme with the words listed.

Word Scramble
- Students will unscramble the letters to make a spelling word.

Grand Tour II, p. 132

Grammar

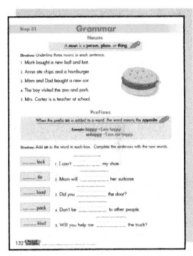

p. 132

Nouns
- Tell students a **noun** is a **person, place** or **thing**.
- Ask a student to tell you if **car** is a **person, place,** or **thing**.
- Tell students you will say a word that is a **noun** and they are to tell you whether the word is a **person, place,** or **thing**.

  Example: car (thing)

- A suggested list of words to say:

school	(place)	thread	(thing)	city	(place)
desk	(thing)	Mr. Jones	(person)	lady	(person)
mom	(person)	apple	(thing)	farm	(place)

- Reverse the procedure. The teacher will say **person (place** or **thing)** and the student will say **boy** or any other reasonable answer.
- On page 132 students will read the sentences and underline three **nouns** in each sentence.

Prefixes
- Tell students a **prefix** is added to the beginning of a root word and changes the meaning of the word.
- When the prefix **un** is added to a word, the word means the **opposite**.

  Example: happy—unhappy

- Ask students to think of words to which the prefix **un** could be added.
- Students will add **un** to each boxed word and complete the sentences with the new words.

Process Writing

Process Writing Lesson #15 for Steps 30 and 31 is found in TM p. 461.

Grand Tour II

Day 4

Getting Started

- Collect homework and put stars on Homework Chart. (See TM p. 26.)
- Administer spelling test with Day 3 spelling words in *Grand Tour II*, p. 131. Sentence for dictation: An egg has a yellow <u>yolk</u>. (See TM p. 100.)

Grand Tour II, pp. 133-134

Spelling Words
Phonetic Grouping: *l*

- Tell students the letter **l** in the middle of a word is sometimes **silent** and the **l** is **silent** in all the words in today's list. Have students mark each word as indicated: **cou/ld**
- As a class, read the 10 spelling words and discuss the meanings.
- Have students copy the 10 spelling words to take home, study, and write in sentences for homework.

Spelling Vocabulary Activities

Crossword Puzzle
- Students will read the clues by the number, think of a spelling word that fits the clue, and write the words in the crossword puzzle.

Singulars
- Tell students **singular** means **one**.
- Students will write a spelling word that is the singular of the words listed.

Contractions
- Students will write a spelling word that is the **contraction** for **could not**.

Rhyming
- Students will write the spelling words that **rhyme** with the words listed.

Word Scramble
- Students will unscramble the letters on p.134 to make a word.

Grand Tour II, p. 134

Story Comprehension

Be Calm! We're Going to the Land of Palms!
Students will:
- Underline the spelling words in the story.
- Read the story silently.
- Complete the activity by filling in the blank or underlining the correct phrase.

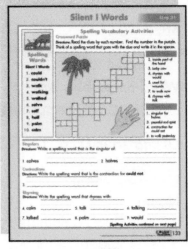

p. 133

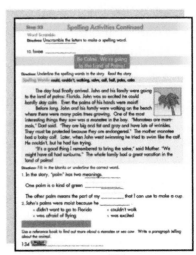

p. 134

Sing-Spell Read&Write.

The Writing Connection

Using Reference Materials

Have students:

- Go to the media center and use reference materials to find out more about a manatee.

- Write a paragraph that includes at least three facts about a manatee.

Grammar Chalkboard Lesson
Plurals

Objective

- The students will know that when a word ends in **y** after a consonant, change the **y** to **i** and add **es** to make a plural.

Practice/Apply

- Write the words on the board. The students will write the correct plurals of the words.

  Example: bunny (bunnies)

1. party	parties	6. baby	babies
2. strawberry	strawberries	7. lady	ladies
3. penny	pennies	8. buggy	buggies
4. pony	ponies	9. city	cities
5. copy	copies	10. grocery	groceries

Process Writing

Process Writing Lesson #15 for Steps 30 and 31 is found in TM p. 461.

Grand Tour II

Day 5

Getting Started

- Collect homework and put stars on Homework Chart. (See TM p. 26.)
- Administer spelling test with Day 4 spelling words in *Grand Tour II*, p. 133. Sentence for dictation: We will cut the apple in <u>half</u>. (See TM p. 100.)

Grand Tour II, pp. 135-136

Learning Cursive Writing

- To introduce the cursive letters $\mathcal{U}u$ and $\mathcal{V}v$, refer to TM pp. 81-82.
- Students will trace over the cursive letters and words and practice writing them on the lines.

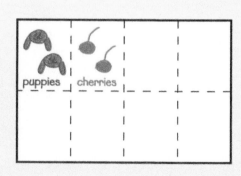

pp. 135 - 136

Process Writing

Process Writing Lesson #15 for Steps 30 and 31 is found in TM p. 461.

Additional Related Activities for Step 31

Listening and Speaking

1. Collections

- Name a set of three objects slowly. Select students to say another object that could belong with the set and tell why the object could be in that collection. Accept any reasonable answers.
  Example: ring, bracelet, earrings, <u>necklace</u> • They are all jewelry.

  Suggestions:
  Bread, meat, potatoes, _____ (food)
  Spring, fall, summer, _____ (seasons)
  Triangle, square, rectangle, _____ (shapes)
  Math, spelling, science, _____ (subjects at school)
  Camel, giraffe, tiger, _____ (zoo animals)
  Thursday, Sunday, Monday, _____ (days)
  Brother, sister, mom, _____ (family)
  Atlanta, New York, Chicago, _____ (cities)
  Right, night, sight, _____ (rhyming words)

2. Plural Pictures

- Give each student a sheet of 12" x 18" newsprint.
- Have students fold the paper to make eight boxes.

- Write eight singular nouns on the chalkboard.
  Suggestions: **puppy, cherry, bush, cat, goose, girl, tooth, box**
- Have students unfold the paper, write the plural form of one word in each box, and illustrate the word.

NOTES

Grand Tour II

Overview for Step 32

Objectives

Spelling: To spell words with **silent b**; **silent g**; **silent h**

Grammar: To know a verb tells something that you do
To know when prefix **dis** is added to a word, the word means the opposite

Comprehension: To read short stories and answer questions requiring higher level thinking skills

Writing: To write a title for a story
To use the Five Steps of Process Writing, focusing on why writers write

Handwriting: To learn how to write cursive letter $\mathscr{W}w$

Suggested Pacing
1 week

Materials
Grand Tour II, pp. 137-146
Cursive Wall Chart

Homework
Daily homework is described in TM p. 99.

Spelling
Daily spelling is described in TM p. 99.

Phonics Games (See TM pp. 40-65.)
Continue to play selected games as needed for reinforcement.

Phonics Songs (See TM pp. 40-65.)
Continue to sing selected songs as needed for reinforcement.

Additional Related Activities
Additional activities are found in TM p. 397.

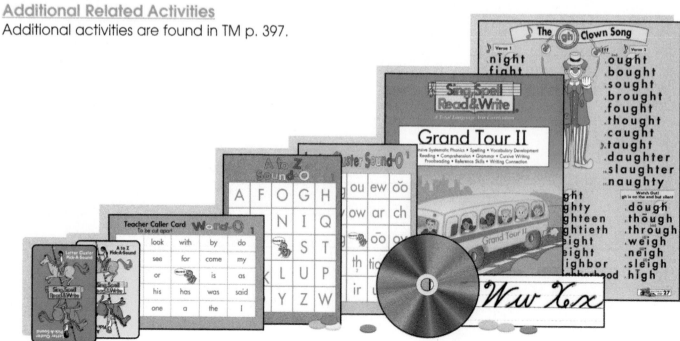

Day 1

Grand Tour II, p. 137

Spelling Words
Phonetic Grouping: b̸

p. 137

* Note that all words have **silent b**. Tell students that sometimes the letter **b** is **silent** in words. Have students mark each word as indicated: **lim**b̸

* As a class, read the 10 spelling words and discuss the meanings.

* Have students copy the 10 spelling words to take home, study, and write in sentences for homework.

Spelling Vocabulary Activities

Silent b Words
* Remind students sometimes the letter **b** is **silent**, especially after the letter **m** or before the letter **t**.

* Have students write the spelling words two times in the spaces provided and cross out the silent **b** as indicated: **lim**b̸.

Suffixes <u>ing</u> and <u>ed</u>
* Explain that when the suffix **ing** is added to a root word, it changes the word to mean "happening now" and **ed** added to a root word means "happened in the past."

* Students will write three spelling words with the suffix **ing**, meaning "happening now."

* Students will write two spelling words with the suffix **ed**, meaning "happened in the past."

Grand Tour II, p. 138

Grammar

Verbs
* Tell students words that tell **something you do** have a group name of their own. They are called **verbs**.
  Examples: action words such as **run**, **play**, **ride**, and **talk**

* Have students say **verbs** telling something they can do.

* Have students read the list of verbs on page 138 and write each verb under the correct picture.

p. 138

Process Writing

Process Writing Lesson #16 for Steps 32 and 33 is found in TM pp. 463.

Grand Tour II

Getting Started

- Collect homework and put stars on Homework Chart. (See TM p. 26.)
- Administer spelling test with Day 1 spelling words in *Grand Tour II*, p. 137. Sentence for dictation: I like <u>climbing</u> big trees. (See TM p. 100.)

Grand Tour II, p. 139

Spelling Words
Phonetic Grouping: b̸

- Note that all words have **silent b**. Remind students that letter **b** is sometimes **silent**, especially when it comes after letter **m** or before letter **t**. Have students mark each word as indicated: **dumb̸**
- As a class, read the 10 spelling words and discuss the meanings.
- Have students copy the 10 spelling words to take home, study, and write in sentences for homework.

Spelling Vocabulary Activities

Break the Code
- Review using a grid to locate the mystery letters. (See TM p. 326.)
- Students will use the symbols to decode letters and fill in the blanks with the correct spelling words.

Silent b Words
- Have students write each spelling word and cross out the **silent b** as indicated: **dumb̸**

Grand Tour II, p. 140

Story Comprehension

The Plumber's Numb Thumb
Have students:
- Underline the seven spelling words in the story.
- Read the story silently.
- Read the sentences and underline the correct answers.

p. 139

p. 140

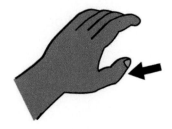

The Writing Connection

Writing a New Title

* Have students tell why *The Plumber's Numb Thumb* is a good title for the story on page 140.
* Explain that authors always give titles to their stories.
* Ask students to pretend they were the author of the plumber story and think of a different title.
* Have students write a different title for the story in the space provided. Remind them to use capital letters for the first word and any other important words in the title.

Grammar Chalkboard Lesson
Verbs

Objective

* Students will know that a **verb** tells something that you do.

Practice/Apply

* Write the sentences on the board. The students will write the sentences and underline the **verbs**.

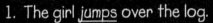

> 1. The girl <u>jumps</u> over the log.
> 2. The baby <u>crawls</u> on the floor.
> 3. The children <u>sing</u> sweetly.
> 4. Alberto <u>rides</u> his skateboard.
> 5. Angela <u>reads</u> her book.

Process Writing

Process Writing Lesson #16 for Steps 32 and 33 is found in TM p. 463.

Grand Tour II

Day 3

Getting Started

- Collect homework and put stars on Homework Chart. (See TM p. 26.)
- Administer spelling test with Day 2 spelling words in *Grand Tour II*, p. 139. Sentence for dictation: A <u>crumb</u> fell on me. (See TM p. 100.)

Grand Tour II, p. 141

Spelling Words
Phonetic Grouping: g

- Note that all the words have **silent g**. Tell students **g** is usually silent if followed by the letter **n**. Have students mark each word as indicated: **siǵn**
- Make sure students do not mark the final **g** in **gnawing**.
- As a class, read the 10 spelling words and discuss the meanings.
- Have students copy the 10 spelling words to take home, study, and write in sentences for homework.

p. 141

Spelling Vocabulary Activities

Cloze
- Students will fill in the blanks with the correct spelling words.

Silent g Words
- Students will write each spelling word and cross out the **silent g** as indicated: **siǵn**

Grand Tour II, p. 142

Grammar

Verbs
- Remind students that a **verb** tells something that you do, such as **sing** or **hop**.
- Have students read the sentences and underline the verb in each sentence.

Prefixes
- Tell students prefixes are added to the beginning of root words and change the meaning of the word. When the prefix **dis** is added to a word, the word means the **opposite**.

  Example: like—dislike

- Have students add **dis** to the word in each box on page 142 and complete the sentences by writing the new words in the blanks.

p. 142

Process Writing

Process Writing Lesson #16 for Steps 32 and 33 is found in TM p. 463.

Day 4

Getting Started

- Collect homework and put stars on Homework Chart. (See TM p. 26).
- Administer spelling test with Day 3 spelling words in *Grand Tour II*, p. 141. Sentence for dictation: The dog is <u>gnawing</u> a bone. (See TM p. 100).

Grand Tour II, p. 143

Spelling Words
Phonetic Grouping: h̷

- Note that all of the words have **silent h**. Have students mark each word as indicated: h̷our
- As a class, read the 10 spelling words and discuss the meanings.
- Have students copy the 10 spelling words to take home, study, and write in sentences for homework.

Spelling Vocabulary Activities

Word Search
- Tell students all the spelling words for this lesson are hidden in the puzzle. The words go across or down.
- Have students circle each word as they find it.

Prefix <u>dis</u>
- Have students add the prefix **dis** to each spelling word given, making it mean "the opposite."
- Students will write the new words in the spaces provided.

Word Clues
- Students will write the spelling words that match the clues.

p. 143

Grand Tour II, p. 144

Story Comprehension

A Parade of Honor
Have students:
- Underline the five spelling words in the story.
- Read the story silently.
- Read the questions and underline the correct answers.

The Writing Connection

Writing a New Title
- Provide drawing paper.
- Have students draw a picture of John leading the parade.
- Have students write a title for their pictures. They will give their picture a title that is different from the story title. Remind students to capitalize the first word and any other important words in the title.

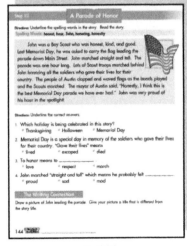

p. 144

(Continued on next page)

Grammar Chalkboard Lesson
Prefixes

Objective

• The students will know that the prefix **mis** means **wrong** or **not correct**.

Practice/Apply

• Write the sentence pairs on the board. The students will write and complete the second sentence of each pair by adding the prefix **mis** to the underlined word in the first sentence.

Example: I can't find where I <u>placed</u> my pencil.
I <u>misplaced</u> my pencil.

I haven't <u>spelled</u> the word correctly. I <u> misspelled </u> the word.

Tim <u>copied</u> the word wrong. Tim <u> miscopied </u> the word.

Do not <u>behave</u> in a wrong way. Do not <u> misbehave </u>.

The dog <u>led</u> me the wrong way. The dog <u> misled </u> me.

My socks do not <u>match</u>. My socks are <u> mismatched </u>.

Process Writing

Process Writing Lesson #16 for Steps 32 and 33 is found in TM p. 463.

Day 5

Getting Started

• Collect homework and put stars on Homework Chart. (See TM p. 26).
• Administer spelling test with Day 4 spelling words in *Grand Tour II*, p. 143. Sentence for dictation: It is good to be <u>honest</u>. (See TM p. 100).

Grand Tour II, p. 145

Learning Cursive Writing

• To introduce the cursive letter *Ww*, refer to TM p. 82.
• Students will trace over the letters and practice writing them on the lines.

Learning Cursive Writing Step 32

p. 145

Grand Tour II, p. 146

Recognizing Cursive Letters in Sequence

- On page 146, students will connect the dots of the cursive capital letters *A - W* in alphabet sequence and then follow the same procedure with lower case letters *a - w*.

- Students will fill in the missing letters in the picture title and trace over the words.

Process Writing

Process Writing Lesson #16 for Steps 32 and 33 is found in TM p. 463.

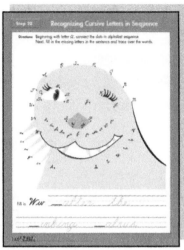

p. 146

Additional Related Activities for Step 32

Listening and Speaking

1. *Word Train* with Verbs

- The teacher or leader starts the game by saying a verb.

- The next player says a different verb and lines up behind the leader to begin a human train.

- Each student in turn adds a new verb and joins the train.

- When all students have become part of the train, the leader leads the train around the room, and students return to their seats.

- For variation, teacher may write words given on the chalkboard. Students draw a train and write a verb on each train car.

2. *Around the World* with Verbs

- Tell students that sentences can be made of just two words, a noun and a verb.
  Example: Dogs bark.

- Play *Around the World* with verbs. First student stands by desk of second student. Teacher says a singular or plural noun. The first student to respond with an appropriate one-word verb moves to the next player.
  Example: Teacher says **dogs**, student responds **bark**.

- Game continues as time permits or until one student goes *Around the World* and back to his/her desk.

- Suggested nouns: **farmers, teachers, children, rabbits, bird, fish, truck, pencils, horn, flowers, babies, cats, cars, dentist**

Grand Tour II

Overview for Step 33

Objectives

Spelling: To spell words with silent **t**; **qu** = **k**; **ph** = **f**

Grammar: To know a verb tells something that you do

To know when **dis** or **un** is added to a word, the word means the opposite

To know an adjective describes a noun

Comprehension: To read a short story and answer questions requiring higher level thinking skills

Writing: To write a story

To use the Five Steps of Process Writing, focusing on why writers write

Proofreading: To use proofreading marks to correct errors

Reference Skills: To know entry words are listed in the dictionary in ABC order.

To alphabetize words to the second letter

Handwriting: To learn how to write cursive letters *Xx* and *Yy*

Suggested Pacing

1 week

Materials

Grand Tour II, pp. 147-156
Cursive Wall Chart

Homework

Daily homework is described in TM p. 99.

Spelling

Daily spelling is described in TM p. 99.

Phonics Games (See TM pp. 40-65.)

Continue to play selected games as needed for reinforcement.

Phonics Songs (See TM pp. 40-65.)

Continue to sing selected songs as needed for reinforcement.

Additional Related Activities

Additional activities are found in TM p. 405.

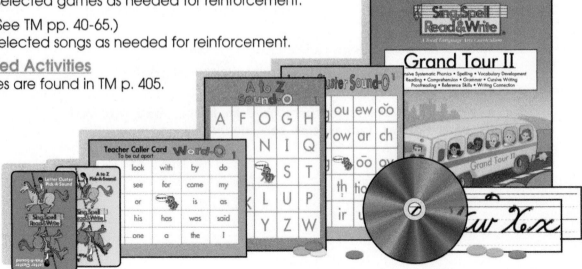

Day 1

Grand Tour II, pp. 147-148

Spelling Words
Phonetic Grouping: t

- Note that all 10 words have **silent t**. Explain to students that letter **t** is sometimes silent. Have students mark each word as indicated: **rustle**

- As a class, read the 10 spelling words and discuss the meanings.

- Have students copy the 10 spelling words to take home, study, and write in sentences for homework.

Spelling Vocabulary Activities

Silent t Words

- Have students write each spelling word two times and cross out the **silent t** as indicated: **rustle.**

Root Words

- Tell students that the root word is what is left when all prefixes and suffixes are taken off.

  Examples: happen**ing** – **ing** = happen (the root word)

- Students will write the root words for the spelling words listed on page 147.

Rhyming

- Students will write two spelling words that rhyme.

Word Clues

- Students will write the spelling words that match the clues.

p. 147

Grand Tour II, p. 148

Grammar

Verbs

- Review **verbs** with students. Tell them a **verb** tells something you do. It can mean "happening now" or "happened in the past." Every sentence has at least one **verb**.

- Students will underline the **verb** in each sentence.

Prefixes

- Explain to students when the prefix **dis** or **un** is added to a word it means the **opposite**. Write these examples on the chalkboard and discuss the meanings: **happy—unhappy   comfortable—uncomfortable   trust—distrust   like—dislike**

- On page 148 have students add **dis** or **un** to the word in each box. Tell them to say the word in their minds with both prefixes and write the prefix they have heard with the root word before. Have them listen to the form of the word that sounds familiar to them.

- Students will complete the sentences by writing the new words in the blanks.

p. 148

Process Writing

Process Writing Lesson #16 for Steps 32 and 33 is found in TM p. 463.

Grand Tour II

Day 2

Getting Started

- Collect homework and put stars on Homework Chart. (See TM p. 26.)
- Administer spelling test with Day 1 spelling words in *Grand Tour II*, p. 147. Sentence for dictation: The king went in the <u>castle</u>. (See TM p. 100.)

Grand Tour II, p. 149

Spelling Words
Phonetic Grouping: *t̸*

- Note that all words have **silent t**. Have students mark each word as indicated: **mois⁄en**
- As a class, read the 10 spelling words and discuss the meanings.
- Have students copy the 10 spelling words to take home, study, and write in sentences for homework.

Spelling Vocabulary Activities

Silent t Words
- Have students write each spelling word two times and cross out the **silent t** as indicated: **mois⁄en**

Root Words
- Students will write the correct root words.

Rhyming
- Students will write four spelling words that rhyme.

Word Clues
- Students will write the spelling words that match the clues.

p. 149

Grand Tour II, p. 150

Story Comprehension

A Glistening World
Have students:
- Underline the five spelling words in the story.
- Read the story silently.
- Underline the correct answers.

The Writing Connection

Writing a Story
- Tell students that writers are good at pretending. They might pretend they are a king or a teacher or a rabbit! They use their imaginations to have pretend adventures.
- Have students pretend they live in a house built over a river, and it rains for four days and nights.
- Students will write a story telling what happened then.

p. 150

Grammar Chalkboard Lesson
Verbs

Objective
• The students will know that a verb tells something that you do.

Practice/Apply
• Write the sentences on the board. The students will write the sentences and underline the verb in each sentence.

> The women shopped for dresses.   The women <u>shopped</u> for dresses.
>
> Todd kicked the ball.   Todd <u>kicked</u> the ball.
>
> Renata played the piano.   Renata <u>played</u> the piano.
>
> The red crayon broke.   The red crayon <u>broke</u>.
>
> My sister went to Boston.   My sister <u>went</u> to Boston.

Process Writing

Process Writing Lesson #16 for Steps 32 and 33 is found in TM p. 463.

Day 3

Getting Started

• Collect homework and put stars on Homework Chart. (See TM p. 26.)
• Administer spelling test with Day 2 spelling words in *Grand Tour II*, p. 149. Sentence for dictation: The man will blow the <u>whistle</u>. (See TM p. 100.)

Grand Tour II, p. 151

Spelling Words
Phonetic Grouping: qu = k

• Note that words #1-6 have **qu = k**. Have students mark each word as indicated: **cro(qu)et**
• Discuss homophones #7-8 and #9-10. (**him—hymn; red—read**)
• As a class, read the 10 spelling words and discuss their meanings.
• Have students copy the 10 spelling words to take home, study, and write in sentences for homework.

p. 151

(Continued on next page)

Day 3 *continued*

Spelling Vocabulary Activities

Homophones
- Call attention to the homophones **him—hymn** and **red—read**.
- Students will fill in the blanks with the correct homophones.

Word Clues
- Students will write a spelling word for each clue.

Word Scrambles
- Students will unscramble the letters to make spelling words.

Grand Tour II, p.152

Grammar

Adjectives
- Review **nouns** and **verbs** with the students. Remind them that there are different kinds of words. The name of a **person, place,** or **thing** is called a **noun**. Something you can do is called a **verb**.
- Tell students that today they will learn about another kind of word. It describes, or tells more about, a **noun**. The new kind of word is called an **adjective**. Adjectives can tell **what kind** of noun. An adjective can also tell **how much** or **how many**. Most **adjectives** come right before a **noun** in a sentence.
- As a class, read the explanations and examples in the shaded boxes on page 152.
- Have students circle the **adjectives** in the phrases and write the **adjectives** on the lines provided.

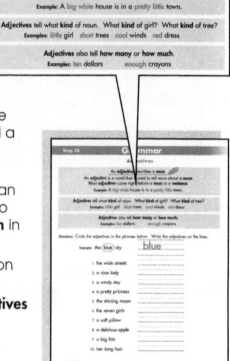

p. 152

Process Writing

Process Writing Lesson #16 for Steps 32 and 33 is found in TM p. 463.

Day 4

Getting Started

- Collect homework and put stars on Homework Chart. (See TM p. 26.)
- Administer spelling test with Day 3 spelling words in *Grand Tour II*, p. 151. Sentence for dictation: A <u>mosquito</u> bit me. (See TM p. 100.)

Grand Tour II, p. 153

Spelling Words
Phonetic Grouping: ph = f

- Note that all 10 spelling words have **ph = f**. Tell students when they see **ph**, it will probably sound like **f**. Have students mark each word as indicated: **nephew**
- Call attention to **photograph** which has **ph** at the beginning and end.
- As a class, read the 10 spelling words and discuss their meanings.
- Have students copy the 10 spelling words to take home, study, and write in sentences for homework.

Spelling Vocabulary Activities

Crossword Puzzle

- Students will read the clues by the number, think of a spelling word that fits the clue, and write the words in the crossword puzzle.

ABC Order

- Review **ABC order** to the **second letter** with students. Write **fell, full,** and **fall** on the chalkboard. Have students tell what order they go in and why.
- Have students read the words in each box on page 153 and write the words in **ABC order**.

Grand Tour II, p. 154

Proofreading

- Review the **proofreading marks** in the box on page 154.
- Students will use the **proofreading marks** to correct three spelling mistakes, insert one capital letter, take out one word, and change a capital letter to a lower case letter.

Reference Skill

Dictionary Entry Words

- Explain that the words listed in the dictionary are called **entry words**. They are in ABC order. When the words begin with the same letter, you must remember to look at the second letter.
- Write these words on the chalkboard: **apple, above, around.** Have students say the word that comes first in the dictionary.
- On page 154, have students circle the word in each group that would come first in the dictionary and write the word.

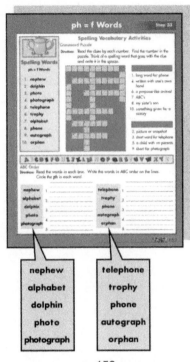

nephew	telephone
alphabet	trophy
dolphin	phone
photo	autograph
photograph	orphan

p. 153

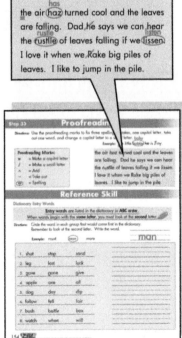

p. 154

(Continued on next page)

Grand Tour II

Grammar Chalkboard Lesson
Prefix pre

Objective

• The students will know that the prefix **pre** means before.

Practice/Apply

• Write the pairs of sentences on the board. The students will write and complete the second sentence of each pair by adding the prefix **pre** to the underlined word in the first sentence of the pair.

Example: We took a spelling test before the real <u>test</u>.
We took a _____.(pretest)

---

1. Some children attend a <u>school</u> before starting kindergarten.
It is called <u>preschool</u> .

2. We went to a football game before the <u>season</u> began.
It was a <u>preseason</u> game.

3. It is the time right before <u>dawn</u>.
It is the <u>predawn</u> .

4. We had a <u>view</u> or showing of the movie before it opened.
We had a <u>preview</u> of the movie.

5. Be sure to <u>heat</u> the oven before you put in the food.
Be sure to <u>preheat</u> the oven.

Process Writing

Process Writing Lesson #16 for Steps 32 and 33 is found in TM p. 463.

Day 5

Getting Started

- Collect homework and put stars on Homework Chart. (See TM p. 26.)
- Administer spelling test with Day 4 spelling words in *Grand Tour II*, p. 153. Sentence for dictation: Did you see her <u>photograph</u>? (See TM p. 100.)

Grand Tour II, pp. 155-156

Learning Cursive Writing

- To introduce the cursive letters *Xx* and *Yy*, refer to TM pp. 82-83.
- Students will trace over the letters and practice writing them on the lines.

Process Writing

Process Writing Lesson #16 for Steps 32 and 33 is found in TM p. 463.

pp. 155 - 156

Additional Related Activities for Step 33

Listening and Speaking

1. Alphabet Chain

- Write a list of 10 words to be alphabetized on the chalkboard.
- Suggested Words: **rustle, bustle, castle, thistle, bristle, croquet, bouquet, nephew, trophy, alphabet**
- Provide each student with 10 strips of 1" x 4 $^1/_2$" paper.
- Students will copy the words from the chalkboard onto the paper strips (one word per strip).
- Students will arrange the words in ABC order and link them together to form a paper chain.

2. "School" of Adjectives

- Provide each student with a sheet of 12" x 18" newsprint paper. Have students fold the newsprint to make eight boxes. Students will number their boxes 1. through 8. as shown.
- Write the following phrases on the chalkboard:

1. **a spotted fish**	5. **a striped fish**
2. **a big fish**	6. **a little fish**
3. **two mean fish**	7. **a red fish**
4. **a round fish**	8. **a purple, green and yellow fish**

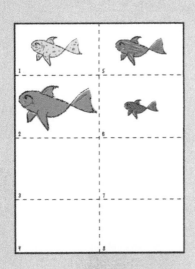

- Tell students that adjectives describe nouns. Call on students to identify the adjectives used to describe the noun **fish**.
- Students will draw and color fish corresponding to the phrases on the chalkboard.

Grand Tour II

Overview for Step 34

Objectives

Spelling: To spell words with **ph = f; ch = k; ss = sh**

Grammar: To identify nouns and adjectives
To know an adjective describes a noun
To know irregular plurals

Writing: To use the Five Steps of Process Writing, focusing on organizing and writing an informational paragraph

Proofreading: To find spelling, capital letter, and punctuation errors
To correct errors using proofreading marks

Reference Skill: To find the right meaning of multiple meaning words

Handwriting: To learn how to write cursive letter *Zz*

Suggested Pacing
1 week

Materials
Grand Tour II, pp. 157-166
Cursive Wall Chart

Homework
Daily homework is described in TM p. 99.

Spelling
Daily spelling is described in TM p. 99.

Phonics Games (See TM pp. 40-65.)
Continue to play selected games as needed for reinforcement.

Phonics Songs (See TM pp. 40-65.)
Continue to sing selected songs as needed for reinforcement.

Additional Related Activities
Additional activities are found in TM p. 412.

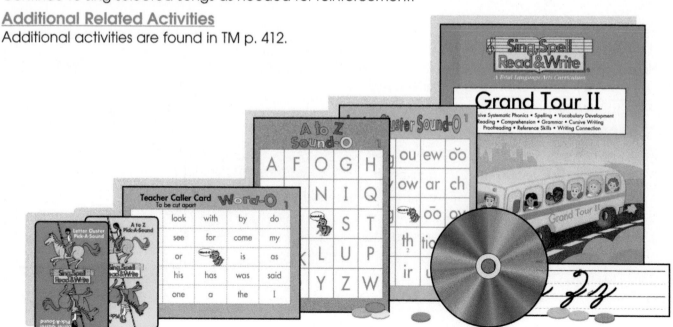

Grand Tour II, p. 157

Spelling Words
Phonetic Grouping: ph = f

- Note that all 10 words have **ph** = **f**. Have students mark each word as indicated: ⓅhiladelⓅhia

- As a class, read the 10 spelling words and discuss the meanings.

- Have students copy the 10 spelling words to take home, study, and write in sentences for homework.

Spelling Vocabulary Activities

Riddles

- Students will answer each riddle with a spelling word.

Syllables

- Remind students that all words are made up of one or more parts called **syllables**.

- Have students write the spelling words, circle the **ph** in each word, and write the number of **syllables** in the word.

p. 157

Grand Tour II, p. 158

Grammar

Adjectives

- Review **nouns** and **adjectives** with students. Tell them that a **noun** names a **person, place** or **thing**. An **adjective** tells more about the **noun**, and it usually comes just before a **noun** in a sentence.

- Hold up a pencil and say, "This is a pencil." Have students add an **adjective** to the sentence and say the new sentence.
  Example: This is a **yellow** pencil.

- On page 158, have students read the sentences in each group and write the **adjectives**.

The Writing Connection

Writing Descriptive Words

- Have students think about adjectives that would describe their own house.

- Students will write "_____ house" six times on a sheet of paper. On each line, the students will write a different adjective describing their house.
  Example: <u>white</u> house

- Have students draw a picture of their house.

Process Writing

Process Writing Lesson #17 for Steps 34 and 35 is found in TM p. 465.

p. 158

Day 2

Getting Started

- Collect homework and put stars on Homework Chart. (See TM p. 26.)
- Administer spelling test with Day 1 spelling words in *Grand Tour II*, p. 157. Sentence for dictation: An <u>elephant</u> is big. (See TM p. 100.)

Grand Tour II, p. 159

Spelling Words
Phonetic Grouping: ch = k

- Note that all 10 words have **ch** = **k**. Have students mark each word as indicated: ⓒhristie (**Ch** occurs twice in **stomachache**).
- As a class, read the 10 spelling words and discuss the meanings.
- Have students copy the 10 spelling words to take home, study, and write in sentences for homework.

Spelling Vocabulary Activities

Word Meanings
- Students will write a spelling word to fit each meaning.

Syllables
- Have students write the spelling words, circle the **ch** in each word, and write the number of syllables in each word.

Grand Tour II, p. 160

Proofreading

- Review the proofreading marks with the students.
- Students will use the proofreading marks to correct one spelling mistake, insert three capital letters, and add one question mark.

Reference Skills

Finding the Right Meaning in the Dictionary
- Explain that some words have more than one meaning. Often a dictionary will give several meanings for a word. Each meaning is numbered and has a sentence to fit it. Sometimes a sentence is written in a different print (*italics*).
- Remind students to read all meanings of a word when they look it up in a dictionary. They will need to decide which meaning to use.
- Have students read the two meanings of **garage** on page 160. Talk about the meanings.
- Students will write 1 or 2 by each sentence to tell which meaning of **garage** is used.

p. 159

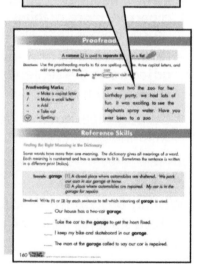

p. 160

Day 2 *continued*

Grammar Chalkboard Lesson
Adjectives

Objective
* The students will know that an adjective is a word that is used to tell more about a noun.

Practice/Apply
* Write the phrases on the board. The students will write the phrases and circle the **adjectives**.

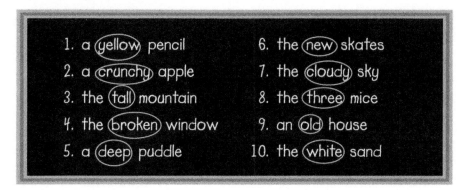

1. a (yellow) pencil
2. a (crunchy) apple
3. the (tall) mountain
4. the (broken) window
5. a (deep) puddle
6. the (new) skates
7. the (cloudy) sky
8. the (three) mice
9. an (old) house
10. the (white) sand

Process Writing

Process Writing Lesson #17 for Steps 34 and 35 is found in TM p. 465.

Day 3

Getting Started
* Collect homework and put stars on Homework Chart. (See TM p. 26.)
* Administer spelling test with Day 2 spelling words in *Grand Tour II*, p. 159. Sentence for dictation: I like to go to <u>school</u>. (See TM p. 100.)

Grand Tour II, p. 161

Spelling Words
Phonetic Grouping: ch = k

p. 161

* Note that all 10 words have **ch = k**. Have students mark each word as indicated: **anchor**
* As a class, read the 10 spelling words and discuss their meanings.
* Have students copy the 10 spelling words to take home, study, and write in sentences for homework.

(Continued on next page)

Day 3 *continued*

Spelling Vocabulary Activities

Cloze
• Students will fill in the blanks with the correct spelling words.

Syllables
• Have students write the spelling words, circle the **ch** in each word, and write the number of syllables in each word.

Grand Tour II, p.162

Grammar

Adjectives and Nouns
• Review **nouns** and **adjectives** with the students. Have students name several **nouns**. List the **nouns** on the chalkboard. Next, have students supply an **adjective** to describe each **noun**. Write the **adjectives** in front of the **nouns**. Call on students to circle the **adjectives** and underline the **nouns**.
Example: (brown) horse

• Have students read the sentences on page 162, then underline the **noun** and circle the **adjectives** in each sentence.

Process Writing

Process Writing Lesson #17 for Steps 34 and 35 is found in TM p. 465.

p. 162

Day 4

Getting Started

• Collect homework and put stars on Homework Chart. (See TM p. 26.)

• Administer spelling test with Day 3 spelling words in *Grand Tour II*, p. 161. Sentence for dictation: My boat has an <u>anchor</u>. See TM p. 100.)

Grand Tour II, pp. 163-164

Spelling Words
Phonetic Grouping: ss = sh

• Note that words #1-6 have **ss = sh**. Tell students that sometimes **ss** has the sound of **sh**, especially when followed by **ion**.

• As a class, read the 10 spelling words and discuss their meanings.

• Have students copy the 10 spelling words to take home, study, and write in sentences for homework.

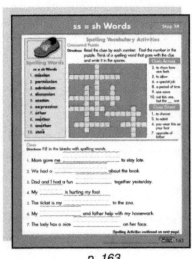

p. 163

Spelling Vocabulary Activities

Crossword Puzzle

- Students will read the clues by the number, think of a spelling word that fits the clue, and write the words in the crossword puzzle.

Cloze

- Students will fill in the blanks with the correct spelling words.

Grand Tour II, p. 164

Grammar

Irregular Plurals

- Tell students that **irregular plurals** are words that do not make their **plurals** in the regular way (adding **s** or **es**). They change their spelling to mean **more than one** in a different way.

- Have students read the **singular words** and **irregular plurals** in the box on page 164. Students will then read the sentences and fill in the blanks with words from the box.

- Be sure students understand that some answers will be **singular** and some **plural**.

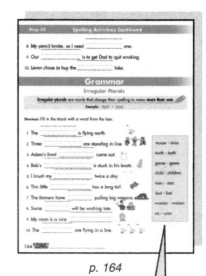

p. 164

mouse	mice
tooth	teeth
goose	geese
child	children
man	men
foot	feet
woman	women
ox	oxen

Grammar Chalkboard Lesson
Adjectives

Objective

- The students will know that an **adjective** is a word that is used to tell more about a **noun**, and it tells **what kind**, **how many**, or **how much**.

Practice/Apply

- Write the phrases on the board. The students will write each phrase, circle the adjective, and write **what kind**, **how many**, or **how much**.
  Example: the red pony (what kind)

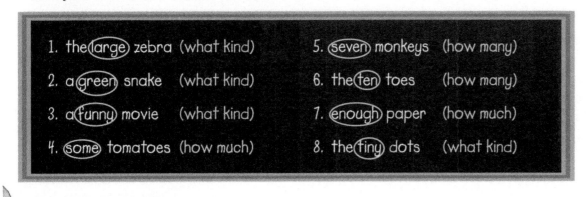

1. the ⟨large⟩ zebra   (what kind)
2. a ⟨green⟩ snake   (what kind)
3. a ⟨funny⟩ movie   (what kind)
4. ⟨some⟩ tomatoes   (how much)
5. ⟨seven⟩ monkeys   (how many)
6. the ⟨ten⟩ toes   (how many)
7. ⟨enough⟩ paper   (how much)
8. the ⟨tiny⟩ dots   (what kind)

Process Writing

Process Writing Lesson #17 for Steps 34 and 35 is found in TM p. 465.

Step 34

Grand Tour II

Day 5

Getting Started

- Collect homework and put stars on Homework Chart. (See TM p. 26.)
- Administer spelling test with Day 4 spelling words in *Grand Tour II*, p. 163. Sentence for dictation: We pay <u>admission</u> to the game. (See TM p. 100.)

Grand Tour II, pp. 165-166

Learning Cursive Writing

- To introduce the cursive letter *Zz*, refer to TM p. 83.
- Students will trace over the cursive letters and words and practice writing them on the lines.

pp. 165 and 166

Process Writing

Process Writing Lesson #17 for Steps 34 and 35 is found in TM p. 465.

Additional Related Activities for Step 34

Listening and Speaking

1. Syllable Addition

- Think of a word with two or more syllables and say the word slowly (**apple**). Have students write the number of syllables as the first part of an addition problem.
- Say another word (**banana**). Have students write the number of syllables as the second part of the addition problem.
- Students add to find the total number of syllables and write the sum.

  Example: **apple** + **banana** = ?
  $$2 + 3 = 5$$

- Repeat with groups of two, three, or four words. Suggested words:

  happiness (3) + caterpillar (4) = 7   sentence (2) + punctuation (4) + prefix (2) = 8
  delight (2) + laughing (2) = 4   consideration (5) + kindness (2) + courtesy (3) = 10
  surprise (2) + spattering (3) = 5   machine (2) + library (3) + January (4) = 9
  sweep (1) + families (3) + president (3) = 7   Constantinople (5) + automatic (4) + dinosaur (3) = 12

- Give recognition for perfect listening.

2. Riddle Sentences

- Review the riddles in *Grand Tour II*, page 157.
- Call on a leader to use the same pattern to say a riddle for a Step 34 spelling word from Day 2, 3, or 4. Leader must use a complete sentence to say the riddle.
  Example: I hold food. What am I? (**stomach**)
- Leader calls on a guesser. Guesser must use a complete sentence when guessing.   **Example:** Are you a stomach?
- Leader replies in a complete sentence.
  Example: Yes, I am a stomach.
- The correct guesser becomes the new Leader.
- Make sure all students have an opportunity to be a guesser during the game.
- If students have trouble guessing the riddles, play with just one day's list of spelling words.

Sing Spell Read & Write

NOTES

Grand Tour II

Overview for Step 35

Objectives

Spelling: To spell **Rulebreakers** and **Wacky Words**;
words with **ch** = **sh**; **ous**

Grammar: To know a pronoun is a word used in place of a noun
To know a pronoun can take the place of a
person's name

Comprehension: To read short stories and answer questions requiring higher
level thinking skills

Writing: To write a story
To write a paragraph about what makes a good leader
To use the Five Steps of Process Writing, focusing on
organizing and writing an informational paragraph

Suggested Pacing
1 week

Materials
Grand Tour II, pp. 167-174

Homework
Daily homework is described in TM p. 99.

Phonics Games (See TM pp. 40-65.)
Continue to play selected games as needed for reinforcement.

Phonics Songs (See TM pp. 40-65.)
Continue to sing selected songs as needed for reinforcement.

Additional Related Activities
Additional activities are found in TM p. 421.

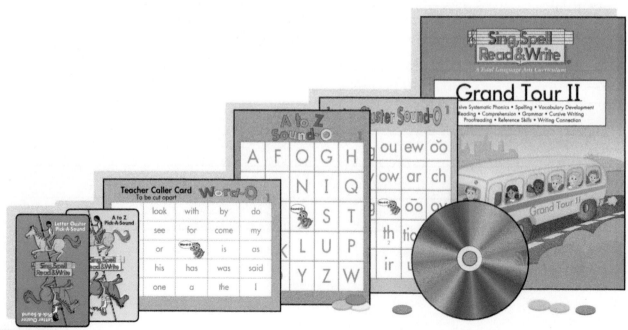

Day 1

Grand Tour II, p. 167

Spelling Words
Rulebreakers and Wacky Words

- Note that all words are **Rulebreakers** and **Wacky Words**. Instead of placing these words in cages, they have been written with helper marks and letters. Call attention to these pronunciation aids.
- As a class, read the 10 spelling words and discuss the meanings.
- Have students copy the 10 spelling words to take home, study, and write in sentences for homework.

Spelling Vocabulary Activities

Word Fun

- Students will cross out every other letter, starting with the second letter, to make a spelling word. Demonstrate this procedure on the chalkboard.
  Example: b ̷i ̷g ̷   big

ABC Order

- Write the words **barn** and **band** on the chalkboard. Ask students to suggest a way to put these words in ABC order since both the first and second letters are the same. Lead students to conclude you would need to go to the **third** letter.
- On page 167, have students read the words in each box and write the words in **ABC order**.

p. 167

Grand Tour II, p. 168

Grammar

Pronouns

- Read the following story to the students:

    I went to **Billy**'s house after school. **Billy** showed me his pet lizard. **Billy** gave me cookies and milk. **Billy** got a baseball bat from his room **Billy** got his baseball. **Billy** said, "Let's go play ball."

- Ask the students if something sounds wrong in the story. (There are too many uses of the word **Billy**.)
- Read the story again, pausing at each **Billy**. Have students suggest words that can take the place of **Billy**. (**He**)
- Tell students that a word used in place of a person's name is called a **pronoun**. Pronouns are words like **he**, **him**, **she**, **her**, **me**, **you**, **I**, **we**, **they**, and **us**. **Pronouns** take the place of **nouns**.
- Have students read each sentence on page 168, underline the **pronoun**, and write the **pronoun** in the space.

p. 168

Process Writing

Process Writing Lesson #17 for Steps 34 and 35 is found in TM p. 465.

Getting Started

- Collect homework and put stars on Homework Chart. (See TM p. 26.)
- Administer spelling test with Day 1 spelling words in *Grand Tour II*, p. 167. Sentence for dictation: My <u>friend</u> gave me a book. (See TM p. 100.)

Grand Tour II, pp. 169-170

Spelling Words
Phonetic Grouping: ch = sh

- Note that all 10 words have **ch = sh**. Have students mark each word as indicated: Ⓒharlotte
- As a class, read the 10 spelling words and discuss the meanings.
- Have students copy the 10 spelling words to take home, study, and write in sentences for homework.

Spelling Vocabulary Activities

Syllables
- Students will write each spelling word, circle the **ch** that makes the **sh** sound in each word, and write the number of syllables in each word.

Riddles
- Have students answer each riddle with a spelling word.

Grand Tour II, p. 170

Story Comprehension

Charlotte at Lake Michigan
Have students:
- Underline the nine spelling words in the story.
- Read the story silently.
- Read the questions and underline the correct answers.

The Writing Connection

Writing a Story
- Brainstorm with students about activities associated with water.
- Have students think about something they have done or would like to do in water.
- Students will choose one water activity and write a story about it.

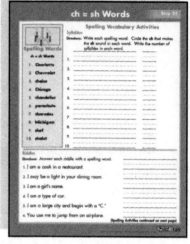

p. 169

p. 170

Day 2 *continued*

Grammar Chalkboard Lesson
Pronouns

Objective
* The students will know that a pronoun is used in place of a noun.

Practice/Apply
* Write the sentences on the board. The students will write the sentences and underline the pronouns.

1. He fell down the steps.	<u>He</u> fell down the steps.
2. Sandy wants to go with him.	Sandy wants to go with <u>him</u>.
3. She is Fran's sister.	<u>She</u> is Fran's sister.
4. Give the books to her.	Give the books to <u>her</u>.
5. Dad took a picture of Vincent and me.	Dad took a picture of Vincent and <u>me</u>.

Process Writing

Process Writing Lesson #17 for Steps 34 and 35 is found in TM p. 465.

Day 3

Getting Started

* Collect homework and put stars on Homework Chart. (See TM p. 26.)
* Administer spelling test with Day 2 spelling words in *Grand Tour II*, p. 169. Sentence for dictation: Our class plays <u>charades</u>. (See TM p. 100.)

Grand Tour II, p. 171

Spelling Words
Rulebreakers and Wacky Words

* Note that all 10 words are **Rulebreakers** and **Wacky Words**. Have students look at the respelling above each word. Explain that the respellings will help them remember how to pronounce the words, but not how to spell them.

* As a class, read the 10 spelling words and discuss their meanings.

* Have students copy the 10 spelling words to take home, study, and write in sentences for homework.

p. 171

(Continued on next page)

Day 3 *continued*

Spelling Vocabulary Activities

Word Association

- Remind students that words go together for many different reasons.
- Have students read words #1-6 and write the spelling word that goes with each word.
- Have students read the directions for #7-9. Explain that **ranks** are **levels of positions in the army**.
- Students will fill in the blanks with the correct spelling words.

Cloze

- Students will fill in the blank with the correct spelling word.

ABC Order

- Students will read the words in each box and write the words in ABC order.

Grand Tour II, p.172

Grammar

Pronouns

- Explain that a pronoun is a word used in place of a **noun**. **She** and **her** take the place of names of women and girls. **He** and **him** take the place of names of men and boys. **They** and **them** take the place of names of more than one person.
- Have students read the sentences on page 172.
- Students will write each sentence, replacing the underlined **noun** with a **pronoun** from the box.

Process Writing

Process Writing Lesson #17 for Steps 34 and 35 is found in TM p. 465.

p. 172

Day 4

Getting Started

- Collect homework and put stars on Homework Chart. (See TM p. 26.)
- Administer spelling test with Day 3 spelling words in *Grand Tour II*, p. 171. Sentence for dictation: The <u>scissors</u> are not sharp. See TM p. 100.)

Grand Tour II, p. 173

Spelling Words
Phonetic Grouping: ous

- Note that all 10 words have **ous**. Have students mark each word as indicated: **famous**
- As a class, read the 10 spelling words and discuss their meanings.
- Have students copy the 10 spelling words to take home, study, and write in sentences for homework.

Spelling Vocabulary Activities

Crossword Puzzle
- Students will read the clues by the number, think of a spelling word that fits the clue, and write the words in the crossword puzzle.

Syllables
- Students will write each spelling word, circle the **ous** in each word, and write the number of syllables in each word.

Grand Tour II, p. 174

Story Comprehension

George Washington
- Have students underline the seven spelling words in the story.
- Read the story aloud with the students.
- Discuss the qualities and accomplishments of George Washington.
- Ask students to tell why Americans say George Washington is "The Father of our Country."
- Discuss the saying, "First in war, first in peace, and first in the hearts of his countrymen."
- Students will read the questions and underline the correct answers.

The Writing Connection

Writing a Paragraph
- Have students think about George Washington. Tell them he was such a good leader that he was made Commander in Chief of the entire army. Discuss the meaning of "good leader."
- Ask students if they think George Washington was a hero.
- Have students write a paragraph about what makes a good leader.

p. 173

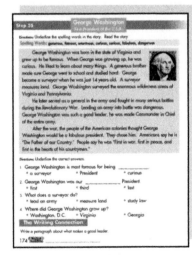

p. 174

(*Continued on next page*)

Day 4 continued

Grammar Chalkboard Lesson
Pronouns

Objective
- The students will know that a pronoun is a word used in place of a noun and that a pronoun can take the place of a person's name.

Practice/Apply
- Write the sentences on the board. The students will write each sentence, replace the underlined word(s) with a pronoun, and underline the pronoun.

1. <u>The girls</u> played chess.
   <u>They</u> played chess.

2. Please take the paper to <u>Mr. Leon</u>.
   Please take the paper to <u>him</u>.

3. The kittens played with <u>Ellen and Tonya</u>.
   The kittens played with <u>them</u>.

4. <u>Aunt Sue</u> is going on vacation.
   <u>She</u> is going on vacation.

5. <u>Donald Jones</u> is very tall.
   <u>He</u> is very tall.

Process Writing

Process Writing Lesson #17 for Steps 34 and 35 is found in TM p. 465.

Day 5

Getting Started

- Collect homework and put stars on Homework Chart. (See TM p. 26.)
- Administer spelling test with Day 4 spelling words in *Grand Tour II*, p. 173. Sentence for dictation: The man was very <u>famous</u>. (See TM p. 100.)

Process Writing

Process Writing Lesson #17 for Steps 34 and 35 is found in TM p. 465.

Additional Related Activities for Step 35

Listening and Speaking

1. Categories

* Students will need lined paper and a pencil for this fun activity.

* Teacher says a category, such as **colors**.

* At a given signal, students make a list of as many words in that category as they can.

* Teacher calls time after 1 or 2 minutes.

* Students count their words. Student with highest total reads his/her list aloud.

* Spelling and handwriting **do not** count.

* Teacher calls on other students to say words they wrote that were not on the longest list.

* Suggested categories: **colors**, **foods**, **animals**, **transportation**, **clothing**, **furniture**, **buildings**, **workers**, **games**, **machines**

2. My Ship Came In

* Leader says, "My ship came in, and it was loaded with_____."
  (Leader says a word that begins with letter **a** that would fit in the blank.
  Example: apples)

* Next person says, "My ship came in and it was loaded with_____."
  (Repeat the **a** word and say a word that begins with letter **b**.
  Example: balls)

* Continue the game, going through the alphabet. Each new player repeats everything previously said and adds an object beginning with the next letter of the alphabet.

* If a student can't remember the sequence of objects, he/she begins the game again by saying a new object beginning with letter **a**.

Grand Tour II

Overview for Step 36

Objectives

Spelling: To spell multi-syllable words

Grammar: To know that quotation marks are used around the words a person says

Writing: To produce a deadline writing story using the skills learned in Process Writing

Suggested Pacing
2 days

Materials
Grand Tour II, pp. 175-176

Homework
Daily homework is described in TM p. 99.

Additional Related Activities
Additional activities are found in TM p. 424.

Day 1

Grand Tour II, pp. 175-176

Spelling Words
Phonetic Grouping: Multisyllable Words

- Note that all 10 spelling words have at least 3 syllables. Tell students that thinking of these words one syllable at a time will make them easier to spell.
- As a class, read the 10 spelling words and discuss the meanings.
- Have students copy the 10 spelling words to take home, study, and write in sentences for homework.

Spelling Vocabulary Activities

Riddles
- Students will use a spelling word to answer each riddle.

Syllables
- On pages 175 and 176, have students write each spelling word in the order of the spelling list and then write the spelling words broken into syllables.
- Encourage students to use their dictionaries if they need help in dividing the words.

p. 175

Grand Tour II, p. 176

Grammar

Punctuation: Quotation Marks
- Tell students that **quotation marks** are used around the words a person says. They always come in pairs.
- Write the following sentences on the chalkboard without the needed quotation marks:
    1. Maria said, I lost my pencil.
    2. Lee said, I found a yellow pencil.
    3. Maria said, I think it is mine.
- With students watching, place the quotation marks in sentence #1. Frame Maria's words with your hands. Have the students read Maria's words aloud.
- Call on students to put the quotation marks in sentences #2 and #3.
- Have students look at the examples on page 176 and read the words the speakers are saying. Call attention to the quotation marks.
- Have students read the 10 sentences, decide what the speaker is saying, and place quotation marks around the words each person says.

p. 176

Process Writing

Process Writing Lesson #18 for Step 36 is found in TM p. 467.

Getting Started

- Collect homework and put stars on Homework Chart. (See TM p. 26.)
- Administer spelling test with Day 1 spelling words in *Grand Tour II*, p. 175. Sentence for dictation: We had fun <u>together</u> this year. (See TM p. 100.)

Grammar Chalkboard Lesson
Punctuation

Objective
- The students will know that quotation marks are used around the words a person says.

Practice/Apply
- Write the sentences on the board. The students will write the sentences correctly.

> 1. Christopher said, "The capital of Florida is Tallahassee."
>
> 2. The doctor said, "Stay in bed for three days."
>
> 3. My teacher asked, "Who wants to play a game?"
>
> 4. Mr. Kornfeld said, "Steven will be absent tomorrow."
>
> 5. The principal said, "Please turn out the lights."

Process Writing

Process Writing Lesson #18 for Step 36 is found in TM p. 467.

Additional Related Activities for Step 36

Listening and Speaking
1. Old Fashioned Spelling Bee
- Explain the procedure for the old fashioned spelling bee carefully. Have at least one practice session with students to avoid misunderstandings.
- Have all students stand side by side in a long line.
- Explain the rules. Students may not talk or help another student. Teacher will select an appropriate step as a starting point and call words in order in the following manner: **"Penny. I have one penny. Penny."** The student will respond: **"Penny, p-e-n-n-y, penny."** If the student spells the word correctly, the teacher calls the next word to the next student. If the word was spelled incorrectly, that student sits down. The teacher calls the same word to the next student. Winner of the spelling bee is the last student remaining.

2. Choose Favorite Activities
- Look at previous **Additional Related Activities** sections and enjoy the class favorites one more time.
- Sing favorite *SSR&W Phonics Songs*.
- Play favorite *SSR&W Phonics Games*.

Process Writing

Pre-Writing

Composing

Revising

Editing

Publishing

Process Writing

The Five Steps of Process Writing

Overview

Helping students become confident and accomplished writers is a challenging task for any teacher. These Process Writing Lessons are designed to make this challenge a rewarding one for both students and teachers.

In this section of the Teacher's Manual you will find **18 Process Writing Lessons**. Each lesson should take about two weeks to complete. Plan on spending approximately 20 minutes each day on writing activities. **Start these lessons the second week of school as you begin teaching Step 2 in** *Grand Tour I*.

The Mini Lesson

Each Process Writing Lesson begins with a Mini Lesson. The Mini Lesson is designed to **focus** the students on the **specific writing skill** to be addressed in that particular Process Writing Lesson. Each Mini Lesson will help the students understand **why** that particular skill is an **essential** part of good writing. As you proceed through the 18 lessons, you will see that each lesson builds on previous lessons. As the year progresses, students will continue to practice and apply the previously learned skills in subsequent lessons.

The Process Writing Lesson

Each Process Writing Lesson contains the following steps:

1. **Pre-Writing**—Helping students generate ideas for writing.
2. **Composing**—Giving students time to write for a sustained period.
3. **Revising**—Having students read, change, and improve their pieces.
4. **Editing**—Learning how to correct capitalization, punctuation, spelling, and grammar errors.
5. **Publishing**—The grand finale!

Teacher Tips for a Successful Year in Writing

- **Provide a print-rich classroom environment**. Surround students with the printed word. Help them look at print from the author's point of view.

- **Provide opportunities for a wide variety of writing every day**. Students may write lists and letters, answer questions, compose stories and poems, keep a journal, publish a newspaper, or create a multitude of other projects in a classroom where written words are valued.

- **Provide meaningful, skill-based instruction**. The 18 Process Writing Lessons will help you do this.

- **Provide encouragement**. Show students that you take their efforts seriously. Conferencing individually with students is a wonderful way to do this. As you "walk the room," stop by students to hear them read their work-in-progress and ask them questions to help them develop their pieces. Sometimes you may prefer to have students sign up for conferences or pass out numbers.

(Continued on next page)

Process Writing *continued*

- **Provide a good role model—you!** Plan for quiet, uninterrupted writing times when <u>everyone</u> sits and writes, you included. Share your piece with the students. Talk about your piece—how you developed it, what you like about it, how you might change it.

- **Provide an audience.** Have a few students share their writing each day. Make sure that even the shy student is heard. When a student has shared, encourage positive comments from the other students. Display published pieces. Make class books. Show students that what they have to say is important, but don't embarrass students by forcing them to share pieces publicly that are meant to be private.

- **Provide time to write.** Plan a daily writing time of about 20 minutes. Calling this time "Writers' Workshop" helps to make it special to the students.

- **Provide a means for students to organize their work-in-progress pieces.** A good idea is to give each student a pocket folder to hold rough drafts. You may want to keep the folders in a file box when they are not in use.

- **Provide interesting ways in which students may publish their work.** Some pieces may be published in students' best handwriting. Some may be published on the computer or other available technology. Some may be published through oral presentation. Publishing encompasses a wide variety of formats. Be creative! The possibilities are endless.

| **publish** (pub' - lish) – **v**. to make known to the public |

speeches	short stories
plays	books
mini-dramas	journals
puppet shows	posters
TV shows	murals
radio broadcasts	notebooks
newspaper articles	video tapes
bulletin boards	audio tapes
craft projects	multimedia presentations
web pages	read-alouds
poems	mobiles

Little House

Suggested Schedule

- Begin with Process Writing Lesson #1 the week you begin Step 2 in *Grand Tour I*.

- This suggested schedule will, of course, need to remain flexible as your daily schedule fluctuates. The two-week format can be applied to all of the Process Writing Lessons as you proceed through *Grand Tour I* and *Grand Tour II*.

Day 1

Mini Lesson

- Teach the Mini Lesson to the whole class. It is designed to focus the students on a specific writing skill.

Day 2

Pre-Writing

- Teach the Pre-Writing Lesson to the whole class. Each lesson is designed to help the students generate ideas for writing. Begin the Composing Lesson if time permits.

Days 3 and 4

Composing

- Review the Pre-Writing Lesson. Restate the topic. Have students begin the silent writing time. Model by writing your own composition. Begin some conferencing.

- Do not expect all the students to complete their compositions in one day. As the year progresses, you will find students working on different pieces and different steps on any given day. This works well once the routine is established. Post a master list of pieces-in-progress and add to it as new topics are added.

Days 5 and 6

Revising

- Teach the Revising Lesson to the whole class. Those finished with composing should move on to this step. Hold conferences with students who are still on the Composing Step. Motivate them to complete the piece.

Day 7

Editing

- Teach the Editing Lesson to the whole class. Have students begin editing if they have completed the previous steps.

(Continued on next page)

Process Writing *continued*

Days 8 and 9

Publishing

- Give instructions for publishing to the whole class. Have students begin this step as they finish editing their work. Provide a new writing topic for students who have published their pieces before Day 10 or have students choose their own topic. Remember, this is <u>writing</u> time!

Day 10

Sharing

- Have students share their work. Encourage positive comments about shared pieces. Talk about the Five Steps of Process Writing and Writers' Workshop. Sometimes share your own piece and talk about how you developed it. Keep building enthusiasm for writing!

Evaluation

Your school may have a pre-determined plan for evaluating student writing. If not, develop your own standards of excellence. You might start by dividing class work into five groups: the weakest stories in Group 1; the best in Group 5; and the rest ranked 2, 3, and 4.

Group 1—This paper lacks meaning. Mechanics and spelling may be very poor. The writer is unable to communicate with the reader.

Group 2—This paper is immature. It may be poorly organized and lacking in details.

Group 3—This is a fairly good paper with good information. It may need improved organization. Language and mechanics may be faulty, but the writer definitely has something to say.

Group 4—This is a paper with good information and language. It will have some flaws, though. It may not be focused. Beginnings and endings may lack excitement. There may be some problems with spelling mechanics.

Group 5—This is an excellent paper. It may have some errors, but it shows strength in all areas.

Keep a folder for each student with copies of selected pieces written throughout the year. Do not expect perfection, but do look for improvement, no matter where the student begins.

Process Writing for *Grand Tour I* and *Grand Tour II*

Curriculum Summary

Lesson #	Steps	Title	Skill Focus
1	2-3	*I'm a Real Writer!*	Writing a Story
2	4-5	*A Pinhole View*	Narrowing the Topic
3	6-7	*Scrambled Breakfast*	Sequencing
4	8-9	*Yum, Yum*	Writing a Good Beginning
5	10-11	*Tell Me a Story*	Recognizing Story Elements
6	12-13	*Happily Ever After*	Writing Story Endings
7	14-15	*Special Treasures*	Correcting Spelling Errors
8	16-17	*As Easy as ABC!*	Correcting Spelling Errors
9	18-19	*Happy Faces*	Editing Run-on Sentences
10	20-21	*Beautiful Places*	Using Descriptive Words
11	22-23	*Someday Boxes*	Developing a List of Self-selected Story Ideas
12	24-25	*My Best Friend*	Developing Supporting Ideas and Specific Details
13	26-27	*Sentence Spiders!*	Using Varied Sentence Structure
14	28-29	*In Other Words*	Making Interesting Word Choices
15	30-31	*As Big as an Elephant*	Using Similes
16	32-33	*Let Me Entertain You!*	Identifying Reasons to Write
17	34-35	*Tell Me Why*	Organizing and Writing an Informational Paragraph
18	36	*Putting It All Together*	Producing a Deadline Writing Piece

NOTES

Process Writing Lesson #1

Skill Focus: Writing a Story

Mini Lesson

Display several of the students' favorite books, both fiction and nonfiction. Have students recall why they like these books. Ask, "Where did these books come from?" Lead students to conclude that real people wrote these books.

Tell students they are all writers, too. Whenever they write a piece, they are sharing their ideas with others. That's what writers do. Tell them that each day in Writers' Workshop they will work on pieces and learn more about what writers do.

Generate enthusiasm for writing!

Pre-Writing

To prepare students for the writing task, tell them that today they will be real writers. A writer needs something to write about. That is called a **topic** or **prompt**. Next, tell students that sometimes they will choose their own topic, and sometimes you will ask them to write about a certain thing.

Tell students that today the topic will be "My Pet." Ask two or three students to tell about their pet. "Who has a pet? Have you ever had a pet? Tell us about a pet that you used to have. What kind of trouble has your pet caused? What do you and your pet enjoy doing together?" Some children may never have had a pet. Help them adapt the topic by saying, "If you've never had a pet, tell what kind of pet you would like to have." Perhaps they can tell about an imaginary pet.

My Pet Fish

Direct students to name things that could be in a piece about a pet. List several of their Ideas on chart paper or the chalkboard. Include items such as the kind of pet, pet's name, appearance, and activities you enjoy with the pet.

Composing

Review the Idea Chart. Restate the topic, "My Pet." Review what students are to write about if they have no pet. Continue by presenting the Composing Lesson. Begin some conferencing. (Do not expect all the students to complete their compositions in one day. As the year progresses, you will find students working on different pieces and different steps on any given day. This works well once the routine is established.)

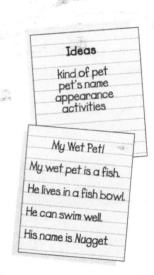

Ideas

kind of pet
pet's name
appearance
activities

My Wet Pet!

My wet pet is a fish.

He lives in a fish bowl.

He can swim well.

His name is Nugget.

Ask children to write their stories on paper. (**Note to the Teacher**: Writing on alternate spaces of wide-lined notebook paper may be easier for the students than using standard handwriting paper.)

Remind students to:

* Write about just one pet.
* Check the list on the chalkboard for things to include.
* Write a title for the story.

(Continued on next page)

Revising

Teach the lesson on Revising to the whole class. Those finished with composing should move on to this step. Continue conferencing with students who are still on the Composing step. Motivate them to complete their pieces.

Ask for a volunteer to read his/her piece. Make positive comments about the story. Invite a few students to tell what part they liked best. Ask one or two questions to clarify the piece. This might be something like, "What is your pet's name?" or, "What is the best thing you and your pet do together?" Suggest that the student add these things.

Direct students to read their stories silently and see if they know something else to tell. Explain that this is called revising—changing a piece to make it better.

Editing

Ask two or three volunteers to read their stories to the group. Direct the group to clap once at the end of each sentence. Instruct students to read their own stories silently and place a punctuation mark (period, question mark, or exclamation point) where the claps would go.

Remind students to:
* Begin each sentence with a capital letter.
* Begin names of people and pets with a capital letter.
* End each sentence with a punctuation mark.

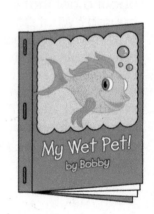

My Wet Pet!
by Bobby

Tell students to make needed changes and not worry if the piece looks messy. Students will recopy pieces another day.

Publishing

Have students make a clean copy of their stories. Remind them their handwriting must be neat so that another person reading the story can understand it.

Provide construction paper to make a cover. Have students decorate the cover. Be sure they include the story title and author's name. Complete by stapling the story inside the cover.

PROCESS WRITING

Pre-Writing
Composing
Revising
Editing
Publishing

Process Writing Lesson #2

Skill Focus: Narrowing the Topic

Mini Lesson

Ask two or three students to orally describe the school building. Remind students to name specific details.

Next, have a few students describe the playground. Ask, "Which could you tell more about?" Lead students to conclude that they could tell more about the playground because it has fewer parts than a whole building, and it is more familiar to them.

Then, give students small pieces of paper. Have each student make a small hole in the center of his/her paper. Say, "Now we are going to see with a writer's eye. Look through the pinhole. Focus on something in the room. Tell exactly what you see." Allow several responses. Lead students to see that the view is small, but they can see many details.

Say, "Real writers like you focus on their pieces. They tell a lot about a topic, but they make the topic small. Which would be better for you to write, a piece about *all* dogs or *your* dog? Would it be better to write about your favorite *park* or your favorite *activity* there? Could you write about cooking everything in a cook book, or would your piece be more focused if you wrote about making a peanut butter sandwich?"

Restate that to **focus** means to **narrow your topic**. Remind students to do this as they begin each new piece.

Pre-Writing

To prepare students for the writing task, remind them they have been describing the playground and something in the classroom. Ask students to name other special places in the school such as the library, cafeteria, and office.

Say, "Think about your very favorite place in the school. That is what your piece will be about today. Where is your favorite place? What does it look like? Do you hear or smell something special there? Use your writer's words to help us see your special place in our minds, and help us to know why it is special to you."

Composing

Ask students to write their stories on paper.

Remind students to:

- Focus—write about just one place.
- Include specific details (words that describe feelings, sights, sounds, smells, and tastes associated with the topic).
- Write a title for the story.

(Continued on next page)

Revising

Ask for two or three volunteers to read their pieces aloud. Invite a few students to make positive comments. Ask other students to name specific details used in the pieces.

Have students recall that real writers revise their pieces to make the pieces better. Direct students to read their pieces silently and add at least one more specific detail somewhere in the story. Demonstrate the use of an insertion mark (∧) when revising. Encourage students to tell how they made their pieces better.

Editing

Have students work in pairs. Ask them to do the following:

* Take turns reading their pieces out loud.
* Read pieces together, looking for beginnings and endings of sentences.
* Start all sentences with capital letters.
* End each sentence with a punctuation mark.
* Begin names of people with capital letters.
* Circle two words that might be spelled incorrectly. Use classroom resources such as a spellchecker, dictionary, or your partner to correct the words.

Publishing

* Have students make a clean copy of their pieces. Remind them that their handwriting must be neat so that another person reading the story can understand it.
* **Note:** Trimming the hole-punched margin off wide-lined notebook paper is an inexpensive way to make "special" paper.
* Finally, have students illustrate their stories. Mount the stories and illustrations on bright paper, and display them in the classroom.

The Playground

Darnelle

The Cafeteria

Robert

The Office

Consuelo

Process Writing Lesson #3

Skill Focus: Sequencing

Mini Lesson

Before beginning the lesson, copy the following sentences onto sentence strips:

- This morning I made scrambled eggs for breakfast.
- I took the eggs out of the refrigerator.
- I cracked them into a bowl and stirred them.
- I cooked them in a pan.
- Then I ate them.

To begin the lesson, tell the students you have written a story about what you did this morning. Display the sentence strips in a mixed-up order, the sillier the better. Ask, "Do you like my story?" Lead students to conclude that the story has been scrambled, too. Have them arrange the sentences into proper order.

Ask students why it is important to tell a story in the order that things really happened. Lead them to conclude that it is much easier to understand what you read if the writer tells the events in order.

Explain that real writers call this putting the story in **sequence**.

Pre-Writing

To prepare students for the writing task, ask them to recall a time when they fell down. Say, "Today you will write a very short piece to tell about your accident. We are going to write this in a special way to help you tell your story in sequence."

At this point you may want to model an appropriate story. Use only four sentences. An example follows:

> I was sitting at my desk working when my earring fell off. I leaned over to get it, but my chair tipped over. I landed on the floor with a bang. I got a little bump, but my class got a <u>big</u> surprise!

Instruct students to fold a sheet of rough draft paper into four sections and to cut the sections apart. Each section is now a small page.

Next, have them number the pages 1-4. Say, "Now you are ready to write about a time when you fell."

(Continued on next page)

Scrambled Breakfast

Composing

Instruct students to write a beginning sentence on page one. Ask students what might go in a good first sentence. Lead them to conclude that the beginning sentence might contain where they were, or what they were doing when they fell.

Have students write a sentence telling what happened next on page two. Remind them they are writing about a fall. Invite a few students to read their first two sentences.

Say, "Now think about what happened next. Remember that your story is almost over. Try to choose something important, and write it on page three." Allow a few minutes writing time. Then ask students to tell what happened last on page four.

Revising

Instruct students to place pages in order on their desktops. Ask them to read their pieces to see if they have told the important parts of the story in sequence.

Invite several students to read their pieces. Comment on any use of transition words such as *first*, *next*, *then*, *last*, and *finally*. Encourage students to rearrange or change their sentences as needed.

Editing

Remind students to:

* Begin each sentence with a capital letter.
* End each sentence with a period, question mark, or exclamation mark.
* Use classroom resources to correct the spelling of any questionable word.

Direct students to show corrected sentences to you or a designated helper before publishing. If there are any words spelled incorrectly, circle them and allow students to make corrections.

Publishing

Students will publish their pieces in accordion-book format.
Materials needed:

* Stiff paper or oak tag—one 4"x12" piece per student
* Hole punch
* Markers
* Colorful yarn—one 20" piece per student

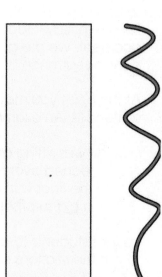

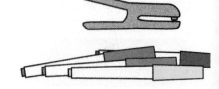

Publishing *(continued)*

Steps:

- Fold stiff paper in half.
- Fold paper in half again so the paper is in quarters.
- Arrange folds in shape of a "W."
- Punch holes as shown.
- Open book and number pages 1-4.

Direct the students to copy one sentence of their piece on each panel of the book. Encourage students to make their handwriting small and neat and to keep the sentences in correct sequence. Students are then to add illustrations to each page of their stories.

When the insides of the books are completed, have students close their books and locate the cover panel. They should then write a title for the story on the cover.

With the book closed, thread yarn through all holes as shown in Diagram 1 and tie the yarn in a bow to keep the book closed. Untie the yarn and spread the book open for reading or display as shown in Diagram 2.

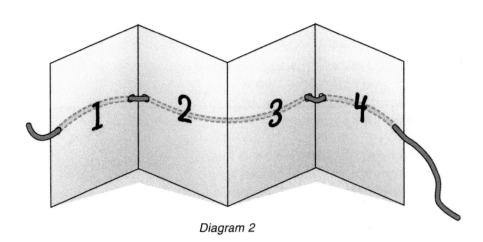

Diagram 2

Yum, Yum

Process Writing Lesson #4

Skill Focus: Writing a Good Beginning

Mini Lesson

Display the following sentences:

* I like hockey.
* Hockey is fun.
* Fast, fun, and exciting! That's my favorite sport, ice hockey.

Invite students to read the sentences. Ask, "Which seems like the best beginning for a piece about someone's favorite sport?" Lead students to conclude that the first two examples have important information, but they are not very interesting. Ask, "What makes the third example better?"

Explain that a good beginning tells what you are writing about. A good beginning also needs to be interesting. That makes a reader want to read the rest of the piece.

Pre-Writing

Materials Needed: One small wrapped treat (such as a chocolate kiss, pretzel, or cube of cheese) per student.

To prepare students for the writing task say, "I am going to give you a surprise. Hold out your hand and close your eyes. No peeking!" Distribute the treats. Then direct students to use all of their senses **except sight** to discover the identity of the objects.

Ask, "What do you think your surprise is? Open your eyes to see if your guess was correct. What senses did you use to help you guess?" Lead children to conclude that touch, smell, and sound could give clues. Say, "We've touched, smelled, felt, and seen the treats. What sense have we skipped?" After the expected response "taste" say, "Well, let's taste that treat!"

Ask, "If you could have any food, what would you choose?" Allow a few responses. Then say, "Today in Writers' Workshop you will write about your favorite food. Remember to start with an interesting beginning sentence that tells what you are writing about. Use all of your senses as you describe the food you like best."

 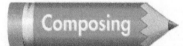 

Process Writing Lesson #4 *continued*

Composing

Have children write their stories on rough draft paper.
Remind them to:

- Focus on one food.
- Make an interesting beginning sentence.
- Use the prompt **favorite food** in the first sentence.
- Write a title for the story.

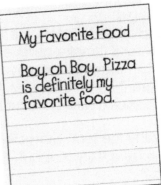

My Favorite Food

Boy, oh Boy. Pizza is definitely my favorite food.

Revising

Working in pairs, have students read their pieces. Instruct students to use markers to highlight all phrases or sentences that describe the sight, smell, feel, taste, or sound of their favorite foods. Encourage students to add more of these specific details.

Invite students to share their good beginning sentences with the class. Allow time for positive comments.

Editing

Ask students to contribute ideas for an "Editing Reminders" chart. Write their suggestions on chart paper. Keep the chart on display for future use.

Instruct students to edit their own pieces, using reminders from the editing chart.

Publishing

Have students make clean copies of their stories. Remind them to use their best handwriting. Providing special paper for publishing pieces does seem to encourage neatness!

Next, have students help construct a food mural. Students are either to draw and color pictures of their favorite foods or to cut appropriate pictures from magazines.

Make a bulletin board heading, "OUR FAVORITE FOODS." Cut a large circle of colored paper. Decorate the edges of the paper to represent a plate. Center this on the bulletin board. Arrange the food pictures on the "plate." Mount the stories on construction paper and display them around the plate.

Tell Me a Story!

Process Writing Lesson #5

Skill Focus: Recognizing Story Elements

Mini Lesson

Read or tell the story *The Three Little Pigs* to the students. Ask, "Is this a true story, or is it make-believe?" Lead children to conclude it is make-believe. Explain that make-believe stories have special parts that make them different from true stories. Posting a chart of the following terms would be helpful as a reference for reading comprehension, as well as process writing.

Display the term **characters**. Explain that characters are the people or animals a story is about. Ask, "Who were the characters in *The Three Little Pigs*?"

Next, display **setting**. Say, "The setting is where the story happens. What was the setting of the story about the pigs?"

Display the term **problem**. Say, "Make-believe characters always seem to have a problem. What is the problem in this story?"

Display the term **events**. Say, "Events are some things that happened in the story. What are some things that happened in *The Three Little Pigs*? Try to tell them in sequence."

Finally, display the term **resolution**. Explain that stories usually tell how the problem works out. This is called the resolution. Ask students to identify the resolution of the problem in *The Three Little Pigs*.

Conclude the Mini Lesson by reviewing the five terms introduced.

Characters

Setting

Problem

Events

Resolution

Pre-Writing

Say, "Today we are going to have some fun writing pig stories of our own. A pig will be the main character. Put an elephant in your story, too, and put in a bouquet of red flowers." Remind students to try to include all the story elements, or parts. Encourage using the Story Elements chart as a reference.

Composing

Ask the students to write their stories on paper. Suggest they circle any words they might not know how to spell. These can be checked as part of the editing process.

Remind students to:

* Write about a pig, an elephant, and a bouquet of red flowers.
* Tell where the story happens.
* Give the characters a problem.
* Tell what they do to solve the problem.
* Tell what happens at the end.
* Write a title for the story.

> The Pig, the Elephant and the Flowers
>
> Once there was a pig and an elephant who lived in a zoo.
>
> They both loved flowers, but there was only one bouquet.

Process Writing Lesson #5 *continued*

Revising

Ask two or three volunteers to read their stories. Make positive comments about the stories. Have students identify the story elements included. Invite all of the students to make their stories even better by adding any missing elements.

Editing

Introduce quotation marks to the students. Using any story available to all the students, ask them to hunt for quotation marks. Invite them to tell why a writer uses quotation marks. Ask the students to read their own pieces, putting quotation marks around what the characters said.

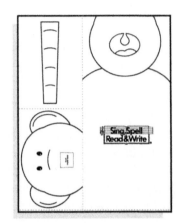

Remind students to:

* Use capital letters to begin sentences.
* Use a period, question mark, or exclamation mark at the end of sentences.
* Make spelling corrections of circled words.

Publishing

Materials Needed:

* Pig and elephant patterns from the Reproducibles Section TM pp. 470 - 471, one of each per student
* Two lunch bags per student
* Scissors, glue, markers and/or crayons

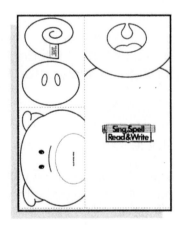

To prepare students for publishing, say, "Now that your stories are done, we are going to share them in a special way. We are going to make puppets of the pig and elephant. We will use them to tell our stories."

Reproduce the pig and elephant patterns. Give all students both patterns and two lunch bags. Students will color and cut out the puppet heads and glue each head to the bottom of a lunch bag, then glue the body part to the side of the bag.

Say, "Work in pairs and practice reading the stories, using the puppets when the characters talk. Make sure the correct character puppet is speaking." Allow plenty of practice time. Finally, students will present their stories to the class.

Happily Ever After!

Process Writing Lesson #6

Skill Focus: Writing Story Endings

Mini Lesson

The purpose of this Mini Lesson is to help students learn to recognize and write story endings.

Begin the lesson by saying, "And they all lived happily ever after." Lead the students to conclude that you only told the ending of a story. Ask them to name some stories that might have this ending. Then, ask if this would be a good ending for *The Three Little Pigs*. Invite the students to suggest other appropriate endings for the story.

Read a favorite short story to the class, but omit the ending. Have students identify the missing part. Read the ending. Ask, "Why do stories need endings?" Lead the students to conclude that the ending completes the story. Say, "Without an ending, we wouldn't know that the story was over. We would wonder what happened next. When we come to the end of a story, we aren't going to write *The End*. Instead, we will write a good ending. That is the signal the piece is finished."

Pre-Writing

To prepare students for writing, ask, "What is a good deed?" Invite responses from several children. Then ask children to recall good deeds they have done. Determine students' understanding of the "good deed" concept through their responses. Praise the good deeds.

Composing

Prior to the "composing" step, prepare a writing booklet for each child. Staple four sheets of notebook paper inside a construction paper cover.

Say, "Today you'll be writing about a good deed you have done. You probably have done many good deeds, but pick just one to write about. Focus on that deed. Help us learn what you did, whom you helped, and how you felt."

Distribute writing booklets to the students. Ask students to leave the cover blank. Explain that they are to write directly into the booklet. They should write neatly since they will not be asked to recopy the piece, as they will be publishing through an oral presentation.

Remind students to:

* Write a good beginning, using the words "good deed" in the first sentence.
* Write a middle part that includes specific details and tells events in sequence.
* Write an ending to the piece. The ending should make the story seem complete.
* Write a title for the piece on the cover of the booklet.

Revising

Ask several students to share their ending sentences with the class. Invite the class to make positive comments. A good way to assure this is to say, "Tell what you liked about the ending." Encourage students to reread their pieces and to change their ending sentences if needed.

Editing

Remind students that editing means correcting capitalization, punctuation, spelling, and grammar. Say, "Good editing will help your readers to understand and enjoy your piece."

Remind students to work neatly as they edit. Finished booklets may be taken home to share with their families. Blank pages may be used for writing additional pieces or for illustrations.

Publishing

Students sometimes become discouraged when asked to recopy every story, and not all pieces need to be recopied. Keep enthusiasm for writing by sometimes using creative ways to publish students' writing.

Plan an oral "publishing" of the good deed pieces as a radio or television show. To prepare for this activity:

I'll be the master of ceremonies.

- Make a list of students who volunteer to participate.
- Have students practice reading their pieces to a partner.
- Prepare a simple stage set of four guest chairs and a special spot for the master of ceremonies.
- You will need a video camera or a tape recorder with microphone or a teacher-made fake microphone on a stand. In a pinch, an upside-down broom anchored in a wastebasket will do just fine.
- Have students name the station and the show.
- Select four volunteers to be the first reader panelists.
- You will be the first master of ceremonies. Select students for the master of ceremonies job in subsequent panels. Use your best acting to make the show lively!
- Panel members will read their pieces to the audience.
- Record the presentation, if desired.
- Continue in this manner until all students that wish to participate have had a turn.

Note to Teachers: This activity will probably be more enjoyable if no more than two groups give presentations on a single day.

Special Treasures

Process Writing Lesson #7

Skill Focus: Correcting Spelling Errors

Mini Lesson

Prepare a chart or overhead transparency, (Reproducible Section, TM p. 477) of the story in the example to the right.

To begin the lesson, display the story. (You will use the chart again in Process Writing Lesson #8.) Say, "We have learned about good beginnings for stories. Here is a story beginning. Please read it to yourself." Then invite a student to read the sentences aloud. Ask students to name the **prompt** (*My Special Treasure*) and tell what clues helped them to identify it. Ask for comments on the selection. Lead students to conclude it is a good beginning, but it has many spelling errors.

Say, "Today in Writers' Workshop we are going to learn some ways to correct spelling errors. The very first thing we'll do is circle any word in the piece that doesn't look right. You've seen most of these words spelled correctly many times. If you are not sure of a word, picture it in your mind. If the written word looks strange, circle it." Have students take turns circling suspect words on the chart as shown in **Example A (words circled in red)**. Accept any responses. Corrections will be made later in the next lesson.

Say, "Sometimes we might accidentally misspell a word that we know. Please look at the words you have circled. Correct any that you are **really sure you know**." Have students make corrections on the chart as shown in **Example B (words printed in purple)**.

Say, "Now the easy words are fixed, but there are still words to correct. Let's try using **sound** to help us. Read each circled word. Are any sounds missing? Put in the **missing sounds**." Continue with students' corrections as shown in **Example C (letters printed in blue)**.

Then say, "Some words are tough. They don't look like they sound. If we can't picture the word or sound it out to get the correct spelling, we can use the dictionary as our helper. We will do some work with the dictionary in our next lesson."

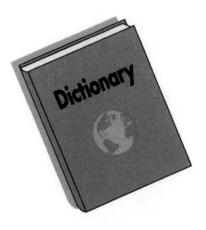

Directions: Circle the spelling errors.

My Sechul Trezure

I hav a sechul trezure that I lov more than piza . It is a butiful rock. That mus seem lik a funny truzure to you, but I will til you why I lick it so mush.

Directions: Circle the spelling errors.

My Sechul Trezure

I hav a sechul trezure that I lov more than piza . It is a butiful rock. That mus seem lik a funny truzure to you, but I will til you why I lick it so mush.

Example A

Directions: Circle the spelling errors.

My Sechul Trezure

have
I hav a sechul trezure that I
love
lov more than piza . It is a
butiful rock. That mus seem
like
lik a funny truzure to you,
but I will til you why I
like
lick it so mush.

Example B

Directions: Circle the spelling errors.

p
My Sechul Trezure

have   p
I hav a sechul trezure that I
love
lov more than piza. It is a
butiful rock. That mus seem
like
lik a funny truzure to you,
but I will til you why I
like
lick it so mush.

Example C

Process Writing Lesson #7 *continued*

Pre-Writing

To prepare students for the writing task, ask them to recall the prompt (*My Special Treasure*) from the Mini Lesson Chart. Invite them to explain what a special treasure is. Lead students to conclude that a special treasure is something that is valuable to the owner, even though others may think it is junk. Give an example of a special treasure of your own.

Say, "Think about something that is very special to you. It doesn't have to be new or expensive, just something that you wouldn't want to be without. Use your writer's skills to tell about your special treasure."

Composing

Ask students to write their treasure stories on paper.

Remind students to:

* Write on alternate lines of rough draft paper.
* Write about just one treasure.
* Write an interesting beginning that mentions the prompt.
* Write a middle part that includes specific details about your treasure.
* Write an ending that makes the story seem complete.
* Write a title for your story.
* Circle any words that might be spelled incorrectly.

Note to the Teacher: Write about your own special treasure while the students are writing. It is important that you model appropriate writing actions. Leave out some important information from your treasure piece. You will be reading it as part of the Revising Lesson, and students will be checking it for missing information.

Revising

Say, "Now it is time to revise our pieces. Remember, revise means change the words to make the piece better."

Ask, "What should be in a piece about a treasure? Let's make a list of questions we would like the treasure pieces to answer." Invite students to suggest questions such as:

* What is the treasure?
* Where did you get it?
* What does it look like?
* When did you get it?
* How did you get it?
* Why is it special to you?

Write their questions on chart paper or the chalkboard.

(Continued on next page)

Revising *(continued)*

Read your own treasure piece to the class. Say, "Let's see how well I answered your questions." Have students answer the charted questions. Add missing information to your piece and read it to the class again, noting improvement of content.

Direct students to reread their own pieces, checking to see that each question on the chart has been answered. Then ask them to revise their pieces by adding missing information in appropriate places.

Editing

Remind students to:

* Begin each sentence and each proper name with a capital letter.
* End each sentence with a period, question mark, or exclamation mark.
* Try to correct spelling of circled words by using visual recall or sounding words.

Publishing

Reproduce the treasure box pattern found in the Reproducible Section, TM p. 478. You will need one for each student and a few extras.

Distribute the copies. Say, "Today you will put your treasure story in a treasure box. Be sure to write the story title on the top writing line. Then copy your piece neatly on the other lines."

When copying is complete, direct students to fold their boxes and decorate them with crayon or marker.

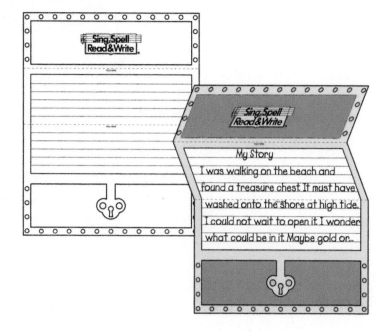

Process Writing Lesson #8

Skill Focus: Correcting Spelling Errors

Mini Lesson

Materials Needed:

- Chart saved from Process Writing Lesson #7
- Several children's dictionaries—preferably one for every two students. Borrow if you don't have enough.

To begin the lesson, display the chart from Process Writing Lesson #7. Words with possible spelling errors should already be circled. Have students tell why some of the words are circled. Ask, "When you are writing and not sure how to spell a word, what should you do?" Lead students to conclude that they should spell the word as best they can, but circle the word for later attention. Remind students that correcting spelling is a part of editing. Ask students to name ways to correct possible spelling errors. Their responses should include picturing the word and sounding the word, techniques taught in the previous lesson.

Say, "We know that using the dictionary is another way to find how words are spelled. Today we will learn some things about using the dictionary."

Arrange students in pairs. Pass out dictionaries. Allow a few minutes for exploration. Invite students to tell what they notice about the dictionary, making sure they say the entries are in alphabetical order.

Present a short list of easily spelled words (e.g., *cat, boy, fox, play*) for students to locate in the dictionary. Invite students to read the entries and tell the page number where each word on the list is found.

Say, "That was as easy as ABC! Let's be word detectives some more. We'll hunt in the dictionary for the words that we circled on the chart (Process Writing Lesson #7). Here's what to do. Sound out the word. Think what the first **three** letters of the word would be. Find the dictionary page with those three letters at the beginning of the entries. Skim the entries on the page to find your word and its correct spelling. You may need to look at more than one page."

Encourage students to use their dictionaries to find the correct spelling of the circled words. Make appropriate corrections. End the Mini Lesson by inviting students to read the corrected chart.

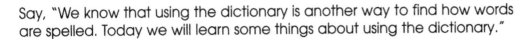

Directions: Circle the spelling errors.

special treasure
My Sechul Trezure

have special treasure
I hav a sechul trezure that I
love   pizza
lov more than pizo. It is a
beautiful   must
butiful rock. That mus seem
like   treasure
lik a funny fruzure to you,
        tell
but I will til you why I
like   much
lick it so mush.

(Continued on next page)

As Easy As ABC

Pre-Writing

Say, "You did a great job finding words in the dictionary. I know you are good at many other things, too. Think about something you're really good at." Invite responses from several students. Write the prompt, "What I'm Good At," on the chalkboard. Say, "Here is the prompt for your next piece. Tell about something you do really well."

Composing

Ask students to write their "What I'm Good At" pieces on paper.

Remind students to:

* Write about just one thing they're good at.
* Include specific details.
* Write a beginning, middle, and ending.
* Circle words that might be spelled incorrectly.
* Write titles for their stories.

Revising

Remind students that a good beginning should mention the prompt. It should also be interesting enough to catch the reader's attention. Suggest that students revise their story beginnings, keeping these things in mind.

Invite students to read their beginnings to the class. Make positive comments about the beginnings. Then have students restate the elements of a good beginning.

Editing

Review ways to correct spelling errors.

Remind students to:

* Begin sentences and names with capital letters.
* End all sentences with a period, question mark, or exclamation mark.
* Correct the spelling of circled words.

Publishing

Materials needed:

* Head and hand pattern in Reproducibles Section, TM p. 480.
* Scissors, crayons or markers, glue
* Lined writing paper

Ask students to copy their pieces neatly on lined writing paper, skipping alternate spaces.

Distribute head and hands pattern. Have students color the parts. They may personalize the head by turning it into a self-portrait. Then have them cut out the parts and glue them to the composition as shown. The finished products will make an interesting bulletin board display with the title, "Yes, I Can!"

Process Writing Lesson #9

Skill Focus: Editing Run-on Sentences

Mini Lesson

- Display the following text:

> I had a very happy time when I rode on the roller coaster at Cedar Point I was scared at first my mom said I should try it so I did and it went as fast as the wind and I screamed and it wasn't scary it was fun and I was happy

> I had a very happy time when I rode on the roller coaster at Cedar Point. I was scared at first. My mom said I should try it, so I did. It went as fast as the wind, and I screamed. It wasn't scary. It was fun, and I was happy.

- Invite students to read the story. Choose a volunteer to read it out loud.

- Ask students to tell what the story is about. Say, "Was this story easy to understand?" Tell students this is an example of a run-on sentence.

- Suggest that students think of a way to make the passage easier to understand. Lead students to conclude that separating the text into smaller parts (sentences) would help. Have students suggest inserting punctuation.

- Ask, "What do you call these groups of words that you have just made?" Elicit the response, "Sentences."

- Say, "You have just done some good editing. You have fixed a run-on sentence. Remember real writers use punctuation and capital letters to separate their stories into sentences. That makes stories easier to understand."

Pre-Writing

- Say, "Happy times are not just exciting things like riding a roller coaster. Yesterday I had a happy time talking to my friend on the telephone. What are some happy times you have had?" Invite a few students to tell about a time when they were happy.

- Say, "I think you can guess what topic you will be writing about today. Tell about a time when you were happy. I'm sure you have been happy lots of times, but remember that a good writer learns to focus. Pick just one of your happy times to write about. Tell us what happened. Help us know why you were happy and how you felt."

(Continued on next page)

Happy Faces

Composing

Ask students to write their stories on rough draft paper.

Remind students to:

* Write about just one happy time.
* Tell at least two reasons why they were happy.
* Write a beginning, middle, and ending.
* Circle words that might be spelled incorrectly.
* Write a title for their stories.

Revising

Remind students that real writers include specific details. Ask students to reread their pieces and add at least one more detail.

Invite a few students to read their pieces, telling what they added. Elicit positive comments from the class.

Editing

Review run-on sentences. Have students work with partners to locate sentence endings.

Instruct students to do the following:

* Together, read one story out loud.
* Place a vertical crayon line in the text at each spot where you take a breath while reading.
* Take turns reading alternate sentences.
* Fix any groups of words that do not make sense.
* Add needed capitalization and punctuation.
* Repeat the procedure for the second story.
* Have students work alone to correct spelling errors.

Publishing

Provide students with an 8 inch circle pattern.

Have students:

* Trace the circle on wide-lined notebook paper.
* Cut out the circle.
* Copy story neatly onto circle, skipping alternate spaces.
* Add additional pages if needed.
* Trace and cut two circles from yellow construction paper.
* Using black marker or crayon, draw a smiley face on one yellow circle.
* Assemble story pages inside cover.
* Staple in book form.

Pre-Writing → Composing

Revising → Editing → **Publishing**

Process Writing Lesson #10

Skill Focus: Using Descriptive Words

Mini Lesson

* Say, "Today we're going to play a describing game. I'll name an object that I'm picturing in my mind. See if you can guess what it looks like. Are you ready? I'm thinking of an apple. What does my apple look like?"

* Encourage several children to respond with guesses such as, "Is it red?" or "Is it shiny?"

* Next, describe the apple as follows:
"The apple in my mind is small and green. It has a hole on the side. A little white worm is crawling out of the hole."

* Compare your description to those of the children's. Repeat the game with other objects.

* Tell the students real writers describe things in their stories. That way the reader can really see what is in the writer's mind.

red

shiny

green

Pre-Writing

* To prepare students for writing, describe a beautiful place you have seen. Start by saying, "The most beautiful place I ever saw was _____." Incorporate as many of the five senses as possible in your description. Ask students to recall describing words that you used.

* Say, "Think about the most beautiful place that you ever saw. Picture it in your mind. Write about that place. Help us see it by using good describing words, just like we did in our game."

Composing

* Have students fold a sheet of notebook paper horizontally three times, dividing the paper into eight strips. Then, have students cut the paper on the folds into eight strips.

* Instruct the students to write a beginning sentence on one strip of paper. Remind them to include the prompt, "The most beautiful place I ever saw was ____," in the sentence. Have students set aside one strip for the ending sentence. On the remaining six strips they are to write sentences describing their beautiful place. Finally, they are to complete the piece by writing a good ending sentence on the remaining strip. Encourage repetition of the prompt as part of the ending.

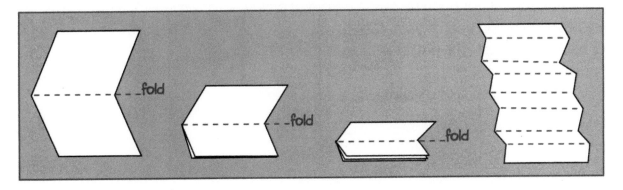

(Continued on next page)

Process Writing Lesson #10 *continued*

Revising

Direct students to display the sentence strips in proper sequence on their work areas. Invite several students to read their pieces. Encourage the class to make positive comments about the pieces. Suggest that students reread their own pieces silently, and change or add words to improve the descriptions.

Editing

Instruct students to do the following:

* Touch the capital letter at the beginning of the first word on each sentence strip.
* Touch the punctuation after the last word on each sentence strip.
* Fix anything that was missing.
* Correct misspelled words. (Give some help by circling misspelled words.)

Publishing

Students will make a coat hanger mobile.

Materials Needed:

* One wire or plastic coat hanger per student
* Construction paper cut into 4 x 6 inch pieces, six per student
* Construction paper, one 6 x 9 inch piece per student
* Drawing paper, one 5 x 8 inch piece per child
* 3 x 5 index cards, eight per student (If cost is a factor, you may use lined paper cut to this size.)
* Glue
* Yarn
* Hole punch

Directions for students:
* Neatly copy one sentence of story on each index card.
* Glue cards to construction paper pieces.
* Make a colorful picture of the beautiful place on the drawing paper.
* Glue the picture to the large piece of construction paper.
* Punch a hole at the top center of each sentence card and picture.
* Thread a piece of yarn through each hole and tie it.
* Tie the yarn to the hanger. Make the pieces different lengths.
* Cut off extra yarn.
* Hang the stories and slide the yarn to distribute the weight evenly.

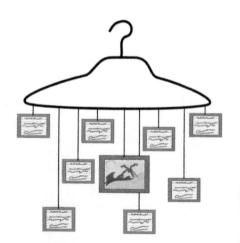

 # Process Writing Lesson #11

Skill Focus: Developing a List of Self-selected Story Ideas

Mini Lesson
Materials Needed:

* One copy per student of Reproducible, TM p. 483.

* Say, "You have written lots of good stories this year. You have learned about good beginnings, good endings, and using describing words. You have learned to focus on just one thing in your stories. You are real writers. So far, I've helped you think of things to write about. Real writers often pick their own topics, though. How do you think writers figure out what to write about?"

* Allow a few minutes to discuss topic selection. Then ask, "What would you write about if you could pick any topic you wanted?"

* Encourage responses. Say, "What good ideas! I call those "someday" ideas, because they are things you might want to write about someday. Real writers keep a list of ideas. They don't want to forget them. Today you'll start your own idea list."

* Distribute copies of "Someday" reproducible. Explain that this is just one way to save ideas. One idea or more can be written in each box. Discuss a few ideas that might go in the boxes. Give students time to write their ideas. Complete sentences are not necessary. Tell students they will have a chance to use their ideas "Someday."

* Students are to save the "Someday" sheets in their writing folders. Encourage them to add new ideas to their sheets during any writing time.

Pre-Writing
* Have students remove the "Someday" papers from their folders. Say, "I promised you that you could use this idea list someday. Well, guess what? "Someday" is here. Choose a topic from one of your "Someday" boxes or use another idea that you have thought about. Remember real writers focus on one idea. They write a good beginning and a good ending, too. Have fun being a real writer!"

Composing
Have students write their pieces on draft paper.
Remind them to:
* Use specific details.
* Write a title for the story.

Uncle Todd

When I hit a homerun

My Grandma's Pool

My New Bike

Clearwater Beach

(Continued on next page)

Someday Boxes

Revising

Invite several students to read their pieces out loud. Ask the class to identify the topic of each piece. Comment on some of the specific details used in the pieces.

Direct students to reread their pieces silently. Suggest they make changes to produce more clearly focused pieces. Ask them to add one or two specific details to make their pieces more interesting.

Editing

Working as a group, have students identify errors to fix when editing. List them on a chart or chalkboard. Be sure to include the following:

- Capital letters
- Punctuation
- Run-on sentences
- Spelling
- Story title

Publishing

- Direct students to copy their corrected stories neatly on special paper (theme paper or notebook paper with hole-punched margins cut off), skipping spaces.
- Mount the stories on construction paper for display.
- An interesting bulletin board idea for this project is to take pictures of students during various writing activities. Include students sharpening pencils and using dictionaries. Display the stories and pictures on a large board with the heading, "CAUTION! WRITERS AT WORK!"

Process Writing Lesson #12

Skill Focus: Developing Supporting Ideas and Specific Details

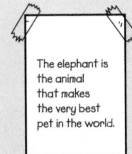

The elephant is the animal that makes the very best pet in the world.

Mini Lesson

Materials Needed:

- Five sheets of chart paper hung side by side

- Say, "Today we're going to learn some ways to make our pieces really interesting. We're going to work together to write a piece about the very best kind of pet. Who has an idea? What kind of animal makes the best pet?"

- Accept the first response. The choice doesn't matter. Have the class help construct a beginning sentence. It should be something like, "The _____ is the animal that makes the very best pet in the world." Write the beginning sentence on the first chart.

- Say, "Now we have a beginning. Next, we need reasons why the _____ is the best pet. You call those supporting ideas."

Reason #1

One reason an elephant is the best pet is because it is so big you can't lose it.

- In the upper left corner, mark the second chart, "Reason #1." Say, "Who can give one reason?" Encourage students to respond. Continue in the same manner with Reason #2 and Reason #3 on the next two charts.

- The next step is to add specific details to the reasons, so go back to Reason #1. Say, "This idea needs some details to go with it. What can we add?" An example follows:

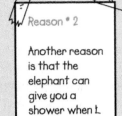

Reason #2

Another reason is that the elephant can give you a shower when you are dirty.

> "An elephant is the best pet in the whole world. One reason is because it is so big. It is bigger than a school bus. It is big enough to carry lots of kids at one time. Because it is so big, you could never lose it."

- Continue this procedure with Reason #2 and Reason #3.

Reason #3

An elephant is also a good pet because you can ride it.

- Invite students to think of a good ending sentence. It should include the name of the animal and the words "best pet."

- Say, "I think we've written a good story. It has supporting ideas and details. It still needs a title, though. Who can think of a good title?" Write the title on the first chart, commenting on the use of capital letters.

- Say, "Let's read our story together and see how it sounds." Conclude the lesson with the group reading the story. Save the charts for the next activity.

Pre-Writing

You can see that the very best pet is an elephant.

- Display the charts from the previous activity. Ask students to recall the steps they followed in writing the pet story. Tell them that today they will be using the same method to write a story of their own, but about a different topic.

- Have students place five sheets of paper on their desks. Tell them their topic will be, "My Best Friend." Explain that they will use their papers just as the charts were used. Remind them they can look at the charts if they forget what each sheet is for.

(Continued on next page)

My Best Friend

Composition

- Have students write their "My Best Friend" pieces as instructed. Review what is to be written on each sheet. Also, remind them to write a title on the first sheet.

Revising

- Suggest that readers might like to know what the best friend looks like or some other interesting fact that wasn't included in the Reasons details. Encourage students to add this to the sheet with the beginning sentence.

- Have students read their completed pieces to partners. Encourage them to make any changes that would make their pieces better.

Editing

Remind students to:

- Look for run-on sentences.
- Begin sentences with capital letters.
- Use periods, question marks, and exclamation marks to end sentences.
- Circle and correct spelling errors.

Publishing

Enlarge the body pattern from the Reproducible Section, TM p. 484 to fit on 18" x 24" oak tag board or other stiff paper. One suggestion for doing this is to make a transparency, project it on 18" x 24" paper, and trace around it to make a master pattern. Use the master pattern to trace one pattern for each student. Have students take their shape home to complete.

Include the following directions:

- Cut out this shape.
- Dress the shape to look like your best friend, using paper, cloth or markers.
- Add a face and hair.
- Return this to school by_____ (give a date).
- At school, have students copy their pieces neatly on special paper. Mount stories on construction paper. Attach the stories to the completed "My Best Friend" figures. These are great for display for any type of open house!

Sentence Spiders Steps 26 & 27

Process Writing Lesson #13

Skill Focus: Using Varied Sentence Structure

Mini Lesson
This is often a difficult skill to teach, since most students naturally use a simple noun/verb sentence pattern. Be patient. The results can be rewarding.

Materials Needed:

A picture of Miss Muffet and a spider. Stick figures drawn on the chalkboard will do. It's the idea that counts.

* Chart paper.

* Have students recall the nursery rhyme about Miss Muffet. Ask, "What is happening in this picture?" Accept the first response that is a complete sentence. Write it on the chart paper.

* Say, "I think I know another way to say that." Write a variation of the sentence on the chart. The lesson will probably proceed as follows:

> Miss Muffet is eating her curds and whey.
> The curds and whey are being eaten by Miss Muffet.

Ask students to suggest other ways to tell the same thing. Write their suggestions on the chart, also. Some possibilities are:

> Sitting on her tuffet, Miss Muffet ate her lunch.
> Miss Muffet sat by the spider while she ate her lunch.

* Try to get as much variety as possible, but keep the meaning the same. The objective is to use a variety of sentence structures, not a variety of adjectives.

* Have students read the completed chart. Ask students which sentences sound the most interesting. Lead students to conclude that there are many ways to say the same thing. Explain that real writers use varied sentences to make their pieces more interesting.

* Save the chart for the next activity.

Pre-Writing
Materials Needed:
* One copy of Reproducible, TM p. 485, cut apart into sentence strips
* One six-inch circle of manila or light-colored construction paper for each student
* Chart from the Mini Lesson

(Continued on next page)

457

Sentence Spiders

Pre-Writing (continued)

To prepare students for the writing task, remind them they have learned that real writers use varied sentences to make their work interesting. Ask for a volunteer to read the Mini Lesson Chart.

Tell the students today they will be writing some varied sentences, maybe as many as a spider has legs. Give each student a paper circle and a sentence strip from the activity sheet. Have them read their sentences.

Say, "Before you make your new sentences, let's have a little fun. Copy the sentence on your strip very neatly onto the circle. Then make a picture in the circle to illustrate your sentence. Later you will write some varied sentences to go with your picture."

Composing

Ask students to read the sentences on their circles. Have them write variations of their original sentences on draft paper. (Ideally, each student should write eight variations. Be happy if everyone can write at least four!) Suggest the students look at their pictures for ideas. Remind them each new sentence needs to tell about the same thing as the original sentence.

Revising

Invite a few students to share their sentences with the class. Have students recall that real writers use varied sentences to make their pieces better. They also revise for the same reason. Suggest that students reread their sentences, making any changes that will make them sound better.

Editing

Have students work in pairs. Ask them to:

- Take turns reading their sentences out loud.
- Start all sentences with a capital letter.
- End each sentence with a punctuation mark.
- Circle misspelled words. Use classroom resources to make corrections.

Publishing

Materials Needed:

- Eight paper strips per student, 1" x 9" each
- Give each student eight strips of paper. Have them turn under a 1/2 inch flap at one end of each strip. These will be glue tabs.
- Next, have students copy their sentences onto the strips, starting at the ends with no folds.
- When all sentences are copied, have the students arrange the strips around their picture circles. (Some strips may be blank. Use them anyway.) Students may then glue the strips to the back of the circle, completing the project.
- The "spiders" will make an interesting display hung from the ceiling or attached to a large paper web or net on a bulletin board.

The dog chases the cat.	The girl reads a book.
A woman drives a car.	A woman walks the dog.
The bird eats a worm.	The bride cuts the cake.
A boy rides a bike.	A bee stings the boy.
A shark eats a fish.	A cat climbs a tree.
The woman pushes a stroller.	The farmer drives a tractor.
The football player throws the ball.	The teacher rings the bell.
The cook makes pizza.	The mother hugs her child.
The policeman blows a whistle.	A horse jumps the fence.
The cowboy rides a horse.	The truck dumps the dirt.
The artist paints a picture.	The man plants flowers.
The author writes a story.	The boy hits the baseball.
The boy sharpens a pencil.	The girl catches the ball.
A man buys hamburgers.	The crossing guard stops the cars.
The saw cuts the tree.	The coach shoots a basket.

The dog chases the cat.

A woman drives a car.

The bird eats a worm.

Process Writing Lesson #14

Skill Focus: Making Interesting Word Choices

Mini Lesson

Materials Needed:

- Chart paper

- Write the word **elephant** on the chalkboard or chart paper. Say, "Today in Writers' Workshop we're going to describe an elephant. Let's think of five words that tell what an elephant is like." List the words in vertical order.

- Next, say, "Those are good words to describe an elephant, but we just might be able to think of some words that are a little more interesting. Sometimes words get tired from being used so much, too. We'll try to think of words that aren't tired!" Explain that a synonym is a word that means the same or nearly the same as another word. Invite students to name synonyms for the five words on the elephant list. Write the new words next to their synonyms.

  Example: big — huge — enormous — gigantic — large

  Note: If you have a children's thesaurus, this would be a good time to introduce its use.

- As an oral activity, have students compose sentences using the original list of words and repeat the sentences, substituting the synonyms.

- Conclude the lesson by reminding the students that real writers try to use words that aren't tired, but instead ones that have pizzazz!

Pre-Writing

- To prepare students for the writing task, tell them that today they will be making a picture. They won't be using paints or markers. They'll be using words to paint a picture of a very special place.

- Say, "Everyone has a special place. I know I do." Relate a little information about a place that is special to you. Then say, "I'm going to write about my special place. I'm going to try to use words that will help you see my place in your mind. I want you to hear it, see it, feel it, and smell it. You might even be able to taste it! I want you to know why it is such a special place to me. I'm writing about my special place. I want you to write about your special place. I can't wait to share."

Composition

Have students write their pieces on rough draft paper.

Remind them to:

- Write about just one place.
- Include specific details.
- Choose interesting words.
- Make a picture with words.
- Write a title for the piece.

Write your own piece and be prepared to share!

(Continued on next page)

Revising

- Share your piece. Mention specific word choices that you made to paint a word picture.
- Review the use of interesting words and varied sentences. Suggest students reread their pieces, add two interesting words to the text, and change the structure of two sentences. Model this with your own piece.
- Allow time for students to share.

Editing

Remind students to:

- Start all sentences with capital letters.
- End all sentences with a period, question mark, or exclamation mark.
- Circle possible misspelled words and try to correct them using classroom resources.

Have students look at printed text in any book. Call their attention to the indenting at the beginning of paragraphs. Demonstrate how to do this at the beginning of a piece. Have them "dent in" the first word in their story. Do not expect them to be able to identify the need for other paragraphs in their writing at this time.

Publishing

Students will make a book cover for their stories.

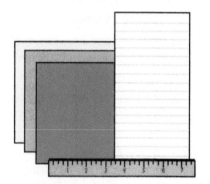

Materials Needed:
- 12" x 18" light-colored construction paper
- Ruler
- Wide-lined notebook paper, hole-punched side removed, cut to 5" x 10" size

Have students:

- Hold the construction paper horizontally and make a vertical fold.
- Use the ruler to mark off a 3" section at both ends of the construction paper. Fold to make flaps.
- Design a book cover on the front of the folder. Make sure the title and author are included.
- Copy their pieces neatly onto the writing paper.
- Mount the completed piece inside the folder.

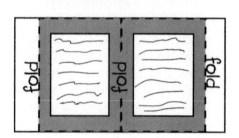

The completed projects will make a nice stand-up display on a table. You may wish to tack stories to a bulletin board with the front flap tucked behind to keep the cover closed.

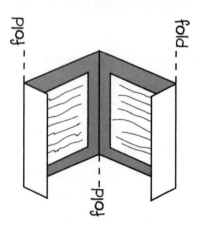

Steps 30 & 31

Process Writing Lesson #15

Skill Focus: Using Similes

Mini Lesson

Have students recall Process Writing Lesson #14, making interesting word choices. Ask, "What were some words we used in that lesson to describe the size of an elephant?"

Tell students that today they will learn another way to describe. On the chalkboard write, "An elephant is as big as _____." Say, "We can describe an elephant by comparing it to something else that is really big, too." Have students name other large things. Use each of their suggestions to complete the elephant simile.

Examples: An elephant is as big as a bus.

An elephant is as big as a house.

An elephant is as big as a mountain.

Say, "This kind of description is called a **simile**. It helps us to make a picture in our minds by **comparing two things**. They don't have to be exactly alike. An elephant isn't really as big as a mountain, is it! It does paint a good picture, though."

Have students complete the following:

* The kitten was as soft as _____.
* The crying baby was as loud as _____.
* The candy was as hard as _____.
* I can run as fast as _____.

Lead students to conclude that similes can be used to describe many things, not just big elephants. Suggest that they try using similes in their next pieces.

Pre-Writing

To prepare the students for writing, ask, "How do real writers like you choose what to write about?" Conduct a discussion, encouraging a variety of responses. Tell the students that they will be free to choose their own topics for a new piece. If no one has mentioned the "Someday" sheets from Process Writing Lesson #11, remind the children to look at them if they need ideas.

Stress that even though they will make their own choice of what to write about, the rules of good writing still apply. The piece will need to focus on one topic. Remind them to include a good beginning, middle, and end.

Have students write their chosen topics and their names on 3 x 5 index cards. Collect these and check them over to make sure the students have made appropriate selections. Hold a conference with any student who has been unable to make a decision. Return the cards at the beginning of the actual composing session.

(Continued on next page)

Process Writing Lesson #15 *continued*

Composing

Distribute the topic cards from the Pre-Writing activity. Remind the students that they are to write about a topic of their own choice. Accept last minute changes.

Ask students to write their stories on rough draft paper.

Remind students to:

- Write about just one thing.
- Make an interesting beginning that mentions the topic.
- Write a middle part that includes specific details and tells events in sequence.
- Try to use a simile in the piece.
- Write an ending that makes the piece seem complete.
- Write a title for the piece.

Revising

Invite several students to share their pieces. Encourage positive comments from the other students. Draw attention to similes or interesting word choices. Encourage students to reread their pieces silently and make at least two changes that will make their pieces more interesting.

Editing

Have students recall errors to look for when editing. Ask them to circle words that may be spelled incorrectly and to make appropriate corrections. Have them highlight all punctuation marks. Suggest that they fix run-on sentences.

Publishing

Materials Needed:
- One large empty cereal box per student
- Construction paper
- Glue
- Scissors

Directions for students:

- Have students copy their pieces neatly on "special" writing paper that is smaller than their cereal boxes. (Cut off the holes from notebook paper.) Be sure that they write only on one side of the paper.
- Trace the top and all four sides of the cereal box on construction paper.
- Cut out construction paper and glue in place to cover the box.
- Plan the placement of the story.
- Glue the first page to the front of the box. If there is a second page, glue it to the back. If the story is really long, stack and hinge the pages.
- Make illustrations to go on the side panels of box.
- Finish the project by gluing a decorated title onto the top of the box.

Process Writing Lesson #16

Skill Focus: Identifying Reasons to Write

Mini Lesson

When asked why writers write, most children respond, "To make money." While that may be true, we want the students to know that there are literary answers to that question. The purpose of this lesson, therefore, is to help students identify various reasons for writing.

Before beginning the lesson, collect examples of the following:

* Advertising copy
* Encyclopedia articles
* Instruction booklets
* Children's fiction books

Also prepare a chart with the following information:

* To entertain
* To inform or describe
* To tell how
* To persuade

Begin the lesson by saying, "Today we're going to talk about real writers. Why do you think they write?" Encourage discussion. Then explain that there are probably lots of reasons, but that when writers write they usually want to communicate with their readers.

Display the chart. Invite students to read it together. Discuss the meaning of each reason listed.

Read aloud excerpts from the writing samples you have collected. Challenge them to match the samples to the reasons on the chart.

> **Why Writers Write**
>
> **To entertain**
>
> **To inform or describe**
>
> **To tell how**
>
> **To persuade**

Pre-Writing

Ask students to recall the reason writers write. Say, "You can entertain by telling a funny story, a scary story, or maybe a fairy tale. Fiction stories are written to entertain." Ask students to name some books that are entertaining. Contrast these with non-fiction works.

Say, "The next piece you will write will be one to entertain your readers. You can really use your imaginations to make a good story. Imagine that you are playing outside. You find an old metal box. You try to open it, but it is locked. In the dirt by a big rock you find a rusty key. You put the key in the lock. It turns. Your job now is to write an entertaining story about what happens next. Have fun imagining!"

(Continued on next page)

Composing

Ask students to write their stories on alternate lines of rough draft paper. Suggest that they mention finding the locked box in the beginning of their stories and that they describe the box. Explain that stories usually have something happen. Since their stories happen to them, the use of the pronouns "**I**" and "**me**" are appropriate.

> I was playing behind the house. I spotted something behind a bush.

Revising

Instruct students to highlight the ending of their stories. Have them write a different ending on a separate paper. Next, have each student read his/her story to a partner twice, trying both endings. Encourage partners to help decide which ending is best. The final choice is up to the author!

Editing

Encourage students to find and correct capitalization, punctuation, and spelling errors. As you conference with the students, focus on one type of error at a time.

3-C	Once i lived in new york.
○	
1-P	Mr Smith lives in Tampa.
2-S	My bother is for years old.

In the margin at the beginning of each line of writing on the students' papers, write a small number and code letter to indicate how many and what kind of corrections need to be made.

Examples:

3-C	Once i lived in new york. (3 capitalization errors)
1-P	Mr Smith lives in Tampa. (1 punctuation error)
2-S	My bother is for years old. (2 spelling errors)

Remember, stick to one kind of error at a time. Don't overwhelm the students.

Publishing

Decorate a large "mystery" box in any manner desired. A large copy paper box would be a good choice for this.

Have students make a clean copy of their stories using their best handwriting. Insert the individual stories into large brown envelopes. Write the story title and the author's name on the front of the envelope. Place the envelopes in the box.

Encourage students to choose stories from the box to read during silent reading time. Have students sign on the outside of the envelope when they have read the story inside. They might also write a brief, <u>positive</u> comment.

PROCESS WRITING

Pre-Writing Composing Revising Editing Publishing

Process Writing Lesson #17

Skill Focus: Organizing and Writing an Informational Paragraph

Mini Lesson

- Review the reasons why writers write, as discussed in Process Writing Lesson #16.

- Say, "Your last piece was about a key in a box. What was the purpose of that piece?" (To entertain)

- Next, say, "We'll write the next piece for a different reason, to inform. What does that mean?" Discuss. Add that writing to inform includes both describing something and telling why.

- Tell the students that this kind of writing starts with a sentence that tells what the piece will be about. It is called a **topic sentence**.

- Say, "When you tell why, you need to give reasons. An example would be writing about your favorite toy and giving reasons why it is your favorite. You may think of lots of reasons, but telling just three is a good rule to follow. Writers call it the Magic Three. Three is just enough, but not too much."

- Explain that an ending sentence is needed to wrap the whole thing up. It often restates the topic sentence.

- **Review the basic five-part paragraph plan:**
  1. **Write a topic sentence.**
  2. **Tell one reason and elaborate.**
  3. **Tell the second reason and elaborate.**
  4. **Tell the third reason and elaborate.**
  5. **Write a concluding sentence.**

- Say, "Try using this plan for the next piece you write. You will still need to add specific details and interesting words, but this will be like a little map to follow as you write to tell why."

Pre-Writing

- What is a hero? Discuss the question and the superior qualities of courage, honesty, and truthfulness that a hero possesses. Help students understand that "successful," "famous," "rich," and "popular" are not synonyms for "hero." Stress that heroes may be male or female, young or old, well-known, or just regular people. One thing that is true, though, is that they are good role models.

- Invite students to name people who are heroes to them.

- Say, "I think you have guessed what the writing topic for your next piece will be, haven't you? Your job in Writers' Workshop today will be to write about your hero. Tell why that person is a hero to you. Use the five-part paragraph plan as your map."

(Continued on next page)

Tell Me Why

Composing

* Ask the students to write their hero pieces on rough draft paper. Remind them to follow the five-part plan as they write.

Revising

* Ask students, working with a partner, to read their hero pieces. Have them highlight as many nouns as they can find. Direct them to change some general nouns to more specific ones. Examples: toy stove—Easy Bake Oven; school—Morgan Woods Elementary; dog—German Shepherd

Editing

* Have students work in two or three person teams to find and correct errors in spelling, grammar, and mechanics. Emphasize the importance of making corrections so others can easily read the piece.

Publishing

* Students usually like to have their pieces read out loud, so plan a performance as the publishing activity for the hero pieces. Ask the students if they would like you to read their pieces to the class. Give them the option of reading their own pieces. If a student is shy or concerned that a piece "isn't good enough," read the piece quietly with the student during conference time.

* To make this a really special activity, invite parents. Make invitations. Rehearse. Consider obtaining amplification for soft voices. (Some "boom boxes" have a place to plug in a microphone.)

* Enjoy this Writers' Roundup and the progress the students have made this year!

Pocahontas

Thomas Jefferson

Hernando De Soto

Process Writing Lesson #18

Skill Focus: Producing a Deadline Writing Piece

Mini Lesson

- Tell students that sometimes real writers have lots of time to think about a piece, compose, revise, and edit. Sometimes, though, they must do all of this quickly to meet a **deadline**. Explain that a deadline means that something must be done by a certain time.

- Say, "Soon you'll do some deadline writing, too. There are some things you need to know so you can do your best."

- It is very important that students understand the deadline writing process. Explain that there will be a starting time and a stopping time. (Thirty minutes is acceptable for second graders, although you may adjust this to as much as 45 minutes according to the capabilities of your students.) Also explain that during the writing time there are no drinks, pencil sharpening, or bathroom breaks, and no conferences. It is a silent work time.

- It is also important that you build confidence! Assure the students that they have learned a lot about good writing. This is a time to show off their skills.

Pre-Writing

- Review the deadline writing procedure. Explain that the students will spend most of their time writing. If they have any time left, they are to use it for revising and editing. They are not to recopy the piece.

- Tell the students that they will be writing on the topic "The Best Thing About School." Ask them to think about the prompt and decide what one thing they think is best. Write the prompt on the chalkboard and read it to the students. Do not discuss the topic further.

- Remind students that this is a time to use everything they have learned about good writing and to write as much as they can.

Composition

- Give the signal for the students to begin writing. The students may reflect briefly, but they need to begin writing quickly. Encourage students who do not start in a reasonable time to just write about anything they like at school.

- Inform students when five minutes remain. When time is up, allow students to finish any sentence they need to complete. Then, collect the papers.

Revising and Editing

There are no specific writing and editing activities for this lesson. They are a part of the deadline writing process.

(Continued on next page)

Publishing

Materials Needed:

- 3 x 5 index cards or drawing paper cut to size

- Class Activity: Prepare a graph showing what the students chose as the best thing about school. Give each student an index card. Have students label the cards and make an illustration to go with their deadline writing pieces.

- Sort the cards into categories. Use them to make a bulletin board graph labeled "THE BEST THING ABOUT SCHOOL."

Evaluation

You may use the deadline piece as one tool in evaluating student writing progress. Compare this work with the piece written in Process Writing Lesson #1 or other selected writings. Look for improvement in skills, effort, and attitude. Develop your own standards of excellence. You might start by dividing class work into five groups, the weakest stories in Group 1, the best in Group 5, and the rest ranked 2, 3, and 4.

Group 1—This paper lacks meaning. Mechanics and spelling may be very poor. The writer is unable to communicate with the reader.

Group 2—This paper is immature. It may be poorly organized and lacking in details.

Group 3—This is a fairly good paper with good information. It may need improved organization. Language and mechanics may be faulty, but the writer definitely has something to say.

Group 4—This is a paper with good information and language. It will have some flaws, though. It may not be focused. Beginnings and endings may lack excitement. There may be some problems with spelling and mechanics.

Group 5—This is an excellent paper. It may have some errors, but it shows strength in all areas.

So, not all your students have papers in Group 5? Are you a failure as a teacher? Not at all. Only a rare second grader will achieve this level. Take pleasure in the gains your students have made this year and a job well done!

Reproducibles

The First Day of School

Dear _____,

Last year, I was **learning to read**. This year, I will be **reading to learn** with a program called *Sing, Spell, Read & Write*.

For the first three weeks of school, we will be reviewing our phonics and reading skills. You'll be hearing me sing some of the phonics songs that helped me learn to read last year.

This year, in Language Arts we will be learning more than 1,400 new Spelling and Vocabulary words, Grammar skills, how to use a dictionary, and how to write good stories.

In Reading, we will be taking an imaginary trip aboard a Grand Tour bus. We're going to travel along the southern and eastern borders of the United States of America. Along the way, we're going to learn what the children are like in all the places we visit. We'll find out what families do for fun and for work, what their weather is like, what their favorite places are, and what makes them most proud of where they live. We'll even learn some of the songs they like to sing. It will be a Grand Tour of reading — and learning — and singing — all rolled into one great school year! Next year in third grade, we'll finish the Grand Tour of the United States.

But before we get on board the Grand Tour bus to read about the United States, we're going to learn how our country began and where all these people came from! For one week, I'll be bringing home coloring pages each day. These pages tell the story of America. I'd like you to display the pages on the refrigerator or on my bedroom door. Each day, I'll share with you what I learned in the story about America.

During the year, every Monday through Thursday, I will bring home a Spelling homework paper. It should take me no more than 10-15 minutes to complete. This will help me learn to be responsible and will show you something I learned in school each day. Please initial my paper. My teacher will collect these papers each morning and give me a star on the *Homework Chart*. Please help me make this a good daily habit.

My Physical Education Day is _____.

My Media Center Day is _____.
(Please help me remember my library book, so I can get a new one.)

My Art Day is _____.

My Music Day is _____.

Lunch is at _____ and it costs $_____.

At Back-to-School Night my teacher, Mrs./Ms./Mr. _____, will explain our *Sing, Spell, Read & Write* Reading and Language Arts program. He/she is looking forward to meeting you.

Love,

_____

FOLD AND GLUE TO BACK OF BAG

GLUE NOSE HERE

Sing, Spell Read & Write

Use with Process Writing Lesson #5   Steps 10 & 11

Sing Spell Read & Write

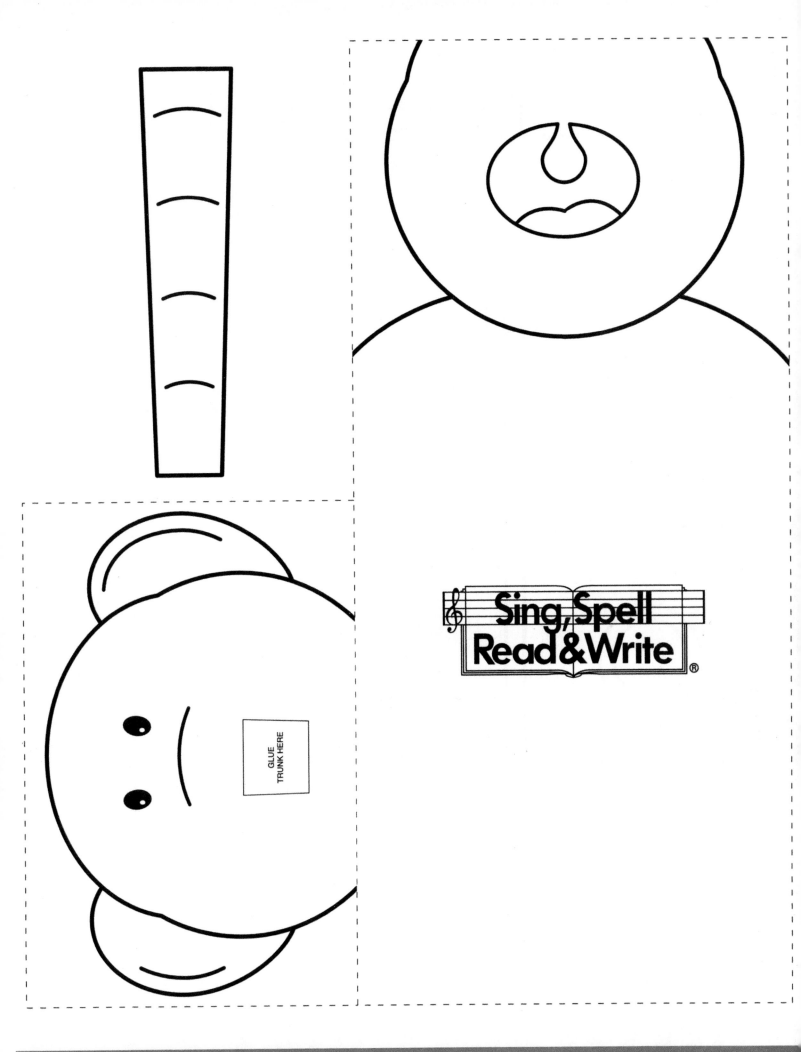

GLUE
TRUNK HERE

Sing, Spell
Read & Write ®

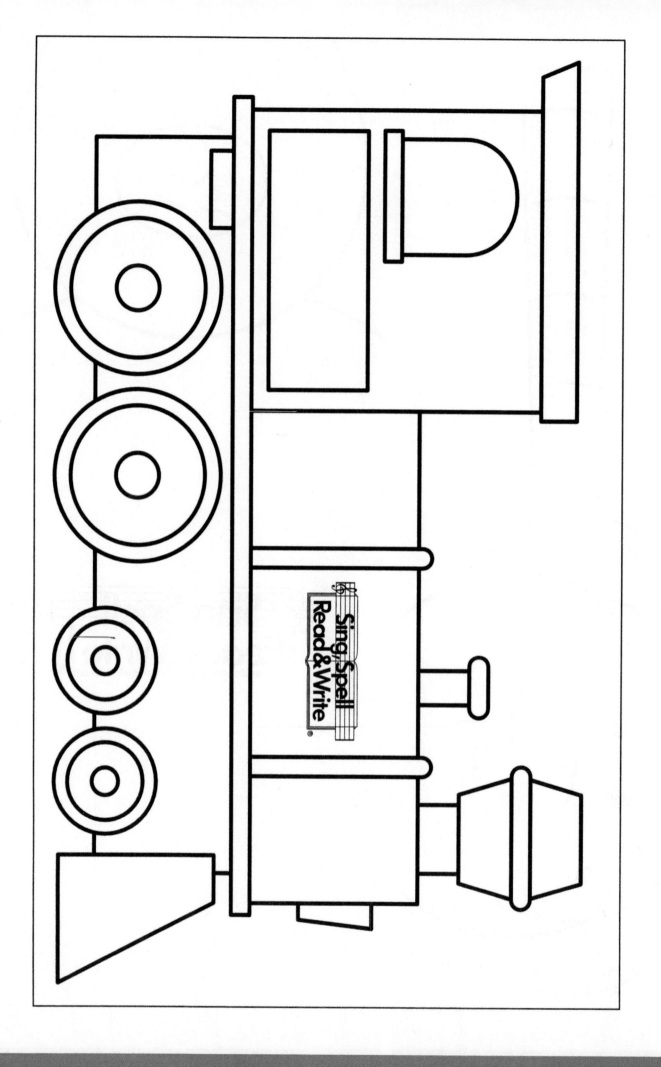

Use with Step 11

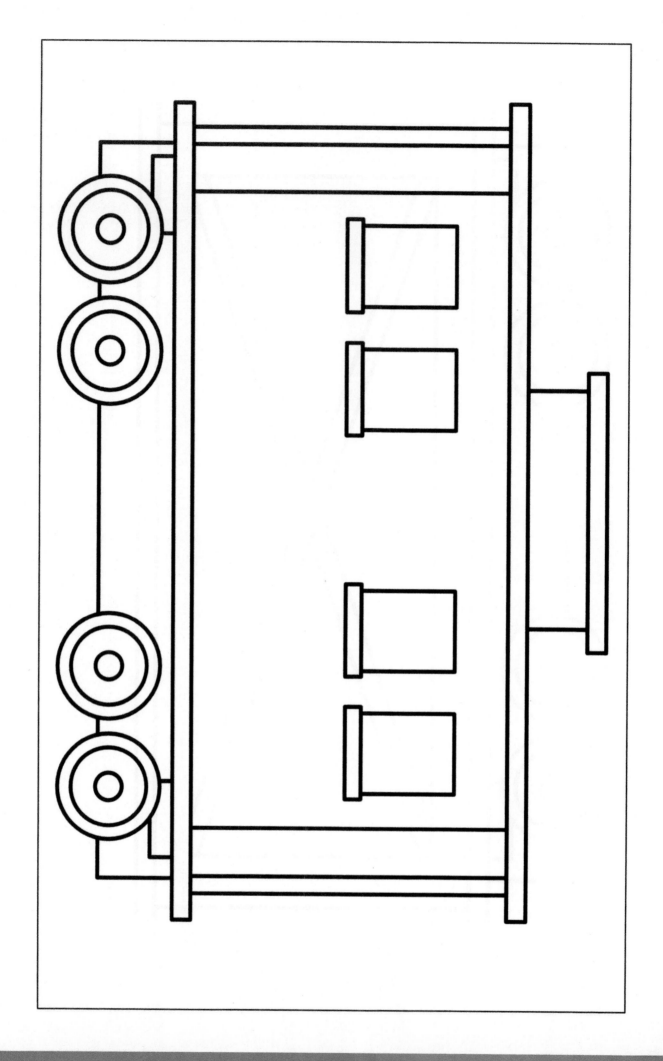

Use with Step 11

Sing Spell Read & Write

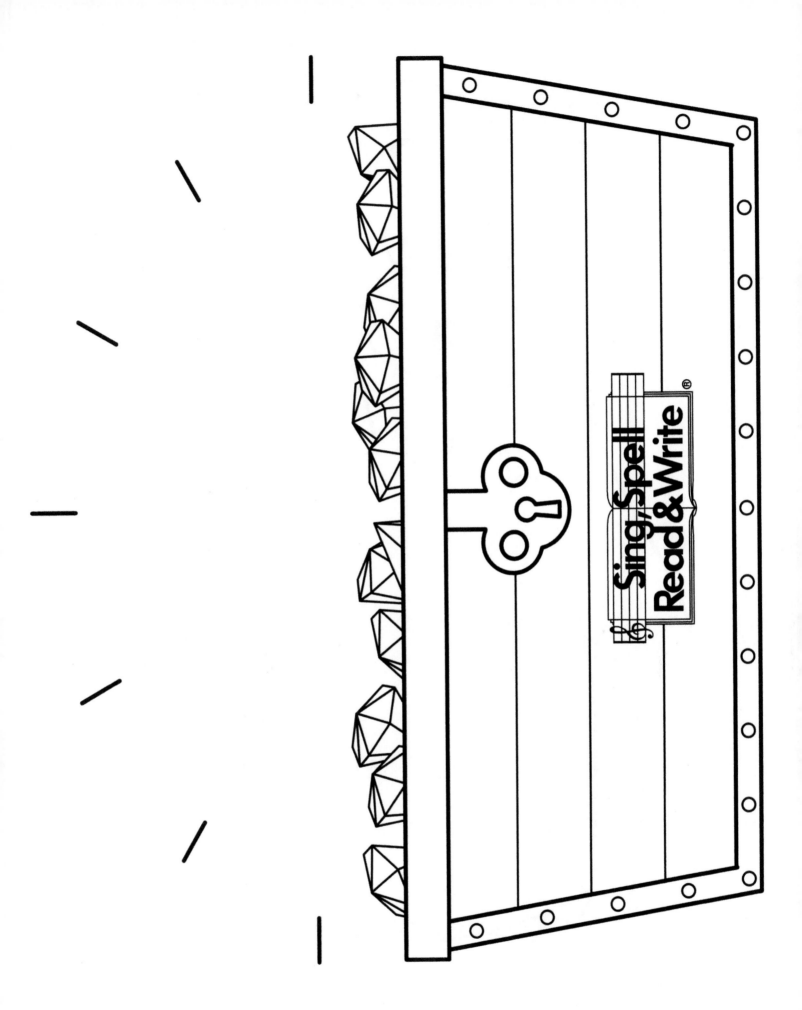

Sing, Spell
Read & Write

475

476

Directions: Circle the spelling errors.

My Sechul Trezure

I hav a sechul trezure that I lov more than piza. It is a butiful rock. That mus seem lik a funny truzure to you, but I will til you why I lick it so mush.

Sing Spel
Read & Write

477

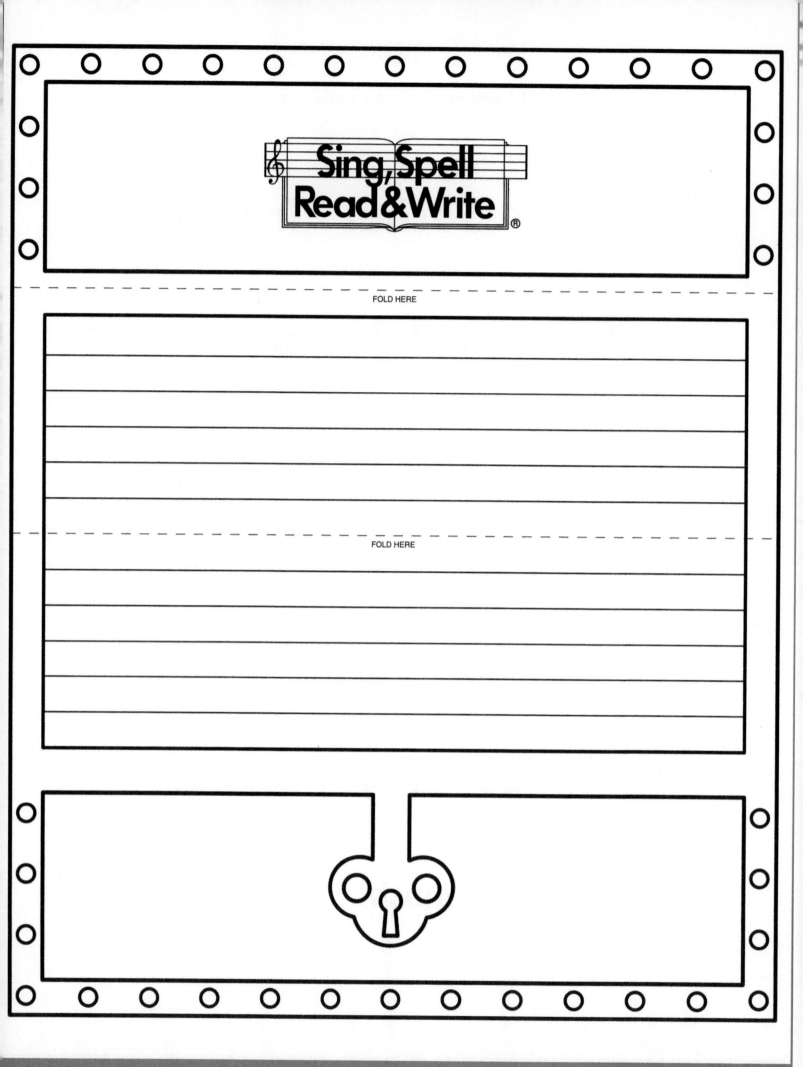

FOLD HERE

FOLD HERE

Use with Process Writing Lesson #7 Steps 14 & 15

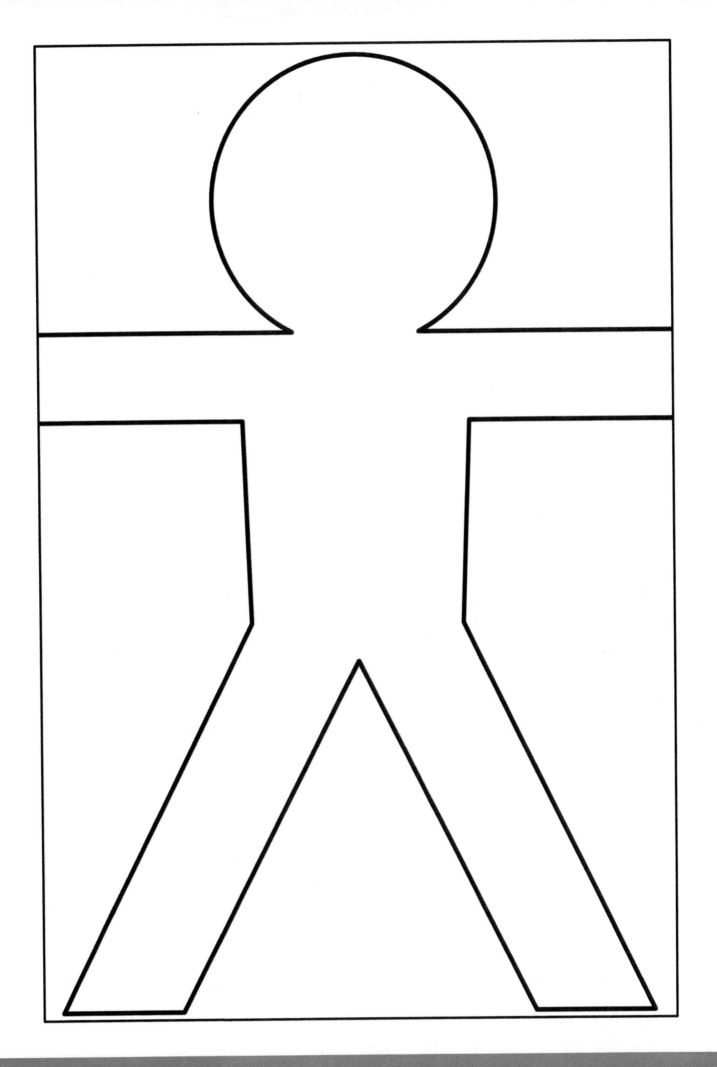

Sing,Spell
Read&Write

479

Use with Steps 16 & 17

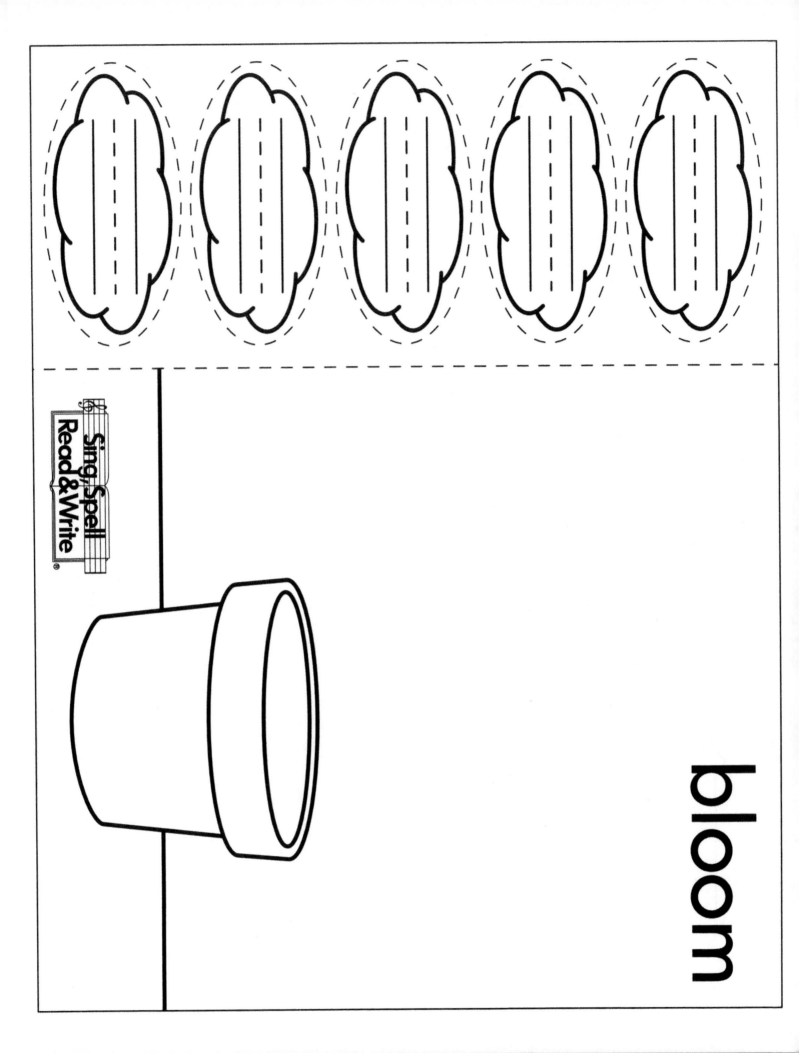

bloom

Sing,Spell
Read & Write

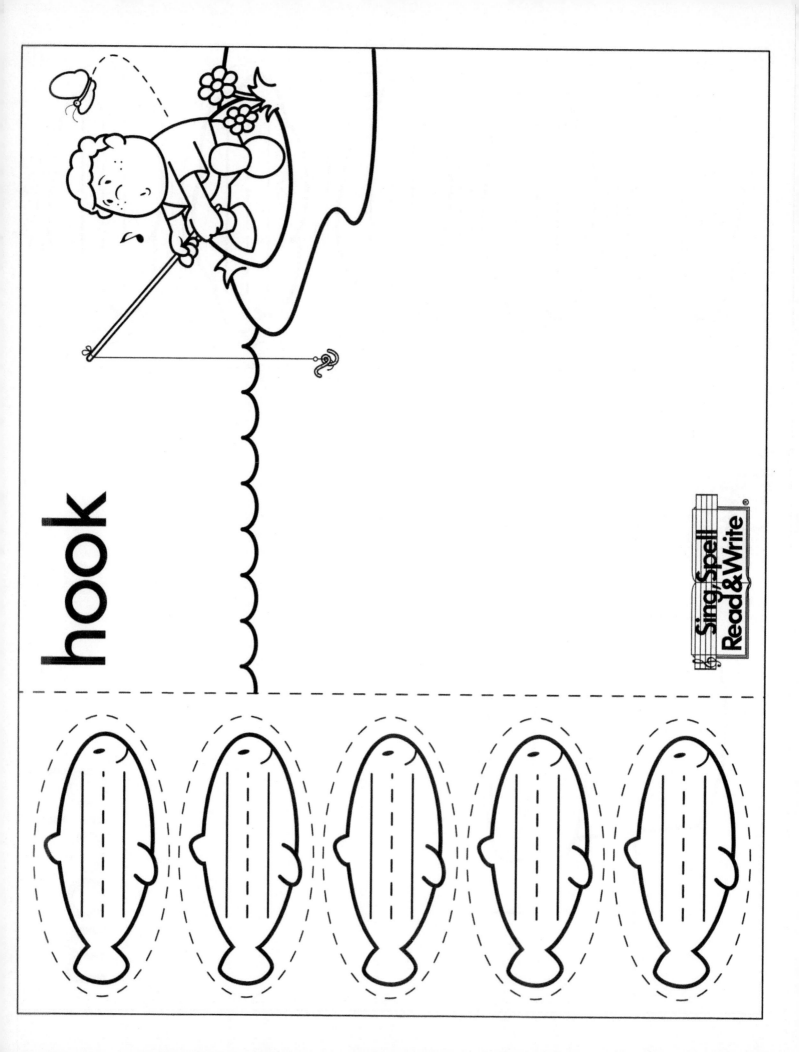

hook

Use with Step 22

Sing Spell Read & Write

Name _____

SOMEDAY

I might write about . . .

People	Feelings
Places	Activities
Things	Ideas

Sing,Spell Read&Write

483

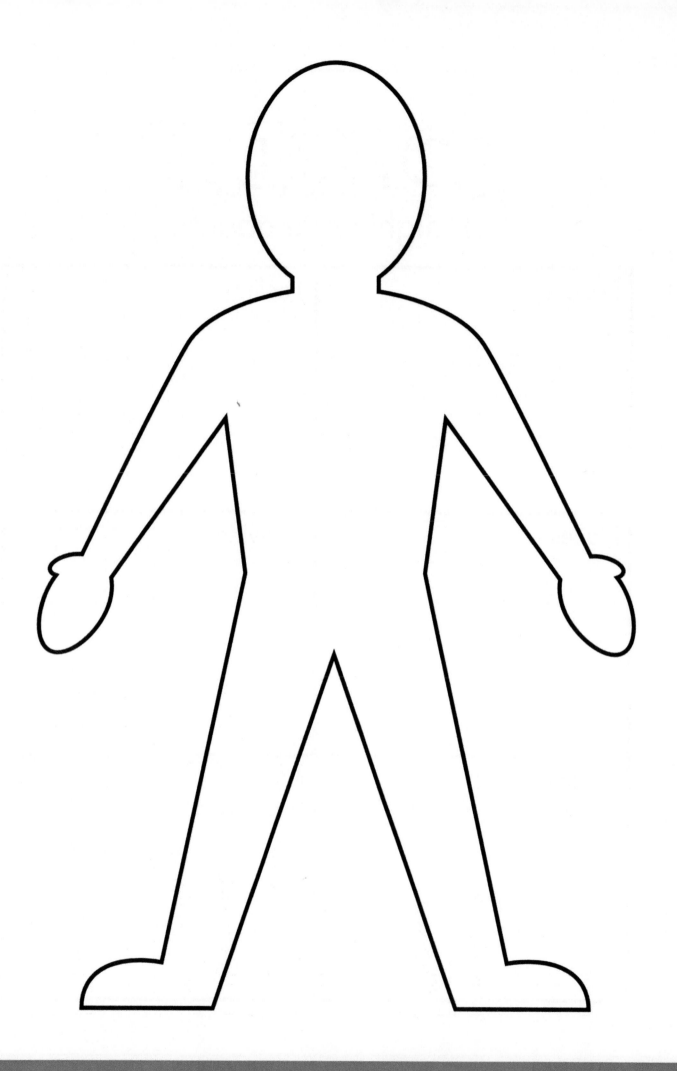

Sing Spell Read & Write

The girl reads a book.	The dog chases the cat.
A woman walks the dog.	A woman drives a car.
The bride cuts the cake.	The bird eats a worm.
A bee stings the boy.	A boy rides a bike.
A cat climbs a tree.	A shark eats a fish.
The farmer drives a tractor.	The woman pushes a stroller.
The teacher rings the bell.	The football player throws the ball.
The mother hugs her child.	The cook makes pizza.
A horse jumps the fence.	The policeman blows a whistle.
The truck dumps the dirt.	The cowboy rides a horse.
The man plants flowers.	The artist paints a picture.
The boy hits the baseball.	The author writes a story.
The girl catches the ball.	The boy sharpens a pencil.
The crossing guard stops the cars.	A man buys hamburgers.
The coach shoots a basket.	The saw cuts the tree.

Use with Process Writing Lesson #13   Steps 26 & 27

Sing, Spell
Read & Write